The Mythology of
the Secret Societies

By the same author

French Revolution Documents (Vol. I)
Europe 1880–1945

The Mythology of
the Secret Societies

J. M. ROBERTS
Fellow of Merton College, Oxford

*Le naturel est presque toujours le dernier point
dont on s'avise dans les sciences de l'homme.*

Charles Nodier

Charles Scribner's Sons · New York

Copyright © 1972 John Roberts

A-1.72 (I)

Printed in Great Britain

Library of Congress Catalog Card Number 70-39353
SBN 684-12904-3

Contents

Preface   vii

I   The Mythology of the Secret Societies
      Disraeli's spectre   1
      Historians and the secret societies   9

II   The masonic legacy
      The first freemasons   17
      The spread of freemasonry abroad   28
      Freemasonry in eighteenth-century France   31
      Freemasonry in other European countries   43
      The character of eighteenth-century freemasonry   47

III   Early anti-masonry
      The original elements of anti-masonry   58
      Early official reactions   64
      The Church and eighteenth-century freemasonry   68
      Unofficial anti-masonry at mid-century   84

IV   Derivation and degeneration: the sects of the later
      eighteenth century
      The golden age of mystification   90
      The disintegration of freemasonry   94
      Occult sources of the secret societies   101
      The Strict Observance   106

V   The Illuminati panic and after
      Weishaupt's achievement   118
      Deepening confusion   134

VI   The Secret Societies and the French Revolution
      The challenge to explanation   146
      Freemasons and the Revolution   154
      Some versions of the plot myth   168
      Barruel and his book   188

VII   The seedtime of the political secret societies

      The reactionary mood   203

      Buonarroti   222

      Secret societies and conspiracy in Italy 1796–9   237

VIII   The Napoleonic era

      Introduction   248

      Opposition and conspiracy in France   250

      Napoleonic Italy   276

      A view from St Petersburg   294

IX   The Restoration and after

      The Restoration atmosphere   300

      Revolutions and exposures   316

      Myth-making: Buonarroti's last years   340

X   Conclusion   347

      Index of Personal Names   361

Preface

As its title specifies, this book is intended to be about what has been believed and said about secret societies, not about secret societies themselves. It is called an essay because it is, so far as I can discover, the first attempt to explore this subject as a whole and claims neither to exhaust it nor to dispose of it definitively. Its aim is to provide some sort of map of a largely unexplored area. As such, even the inadequate reconnaissance on which it is based may be useful; it can be a basis for work which will have to be done much more closely and in much greater detail by other historians.

The subject is important because what has been said about secret societies is an outstanding example of a view of politics shaped by nonsense, though unhappily not the only one. Its boundaries could be drawn more widely than in this book, but I have purposely limited myself to a period, not very precisely defined, in which the ideas with which I am concerned coagulated into a recognisably complete structure. In this period they were for practical purposes confined to continental Europe; this particular mythology has mattered hardly at all in the politics of our own country—and why that should be so still invites exploration. It was expressed sometimes in conscious and formal statements, both published and unpublished, sometimes in casual responses in words and acts to imagined dangers and illusory prospects. Sometimes the mythology was embodied in secret societies themselves. This means that the student of it faces a chaotic and almost boundless mass of evidence. It has only been sampled, not exhausted, in these pages.

At many points its boundary is vague because there is no clear line between the mythological and positive history of the secret societies. I have often had to cross it and to draw when I did so on the works of scholars to whom we owe our knowledge of early freemasonry and secret societies. Where I have done so, I hope my references will make clear my obligations to them and that they will excuse errors and shortcomings which arise from my unfamiliarity with their specialisations. Only someone who is himself a freemason or a member of one of the secret societies has a sporting chance of avoiding error among the arcana of such bodies. I have also endeavoured to register at appropriate places the practical help given me in person by some other scholars.

In different contexts, my thanks are also due to Mrs E. Silk for her outstanding help as my secretary during a year and a half when other duties were pressing me heavily, and to Miss J. Hetherington who always gave me most efficient service though asked to type drafts under very heavy pressure. My college paid for the typing of this book and I wish warmly to thank the Warden and Fellows for their generosity in this matter. I am grateful to the Trustees of the Rockefeller Foundation who at one stage of the book's preparation allowed me to stay, most usefully, at the Villa Serbelloni; to Mr and Mrs Marshall, who made that stay so pleasant; and to the staff of the Bodleian Library, who are efficient and helpful, and avoid churlishness, in a manner which ought to be exemplary to the staffs of some other great libraries, but seems not to be. There is also something more than conventional thanks due to my wife, who has had to tolerate an unusual amount of disruption of our domestic life because this book was written at a time when other demands on my time were exceptionally heavy; and to my colleague Dr J. M. Wallace-Hadrill, who was good enough to take the time to read the text in draft and give me his comments upon it. I wish also to thank Mr Harold Kurtz and Mr Richard Cobb, both of whom read a part of the book in proof and made helpful suggestions.

Finally, although (as must appear in what follows) the work which has resulted in this book was far from totally pleasurable—prolonged exposure to the things said about secret societies easily brings on deep depression—it was something I am glad to have done. It follows that I owe a considerable debt in this, as in so many other things, to my friend, Professor John Bromley, who first, unwittingly, directed my attention along the route which eventually led to it twenty years ago, by telling me in a tutorial to read a book on the Carbonari by the American, R. M. Johnston. This can only register my many obligations to him, since they cannot be discharged, but I wish to recall them in this preface since it is an appropriate place.

Merton College

                                                        J. M. Roberts

References

W HEN I began this study I had hoped to provide it with a reasonably complete bibliography, but I have come to the conclusion that this is impossible. By its nature, which is exploratory and not exhaustive, this book cannot suitably be given a bibliography. Its subject-matter is too imprecisely demarcated for one to take the reader usefully beyond such standard guides to masonic literature as Wolfstieg; the other secret societies, moreover, have no such authorities (although some individual studies have useful suggestions to make on specific points) and a huge effort would be required to compile a systematic bibliography of them. Moreover, even if this were done, we would only have a guide to the positive history of the secret societies, not to the legends and mythology which they generated and which is embodied in a vast mass of often ephemeral publication. This is the main source of this study. The materials used in it inevitably represent only a selection from this huge corpus, much of which still remains to be explored from the point of view expressed in these pages. I have therefore chosen not to supply a consolidated bibliography, but to provide full references to the material I have used. In many cases these include secondary works which themselves provide helpful guidance to sources. Full titles, place and date of publication (when available) are given for all the works cited in references at their first (and sometimes at a later) appearance. In the case of many words in foreign languages, regular spellings and accentuation had not been established when passages quoted in this book were written. I have tried wherever possible to retain archaic spelling if that seems to me to help in keeping the flavour of the original, but I have not hesitated to modernise when this seemed likely to do no harm.

The abbreviations employed throughout are as follows:

AHRF: *Annales historiques de la Révolution française*
AN: Archives Nationales, Paris
AQC: *Ars Quattuor Coronatorum. Transactions of the Quattuor Coronati lodge, Margate*
AR: *Annales révolutionnaires*

ASJP: Archives of the Society of Jesus, province of Paris
ASPN: *Archivio storico per le provincie napoletane*
BIHR: *Bulletin of the Institute of Historical Research*
CS: *Critica Storica*
NRS: *Nuova Rivista Storica*
RF: *La Révolution française*
RH: *Revue Historique*
RI: *Risorgimento italiano*
RISS: *Revue internationale des Sociétés Secrètes*

Chapter I

The Mythology of the Secret Societies

DISRAELI'S SPECTRE

THOUGH sometimes amusing, it is always disturbing when intelligent people seriously talk nonsense. This is true even of the dead; we are always surprised at the credulity of our forebears. Sometimes it shocks us; they often held views which seem wicked as well as false, and they sometimes acted on them. It ought to be merely a truism that bad ideas can be as effective and influential as good, but obviously it is not, since we are so surprised by this. The hardest things to understand about much of the past are its errors and delusions. We are shut off from understanding them not only by the difficulties of research and by insensibility, for these are only general and preliminary obstacles to any discovery of the past, but also by the particular, anachronistic incredulity which we bring to anything which does not rest on our own intellectual assumptions.

This book is an attempt to enter one unexplored ruin of the historical landscape, the relics left behind by a set of beliefs once acceptable. They were held by men who were socially and intellectually respectable and who prided themselves, often, on their practical grasp of public affairs. They are ideas now generally thought to be nonsense, but they were once effective and influential. Moreover, they were often elaborately articulated; this essay is a reconnaissance in an area of highly organised nonsense. Even now, too, some people would deny that it is nonsense. There are still those who think that secret societies are operating in the world about us and operating to such effect that virtually everything unpleasant which happens can be attributed to them. (The view that the pleasant things can be attributed to them is only held by a still smaller number among those who actually belong to secret societies.) Nevertheless, such believers are a minority. They are not esteemed for holding their views, which rarely win a hearing in the authoritative journals of opinion, still less in those of scholarship. The intellectual tone of our society is against them; it prefers other mythologies.

The justification for this essay is that it is overlooked that this has not always, or even long, been so. For about a century and a half large numbers of intelligent Europeans believed that much of what was happening in the world around them only happened because secret societies planned it so. An enormous literature embodied and reflected this view. Hundreds of books and pamphlets in every major European language drove home the message in many variants and ludicrous detail: the author of a successful book on the secret societies published in 1877 could point to both the unification of Germany and the 'Kulturkampf' as evidence of the domination of Prussian policy by freemasons and assert that: 'Lord Palmerston fut pendant de longues années et jusqu'à sa mort un de ces quatre ou cinq grands chefs des sociétés secrètes et c'est autour de lui qu'ils se réunissaient.'[1] More believed such nonsense, probably, between 1815 and 1914 than at any other time. It is, therefore, an aberration of maturing bourgeois society and had some expressions characteristic of this. The adherents of these beliefs always included numbers of otherwise well-informed, sane and sensible men who sought authoritative support. A *Revue internationale des Sociétés Secrètes* which began to come out in 1912 in Paris is, in appearance, a solid and even massive periodical which must have demanded lavish financial support and devoted readers. At first glance it has all the austerity, but also the appeal, of a scholarly journal. Yet 'Notre programme', printed in the first volume, asserts with quiet assurance the astonishing proposition that 'de nos jours, la société secrète est la maîtresse du monde'.[2] It is worth repeating: this was in 1912. If they could swallow this, there is of course no reason to suppose that the readers of the *Revue* would be troubled by its later articles on 'Les "Boy-Scouts"' (which raised grave suspicions of that body and condemned it as unfit for Catholic membership), the Hague Peace Conference ('un fiasco maçonnique') and Esperanto (another subversive idea).[3] They may even have been convinced by the assertion in July 1914 that the Sarajevo assassination was not the result of a nation-

---

[1] C. Jannet, *Les sociétés secrètes* (Paris, 1881), p. 38. See also pp. 98, 106 for more of the legend about Palmerston, which did not originate with Jannet. In a Belgian edition of 1854 of a German book we find Palmerston described as 'Grand-Maître de tous les Maçons de l'univers'. From this it follows that British policy is dictated by freemasonry: 'Nous avons vu, sous l'impulsion de lord Palmerston, la révolution bouleverser l'Italie, la Sardaigne et surtout la Hongrie' (E. E. Eckert, *La Franc-Maçonnerie dans sa véritable signification* (Liège, 1854), ii, pp. 242–3). Though stated more discreetly in recent times, the story has had a long life. See, e.g., J. Berteloot, *La franc-maçonnerie et l'église catholique* (Paris, 1947), pp. 132–3: 'en 1859 . . . le ministre franc-maçon Lord Palmerston et l'empereur franc-maçon Napoléon III s'entendirent . . . Le gouvernement libéral anglais ne fut-il pas le premier à reconnaître le nouveau royaume du Piémont?'—and, of course, the despoiler of the Papacy.

[2] *RISS*, I, p. 3.   [3] *RISS*, I, pp. 245, 332, 855.

alist plot, whether Serb, Croat or Albanian, but bore 'le signe certain de l'anticatholicisme et de l'antipapauté: c'est là ce qu'on veut faire oublier'.[4] They would certainly not have been surprised to learn from the *Revue* after the Great War that Lenin had belonged to a secret masonic lodge in Switzerland.[5]

Credulity in these matters has not been confined to continental Europe. An English lady has revealed in her autobiography how an academic study of the French Revolution gave her the key to the great events of her own times. Bolshevism, she quickly saw, was only 'Jacobinism under another name, the same aims, the same methods'. It was part of the same 'gigantic conspiracy of the same dark directorate against the whole structure of Christian civilisation'. In work she had believed to be only historical she had unwittingly 'entered the lists against terrific living forces of which I had not guessed the existence. My whole life was now to become a prolonged contest with these unseen powers.'[6] Nesta Webster waged this struggle with such vigour and success that a stream of popular books resulted. One on *Secret societies and subversive movements*, first published in 1924, went into an eighth edition as late as 1964. In *World Revolution. The plot against civilisation*[7] she traced all the great revolutionary upheavals since 1789 back to a common source in an eighteenth-century Bavarian society. In *Surrender of an Empire*,[8] the Wafd, Sinn Fein, Zionism and Bolshevism are all seen as examples of the same great threat. The acceptability of these ideas to the British and American public was shown by the reprinting of her books.

Another way of bringing this world of fantasy into historical perspective and of conceiving the impression it could produce is to recall how much of it was believed by very eminent and powerful people, in positions of great responsibility. Bismarck's fears of social revolution after the Paris Commune may be thought exceptional, and the pronouncements of the Vatican too specially interested, but a sufficiently startling example can be found at the very centre of British nineteenth-century government. It was in 1870, the year before the Paris Commune, that a former Prime Minister of the United Kingdom wrote the words: 'It is the Church against the secret societies. They are the only two strong things in Europe, and will survive Kings, Emperors or parliaments.'

[4] *RISS*, VIII, p. 12. See also IX, p. 231.
[5] *RISS*, VIII, p. 702.
[6] Nesta H. Webster, *Spacious Days* (London, 1949), p. 191.
[7] London, 1921.   [8] London, 1931.

Admittedly, Disraeli put these words into the mouth of a character in one of his novels, but he certainly held views like these for most of his life. In 1870 he still had nearly six years further office as Prime Minister ahead of him; such assumptions, therefore, have been practically important. There is at least as much reason for taking them into account in assessing him as for considering, say, Mackenzie King's fondness for discovering messages in the patterns left by tea-leaves in teacups. Perhaps fortunately, perhaps unfortunately, prime ministers are not more immune to irrational conviction than other men. But for present purposes, this is not the main interest of Disraeli's views. The best reason for paying attention to them here lies not in their possible effect on his behaviour but in the acceptability he felt they would command. Such ideas were the common intellectual furniture of the minds of his contemporaries; this is why they provided a good focus for his novel. For once, Disraeli is significant as a typical rather than as an eccentric figure. His words expressed a widely held mythology and *Lothair*, the novel from which they are taken, became, almost at once, a best-seller in both England and the United States.

Some of its success must have been due to the eminence of the author and his known skill in writing an entertaining tale. It also probably owed something to the topicality of its theme, the spiritual turmoil of a young English nobleman oppressed by religious uncertainty and obsessed by the need to make proper use of his vast fortune. He thinks of building a huge cathedral, but, unfortunately, cannot make up his mind who should minister in it. His religious allegiance is in fact disputed between Rome, Canterbury, and what may be called natural religion. Each of these is represented by a female protagonist. Theodora, the exponent of natural religion, is one of Disraeli's most attractive creations, but in the end Lothair remains true to Anglicanism, though held to it by the least colourful of the three ladies. In this choice of a subject, Disraeli reflected and exploited the excitement of the middle decades of the century over an apparent resurgence of Roman Catholicism in England, which came to a social climax with the spectacular conversion of the Marquess of Bute.[9] But there was in his book much more of contemporary relevance than just this. Its background is the closing spasm of the Italian Risorgimento, the struggle for the occupation of Rome and the overthrow of the Temporal Power. Mazzini (dis-

---

[9] John Patrick, third Marquess, twice Mayor of Cardiff, joined the Roman communion in 1869. It is interesting to note the even greater sensation of 1874, when Lord Ripon, who had resigned from the Cabinet the year before, vacated his office as Grand Master of the freemasons of England and was received as a Roman Catholic a month later.

guised as a fictional character) and Garibaldi appear in its pages and in their struggle Lothair takes part. He is wounded at Mentana (the skirmish in November 1867 in which Garibaldi's invasion of the Papal States was defeated) and is then carried to Rome as a prisoner. There, he narrowly escapes the blandishments and plots of Papal agents who covet his adherence; he is saved by the apparition at night in the Coliseum of a vision of Theodora, who has been killed at Mentana. By way of Palestine, he returns eventually to England and marriage.

Throughout the book this romantic tale is unwound against a background of high society and high politics into which the myth of the secret societies is closely woven. In numerous passages they are talked about as a fundamental datum of the European political scene. The words already quoted are spoken by a Papal minister (tipped by another character as a possible successor to Antonelli, the Papal Secretary of State) to someone who seems to be the French ambassador at the Court of St James.[10] Elsewhere, another prelate tells Lothair that the secret societies for which he has been fighting 'have declared war against the Church, the State, and the domestic principle. All the great truths and laws on which the family reposes are denounced. Their religion is the religion of science.'[11] Equally dramatic claims for the societies are put into the mouth of one of the revolutionaries in the book, Captain Bruges, whom Disraeli seems to have modelled on Cluseret, a soldier of fortune who was to play a large part in the defence of Communard Paris in 1871. Talking of Marianne, a legendary French secret society, he says that 'there are more secret societies in France at this moment than at any period since '85, though you hear nothing of them'.[12] As *Lothair* was the first novel Disraeli had written for twenty years, a theme which he made as central as this must have impressed him powerfully.

Earlier writings show that the secret societies and the threat they presented were not new fears for Disraeli. He had already broached the theme twenty years before, in his remarkable life of Lord George Bentinck, a book as revealing of its author as of its subject, the horse-racing, upright aristocrat who had led and focused Tory opposition to Sir Robert Peel. It appeared soon after the revolutionary year, 1848, and Disraeli looked back on that great upheaval and tried to analyse its meaning in a long passage, worth quotation in full.

[10] *Lothair* (Hughenden edn., 1881), p. 275.
[11] *Lothair*, p. 150.
[12] *Lothair*, p. 169. For the significance of 1785, see below, Ch. V.

'It was neither parliaments nor populations, nor the course of nature nor the course of events, that overthrew the throne of Louis Philippe. Amid one of those discontents which are appeased by the sacrifice of a favourite or the change of a ministry, the sovereign and the subjects both in confusion, the king deprived of his wonted energy by a prostrating illness and the citizens murmuring without convictions, the throne was surprised by the secret societies, ever prepared to ravage Europe.

'The origin of the secret societies that prevail in Europe is very remote. It is probable that they were originally confederations of conquered races organised in a great measure by the abrogated hierarchies. In Italy they have never ceased, although they have at times been obliged to take various forms; sometimes it was a literary academy, sometimes a charitable brotherhood; freemasonry was always a convenient guise. The Inquisition in its great day boasted that it had extirpated them in Spain, but their activity in that country after the first French revolution rather indicates a suspension of vitality than an extinction of life. The reformation gave them a great impulse in Germany, and towards the middle of the eighteenth century, they had not only spread in every portion of the north of that region but had crossed the Rhine.

'The two characteristics of these confederations, which now cover Europe like a network, are war against property and hatred of the Semitic revelation. These are the legacies of their founders; a proprietary despoiled and the servants of altars that have been overthrown. Alone, the secret societies can disturb, but they cannot control, Europe. Acting in unison with a great popular movement they may destroy society, as they did at the end of the last century. The French disturbance of '48 was not a great popular movement. It was a discontent which required nothing more for its solution than a change of ministry: but the sovereign and his subjects were in sudden confusion; the secret associations are always vigilant and always prepared; they took society by surprise, but having nothing really to rely upon except their own resources, the movement however disastrous has been an abortion.

'It is the manoeuvres of these men, who are striking at property and Christ, which the good people of this country, who are so accumulative and so religious, recognise and applaud as the progress of the liberal cause.'[13]

Such thoughts have been uttered by other, less distinguished men; historians have tended to pass them by because they believed them

[13] *Lord George Bentinck, A Political Biography* (London, 1852), pp. 553-4.

baseless rubbish. Yet they are worth pondering; this passage, after all, was written by an observer who, although his imagination was rarely held in check unless his political interests provided the rein, nevertheless looked at the European revolutions from the outside. Disraeli could pretend to some degree of objectivity in considering 1848; he did not have to introduce the secret societies as deus ex machina in a book about the Corn Law controversy. They had nothing to do with English party politics, and are irrelevant to the biography (although Disraeli incorporated them in an argument about the importance of traditional institutions which fitted into praise of Bentinck). Nor was it only in his books that Disraeli had harped on the secret societies. In 1856 he warned the House of Commons of the dangers of encouraging revolution in Italy because of the readiness of the secret societies to take advantage of disorder both there and in France.[14] No doubt his experience of the Fenians in the 1860s helped to confirm his views. As late as 1876, when he was again Prime Minister and knew that great attention would be given to his words, after decades of political experience and years of cabinet office, he again spoke about them in public.[15]

Disraeli can be left here. He is an outstanding example of the extraordinary state of mind into which otherwise shrewd and intelligent men could be transported by a belief in secret societies. Paradoxically, he establishes the respectability of our subject. Something so gripping is worth examination. Its obsessive power has been richly illustrated

[14] Hansard, H. of C. debates, III series, cxliii, 773–1, 14 July 1856. He again stressed the importance of 1848 in revealing the strength and aims of the societies and continued: 'a great part of Europe—the whole of Italy and France and a great portion of Germany, to say nothing of other countries, are covered with a network of these secret societies, just as the superficies of the earth is now being covered with railroads. And what are their objects? They do not attempt to conceal them. They do not want constitutional government; they do not want ameliorated institutions; they do not want provincial councils nor the recording of votes;—they want to change the tenure of the land, to drive out the present owners of the soil, and to put an end to ecclesiastical establishments. Some of them may go further. . . .'

[15] The speech of 1876 was made at the annual dinner of the Royal and Central Bucks Agricultural Association at Aylesbury on 20 September. After attributing the Serbian attack on Turkey of that year to the secret societies, Beaconsfield went on to say that 'in the attempt to conduct the government of this world there are now elements to be considered which our predecessors had not to deal with. . . . These are the Secret Societies . . . which at the last moment may baffle all our arrangements—Societies which have regular agents everywhere, which countenance assassination, and which, if necessary, could produce a massacre.' I am indebted to the Editor of the *Bucks Herald* for help in consulting a report of the speech in that newspaper (23 September 1876) which, somewhat surprisingly, tells us that the last statement was greeted with cheers.

since Disraeli, moreover. Other novelists greater than he turned to the conspiratorial world for their matter or exploited it as a background.[16] The stream of bogus revelations and witch-hunting literature has continued to flow right down to our own day and has had great political importance. It affected many conservatives' views of the nature of the event which defined European politics for nearly a century and a half, the French Revolution. It also inspired liberals to particular kinds of organisation and action. The history of church and state would in most countries have read very differently without it even as late as the middle of this century. The politics of the Third Republic and of united Italy seem at times to have expressed themselves quintessentially in the struggle of clericals and freemasons. Elsewhere—in Spain, for example, or Spanish America—the history of political radicalism is riddled with fear of secret societies. Finally, it was above all in Nazi Germany, Soviet Russia and Vichy France, that these conspiratorial and sectarian obsessions took their most sinister form and showed most strongly the power of the collective dream—or nightmare—of the modern European mind which Disraeli shared and exploited.

Such examples suggest, too, that though this essay is above all about the delusions of the directing classes—we are not dealing with a mass phenomenon such as popular anti-semitism or a witch-craze—it is not one whose significance is limited to the margins of intellectual history. It is more than the aberration of a few hundred writers. The myth was able to have great practical and political effects, though indirectly. It may be that there has been in Western society a latent tendency to personify and dramatise its problems, to identify an Enemy, and that this can be evoked very easily. It is at least a possible explanation of the power of men who are themselves believers in mythologies to move masses who are not. Sometimes this is open and explicit: Hitler's anti-semitism went far beyond political calculation, shrewd though his exploitation of it may have been. The classical Marxism of the first half of this century contained mythological elements whose influence went down deep into labour movements, sometimes driving them in directions wholly opposed to the objective and observable trends of industrial society. No doubt, too, many Russians found it quite credible that their own security service, army and party should have been led for years by the agents of counter-revolution and capitalism, just because of their absorption of the myth of irreconcilable conflict between social systems. In such instances, it is not necessary that many

---

[16] *The Possessed, The Princess Casamassima* and *The Secret Agent* are obvious examples.

people should grasp and enunciate the whole detail of the myth. Enough will get through to have political effect as a few simple images and polarisations of the emotions.

It is the resonances which await the successful exploiter of mythology which redeem the subject-matter of this essay from triviality. The particular intellectual errors embodied in the mythology of the secret societies are more than mere picturesque embellishments of political debate: they are cultural facts of great significance. Yet the assertions which seemed incontrovertible to Disraeli—and which were shared at the time and have been shared before and since by thousands of other men—have properly been treated by historians as rubbish, and therefore uninteresting. The neglect was proper because the assertions themselves were so obviously based on fantasy: only occasionally and briefly, at moments when the particular acts of particular societies seemed important (as they were in Italy during the Restoration after 1815, or in the United States in the days of the Ku Klux Klan), were they thought to be worth study. For the most part, therefore, the books written about secret societies have been unscientific, sensational, frivolous, infatuated publications. The professional historian has been unperturbed and since he has been so little interested in the positive history of secret societies, it is hardly surprising that their mythical dimension, which is of importance, has been completely ignored. Yet it may be that it was just here, in the illusions and fears they created, and in the dreams cherished about them, that the secret societies exercised their greatest power. The widespread belief in the rubbish talked about them is their most important as well as most interesting feature and it is this belief, and not the societies themselves, which is the subject of this essay.

HISTORIANS AND THE SECRET SOCIETIES

One reason why historians have tended to neglect secret societies is, paradoxically, the very strength of the mythology which grew up about them. Early in the nineteenth century it was still possible for the belief in secret societies to rest on assumptions acceptable to most educated people, even if they did not draw from them the same conclusions. In seeking an explanation of great changes in European society many people accepted the explanation that secret societies were behind them because it was coherent with widespread views about the origins and springs of historical change. Much which seemed mysterious had, traditionally, been explained in terms of plots and conspiracies—in terms, that is, of conscious human agency—and the supposed misdeeds of secret societies fitted easily into this general assumption. Between 1789 and 1848 there was almost everywhere in Europe a great general acceleration of social and political change, a spread of certain common institutions in the place of particular and local ones, and a generalising of certain ideas which may loosely be called liberal. Educated and conservative men raised in the tradition of Christianity, with its stress on individual responsibility and the independence of the will, found conspiracy theories plausible as an explanation of such change: it must have come about, they thought, because somebody planned it so. Throw in on one side vanity and on the other fear, and the appeal of a theory of historical change based on the activity of secret societies is understandable.

This background has now almost completely vanished. In academic circles it disappeared a long time ago. It increasingly affronted the trend of historical thinking. Modern historical scholarship has evolved canons of explanation which make it ab initio unsympathetic to arguments about secret societies or conspiracy except in closely defined and delimited contexts. (It may even be thought to have gone a little too far in this direction.) Historians have long found explanations of historical change satisfactory only if they take account of many considerations other than conscious design. The historian faced with a big change in society now often looks first to social structure and economic patterns; he is sceptical about individual agency except within the firmly delimited framework they provide. He is bound from the start, therefore, to be sceptical about so melodramatic a theory as that of the secret societies. His scepticism easily runs on from merely saying they are not of much importance—which is, perhaps, justifiable in an overwhelming majority of cases—to become an unexamined and dogmatic judgment that they are not worth examination at all, at any level.

This predisposition to ignore subsequently set up a process in which neglect and contempt have been perpetuated by feedback. With the notable exception of some masonic historians and a few Italians excavating the roots of the Risorgimento the whole subject of secret societies was neglected as an area for serious investigation until twenty or thirty years ago. Because the historian passed by, the charlatan, the axe-grinder and the paranoiac long had the field to themselves. In due course, the assertions of terrifying conspiracy and demoniacal subversion which they produced (and sustained so badly by evidence and argument) made historians even less inclined to take the subject seriously. The result has been the mountain of rubbish—still growing, though now more slowly—which explains everything from the collapse of the Roman Empire to the Russian Revolution in terms of secret societies. If the mountain has contained an occasional grain of truth and has absorbed a few fragments of serious and objective research, these have until very recently been almost lost to sight. Intelligent men have preferred to treat secret societies as, until recently, they treated anti-semitism: as an aberration whose roots lay in an irrationality which disqualified it for serious study. At best it was a footnote to the 'real' history of political and economic change. Only since 1945 have scholars been sufficiently disabused of the presuppositions of liberal, positivist history to treat a fundamentally irrational subject such as anti-semitism with the attention it deserves. The myth of the secret societies is another irrational topic, though, fortunately, one whose positive expression in history has been less atrocious than, say, 'The Protocols of the Elders of Zion'.[17]

This parallel suggests another point. Like the secret societies, anti-semitism is a historical phenomenon which embodies both positive and mythological elements. This book is above all about myth—about what people believed to be the role of the secret societies, however remote this was from reality. Yet scholarly study of any institution usually begins and ends with its positive reality, with what it actually was. In the case of the secret societies, there are important obstacles to arriving at a correct view of this which have contributed to the primary neglect of them by historians. There is in the first place the nature of such hard evidence as does exist about the political secret societies. It is usually slight and scrappy. The point of a secret organisation, after all, is that it is secret; it is not likely either to keep a considerable body of records or to allow the profane to have access to them.[18] In many cases the best documentary evidence about secret societies can only be that put together by the police and judiciary in the course of investigation and interrogation. But such evidence is patchy and occasional. Even where it is relatively plentiful—one example would be the mass of material brought to light after the Lombard and Venetian trials of

[17] The secret societies mythology has, of course, often appeared in anti-semitic forms. Few people have been impressed, it seems, by Disraeli's vision of the societies' 'hatred of the Semitic revolution'. More have sympathised with the view propounded in 1912 by a contributor to the *Revue internationale des Sociétés Secrètes*: 'de nos jours, l'histoire des sociétés secrètes est la page magistrale de l'histoire juive' (I, p. 9). That journal began in 1914 to publish a monthly *Partie Judéo-Occultiste*. See also below, pp. 274–5.

[18] A non-political secret society, of course, may keep voluminous archives to which outsiders may sometimes obtain some access. Freemasonry is an obvious example.

the 1820s—the recorders and investigators had interests different from those of the historian, and a long and very laborious process of accumulation and piecing together of scraps of evidence from scattered sources is necessary before very much solid information about the whole picture can emerge. Even then there are huge gaps in it. It may properly be said that this is not decisive. Historians meet similar difficulties in investigating other problems. Although this is true, the difficulties of getting together evidence are more important in the case of the secret societies because, as we have seen, grave doubts are likely to exist from the start in the minds of historians about whether the subject is worth studying at all.

Another difficulty about evidence arises not in connexion with its availability, but with its status and the scepticism it is likely to breed in those who use it. The point on which both the secret societies and the policemen who pursued them could agree was that they were very important. In consequence, a steady factor of exaggeration is usual in the records. Moreover, these difficulties increase the further one goes back. Between the wars, a historian could interrogate for himself surviving members of the Black Hand; for the Carbonari, the positive statements of alarmed policemen and self-important conspirators are a priori suspect, and cannot always be tested against other sources.

The content of the evidence about secret societies has also presented a difficulty arising from unfamiliarity. It has required for its interpretation an awareness of a penumbra of assumptions and ideas not always easily recreated. This is especially true of their great age, the period running from the late eighteenth to the mid-nineteenth century, when secret societies actually existed in many countries. We have been, perhaps, only too ready to accept a purely political interpretation of them. We see them as conspiracies arising in response to political needs. But when the whole spectrum of such organisations is kept in view and when the activities of individual societies are studied closely, the importance of their non-political and mythical components is also very striking. The ritual and symbolic elements are very important; the wide and long-enduring diffusion of a masonic element in these seems, as we shall see, to go far beyond the point at which any merely utilitarian purpose could be served by borrowing. The historian of modern politics is not always well-equipped to deal with such matters. A medievalist, an anthropologist, or a historian of art might sometimes be better able to assess the importance of some of the apparently trivial and subsidiary evidence which comes to light in this connexion. All of us have presuppositions which make it difficult for us to appreciate social purposes when they are expressed in an unfamiliar idiom and these constantly ensnare and divert us when dealing with a topic so rich in irrational elements as this. The memory of Mau-Mau is recent and the hints it provides about the risks of interpretation should be present in our minds, but we still find it hard to assess the true dimensions of the oathing rituals of the late eighteenth-century and early nineteenth-century secret societies. We cannot even easily come to grips in our own day with such a notion as the Mafia's institution of 'omertà'. We should remember these things, but too often forget them when assessing the intellectual world of the secret societies. It may seem ridiculous to us, but to many intelligent men in the early nineteenth-century freemasonry was as shocking and alarming as Mau-Mau to us a few years ago.

These difficulties seem to me to explain much of the neglect of the secret societies by professional historians. Such difficulties could argue for and justify many very different books from this one, which does not aim to fill any of the gaps in our positive knowledge of secret societies themselves. It is an essay, essentially tentative, in tracing the outlines of a subject so far not recognised to exist. It is about the secret societies only in so far as they are the origin of a myth and in dealing with them it is very selective. No one should hope to find here a history of the Carbonari or the Illuminati. It is an attempt to clarify the evolution of a mythology and no doubt the sketch-map which I hope it will provide will soon be corrected, improved and then abandoned altogether. Only in speculating about the reasons why the map seems to be of a particular shape should it be thought to go beyond this modest aim.

Yet although what follows is not, therefore, a history of secret societies, much of their positive history has had to come in, if only to make it easier to draw the line between myth and reality. The positive and direct impact on politics of secret societies should only be relevant to this book in so far as it shaped the views men took of them and the fears and dreams which resulted, but this line cannot be a clean one and has often had to be crossed in what follows. From time to time, questions about what was believed about secret societies cannot be separated from questions about what they did to give rise to these beliefs, but I have always tried to say as little about positive institutions and events as is necessary to make the mythology comprehensible. Nonetheless, this has often forced me to say quite a lot about subjects where I have had to follow other scholars as best I could. No doubt I have made mistakes in the process, but they should not affect the core of the story. It is the myth which is the mainstream of this book, and it is my own view that its dominance was the most important thing about the secret societies. It is here that I have tried to make an original contribution of my own by disentangling the relationships of its most important expressions. This seems to me a worthy theme. The mythology was far more important than any of the positive achievements of the secret societies because its grip on the European imagination has had so many and such long-lived consequences.

It kept this grip during a period running roughly from the French to the Russian revolutions, and was at the peak of its strength between 1815 and 1848. It is, in fact, as characteristic a cultural product of the age of revolution in Europe as, say, liberalism and has been exported with as much success to other continents. Freemasonry dogged the politics of nineteenth-century Latin America and the Dutch Reformed Church of South Africa retains a deep suspicion of it. Yet Europe is the cradle of the mythology, and to Europe this book is confined. All that remains to be done before considering the first appearance of the elements of that mythology is to sketch its characteristic outline so that we have an idea of what we seek.

The mythology of the secret societies has many different specific embodiments, religious and non-religious, liberal and conservative, but it is always an example of the 'puppet' theory of politics. It claims that the real makers of events are not the statesmen who strut before the public, but secret directors who manipulate them, sometimes with, sometimes without, their knowledge. These manipulators use their puppets as the instruments of great and usually sinister designs. Sometimes, too, the masses are the puppets and are stirred up to violence by hidden hands. Examination of the events in many countries in the light of this theory reveals (it is believed) that the same patterns are to be seen everywhere, running through both methods and aims. We may therefore predicate not a scattered inexplicable series of manipulations, but a central directing plan, a secret organisation which is international and integrates its agents in many countries. Many different versions of this secret force have been identified. The freemasons, the Jesuits, the Carbonari, the Comintern have all had the blame placed on them at different times. The most ambitious theorists in this tradition have identified conspiracies stretching historically in time across centuries and linking organisations as remote from one another as the Templars and Sinn Fein. But the most popular form of the myth is to identify the enduring secret societies as primarily the agents of political and social revolution. Their great aim, it is asserted, is to sap the stabilising certainties of society—Church, State, Morality, Property, the Family—and set up a new order. But in all these versions, whatever the particular assertions of any one of them, the same fundamental claim appears beneath the variants—that there is an occult force operating behind the seemingly real outward forms of political life. No discovery, no penetration of the veils of secrecy can ever be assumed to have revealed the full truth about the hidden directors who are, in extreme statements, said to preside even over societies which appear to be in conflict with one another.

On the whole, the myth has had an anti-liberal cast, though this has never prevented the emergence of it in liberal versions. Left-wing versions also exist. This is a reflexion of the fact that the myth emerged as an attempt to impose some sort of order on the bewildering variety of changes which suddenly showered upon Europe at the end of the eighteenth and the beginning of the nineteenth centuries and an ordered view was as attractive on one side as the other. This was the age of the invention of modern politics and of the imposition of the Left-versus-Right model which after a long life only began to lose its usefulness between the two World Wars. It was an age in which European society was changed by economic and technological forces at an accelerating pace. It was one in which the European map was redrawn, the principle of nationality replacing that of proprietorship as the foundation of states, and in which the mass of the population for the first time entered conscious political life. It was also (in part because of these transformations) punctuated violently by war and revolution. On the whole it was people who disliked these changes who felt the greatest need of some exceptional explanation to account for them and they found to hand and eagerly took up elements already in existence since the eighteenth century. These primitive elements, moreover, themselves had a generative force: they actually contributed to the creation and shaping of real secret societies. When these came to light, of course, they gave added plausibility to the myth.

In Western Europe in the half-century before 1848 there were indeed real secret societies at work with political aims; they were most important, and most celebrated and feared, in Italy and France. Some of them owed much in their organisation, tradition and procedure to a much older movement which had already attracted public attention and distrust. It has always provided the most important and enduring themes in the mythology of the secret societies. Through almost the whole history of the myth, from the prurient suspicions of what really went on at eighteenth-century masonic suppers to their condemnation by the nineteenth-century Papacy and the attacks on the movement launched by the Nazis and the Bolsheviks, the freemasons are given a special role and emphasis.[19] Although most of the story now to be unravelled runs through an unreal twilit world of legend, fancy, nightmare and paranoia, its beginnings lie in the commonsensical, enlightened world of the early English freemasons. It is with them that it is best to begin.

[19] Some of the Papal condemnations are discussed in what follows. The most important is as recent as 1884; this is Leo XIII's *Humanum Genus*, the last doctrinal encyclical against freemasonry in which, it says, 'in our time' all sorts of evildoers seem to have come together. It was not the last Papal condemnation of secret societies, which have been, according to one authority, the object of fifteen separate condemnations since 1738. (A. Mellor, *Our Separated Brethren* (London, 1964), p. 287. This book is a translation from the author's *Nos Frères séparés* (Paris, 1961), and all references which follow are to the English edition.)

Chapter II

The masonic legacy

THE FIRST FREEMASONS

MANY institutions and ideas which have shaped Western society, and therefore the world ever since, were first crystallised in the eighteenth century. The central issues of European politics for much of the next two centuries were then defined for the first time. Men began to turn away from the hope of building community on inherited subordination or confessional unity; they began instead to envisage a secular and voluntary society which would be a true community. Sometimes they saw this society as the inevitable result of the operation of natural laws: one such school of thought (which had great success) sketched out the theoretical principles which lay behind the emerging institutions of market society, with its emphasis on the contractual and rational nature of ties between man and man. The evolution of a new idea of the individual was a part of this. Such changes were to be rapidly accelerated after 1789 when, it is not too much to say, the end of the Middle Ages at last came into sight for all Europe.

One expression of these very important changes was a new respect for private and informal activity. Outside the family—itself still a highly formalised and demanding institution—there was little scope for wholly private activity or, indeed, tolerance of it, in the corporate structure of the ancien régime. In some countries, notably England, the English colonies and the United Provinces, this had begun to change even before 1700. Elsewhere, the institutions which appeared to meet new demands and new tastes took root more slowly and were not common until well into the nineteenth century. But the appearance of such informal meeting-places as coffee-houses, clubs and salons gives a rough guide to the timing of the advance of a new cultural wave. They were the inventions of men and women making new demands on society and discovering new capacities in themselves which could not be given expression within the historic unities of blood, locality, religion, occupation and legal subordination. Some of the most remarkable of the social inventions thrown up in this way were to be the first 'secret societies', in the modern sense of that phrase. Sometimes they were light-hearted and convivial, sometimes they were not. They jealously guarded their secrets and took elaborate precautions against the approach of the profane and uninitiated.[1] Such caution showed the confidence of their members that they had hit upon an important device for the satisfaction of needs of whose full extent and nature they may have been unaware. Of these societies, immeasurably the most important were those of the freemasons. They quickly became the most widespread and numerous. For all their talk of ancient origins, they are a product of the early modern age and the traditional accounts of their origins were first settled in the early decades of the eighteenth century. They then took the form in which they came to be generally accepted by freemasons. Both manuscripts and oral tradition can take us back much further than this, but there is no need to follow up the investigations of these which have been carried out with diligence by masonic antiquarians. We need only remark in the first place that there is a large core of mainly baseless legend and tradition common to all these accounts: most of them attribute crucial significance to the work of Hiram, the master-mason of Solomon's Temple, murdered because he would not reveal the masonic secrets. The origins of the story are taken back in the original Constitutions to the sons of Adam and almost no important event from the Flood to the collapse of the Roman Empire fails to find a place in it.[2] In due course the Gothic style and the great masters of the Renaissance were also incorporated in the story. Other accretions to this central tradition talk of four crowned martyrs who died to preserve their secret, of Eleusinian mysteries, of Essenes, Druids, Roman cults and the Templars; most of these stories were current at a very early date.

The second thing to note about this is that, as modern masonic

---

[1] An example recently brought to light is a group of French refugees in London in 1710, seemingly connected with the English freethinker Toland. It is interesting because it demonstrates the possible existence in one body of very different purposes, in this case pure conviviality and good fellowship with the possible circulation of clandestine literature. See M. C. Jacob, 'An Unpublished Record of a Masonic [sic] Lodge in England: 1710', *Zeitschrift für Religions- und Geistesgeschichte*, XXII, 1970, p. 168. Whether 'Masonic' is or is not an appropriate description of this body is largely a matter of definition. It certainly seems to have analogies in structure with early freemasonry, but it does not show any precise filiation to the traditional body of legend and ritual which characterises the Craft and are glanced at below. Mrs Jacob's use of the word requires qualification and explanation which does not appear in her paper. But this, of course, only shows the confusion which surrounds the early history of such bodies as these.

[2] *The Constitutions of the Free-Masons containing the History, Changes, Regulations, etc. of that now Ancient and Right Worshipful Fraternity. For the Use of the Lodges,* London, 1723.

historians allow, it is almost entirely rubbish, mumbo-jumbo to which
modern masons only give veneration or lip-service because it is traditional to the Craft. Yet in the eighteenth century much more weight
was given to these legends (some of them only appeared then), and
they were influential in shaping both the characteristic masonic
ideology and the image of masonry formed by its detractors. As a
guide to the positive history of freemasonry, on the other hand, they
are valueless. 'The history of Freemasonry begins, not in the Holy
Land, not in Egypt, Greece or Rome, but here in England.'[3] That
history has its roots in the Middle Ages, though this is not very significant for our purpose. Briefly, the working masons of England and
Scotland had certain practices and organisations peculiar to their
craft which seem to have taken their basic shape in the fourteenth and
fifteenth centuries. One important example was the lodge organisation
which grew up outside the more usual gild structure in which masons,
like other craftsmen, first grouped themselves. The lodge structure
was functional; it met the needs of a craft whose members were often
itinerant, assembling sometimes for limited, even if for long, periods
on building sites where no urban craft organisation existed. Masons
moved about all over the country, as the distribution of their 'marks'
shows, and this mobility led to the generalisation of practices such as
the formation of lodges, and the evolution of rudimentary codes of
mutual help and an internal discipline operating through the lodges.
The legendary history of the Craft—whose origins can be traced back
as far as the fourteenth century—was later woven into the ritual of
the first lodges of freemasons.

It may also have been the itinerant nature of the Craft which explained the early evolution of a secret system of signs for mutual
recognition of its members. This was to become known as 'The Mason
Word', and great importance has long been attached to it by non-
masons. 'Secret signs' were one of the things which struck the antiquarian Plot who provides one of the earliest comments on freemasonry in the age in which it took its modern form.[4] Masons linked

---

[3] *Grand Lodge, 1717–1967* (London, 1967), p. 2. See also the similar judgment of
D. Ligou, 'La Franc-Maçonnerie française au XVIIIe siècle (Position des problèmes
et état des questions)', *Information Historique*, 1964, p. 99. The best account of the
origins of freemasonry is to be found in D. Knoop and G. P. Jones, *The Genesis of
Freemasonry* (Manchester, 1947). There is also much information in the old standard
History of Freemasonry, by R. F. Gould, which has been many times re-published and
revised. I have used the undated edition 'revised, edited, and brought up-to-date'
by Dudley Wright, in five volumes and attributed by the catalogue of the Bodleian
Library to 1932. All references which follow are to this edition.
[4] R. Plot, *The Natural History of Staffordshire* (Oxford, 1686), pp. 316–17. Although

the 'Word' with the legends of Hiram and the four 'coronati' who where supposed to have been murdered in the defence of their secrets. This association had from an early date led to a heightening and dramatising of the language of initiation: the aspirants' oaths were couched in terrifying terms in order to bring home to them the importance of preserving secrecy about trade practices and signs of recognition in whose defence the 'martyrs' were supposed to have died.

This complex of craft practices has traditionally been designated 'operative' masonry, to distinguish it from what followed. It was not static and continued to evolve—by the sixteenth century Scotland already had some lodges firmly established on a permanent basis and this became more common as the occasional assembly of many masons on great architectural projects became rarer with the close of the great era of ecclesiastical building—but the records are thin. The first operative lodge whose records are known to survive was at Alnwick, but its documentation begins only in 1701.

By that date, the birth of freemasonry in its modern sense was already under way. In brief, it was a matter of non-professionals first joining the lodges of operative masons and, later, founding their own, in which it might be that there would be no operative mason at all. This process went on at different speeds in different places. The lodge at Alnwick remained operative until 1748, but a celebrated lodge at Warrington in which Ashmole was made a freemason, was held in 1646, more than a century before this; the occasion provides the earliest known record of non-operative masonry in an English lodge.[5] There also exists evidence of lodges where the state of transition can be measured at some points by the occupational status of their members.[6] Fortunately, exact chronology is not important here. What is clear is that in the second half of the seventeenth century changes were going forward rapidly within operative masonry which were to lead to its virtual extinction and replacement by a new kind of masonry in the early eighteenth century. By 1717, the date when the first Grand Lodge met, we know certainly of only one clearly operative lodge still in existence, and the change can be regarded as consummated.

---

he knew the Craft to be spread throughout the country, Plot says, 'here I found persons of the most eminent quality, that did not disdain to be of this Fellowship'. He was scathing on the legendary history of the Craft, 'than which there was nothing I ever met with, more false and incoherent'.

[5] C. H. Josten, *Elias Ashmole (1617–1692)* (Oxford, 1966), i, p. 34, and ii, pp. 395–6.

[6] e.g. that at Chester, which c. 1670 seems to have had no continuing operative functions, but which still had as eighteen or nineteen of its twenty-six members persons connected with the building trade (*Grand Lodge*, p. 30).

What had begun with the admission of non-operatives to operative lodges had led first to change in the status of these lodges as the number of what were soon called 'accepted masons' grew, and then to the rise of wholly non-operative lodges, sharing the ritual and traditions of their ancestors, but brought into being for other purposes. These opened the way to the modern phenomenon which appears clearly in the eighteenth century, 'speculative' masonry, wholly non-operative and having, as its essence, a morality peculiar to itself, veiled in allegory and cloaked in traditional ritual and symbol. The trade secrets of the operative masons became the esoteric secrets of the speculative masons. This was the freemasonry whose great age was to be the eighteenth century. Little of its history concerns us. Freemasons show an intense interest in the first decades of speculative masonry because of the constitutional and ritual developments which then took place. For the rest of us, the interest of these years lies in the rapidity of the spread of the Craft and the light this throws on the character of eighteenth-century society.

The spread of masonry was made easier by constitutional and organisational changes. These, too, helped for the first time to bring freemasonry to the surface of history and provide the first plentiful evidence about it. The story begins with the foundation of the first Grand Lodge. In 1716, a meeting of masons from a few London lodges took place in the Apple Tree Tavern, Covent Garden. At that meeting, it was resolved that future Annual Assemblies and Feasts should be held on St John's Day; it appears that the desire for improved social arrangements and greater opportunities for conviviality thus lies at the root of the modern movement. A year later, on 4 June 1717, the masters of the same few lodges met at the Goose and Gridiron and constituted the first Grand Lodge. Its significance was merely symbolic and local, but it was presided over by the first of masonic Grand Masters, who was elected at this meeting.

Annual meetings in Grand Lodge seem rapidly to have attracted the attention of other lodges. By 1722, twenty-four lodges were represented, but the significance of Grand Lodge was still only local. It had begun to assume some regulatory powers, but their exercise and the acceptance of its authority was confined to London. The exact status of Grand Lodge is hard to establish before its official records begin (in 1723); after that, it is clear that in the third and fourth decades of the century its authority was more and more widely accepted. It claimed authority over some provincial lodges for the first time in 1725 and ten years later over the whole kingdom. This was recognised by a growing number of lodges. The fast early rate of growth was not sustained in the 1740s, but the slowing was only temporary.[7] Meanwhile, other masonic institutions were appearing which entrenched it still more solidly. The general charity scheme, which was to be so important in giving a character to English freemasonry, was begun in 1726. Dress, regalia and rituals were regulated more closely. Freemasons' Hall, however, was not opened until 1776: only then did English masonry have a permanent headquarters.

There is no need here to trace the detailed evolutions of English freemasonry further or more precisely than this. By 1740 it was an accepted and well-known feature of English life. Not all masons recognised Grand Lodge and some lodges continued independently, but it was a solid enough institution to provide an inspiration and example to the world-wide masonic movement of the eighteenth century.

Some of this success was due to the efforts of the masons to put their history and rites into decent written order. This gave a new coherence and stability to masonic doctrine. Its most important expression was the re-editing of the traditional manuscripts, the *Old Charges* or *Constitutions*, of which something like a hundred versions existed in the early eighteenth century. This work was commissioned by Grand Lodge in 1721 and carried out by Dr Anderson, a minister of the Church of Scotland.[8] His editorial skills were not great and the result, *The Constitutions of the Freemasons* which appeared in 1723, not very satisfactory. Masonic scholars have regretted Anderson's 'fertile imagination' and find his work an excellent illustration of 'learned credulity';[9] it cannot be said that the legendary history with which he prefaced his Charges, or regulations of masonic conduct, inspires confidence either in his scholarship or his judgment. Nevertheless, the Charges themselves have remained the core of English masonry and the major source of masonic ideology throughout the world. So much was later to be said about the fundamental purposes and designs of masons by their detractors that their main heads must be summarised at this point.

They begin with a reassuringly emphatic assertion: 'A Mason is obliged, by his Tenure, to obey the moral law; and if he rightly understands the Art, he will never be a stupid Atheist, nor an irreligious

---

[7] *Grand Lodge* (pp. 85, 88) gives these figures for lodges dependent on Grand Lodge: 1729, 61; 1739, 175; 1741, 189; 1748, 157.

[8] Knoop and Jones, pp. 1–2. There is a long discussion of the surviving manuscripts of the Old Charges in Gould (1932 edn.), I, pp. 27–63.

[9] *Grand Lodge*, p. 47; Gould, I, p. 63.

Libertine.' This is immediately followed by an endorsement of the principle of religious toleration; although already partly embodied in English law, this principle was novel enough to be worth reiteration in a country which had spent most of the previous century quarrelling bitterly about confessional differences. 'Though in ancient Times Masons were charged in every country to be of the religion of that Country or Nation, whatever it was, yet 'tis now thought more expedient only to oblige them to that Religion in which all men agree, leaving their particular Opinions to themselves; that is, to be *good Men and true*, or Men of Honour and Honesty, by whatever Denominations or Persuasions they may be distinguished.' By these means, the Charge continues, Masonry becomes an instrument of social union 'and the means of conciliating true Friendships among Persons that must have remained at a perpetual Distance'.

There is little enough theology in this. It does, just, demand a specific belief in God (though we should also read it against the background of a legendary masonic history whose main early support was the Bible). It is not surprising, in the light of it, that so many critics in more theologically-minded times were to claim that the spirit and tendency of freemasonry is anti-Christian. Yet it is best not to read the words of the Charges too strictly. Their intellectual setting was the age of Toland and Newtonian Christianity.[10] It is significant of masonic priorities that the Charge from which words have been quoted is the first, and is entitled 'Concerning God and Religion'. Furthermore, practising Christians of many denominations from the start found it possible to be freemasons. One of the most famous was the Huguenot John Theophilus Desaguliers, Student of Christ Church, Doctor of Laws of Oxford University, and priest of the Church of England. Another, the Roman Catholic eighth Duke of Norfolk, became Grand Master in 1730. And it is interesting that prominent freemasons were involved in Archbishop Wake's scheme for union of the Anglican and Gallican churches. Nor has this association of official English

[10] Mellor (*Our Separated Brethren*, pp. 81–2) has suggested that Anderson's language reflects the ideas and terminology of Sprat's *History of the Royal Society*. John Toland, sometime Roman Catholic, later deist, defender of the Act of Succession and protégé of Lord Shaftesbury, caused a sensation by the publication of his book, *Christianity not Mysterious*, in 1696. He is a figure of importance in the history of free thought and it is interesting that attention has recently been drawn by Mrs M. C. Jacob to his possible connexion with masonic and quasi-masonic bodies in the article cited above, p. 18. See also Mrs Jacob's 'John Toland and the Newtonian Ideology', *Journal of the Warburg and Courtauld Institutes*, 1969, where, in the course of a general discussion of Toland, she first drew attention to the 'Masonic' group to which he belonged.

B

freemasonry with belief in a theocentric universe been weakened. It was the determination of the French Grand Orient in 1877 that it would no longer demand of its members belief in a Grand Architect of the Universe that led to the severance of its ties with the English Grand Lodge.

Religious and civil discord were closely linked in that age. Popery and Dissent were plague-spots in the body politic to many Englishmen who looked back to more than half a century of upheaval and blamed it on one or the other. The Revolution Settlement had by no means settled everyone's fears for there was a Papist king over the water to threaten the Protestant succession. On the other flank, Anglicans under Queen Anne increasingly saw the 'Church in danger' from Whig bishops too tolerant of the overweening ambition of nonconformity. When the High Church Dr Sacheverell preached in 1709 on the theme at St Paul's and appeared to deny the foundation of the Revolution Settlement in the process, the government impeached him, but this only made him a martyr and released a storm of popular clamour and violent rioting. Such a background makes masonic caution in these matters readily understandable. The second Charge, entitled 'Of the Civil Magistrate supreme and subordinate' begins by enjoining civil obedience on the mason, who is 'never to be concerned in Plots and Conspiracies against the Peace and Welfare of the Nation, nor to behave himself undutifully to inferior Magistrates'. This should have removed any cause for misgivings, but it was followed by a qualification which strikingly reveals the practical difficulties facing a body of men who had undertaken voluntary obligations to one another in an age when a new dynasty could not expect at once to feel firm in the saddle and a pretender was always waiting off-stage. It provided that 'if a Brother should be a Rebel against the State, he is not to be countenanced in his Rebellion, however, he may be pitied as an unhappy Man; and, if convicted of no other Crime, though the loyal Brotherhood must and ought to discover his Rebellion, and give no Umbrage or Ground of political jealousy to the Government for the time being; they cannot expel him from the *Lodge*, and his Relation to it remains indefeasible.'

A pious and moral tolerance in matters of belief and a corporate disavowal of a rebel which was not to extend to depriving him of the advantages of fellowship in the Craft—such principles of corporate behaviour safeguarded unity and made growth easy. They were reinforced by a fourth Charge, 'Of Behaviour', which insisted that 'no private Piques or Quarrels' should be brought into the lodge, far less religious or political disagreement, for 'we . . . are resolved against all Politicks, as what never yet conducted to the welfare of the *Lodge*, nor ever will'.[11]

These and other principles (which were quickly publicised) go a long way towards explaining the respectability which English free-masonry at once attained and has never lost. The seventeenth-century records show that the early non-operative masons included a few men of rank and station but that such persons joined new and old lodges in much greater numbers after the foundation of Grand Lodge. Only the first three Grand Masters of the Craft in England were commoners and the third of them, Desaguliers, may be regarded as a figure of some social eminence. Besides his academic distinctions and his Fellowship of the Royal Society, he was a chaplain to the Prince of Wales. He had lectured in public and before the Court on 'mechanical and experi-mental philosophy'.[12] Desaguliers was thus a link between learned and fashionable society and the Craft. It is reasonable to believe that by this he contributed importantly to the rapid growth of freemasonry,[13] but it may also owe more to him as the driving force behind the editing and publishing of the *Constitutions*. There can be seen in them the influence of ideas which would have been familiar to someone who (like Desaguliers) shared the philosophical assumptions of Newtonian Christianity. Such assumptions could provide an intellectual basis for the practical tolerance which Englishmen badly needed to establish if a repetition of the upheavals of the previous century, and their threat of social disorder, was to be avoided.

With this useful and reassuring ideology was combined the patron-age by the great which was almost certain to secure for freemasonry a quick growth, even if we leave out of account the Craft's ritual and esoteric attractions. Desaguliers was succeeded in 1721 by the Duke of Montagu and from that time English Grand Masters have always been noblemen. The distinction of the office—and therefore of the Craft—was so firmly established that it survived even the Grand Mastership of the Duke of Wharton (who followed Montagu), and from 1782 to

[11] It has been remarked of Ashmole's record of his own admission in 1646, where he gives the names of those also of the lodge, that it is 'most valuable as a testi-monial of the non-political and non-denominational character of seventeenth-century freemasonry' (Josten, *op. cit.*, ii, 396, footnote 2) and it would seem reason-able to believe, therefore, that the fourth Charge reflects masonic tradition, as well as current and practical concern.

[12] On Desaguliers' lectures, see A. E. Musson and Eric Robinson, *Science and Technology in the Industrial Revolution* (Manchester, 1969), pp. 37-40.

[13] He himself admitted the Prince of Wales freemason.

1843 it was held continuously by three members of the Royal family.[14] The movement of meetings of Grand Lodge from taverns to the halls of livery companies, and the annual processions on St John's Day in which the freemasons marched in state to their feasts, were other signs of the public standing of the Craft.

Rapid growth and conspicuous patronage gave the freemasons publicity. Newspapers reported their processions and meetings. Imitations also appeared and freemasons soon had to take precautions against irregular organisations laying claim to masonic secrets and rituals. This led to renewed attention to secret signs and methods of recognition. It also helped to stir up the first important printed attacks on the freemasons, the ancestors of a whole literature to come.[15] But no criticisms could fundamentally weaken the position the Craft had so quickly won in English society. Both this fact and the lack of precedent for a craze so successful pose the question: why did people become masons? A complete answer would have to be very detailed and will not be attempted here. There is great difficulty in extracting clear information about motives from the fragmentary non-official evidence about masonry and the formal utterances of the Craft itself. Yet four themes seem to stand out. One is the simple social urge which culminates in the conviviality of the Lodge and the banquet. Modern masonic writers have happily defined it as 'that compound of refreshment, smoking and conversation, in circumstances of ease rather than elegance, and undisturbed by the society of women, in which many men can take a rational pleasure'.[16] In joining lodges for this, of course, the freemasons were only doing what many other men of their time were doing: the early eighteenth century was a great age for the formation of small assemblies and clubs for social enjoyment.

More distinctive, but still very much of the era, was the ideological motivation supplied by the tolerant, latitudinarian atmosphere of the lodges. This, buttressed by the Charges, removed the unpleasant possibilities of religious or political friction, but also did more: it was a positive attraction to enlightened men seeking a society where up-to-date ideas were current and where they could be discussed with understanding. This was to appeal even more strongly when masonry spread to Europe. Because it implied the recognition of moral duties and an attitude of general benevolence it may be united with a third motive for joining the Craft, that of the charitable feelings awoken

---

[14] The Duke of Cumberland (1782–90), the Prince of Wales (1790–1813), the Duke of Sussex (1813–43).

[15] See below, pp. 58–63.   [16] Knoop and Jones, p. 315.

by the spectacle of masonic mutual aid (and strengthened after the setting up of a general charity scheme).

Finally, there is the appeal of the occult. This is even more difficult to assess. It arose not only from the perpetual fascination of 'being on the inside' but also, as the eighteenth century advanced, from a growing taste for and appreciation of the non-rational and mysterious. Speculation is dangerous, but on the continent such appreciation can be seen growing as the observances and ritual of established religion came to be felt to be less and less satisfying. Whether a direct connexion can be shown is another matter: what is indisputable is that ritual and ceremony have always proved satisfying ways of meeting some emotional needs and secrecy seems often to give them an added potency. Expressions of this recur throughout history. Alchemists, cabbalists, Rosicrucians and operative masonry itself had long attracted the attention of antiquarians, and many people linked them or mixed them up with one another. In the late seventeenth century, speculative masonry drew some of its power from its ability to tap the same interests and the result was the great elaboration of 'Craft Working'—that is, of ritual practices—which characterised the first four decades of the eighteenth century.[17]

In leaving the question of motivation, it must be remembered that we need suppose no general or consistent pattern of motives in individual masons. They joined for many different reasons and were to go on doing so. The emphasis of masonic activity often changed, in consequence. This reservation is important because the opposite assumption —of consistent, unswerving purpose—lies at the heart of almost all anti-masonic propaganda. Such, for example, was the view soon held abroad that the organisation of Grand Lodge and the re-editing of the *Constitutions* was a political act of adherents of the Hanoverian dynasty.[18] It was suggested that after 1688, Jacobite, Roman Catholic elements had remained strongly influential in the London operative lodges. Of the intermittent evidence of the existence of 'Grand Lodges' at York and in Scotland at the beginning of the eighteenth century it has been alleged that the best explanation is the existence of a Scottish, Roman Catholic and Jacobite freemasonry to which the foundation of a 'Protestant' Grand Lodge in 1717 was a reply. The story is from several points of view interesting, not least because it introduces at the very beginning

---

[17] The recent and posthumous book by R. Le Forestier, *La franc-maçonnerie Templière et occultiste* (Paris and Louvain, 1970), discusses in its first chapter the (in Le Forestier's view) underrated and underemphasised mystical elements in early English freemasonry.   [18] See Ligou, p. 100.

of the modern history of secret societies an element of that political mystery which was to be central to the later myth. But it is not necessary to rely on any such arguments to explain the rapid growth of English freemasonry in the eighteenth century.

Here we can leave its history; from this point English freemasonry will have little but incidental interest for us. Its importance to the myths of the secret societies is that it was the character and ritual of the movement so solidly grounded in England in the first decades of the eighteenth century which shaped directly or indirectly almost every secret society in Western Europe or America down to the nineteenth century. The myths about those secret societies, too, were shaped not only by knowledge of this affiliation—however misconceived—but by the interpretation of the details of early English freemasonry. Secrets, signs and passwords, symbolic rituals, an inflated rhetoric of moral purpose, a hierarchy of initiates of various degrees: these were some of the elements which were to be woven again and again into the fantastic speculations of the myth-makers of the next two hundred years. Meanwhile, English freemasonry was to continue its respectable, blameless and increasingly insular course. It survived a great quarrel in the second half of the eighteenth century, negotiated with no more than temporary alarm the panics of the revolutionary wars and emerged into the next century as firmly non-political and as staunchly attached to a vague non-sectarian Christianity as ever. Its social prestige was undiminished: between 1737 and 1907, sixteen princes of the blood were freemasons, and four of them became kings. It was in continental Europe that the consequences of a lack of firm guidance such as that provided by Grand Lodge were to appear in a luxuriant growth of ritual and sectarianism. From this were to spring further opportunities of misunderstanding and, therefore, yet more suspicion that something sinister was afoot. In the story of English freemasonry such developments and such suspicion were to remain inconsiderable and little need be said of it in what follows.

THE SPREAD OF FREEMASONRY ABROAD

England was à la mode in the second and third decades of the eighteenth century. She had the prestige of power: after successfully sustaining a great war and achieving a victorious peace, her own strength and judicious alliance gave her a large measure of control of Western European and Mediterranean affairs until about 1730. These years have been called 'la prépondérance anglaise', and this international

achievement was matched at home. There, a long drawn-out constitutional and dynastic crisis was successfully resolved, a union with
Scotland closed a century of bickering and war, a rebellion was suppressed and a set of new institutions was created under which Britons
were to live for the next two centuries and reach the peak of their power.
And this was all borne by a striking increase in the country's wealth
which, in spite of misgivings about high taxation and national in-
debtedness, formed a solid foundation for the new burdens of power.

Many foreign observers linked this achievement to an accompanying
cultural and social renovation so striking that it might have been
called revolution, had that use of the word then been accepted. Not only
was England the country of Newton and Locke; it was also the
citadel of religious toleration, now embodied in the law, and it was
a community in which differences of birth counted for somewhat less
than in other European countries and in which a wide measure of legal
equality was a reality. Englishmen, it appeared, had somehow, after a
half-century of turmoil, learnt to live together in harmony and to do
without the devices of despotism thought to be necessary in Europe.
The result was an admiration for England among men of letters which
was to earn itself the distinction of having a new word invented to
describe it: anglomania.[19]

Anglomania was fed by travel and commerce, both of which brought
Europeans into contact with Englishmen and English ideas. Paradoxically, it was also helped by the presence in Europe, and especially
in France, of Jacobite exiles. This was a paradox not only because many
of these exiles were Scottish or Irish (who often cherished social and
cultural ideals very different from those admired by foreign visitors to
England), but also because the core of Jacobitism was, after all, a wish
to return to an ancien régime which had been swept away. Nevertheless, the literary success of Hamilton's *Memoirs*, the wit and address of
a Bolingbroke in exile or the tarnished glamour of the Pretender's
court helped to keep the fashionable public aware of the interest and
excitement of English cultural life under the first two Hanoverians.

In this context it is easy to see why something so successful in
England as freemasonry—but also something so peculiarly English—
should have so quickly crossed the Channel. Fashion alone explains
much of its appeal. It is also obvious that the attractions which had

---

[19] There is a good general survey of this phenomenon in one country in A. Graf,
L'Anglomania e l'influsso inglese in Italia nel secolo XVIII (Turin, 1911). Its French
expressions can be appreciated by reading two major works of the period, Voltaire's
Lettres Philosophiques and Montesquieu's *De l'Esprit des Lois*.

helped freemasonry to spend itself in England would exercise just as powerful an influence abroad; at the lowest level, freemasonry offered an escape from the stupefying boredom of early eighteenth-century society anywhere outside the capital and court in an age when such escapes were few. There were also some things in masonry, certain masonic tenets and attitudes, which were likely to appeal even more in Europe than they did in England because they implied criticisms of official assumptions and established institutions in less advanced societies. Some people found religious tolerance a very attractive ideal in a France whose Church was rent by bitter struggles against Jansenists and where Protestants' children were ipso facto illegitimate.[20] The equality of brother masons was a much more startling and attractive idea in the complex and elaborate hierarchy of most European countries where men were divided into Estates and Estates were only slightly less sharply divided within themselves, than in the looser texture of English hierarchies. Where the baroque exuberance of the Counter-Reformation was still the pervading ideological force, the idea of a great Architect of the Universe seemed attractive in its simplicity and restraint. In short, freemasonry was likely to appeal to cultivated Europeans in the early eighteenth century just because it embodied elements of that Enlightenment attitude which was about to establish itself as the outstanding cultural fact of the age.

This context favoured the spread of freemasonry outside England. There are good grounds—as will appear—for saying that it is one of the most important, as well as one of the most underrated of English cultural influences on Europe in the last two-and-a-half centuries. The structure of lodges, their subordination to grand lodges, the three grades, the basic rituals and traditions, the emphasis on works of benevolence, the ideological latitudinarianism and the social prestige of freemasonry were all to spread all over the world. Other countries were to elaborate, to distort and borrow from the English masonic tradition. They were also, it appears (though certainty in this matter is very difficult to obtain), to draw directly upon Scottish sources when the English tradition was, for one reason or another, unsatisfying.[21]

---

[20] The special attractiveness to Protestants in France of adherence to the Craft, it has been recently suggested, might go far beyond the abstract appeal of tolerance. See the exploratory article of G. Gayot, 'Les problèmes de la double appartenance: Protestants et Francs-maçons à Sedan au XVIIIe siècle', *Revue d'histoire moderne et contemporaire*, 1971, pp. 415–29.

[21] The difficult question of Scottish origins for continental freemasonry has recently been reopened in a paper by C. H. Chevalier, 'Maçons écossais au XVIIIe siècle', *AHRF*, 1969, pp. 393–408.

Yet they were never to evolve masonry directly from operative survivals as English and Scottish masons had done. Their masonry was always derivative; its English components were always to remain obvious, even if dilute, and the English connexion was, in most countries, long to be the test of masonic orthodoxy.

Not surprisingly, some of the first traces of freemasonry's diffusion from England reflect the influence of trade and empire; overseas lodges appeared quickly in seaports and colonies. Provincial Grand Masters began to be appointed in 1726, primarily for overseas lodges, and Gambia and Bengal were by then on the list. Gibraltar had a lodge in 1729; Charleston, South Carolina, had one in 1735. But our concern is with Europe. The earliest lodges there have obscure and ill-documented histories. Many problems arise in connexion with the order of their establishment and it is simplest not to follow a strict chronological method in tracing their early history. The main point of importance is that such evidence as we have usually points to the important influence in the early years of direct contact with England. By 1738, the English *Constitutions* refer to Grand Lodges in Scotland, Ireland, France and Italy. The last two countries are those with which this book will be mainly concerned since so much came to be voiced and felt in them about the threats posed by secret societies; it is interesting and significant that they should have been among the first to acquire a mature masonic society of their own.

FREEMASONRY IN EIGHTEENTH-CENTURY FRANCE

There are good reasons for looking at France most closely of all. It was the first continental country in which freemasonry enjoyed the widespread and fashionable success it had already achieved in England. French freemasonry was also to make one important original contribution to the history of the secret societies, the appearance of 'Scottish' masonry. Finally, a good reason for looking in some detail at it is what followed: the French Revolution and the furious arguments over the part played in it by masons. We are fortunate that French freemasonry has had longer scientific study than that of other nations, and to that extent our data are better.[22]

[22] The best starting-point is the article by D. Ligou, 'La Franc-Maçonnerie française au XVIIIe siècle (Position des problèmes et état des questions)', *Information Historique*, 1964, p. 98, which describes the bibliography down to that date. Since this article appeared, P. Chevallier has published two important monographs, *Les ducs sous l'acacia ou les premiers pas de la Franc-Maçonnerie française 1725–1743* (Paris, 1964), and *La première profanation du temple maçonnique* (Paris, 1968), and A. Le

There are nevertheless big gaps in our knowledge of its early history. Before 1730 there is little documentation: the earliest claims for ancient foundation among the French lodges were made when lodges were trying to regularise themselves in the 1760s. One lodge then claimed to go back to 1688, when allegedly it was founded in an Irish regiment in the service of France; the claim was later accepted by the masonic authorities. The claim of a Dunkirk lodge to have been founded in 1721 is still asserted and still in doubt.[23] Traditionally, too, 1725 is the date of the founding of the first Parisian lodge, by Charles Radcliffe, secretary to the Young Pretender.[24] The most recent studies are cautious, admitting simply that Parisian masonry appears somewhere between 1725 and 1730.[25]

The years before the mid-1730s therefore form the first distinct period of French masonic history, or, perhaps, of its pre-history. In spite of the unsatisfactory nature of the evidence it contains a recurrent theme which springs at once to the eye, that of Jacobite connexion; the Irish regiment and Radcliffe's role make it clear, and it was widely remarked at the time. It has been claimed that because freemasonry was brought to France by Jacobites there existed in French freemasonry from the start a senior tradition and affiliation opposed to that deriving from the London Grand Lodge. It has also been claimed that the Dunkirk lodge, supposedly founded from the Grand Lodge of England, was replaced in 1732 by another under Jacobite influence. However this may be, the evidence both from the earliest period and from the decade of 1730s when more information is available, makes it clear

---

Bihan has compiled two valuable reference works, *Francs-Maçons parisiens du Grand Orient de France* (Paris, 1966), and *Loges et Chapitres de la Grande Loge et du Grand Orient de France* (Paris, 1967). Each of these books contains bibliographical references not included in M. Ligou's invaluable summary. Finally, mention should be made of the collection of articles (of very varied quality, it is true) in *AHRF*, 1969, no. 197, pp. 373–548.

[23] See notes in Le Bihan, *Loges*, p. 82 on the lodge 'L'Amitié et Fraternité' where references are given; for the Irish regimental lodge, 'La Parfaite Egalité', p. 329.

[24] Knoop and Jones, p. 320. Brother of James Radcliffe, third Earl of Derwentwater, who was executed after impeachment and attainder in 1716 for his part in the '15. In spite of the attainder, his son assumed his title and so, in turn, did Charles Radcliffe, after his nephew's death in 1731. He too was executed on Tower Hill in 1746 after capture at sea by an English ship. More information about Charles can be found in the *D.N.B.*, s.v. James Radcliffe; there is no separate article on him.

[25] Le Bihan, *Loges*, p. vii. 'Il est difficile de remonter au delà.' The arguments of Chevallier (*Les ducs*, pp. 17–18), suggest that although lodges of exiled Jacobites probably existed in Paris even in the early 1720s, they led 'une existence discrète et effacée' and only emerged from 'la pénombre volontaire' after 1730.

that French freemasonry was at the start believed to be closely connected with the Jacobite exiles and their sympathisers. The importance of this was that some elements in French masonry were, therefore, thought to be potentially schismatic and possibly the vehicle of political purposes.

1730 was the year in which publicity was given to the initiation of Montesquieu in London.[26] It may be that this publicity in part explains the increasing attention paid to freemasonry in France and the more frequent references to it in the following years. But there is also internal evidence of growth, such as the issue of patents by the Grand Master in London for lodges at Paris (1732) and Valenciennes (1733). A lodge at Bordeaux, called 'la loge anglaise' and perhaps for English merchants, appeared in 1732 although its history was soon broken; other lodges of the decade whose establishment is well authenticated appeared at Lyon, Rouen, Marseille, Caen, Montpellier. A Jacobite lodge in the Papal enclave of Avignon was set up in 1736.[27] One at Metz in 1735 is alleged to have been working 'sur les fondements d'une trés ancienne loge'.[28] The culmination of this decade of development was the appearance of a Grand Lodge at Paris: it is first mentioned in 1737 and the first Grand Masters seem not to have been Frenchmen.[29] Persons of quality were nonetheless known to be masons and it was in 1735 that Desaguliers was reported to have admitted the Comte de St Florentin a mason.[30] Then, in 1738, the Duc d'Antin became Grand Master, an elevation symbolising both the independence of French freemasonry and its social success. A masonic account (written later in the century) says that five lodges in Paris in 1735 had become twenty-two seven years later.[31]

Several further developments of importance occurred towards the end of this period. One was the supersession of Jacobite influences by others drawn from the revivified English freemasonry.[32] Only in 1732

[26] Robert Shackleton, *Montesquieu: a Critical Biography* (Oxford, 1961), p. 140.

[27] Le Bihan, *Loges*, p. 39 (s.v. 'L'Anglaise'), vii, 421–2. G. Hubrecht, 'Notes pour servir à l'histoire de la franc-maçonnerie à Bordeaux' (*Revue historique de Bordeaux et du departement de la Gironde*, 1954, pp. 143–50) is useful on this city. For Avignon see G. Gautherot, 'La Franc-maçonnerie à Avignon au milieu du XVIIIe siècle. La Loge Saint-Jean de Jerusalem, statuts et procès-verbaux', *RISS*, IX, pp. 113–217. (The date 1737, however, is asserted by C. Mesliand in 'Franc-maçonnerie et religion à Avignon au XVIIIe siècle', *AHRF*, 1969, p. 447.)

[28] Le Bihan, *Loges*, p. 128.

[29] Derwentwater, James Hector Maclean and (strongly presumptive) the Duke of Wharton are the names given by Le Bihan, *Loges*, p. vii; for Maclean see Chevallier, *Les ducs*, p. 27.

[30] R. Priouret, *La franc-maçonnerie sous les lys* (Paris, 1953), p. 17.

[31] Ligou, p. 101.

[32] Later, recognised English origins were to be regarded as a sign of authenticity

does a lodge directly dependent on London for its origins appear to have been successfully established. This has been said to be the origin of a tension within the Craft in France between two 'tendencies', described by a contemporary as 'freemaçons catoliques, royalistes et jacobites' and 'freemaçons hérétiques apostats et républicains'.[33] The lodges of the two tendencies looked respectively to the Jacobite-dominated Grand Mastership or to London for guidance. But both tendencies remained in relations with one another and Derwentwater, installed as Grand Master in 1736, was accepted by all lodges. The next election, that of d'Antin two years later, was, it is said, the mark of a victory of the 'Hanoverian' tendency over the other for the control of French freemasonry.

The arguments about this issue are complicated and in some degree speculative. Nor is it easy to see what might be implied by such a thesis. Nevertheless, argument of this sort provides a plausible thread through the fragmentary evidence and a better explanation of the known facts than any other in that it accounts for more of them. It fits, too, other indications that the years 1736–8 were in many ways crucial. These are not only the years of sudden publicity and a spectacular growth of the Craft's influence in the higher ranks of society; they are also those in which the French government's official actions towards freemasonry seem to indicate that something in the nature of a conflict between different views of freemasonry is taking place.[34] It has been suggested, too, that the publication in 1738 of a Papal Bull condemning freemasonry sharpened the desire of some French freemasons to emphasise the Catholic and legitimist nature of their inheritance at the expense of the London connexion.[35] It was also at this time that, possibly because of publicity, there were clear signs of a

---

of great weight in establishing the antiquity of a lodge. See, e.g., the comments of the Beaucaire Lodge quoted in Le Bihan, *Loges*, p. 31.

[33] Ramsay, quoted in Chevallier, *Les ducs*, p. 216. Elsewhere (*Mémoires de la Société Académique de L'Aube*, CIV, 1964–6, p. 184) M. Chevallier remarks on the roots of 'la vieille maçonnerie parisienne' as lying in the 'milieux bourgeois et commerçants de Paris à partir de 1737–40'. This tendency later divided itself from more aristocratic masonry (see below). It was always more Catholic, more conservative and prided itself on its origins in figures like Maclean. Perhaps we can infer a certain social resonance in the two tendencies M. Chevallier here distinguishes ideologically.

[34] See below, Ch. III. There is also the interesting suggestion (Chevallier, *Les ducs*, p. 110) of a close involvement of the British ambassador, Waldegrave, in official transactions affecting masonry.

[35] Notably by R. S. Lindsay, 'Le rite écossais pour l'Ecosse', *Le Symbolisme*, 1961, p. 7. On the Bull, see below, pp. 68–71.

sudden spurt of growth in freemasonry outside Paris.[36] Finally, it was in 1737 that a document was published which gave resounding publicity to the movement and which shaped its history profoundly. This was the speech of the Chancellor of the Grand Lodge of France, the Chevalier Ramsay.

Andrew Michael Ramsay is an ambiguous and interesting figure. There is something of the eighteenth-century adventurer about him and something of the spiritual pilgrim. Born at Ayr in 1696, the son of a baker, he went to Edinburgh University and then acted as tutor to a nobleman's sons before going to London. There he learnt French, and encountered the writings of Fénelon. In 1709 he went to Holland, where he attended lectures at Leiden before moving on in August to Cambrai, Fénelon's diocese, where he met the archbishop and joined the Roman Catholic Church. Ramsay remained there until Fénelon's death in 1715. (He was later to write the archbishop's life, using the papers which his patron had left him.) Ramsay then went to Paris in the household of a great nobleman. A friendship with the Duke of Orléans, then Regent for the child king Louis XV, won him his title, as a Chevalier of the Order of St Lazare, and a pension.

He was now a figure of some social distinction. It may have been the publication of his life of Fénelon in 1720 which led to his appointment, in 1724, as tutor to the Old Pretender's sons in Rome. After some fifteen months he resigned and returned to Paris. He refused another post as tutor—this time to the Duke of Cumberland, the third son of George II—and in the light of his Jacobite associations it is interesting that his standing should at this time have been sufficiently ambiguous for this offer to be made to him and for him to be given a safe-conduct to the United Kingdom. In 1728 he went there as the guest of the Duke of Argyll at Inverary. He is recorded in 1729 at Spalding as a member of the celebrated Gentlemen's Society (whose membership included many freemasons) and in 1730 he was given a doctorate of civil law at Oxford. This degree was opposed on grounds of religion and political sympathy but, once again, his position seems to have brought him support in quarters where he might have been expected to provoke hostility. There is something of a mystery here; perhaps he was some sort of double agent. It is at least odd that he should enjoy the patronage of the Pretender *and*, at the same time, that of the Regent, Orléans,

---

[36] It seems to have been in 1737 that Nancy, the residence of the Dukes of Lorraine, was first reported to be a masonic centre (Chevallier, *Les ducs*, p. 163). The first evidence from Orléans is in 1743, but may refer to an earlier date (*AHRF*, 1969, pp. 425–6).

whose alliance with England was meant to keep the Stuarts off the English throne.

Ramsay's association with freemasonry is believed to date at least from 1728. In that year he was probably admitted to a London lodge. Certainly he was by then associated with many prominent English masons and he began soon after his return to France to stand out in French freemasonry as well. In 1736 he was Chancellor, or Orator, of the Grand Lodge of France and in the following year publicity was given to his sensational speech. It appeared in English in Dublin in 1738 as the *Apology for the Free and Accepted Masons* and was long said to have achieved the distinction of being burnt at Rome that year, but this is no longer thought likely.[37] Its wide circulation was guaranteed when in 1742 it was issued together with a French translation of Anderson's *Constitutions*. Although he continued to write and publish—his literary and philosophical works form a sizeable corpus—nothing that he subsequently wrote was ever so influential and he disappears completely from masonic history. He died in 1743 at St Germain-en-Laye.[38]

In its final form, Ramsay's speech should have been delivered to a general assembly at Grand Lodge on 24 March 1737, but it now seems unlikely that it was. An earlier and shorter version had been presented at a lodge held in the previous December. It seems also to have been read on other occasions, at the admission of new freemasons, and Ramsay clearly regarded it as a chef d'oeuvre which he was at pains to embody in print.[39] Its tone is defensive and it represents Ramsay's considered view of the purpose and justification of the Order. As such, it was to be of great importance both to those who feared the Order and and to those who sought to uphold it.

Ramsay's general tenor was unexceptionable and unsurprising.

[37] There is an ingenious discussion of the document which was burnt at Rome by W. E. Moss, 'A note on the Relation Apologique et historique de la société des franc-maçons', *AQC*, li, 1940, p. 226.

[38] For Ramsay's biography, we must still rely mainly on A. Chérel, *Un aventurier religieux au xviiie siècle, André-Michel Ramsay* (Paris, 1926), supplemented by additional information in Chevallier, *Les ducs*, pp. 133–7. The earlier and now out-dated discussion by Gould (*History of Freemasonry*, IV, pp. 3–19) is mainly concerned with defending Ramsay against the charge of exploiting masonry in the Stuart interest.

[39] Chevallier, *Les ducs*, pp. 144–54, has a thorough examination of the complicated question of the provenance of the speech and its importance for the historian of the internal tendencies of French freemasonry (a theme of some complexity which, fortunately, need not concern us here). He shows that the final version dispensed with much pseudo-historical material linking the Craft with early Jewish history and the Patriarchs. Gould (IV, pp. 10–15) gives a translation of the speech in its final form from which I quote.

Building on and elaborating Anderson, he presents the Order as the embodiment, promoter and diffuser of social and individual virtue; the Order was set up, he says, 'to make men lovable men, good citizens, good subjects, inviolable in their promises, faithful adorers of the God of Love, lovers of virtue rather than reward'.[40] His cautious assertion of the innocence of masonic feasting is only significant as evidence of the sort of criticisms which were at that time being made of the Order.[41] The same may be said of his defence of the exclusion of women from masonic assemblies and of his explicit assertion that the penalties for the breaking of masonic oaths were moral and social, not physical. It was not in such passages as these, but in the antiquarian embellishment of this theme that Ramsay was to give so much scope for future suspicion of the freemasons and to justify the title of 'Homer of masonry' given to him by one modern scholar.[42]

Ramsay returns in his speech several times to the legendary theme of masonic origins in the Crusades, alluding respectfully, certainly, to the more ancient traditional ancestry of the Order, but identifying the crusading era as the great period of revival. Then, he says, 'many princes, lords and citizens associated themselves and vowed to restore the Temple of the Christians in the Holy Land, to employ themselves in bringing back their architecture to its first institution. They agreed upon several ancient signs and symbolic words drawn from the well of religion in order to recognise themselves amongst the heathen and Saracens. These signs and words were only communicated to those who promised solemnly, even sometimes at the foot of the altar, never to reveal them. This sacred promise was therefore not an execrable oath, as it has been called, but a respectable bond to unite Christians of all nationalities in one confraternity. Some time afterwards our Order formed an intimate union with the Knights of St John of Jerusalem. This union was made after the example set by the Israelites when they erected the second Temple who, whilst they handled the trowel and mortar with one hand, in the other held the sword and buckler.'[43] In this emphasis and in the specific references to the Knights of St John lay the roots of a legendary connexion of masonry with the Templars which was to animate both a great flowering of masonic activity and a rich heritage of misrepresentation and misinterpretation.

[40] Gould, IV, p. 11.
[41] See below, pp. 58–61.
[42] The term is Chevallier's (Les ducs, p. 152); it becomes even more apposite if we take into account the biblical material from Ramsay's early draft which was omitted from the printed versions.
[43] Gould, IV, pp. 13–14.

In the Templar association lay the germs of a mythology of revolt and vengeance.[44]

The idea of masons who strove sword in hand to rebuild the Temple was the taproot of the tradition to become known as 'Scottish' masonry, a name which owes much to another of Ramsay's flights of fancy. This was contained in assertions he made both of the superior antiquity of the Scots lodges and of the role of other Scotchmen in the era which followed the end of the Crusades. Then, says Ramsay, the lodges and rites fell in most places into neglect. 'This is why of so many historians only those of Great Britain speak of our Order. Nevertheless, it preserved its splendour among those Scotsmen of (*sic*) whom the Kings of France confided during many centuries the safeguard of their royal persons.'[45] The specific assertion of the existence of a thirteenth-century Scots lodge ignited generations of debate within the Craft about the standing of lodges claiming to belong to the 'Scots Rite'.[46] Generally, a prestige came to be attached to imagined or real Scottish connexions which was of high importance in that fashion-conscious age. From it was to flow a huge elaboration and proliferation of rites within masonry; this, in turn, was to generate further grounds for suspicion of the Craft as a whole. We need not anticipate these consequences and implications. Nonetheless, the public attention soon given to Ramsay's address marks its significance. He contributed, unknowingly, a seminal element to the later secret society mythology, though decades were to pass before its outlines were to become clear.[47] More immediately, a tendency in continental European freemasonry to justify and seek prestige for any innovation by tacking on to it a legendary Scottish origin became apparent and spread rapidly. The freemasonry which accepted higher degrees beyond the original three came to be referred to as 'Scottish' freemasonry, and claimed independence from the tradition drawing authority from England.[48]

Such legends favoured a new wave of inventiveness in freemasonry in the twenty years after 1740. In France, a luxuriant but anarchic growth showed itself both in an elaboration of ritual and in the

[44] These themes are discussed below; see especially pp. 98–100.

[45] Gould, IV, p. 14.

[46] See C. H. Chevalier (*AHRF*, 1969), already cited. See fn. 21.

[47] For other details of Ramsay's speech which the later mythology was to draw on, see below, p. 55.

[48] See below, pp. 96 ff., for a discussion of this phenomenon. The three 'original' degrees were those of Apprentice, Fellow Craft and Master, but it should be noted that masonic historians have long and nicely disputed the records which throw light on their origins and exact distinctions. For one authoritative discussion see Gould, II, pp. 204–11.

appearance of new higher degrees. The prosperity of the Craft was shown by its success in recruiting persons of respectability and station. There are even grounds for believing that Louis XV may himself have become a freemason.[49] Lodges appeared all over France. But it was not a sign of health that some of them had very suspicious credentials. Their names were often exotic and pretentious. At Bordeaux there met the 'Sublimes Princes du Royal Secret' and at Carcassonne the 'Cour des Souverains Commandeurs du Temple' (these names were not untypical of many which now began to reflect the themes of the great secret and the Templar connexion which were given currency by Ramsay's speech). At Paris there was from 1758 the 'Conseil des Empereurs d'Orient et d'Occident', claiming a Scottish descent. Such high-flown language later became a commonplace and ceased to alarm or impress, just as people are nowadays as little worried by the titles of the dignitaries of the Ku Klux Klan as by those of the Shriners. Nevertheless, the publicity given to such names in the eighteenth century could awake uneasiness. In that more innocent era they seemed portentous and alarming. Furthermore, the organisations that bore them presented French freemasonry with a grave disciplinary and organisational problem. Especially after the formation in 1754 of the Chapitre de Clermont,[50] the Paris Grand Lodge was increasingly unable to win acceptance from most French freemasons as the unique centre of their craft. The result, after deepening disorders, was a crisis within French masonry which lasted roughly from 1760 to 1799.

Dissidence within freemasonry crystallised slowly during this period around the issue of reform. At one meeting of Grande Loge, the supporters of reform actually came to blows with the supporters of the Grand Master. His rival succeeded him but disputes continued to rage. Meanwhile, most lodges were living more or less autonomously, but when in 1767 the Grand Master, the Duc de Clermont, ordered Grande Loge on the royal authority to adjourn sine die, he was in fact removing one of the few feeble barriers to further disintegration, because it had attempted to regulate and resist the flood of new higher grades. Meanwhile, lodges continued to spring up, sometimes from disreputable origins. Ageing and penniless Jacobites had for years been conferring irregular patents on credulous masons in return for fees; each 'obedience' had sought to extend its influence by authorising new

---

[49] See Chevallier, Les ducs, pp. 173–9.

[50] A terminological point may be conveniently made here: the custom arose of applying the word 'Chapter' to masonic assemblies at which other grades than the three established by English practice were present.

lodges; individual lodges had engendered daughter lodges. In this luxuriant tangle, the thread of orthodox masonry was often lost.

The turning-point was the death of Clermont, in 1771. This was followed not only by the election of a new Grand Master, the Duc de Chartres, but by the coming together of the two factions in Grande Loge and their agreement to seek reform under him. Famous later (and important in anti-masonic mythology) as Philippe Egalité, Duc d'Orléans of the revolutionary era, Chartres was, in fact, not a significant figure in what followed. The real regenerator of French masonry was the Duc de Montmorency-Luxembourg, who became 'administrateur-général' in 1772 and pressed forward without scruple towards a reformed French masonry firmly based on one centre of authority. The result was the emergence in 1773 of a new body, based on the old Grand Lodge, and augmented by the masters of other lodges: the Grand Orient. Its creation was forced through, police being employed to seize the seals of the old Grand Lodge. Circulars were sent to provincial lodges to acquaint them with an accomplished change. It was not the end of the troubles of French freemasonry, but it was the turning-point. Henceforth, at least the 'blue' lodges (as those which stuck to the three grades of English masonry were soon called) had a central authority recognised by the majority of them.

Gradually, the supremacy of Grand Orient was established over a majority of 'blue' lodges. Schism persisted; many lodges refused its authority and, laying claims to be the true heirs of Grande Loge, set up a new Grand Loge de France which did not come to terms with the Grand Orient until 1799 and provided a rival authority.[51] And of course, there were by now many 'Scottish' rites, to say nothing of fringe masonic or crypto-masonic lodges not all of which would enter the new obedience.[52] One importance of this, for our purposes, is that the fact of schism generated publicity and attention because of the publication of books and pamphlets setting out the claims of rival obediences. More 'secrets' thus entered circulation and were available to the myth-makers.

Nevertheless, the long and careful effort of Montmorency's Grand Orient bore fruit in a large measure of stabilisation and reform. The main instrument of this reform was insistence that all lodges should submit their constitutions for inspection and verification to the Grand Orient which then determined the validity or invalidity of their titles. In this way common adherence to the basic tenets of orthodox masonry

[51] And even then the reconciliation was not to prove lasting.
[52] For example, the French affiliations of the German 'Strict Observance', to which we return below, pp. 106 ff.

was achieved. In January 1777 the Grand Orient ruled that all constitutions which had not survived this process were irregular; although it
is not likely that this could have been completely effective, in that individual lodges or masons might still have chosen to recognise as a
brother-mason someone from an irregular lodge, it went far to diminish the confusion left by the middle decades of the century. The core
of the Grand Orient's requirements was an insistence that lodges
should only adhere to traditional, symbolic masonry, with its three
grades.[53] Perpetual masterships of lodges were ended and hencefor-
ward all lodges were to elect their master annually. A permanent headquarters was acquired when the Grand Orient installed itself in a former
house of Jesuit novices in the Rue Pot-de-Fer; it was often referred to
subsequently as the 'Orient pot de fer'.

The number of lodges which were brought under the aegis of the
Grand Orient in this way was very large.[54] It is important to remember,
of course, that many had only a discontinuous and even a fleeting
existence. Many applications, too, were rejected. Meanwhile, as a
second best, the Grand Orient negotiated concordats with those rites
which it could not control.

Unfortunately even such data as are furnished by the substantial
records left by these proceedings—the biggest single collection of
material for the documentation of early freemasonry—still remains an
imperfect guide to the important question of the size of the masonic
movement in France at the end of the century. One authoritative
estimate is that there were some 20,000 to 30,000 freemasons grouped in
over 600 lodges in 1789.[55] Another, on a different basis, suggests that
between 35,000 and 50,000 masons were grouped under the Grand
Orient in that year.[56] The latest studies permit more precise statements
about the number of lodges subordinate to the Grand Orient. But
outside this obedience lie first the lodges adhering to Grande Loge and
then the huge twilight area of lodges of doubtful status but not always
clearly distinct from regular masonry to the uninitiated (or even, in
some cases, to the initiated).[57] Membership often overlapped. This

[53] Since the early 1720s three, though the first edition of the English *Constitutions*
specified only two and the third grade (Master) was only formally recognised by
Grand Lodge in 1730.

[54] Le Bihan (*Francs-maçons parisiens*, p. 7) says that nearly a hundred lodges at Paris
and the court alone were constituted or reconstituted by the Grand Orient between
1773 and 1793.

[55] D. Mornet, *Les origines intellectuelles de la Révolution française* (Paris, 1934), p. 36.

[56] Ligou, p. 108.

[57] Le Bihan, in a useful attack on the question of social composition ('Maçons du
XVIIIᵉ siècle. Personnalité et milieux sociaux des maîtres de loge de la Grande Loge

confused situation was now only to make it even harder for regular freemasons to shake off the suspicions which they attracted even before 1789 and also make it hard even to pose in precise terms questions about masonic numbers in France. There is also the problem of the so-called 'lodges of adoption' for women, of which there seem to have been some hundreds. Nevertheless, a series of general statements can be made which the evidence does not invalidate.

In the first place, masonic lodges or other organisations with sufficient self-confidence to call themselves masonic were so widespread in France by 1789 that few towns, even the smallest, were without them.[58] Although many of them had interrupted and sporadic lives, they survived and prospered sufficiently for freemasonry to be a familiar social fact to most Frenchmen of the literate classes.[59] In theory, the movement attracted and recruited men of every class, but there were important qualifications of this general principle. Lodges did not always span social barriers. The Grand Orient and Grande Loge were the foci of different social interests, the direction of the first being predominantly aristocratic while that of the second was restricted mainly to the professional and commercial classes of Paris and a few provincial areas.[60] Sometimes the presence of two lodges in the same town, one belonging to one obedience and one to another, could reflect this social distinction.[61] The Grand Orient, also, had made attempts to have artisans excluded from lodges under its authority. Nevertheless, numbers alone ensured that the masonic connexions as a whole did something to cut across social barriers between French-

---

de France', *AHRF*, 1969, p. 418) says that 119 lodges were constituted by Grande Loge between 1773 and 1799.

[58] On the eve of the Revolution, says P. Chevallier, 'l'ordre connaît en France un développement dont l'équivalent peut à peine se retrouver lors des plus belles années de la IIIᵉ République' (in 'Les Origines de la Franc-Maçonnerie à Nogent-sur-Seine', *Mémoires de la Société Académique de l'Aube*, CIV, 1964–6, p. 179).

[59] 'En 1789, surtout dans les villes de moyenne importance et dans les petites villes, tout ce qui "compte" sérieusement a été ou est maçon.' Ligou, p. 108. G. Gayot's article on Sedan already cited (p. 30) shows both the importance and some of the limitations of the Craft's social comprehensiveness. See also P. Leuilliot's comments in a review, 'La franc-maçonnerie, "fait social"', *Annales E.S.C.*, 1953, pp. 241–2.   [60] Le Bihan, 'Maçons du XVIIIᵉ siècle', pp. 419–20.

[61] Chevallier, *Mémoires de la Société Académique de l'Aube*, pp. 180–2. He also prints, pp. 182–4, an amusing letter (from the Directory period) in which a loyal adherent of Grande Loge comments sardonically on the way in which nobles 'ainsi que des chevaliers d'industrie' attracted some masons to the Grand Orient who '[se] laissent maîtriser comme des esclaves parce qu'ils étoient flatté[s] de fraterniser avec des nobles . . . et ne [croyaient] pas être sous leur joug'. Many bourgeois were, of course, members of lodges in the Grand Orient obedience, as has been shown by M. Le Bihan's *Francs-maçons parisiens*.

men of the directing classes. Perhaps one hundred thousand Frenchmen were masons of one sort or the other on the eve of the Revolution. The French were then the most substantial, the best-organised and the most respectable of the continental masonic connexions.[62] Their vitality and independence left them therefore in no need to pay more than formal and polite acknowledgement to the English freemasonry from which they had originally sprung. Many of them, in any case, were by then unwilling to do even that.

FREEMASONRY IN OTHER EUROPEAN COUNTRIES

In every European country, local circumstances produced significant differences in the success and social influence of freemasonry and these are worth some consideration. Almost everywhere (as in England, Scotland and France) the details of masonic origins are obscure, but research is gradually bringing more facts to light. It is clear that freemasonry spread by two means: freemasons and lodges were either initiated and founded directly by persons originally connected with English freemasonry, or else they came via other, continental intermediaries of which the most important were the masonic movements of France and the court of Lorraine (which may be considered as a part of French freemasonry). How quickly the French lodges began to exercise a cosmopolitan influence is shown by a Paris lodge in 1736-7 which had forty-one foreign members to only twenty-seven French; among the foreigners, Germans and Scandinavians predominated (this is not, of course, to say how many of these had made their first contacts with the Craft in France, rather than elsewhere).[63]

The earliest continental lodges outside France for which there are claims with some colour go back to 1721, when there were supposed to have been lodges at Mons and Liège.[64] This is plausible; there may have been masonic influences hanging over from the comings and goings of the Marlborough wars. After that date, Spain seems to have been the next area of growth. A Gibraltar lodge in 1727 was almost certainly the starting-point for freemasonry in southern Spain, but it seems that the Duke of Wharton—by then a Roman Catholic and agent of the Pretender—presided over the first lodge in Madrid in 1728 and

---

[62] Nonetheless, we should not overlook the harsh but authoritative judgment of R. Le Forestier: 'Si l'on tentait d'indiquer d'un mot le caractère dominant de la Maçonnerie française au XVIIIe siècle, un seul conviendrait: dilettantisme.' (La franc-maçonnerie Templière et occultiste, p. 49.)

[63] Chevallier, Les ducs, pp. 72-7. Sixteen of these foreigners were admitted in 1737.

[64] An early claim for a lodge at Naples is regarded sceptically.

that it was attended only by Englishmen. A rapid spread is said to have followed. By 1749 a Cadiz lodge with eight hundred members is reported (the strength of a seaport's freemasonry is suggestive) and there is talk of over a hundred lodges by 1750, when a list of ninety-seven was handed to the Inquisition. A burst of persecution in the middle of the century does not seem to have prevented the movement from receiving fashionable patronage later; the lodge La bella Unión seems to have been very much a part of Spanish aristocratic society. But our information is not good. We know that there was an independent Grand Lodge during the reign of Charles III and that there was subsequently to be much exaggeration about freemasonry in eighteenth-century Spain. A recent study of the Inquisition (one of whose tasks was to initiate prosecutions against freemasons) inclines to the view that it was not until the arrival of British and French armies in the Peninsular wars that freemasonry spread widely in Spain.[65]

With the 1730s proliferation is much more rapid and priority is still harder to establish. Italian masonry was fed both by English diplomatic agents, travellers and merchants, and by direct trans-Alpine contact with France through Savoy. This combines with the fragmentation of the peninsula into many small states to make early Italian masonry especially difficult to trace. There is still lacking in many places a foundation in firm, detailed research. It is known that in the 1730s, perhaps as early as 1732, a Jacobite lodge existed at Rome which was closed in 1737.[66] In Tuscany, a lodge founded in 1732 or 1733 by Lord Middlesex and operating under the protection of the Grand Duke was anti-Jacobite in origin, and soon included several Italians.[67] The grand duchy, it has been claimed, was the Italian state where masonry was most widely diffused in this decade and there were lodges at Siena, Pisa and Leghorn later in the century.[68] Elba had one by the 1770s.[69]

[65] H. Kamen, *The Spanish Inquisition* (London, 1965), p. 264, which, on this point, concurs with the older judgment of F. Rousseau, *Règne de Charles III d'Espagne* (Paris, 1907), I, p. 169.

[66] W. Hughan, *The Jacobite Lodge at Rome 1735-37* (Torquay, 1910).

[67] J. H. Lepper, 'The Earl of Middlesex and the English Lodge at Florence', *AQC*, lviii, 1947, p. 4. The earlier date is suggested by N. Hans, 'The masonic lodge at Florence in the eighteenth century', *AQC*, lxxi, 1958, p. 109.

[68] F. Venturi, *Settecento riformatore. Da Muratori a Beccaria* (Turin, 1969), p. 54; C. Francovich, *Albori socialisti nel Risorgimento* (Florence, 1962), p. 89. The latter author (p. 139) says that the Leghorn lodge was founded about 1730 and may have been the first in Italy. Benedict XIV, writing in 1751 in a hostile mood, thought 'il grand male e nella Toscana' (quoted in I. Rinieri, *Della rovina di una monarchia* (Rome, 1901), p. 609).   [69] Francovich, p. 100.

Further north, the Marquis of Bellegarde received his (English) patent as Grand Master for the territories of the King of Sardinia in 1739. Soon, the royal court at Turin is said to have had a lodge (Victor Amadeus III was later a member) and the mother lodge of Savoy, the Trois Mortiers at Chambéry, was founded in 1749.[70]

It was long said that freemasonry was introduced to Naples in the middle of the century under Austrian auspices, but the first date of foundation for a Neapolitan lodge is 1745, when a Piedmontese and a Frenchman set one up.[71] It soon attracted attention and the Prince of San Severo became Grand Master. At the end of the 1740s the foundation of new lodges quickened although this was followed by a royal ban in 1751.[72] Meetings seem to have been resumed in the mid-1750s. In Sicily there is evidence of a lodge at Palermo in the 1750s and we may conclude that a flourishing masonry still existed in the Two Sicilies from the holding of a National Grand Lodge for Naples and Sicily in which eight lodges joined. The allegiance to London was thrown off and relations opened with the German 'Strict Observance' rite.[73] The Craft appears to have enjoyed greater success in the south than in any other part of the peninsula. It was honoured by a visit from Montmorency-Luxembourg in 1772, and the queen, Maria Carolina, favoured it too (both her father and brothers were masons).

There is also evidence of activity in Venice and Lombardy. Clearly by mid-century Italian freemasonry was well-established and prosperous. When Pivati published an article on freemasonry in his dictionary in 1741, it seemed to him to be worth devoting thirty pages to the subject.[74] This must have given the Craft useful publicity, though the article also indicates some suspiciousness and certain reserves.

In the diffusion of freemasonry in central Europe, Francis, Duke

[70] F. Vermale, *La Franc-maçonnerie savoisienne à l'époque révolutionnaire d'après ses registres secrets* (Paris, 1912), pp. 4–6. An excellent survey of eighteenth-century freemasonry in Savoy was printed by W. K. Firminger in *AQC*, xlvi, 1937, pp. 325–54. See also notes of a discussion, *AHRF*, 1969, pp. 391–2.

[71] The memorandum of Father Orlando referred to below (p. 75) alleged English origins; M. d'Ayala, 'I liberi muratori di Napoli nel secolo XVIII' (*ASPN*, 1897, pp. 417–18), dates the Lodge. A (presumably Jacobite) captain in the Neapolitan army, Thomas Archdeacon, was admitted a freemason at the Rome lodge in 1736 (Hughan, p. 45). But we cannot assume that this is the beginning of the story of Neapolitan freemasonry. See also the document printed in *ASPN*, 1905, pp. 243–52, which appears to date from the 1750s and to be based on contemporary information.

[72] See below, p. 74.

[73] d'Ayala, p. 452. On the Strict Observance, see below, pp. 106 ff.

[74] *Nuovo Dizionario Scientifico e Curioso Sacro-Profano* (Venice, 1747), VI, s.v. 'Muratori Liberi'.

of Lorraine, husband of Maria Theresa and as such later crowned Holy Roman Emperor, is a key-figure. He was initiated by Lord Chesterfield at The Hague in 1731 and admitted a master in the same year at a lodge held in Sir Robert Walpole's Norfolk house, Houghton Hall, in a ceremony which included the admission of the Duke of Newcastle.[75] Under his patronage and protection, the Craft prospered both in Tuscany (to which he went as Grand Duke in 1737) and to Vienna (to which he removed in 1739), in spite of suspicions entertained of it by others, including his wife. The first lodge at Vienna appears to have been an offshoot of one at Breslau and opened in 1742. In spite of some evidence from police sources that masonic activity was already going on in Budapest, it is also only in 1742 that the first lodge appears in Hungary.[76] In all parts of the Habsburg dominions, the lodges were to spread rapidly under Joseph II, who, though not himself a mason, looked benevolently on the Craft for most of his reign.[77]

Swiss masonry appears on the scene when a Scotsman opened a lodge at Geneva in 1736. The Craft spread quickly through the cantons and London appointed a Grand Master for the area in the following year. Meanwhile, freemasonry was already spreading in Germany outside the Habsburg lands. This was important, because it was to be in Germany that there occurred subsequently the most luxuriant growth of deviations and offshoots of the masonic order.[78] Again, we find claims of masonic activity as early as the 1720s, and they are not inherently improbable, given the presence of English merchants and travellers. But our first clear documentation comes from 1730, when London granted a patent for a Provincial Grand Master for Saxony. In 1737 we have the first indisputable evidence for the existence of a particular and identifiable lodge, one at Hamburg which may have been founded by English merchants. Hamburg was the first important centre of German freemasonry and it was a deputation from this lodge which initiated the Prussian Crown Prince (the future Frederick the Great) in 1738. In that year a lodge appears in Saxony at Dresden. The spread in the following decade was rapid; lodges can be identified at Frankfurt and in Bavaria, Brandenburg, Brunswick and Hanover, as well as in growing numbers in Saxony. There is no need to dwell on the details; the picture is one of almost irresistible advance. The im-

[75] Gould, IV, p. 161. Desaguliers is said to have been present.

[76] Gould, IV, p. 290.

[77] A brief sketch of masonry's prosperous years in Vienna during his reign is available in H. Bradley, 'Bro. Mozart and some of his masonic friends', *AQC*, xxvi, 1913, pp. 241–63.

[78] Gould, IV, pp. 89–102.

plications of this for the future were many; Germany was already showing a responsiveness which anticipates the rich later growth there of irregular and sub-masonic societies.

In northern Europe, the initiation of the Duke of Lorraine throws some light on the start of Dutch masonry, since there was a Dutch mason present; a condemnation by the States-General in the previous year confirms that freemasonry was already under way there before this. The first authentic record of a lodge is in 1734 at The Hague. The earliest claims of foundations in the Austrian Netherlands and the archbishopric of Liège have already been mentioned and the number of lodges seems to have grown steadily in these territories, especially in the 1770s. In 1786 there are said to have been twenty-six.[79] The Scandinavian countries had their first masonic activity in the 1730s. A Swede was initiated at Paris in 1731, but the first lodges only appeared in Stockholm in 1735 and at Copenhagen in 1743.[80] Finland's first lodge was not established until 1756.

Finally, there is Russia. It must be regarded as a legend only that Peter the Great was initiated during his visit to England by Sir Christopher Wren.[81] It is certain, on the other hand, that in 1731 a Provincial Grand Master was appointed for Russia from London, even though this does not imply that there were at that time already working lodges in Russia.[82] There may have been a lodge at St Petersburg in the next few years founded by a Jacobite exile, but the London influence was soon to be dominant until the elaboration of new rites around the middle of the century, though it is only in 1771 that we have clear evidence of a regular lodge under the English obedience.

THE CHARACTER OF EIGHTEENTH-CENTURY FREEMASONRY

A list of dates and places is not only boring, but is only half the story of the growth and spread of freemasonry. Yet it is necessary to grasp the pattern it contains, because the rapidity with which the Craft spread and the mystery of its origins in some places were later to contribute importantly to suspicion of what freemasonry was. Some other points, too, need to be appreciated before the image of freemasonry formed by eighteenth-century observers can be understood. We need to try to estimate what the rapid growth meant, what it was that was diffused

[79] J. Bartier, 'Regards sur la franc-maçonnerie belge du XVIIIe siécle', *AHRF*, 1969, p. 469.
[80] Chevallier, *Les ducs*, p. 26.
[81] Gould, IV, p. 173.
[82] *Grand Lodge*, p. 232.

through the lodges and what men sought in them. However summarily, we have to try to recreate the social and intellectual world of eighteenth-century freemasonry. This done, it may be a little easier to see what it was that freemasonry contributed to the myth of the secret societies.[83]

The key question is obvious: who were the masons? And, we may add, why did they join the lodges? At first sight, no one was ineligible, though evidence has already been mentioned which seems to show that the egalitarianism of masonic precepts was much qualified in practice. The Craft, although widespread, did not appeal to everyone; recruits did not come forward on a random basis from every class and group. It is also clear that there was some conscious selection by the lodges themselves. Although the *Constitutions* laid down no formal social restrictions on admission there are many instances of such restrictions in practice. The Grande Loge made its recognition of the constitutions of lodges conditional upon their agreement to admit no servants, but only persons with an independent livelihood, after careful scrutiny and the payment of substantial dues.[84] This was enough to take one a long way down the social scale from the vantage point of a peer of France, but it was far from democratic. M. Le Bihan's list of members of Parisian lodges of the Grand Orient is studded with qualifications like 'peintre', 'professeur', 'marchand bonnetier', 'commis aux finances' or 'négociant', but there are no labourers to be found in it. In the small provincial towns the proportion of small businessmen and clerks might be greater than in Paris, but it could be almost as restricted; in either instance we are still dealing only with a small élite in a society of twenty millions. The spectacular examples of crossing class-barriers which occasionally turn up—the opera singer who was the rival in love of the Prince de Conti, or the fashionable dancing-master who was Grand Master—show only that fashionable society could always relax its standards if it wished.

Nor are there grounds for believing that the position was more relaxed in other European countries. The impression is to the contrary. Social exclusiveness and cachet is the recurrent impression left by early freemasonry. While members of all classes could be found in the lodges, a judgment on Belgian freemasonry seems applicable to all countries: 'dans l'ensemble pourtant, le recrutement fut de bonne

[83] Here I deal only with orthodox freemasonry, as I have done in the main above. Heterodox and breakaway derivations will be discussed in Chapter IV.

[84] Le Bihan, *Loges*, p. ix ('mais bien tous marchands, maîtres ou bourgeois pourvues de charges ou d'un état distingué').

qualité'.[85] This was also conclusively demonstrated by the adherence to freemasonry of several monarchs. Francis of Lorraine, Stanislas, Frederick the Great, Joseph II were outstanding examples, and it now seems likely that Louis XV too was a freemason.[86] The French court circle had succumbed rapidly to the new craze; Ramsay was probably not boasting vainly when he said his speech was 'made at the acception at different times of eight dukes and peers and two hundred officers of the first rank and highest nobility' of France.[87] Nor was the Craft's social success in France confined to Paris and the royal court. Already in the 1740s there are many examples of provincial notables—country noblemen, parlementaires—in the Craft. The Intendant of the Orléanais founded one of the lodges of Orléans, and in the Parlement town of Dijon twenty-two out of forty-one lodge members who have been identified were officers of justice or finance.[88]

This social success further prejudiced the dogmatic egalitarianism of freemasonry. It also produced internal strains within lodges. Sometimes these could be, and were, avoided by social segregation in separate lodges. Le Mans and Laval had distinct lodges of noblemen and magistrates on the one hand, and of lesser bourgeois and artisans on the other.[89] This solution was not always available or at first sight attractive and it has been suggested that one aspect of what happened in the late 1730s to Parisian freemasonry was that there was something very like a 'takeover' of masonry by great noblemen. The Jacobite gentry who had hitherto dominated it were squeezed out and so were members of the bourgeoisie. Clearly irritation was felt when, for example, a duke gave a dinner for fellow-masons but only invited noblemen to it, ignoring the 'tiers état'.[90] So elevated a personage as the Duc d'Aumont may be thought untypical, but there is much evidence of just this sort of exclusiveness. The point of view of many

[85] J. Bartier, *AHRF*, 1969, p. 471. An impressive list of aristocratic names in Italian lodges is printed by R. Sòriga (*Le Società segrete, l'emigrazione politica e i primi moti per l'indipendenza* (Modena, 1942), pp. 28–33) in support of his argument that freemasonry in Italy before 1789 was, by and large, an aristocratic phenomenon.

[86] Chevallier, *Les ducs*, pp. 175–9.   [87] Chevallier, *Les ducs*, p. 182.

[88] *AHRF*, 1969, pp. 429 and 433–4. In her article on 'La Loge "La Concorde" de Dijon', Mme R. Robin stresses that the merchant middle class formed no part of this lodge, but formed another, apart. Of the nine bourgeois in the Concorde lodge, 'il s'agit donc d'une bourgeoisie de rentes, des professions libérales, largement intégrée objectivement et subjectivement au système seigneuriale'. Concorde was a very aristocratic lodge.

[89] *AHRF*, 1969, p. 487. Similar distinctions between lodges have been noted at Bordeaux; see the article (already cited in fn. 27) by G. Hubrecht (*Rev. Hist. de Bordeaux*, 1954), p. 149.

[90] Chevallier, *Les ducs*, p. 68.

noble masons is expressed in the disapproval shown much later in the century by a parlementaire who was master of a Bordeaux lodge. When, in 1785, a new lodge was proposed he ran down the suggestion, saying '. . . tous ces soi-disant maçons sont des Ouvriers, la pluspart aux gages des negotians de l'état desquels ils se sont revêtus. . . . Ce seroit aviler, anéantir, ou au moins humilier l'art Royal, que de admettre de pareils sujets dans le sein de la maçonnerie, dont le privilège de l'Égalité deviendroit un abus bien dangereux, si sous ce prétexte on admettrait indifféremment tous les états.'[91] There is more than a whiff in this of the aristocratic resurgence which characterised the French nobility under the last pre-revolutionary kings.[92] Even a progressively minded nobleman, seeking to utilize masonry for political ends, urged 'gens de qualité' who felt uneasy about the generalisation of liberal principles to consider the position of the ruling class in England: 'les lords ont-ils perdu de leurs droits et leur éclat parce qu'ils n'ont pas droit de commettre des injustices et d'opprimer?'[93] The 'cascade de méprise' did not leave freemasonry unsprinkled.

A special group from which recruitment took place was the clergy. There is evidence that many clergy in both France and Germany joined the Craft; far fewer seem to have done so in Italy and Spain. Nevertheless, at least one Italian lodge, at Portoferraio (Elba), apparently had a Franciscan friar as its master, and clerical membership of the lodges seems to have been notorious in the Papal enclave of Avignon.[94] In the Austrian Netherlands, there was a lodge at Mons composed exclusively of ecclesiastics.[95] There were both secular and regular clergy among these freemasons, the only notable absentees among the religious Orders being the Jesuits.[96] Once again, the evidence of social composition, widely differentiated by origin though clerics might be, emphasises the extent to which eighteenth-century freemasonry was

[91] I am grateful to Mr W. Doyle for allowing me to borrow this quotation from p. 338 of his unpublished Oxford D. Phil. thesis, *The Parlementaires of Bordeaux at the end of the Eighteenth Century 1775–1790* (1967).

[92] See also the interesting gloss on the masonic principle of equality by a master of a Dijon lodge, quoted in *AHRF*, 1969, p. 441 (incredibly, without any indication of date).

[93] Mirabeau, *RF*, iii 1882, p. 300.

[94] Francovich, p. 101; *AHRF*, 1969, pp. 453, 462, 466.

[95] *AHRF*, 1969, p. 471.

[96] Ligou, p. 108. The lodge of *St Jean dite de St Germain* appears to have had many religious people of several orders in its ranks (Le Bihan, *Loges*, p. 71). Another lodge had a Benedictine as master (Le Bihan, p. 161) and the masonic career of a bishop has been traced by P. Chevallier in 'Un Evêque de Troyes Franc-Maçon', *Mémoires de la Société Académique de l'Aube*, CIV, 1964–6, pp. 187–94. Some Bordeaux lodges had chaplains (Hubrecht, p. 145).

in the main a resort for members of the directing classes. Poor though clergymen often were, they were men with some social and cultural leverage. In small towns they must have found the lodge very much a gathering of their fellow notables. The whole question of clerical participation, of course, was complicated by the condemnation of freemasonry by the Pope.[97]

Freemasonry's recruitment, then, if far from democratic, took place within generously drawn social limits. Anyone with claims to some social standing could probably have been a mason somewhere. It is also worth emphasising for a moment that masonic fraternity and equality was emphatically successful in cutting across national boundaries, whatever other limitations confined them. In the modern sense of implying controls on movement and legal rights, frontiers mattered less than they do today. It is true, too, that educated Europe was then in some ways a more compact and intimately connected society than now. Nevertheless, the internationalism of freemasonry may have been important in offsetting obstacles to communication which loomed large in those days. Freemasons passed easily from country to country, assured of reception and help. This brought American lodges, for example, into contact with European, and, even more strikingly, Moslem freemasons into French lodges. The only formal racial exclusions which modify this picture affected Jews and these were local: lodges in Alsace restricted their membership, and there was for a long time at Frankfurt-on-Main a lodge distinguished for its loyalty to the English system of only three degrees which excluded Jews.[98]

Another exclusion which was important was that of women. It is not easy to be sure of the exact state of affairs. Certainly very few lodges of men formally accepted women and the furthest that English freemasonry (always the best regulated) seems to have relaxed its practice was in holding dinners of freemasons at which ladies were present, though not in lodge. It is clear on the other hand that the eighteenth-century lodges were often under considerable pressure to admit women.[99] On the whole the sex line may be said to have held

---

[97] See Ch. III.

[98] Gould, IV, p. 97. At Bordeaux, the aristocratic 'loge anglaise' excluded Jews along with actors (Hubrecht, p. 145).

[99] Le Bihan, Loges, p. xv. See d'Ayala, p. 453, on women masons at Naples. The author of La Franc-Maçonne ou révélation des mystères des franc-maçons (Brussels, 1744), pp. 11-15, says that such lodges were not true lodges, but only devices for beguiling women into thinking they had penetrated the secrets and also, perhaps, for immoral purposes.

successfully, but the defence was by no means perfect. There is evidence that women occasionally attended early lodges and there were hundreds of women's 'loges d'adoption' whose status was ambiguous. One thing is certain about these, that their members were women drawn from the same groups as freemasonry proper. We are still dealing with a relatively small élite.

But this selection from an élite, though small, was still one which extended further than any other eighteenth-century social groups except the major religious confessions, and in many places it could be joined at least as easily as the churches. Because of this, its ideology and attitudes illuminate a very wide range of European history; this is why they must interest the historian and excited such hopes and fears among contemporaries.

Masonic aspirations were high, as the *Constitutions* show, and they retained their quality when they crossed the Channel. The language of the Duc de Montmorency-Luxembourg in 1773 was not uncharacteristic of masonic rhetoric: 'Le but que nous poursuivons consiste à établir entre tous nos prosélytes une communication active de sentiments de fraternité et de secours en tout genre, à faire revivre les vertus sociales, à en rappeler la pratique, enfin à rendre notre association utile à chacun des individus qui la composent, utile à l'Humanité même.'[100] Such language, stale as it sometimes became, is symptomatic of widely shared attitudes. Benevolence, fraternity, utility, morality: these were what freemasonry was about for anybody who took it seriously, and there is much evidence that many did. Around these principles there clustered also masonic symbolism and imagery, growing steadily richer and more encrusted as the century progressed.

The antiquity of the craft was a fundamental dogma, lightly though cultivated masons might pass over the obscurer origins. The symbolism of this was important; the pillars of the Temple, and the fidelity to the Secret expressed in the Hiram legend were powerfully evocative. They emphasised the moral virtues of solidarity, integrity and reliability upon which the brothers prided themselves no less than their corporate loyalty. Similarly, the symbols used in the ritual and iconography of masonry embody the types of moral virtues. Level, compass and plumb-line were evocative of solidarity, rectitude, directness, good craftsmanship, and these qualities were continually recalled to the brothers in their ceremonies. Masonic hymns, songs and poems took up the same themes.

[100] Quoted in P. Sagnac, *La fin de l'ancien régime et la Révolution américaine* (Paris, 1947), p. 447.

To this basic system of symbolism and morality, enriched by internal development and deduction, must be added the extra contribution made to European masonry by other traditions and, above all, by the suggestions of Ramsay's oration. It was important both because of the publicity which it received almost at once, and because of the material in it which was to inspire future masonic flights of fancy. Ramsay deliberately sought a comprehensive ideal which would reunite masons irritated against one another by the strains and cross-currents within the Parisian lodges. This was why he drew attention to legends emphasising the Scottish and European antecedents of the Craft rather than the English (though he acknowledged the importance of the English role). Hence also the emphasis on the chivalric myth in his allusion to the Crusades, an emphasis to be enormously fertile in provoking new divisions within masonic systems and the rise of rivals outside them. Linked to the suggestion of superior chivalric grades was that of hidden, higher secrets.[101] From these suggestions were to flow 'Scottish' masonry and all its derivations and complications. It was also to add to the excitement of those masons and aspiring masons who sought in the Craft esoteric knowledge and mystical systems.

Many of those stirred by the ritual and symbolic in masonry were content to go no further than enjoyment of the satisfaction they afforded and observation of the internal disciplines of the Craft. But many freemasons sought an expression of masonic morality and speculation in action. Their philanthropic and benevolent work in this country is well known and similar examples can be found in other countries. On the other hand, involvement in public affairs which might be termed political was a thing English freemasons shunned. The *Constitutions* show how, from the first, they stressed political neutrality and it has been hazarded that this was because an earlier domination of the English lodges by Stuart sympathisers had left impressions of disaffection which had to be dispelled. A similar indifference to politics is suggested by the archives of the eighteenth-century Grand Orient; virtually bare of anything of political interest, they contain no references, we are told, to the stirring politics of the decade in which it was set up. At lodge level, however, there seem to have been moments when freemasons did find themselves engaged in political acts, or in actions with political implications. There is the possibility, already mentioned, that there was a political dimension to the change of Grand

[101] According to a letter to a private correspondent printed first by Mlle Weil and reprinted by Chevallier (*Les ducs*, pp. 215–16) Ramsay seems to have taken this very seriously indeed.

Masters in French freemasonry in 1738, but more explicit instances can be found. The lodges of Bordeaux, for example, publicly celebrated the victory of the local Parlement in its struggle with the crown.[102] A more surprising example of masonic propaganda activity is the protest of an Arras lodge against the expulsion of the Jesuits, for which the Artésien masons tried to get the support of their Parisian brothers (they were worried about the effects of the expulsion on local schooling).[103] Nevertheless, these were local matters in which freemasons were involved personally through their friends and connexions; no question of a masonic political principle arises. The official attitude of the Craft remained apolitical. Anderson's teaching was simply spelt out all the more fully as the century wore on. There is a good comprehensive statement of the masonic political and religious conformity in the words of the oath taken by the master of a lodge in 1776: 'je jure par la fer et sur la Sainte Ecriture, à la face du Grand Architecte de l'Univers, et de cette auguste Loge, de vivre et mourir dans la religion Catholique Apostolique et romaine, dans laquelle je suis né, d'être fidel à mon roy contre lequel je ne porterai jamais les armes, de n'entrer dans aucune Conspiration contre l'Etat, comme aussi de ne jamais m'écarter des lois de la maçonnerie en général.'[104] All that can be said in favour of later allegations about conscious political action by the Craft is that some of its members would not have gone so far as this.[105]

Before the Revolution, therefore, overt political activity by masons remains exceptional and easily explicable on non-masonic grounds—or appears to be so in our present state of knowledge. Probably a more usual expression of masonic ideology was the informal discussion which must have gone on, in many lodges as important as formal activity.

We suffer here from a grave lack of information about what proceedings at the lodges actually were and how they might specially favour the communication of 'lumières'. Much has been read into another

[102] Doyle, p. 340.
[103] Priouret, La franc-maçonnerie sous les lys, p. 68.
[104] Quoted in H. Soanen, AHRF, 1928, p. 70.
[105] One example can be found in a project for an 'association intime' of truly dedicated freemasons which Mirabeau drew up in 1776, printed in RF, iii, 1882, pp. 209–306. In it he stipulated that 'le second grand pivot de l'association devrait être la correction du système présent des gouvernements et des législations' and the second principle of the association to be revealed to those who became members of its second and superior grade was 'la correction des gouvernements et de la législation, et l'établissement d'une juste liberté parmi les hommes'. This was spelt out much more precisely later in the scheme as a set of specific reforms. Mirabeau's proposal was first published in 1834.

reference in Ramsay's speech to the preparation of a great compendium of knowledge under way in London. When it began to be believed that the century had seen a widespread conspiracy of intellectuals against faith and morals it was often to be said that this was a direct reference to the *Encyclopédie*. Close investigation of the problem of masonic participation in the *Encyclopédie* reveals no such conscious intention and connexions.[106] Yet the masons could have had an important part to play in the process which we term the Enlightenment because the lodges must have been one of the agencies at work generalising and diffusing enlightened ideas. Some freemasons (the young Mirabeau was one) thought this should be done consciously.[107] This is not surprising. In any individual lodge, the presupposition of a shared social background would have made frank and relaxed discussion easier. Many lodges too, especially those in large metropolitan or court centres, would draw members from circles aware of new ideas and receptive to them. In some, Protestants were well-represented. Interpenetration of lodge memberships and the exchange of visits made it likely that ideas were likely to circulate fairly quickly.

These probabilities, a priori plausible and convincing, must be balanced by others. There is much evidence of masons holding unexceptionably conventional views on many topics. Not only were clergymen often freemasons but some lodges would attend religious services in some state.[108] Freemasons were for the most part very consciously members of established society, and they celebrated their feasts (as did most other corporate bodies) by going to church. Some positively and explicitly denounced impiety and the Philosophes.[109] Others took pains to give the workings of their lodges a religious (or at least non-atheistical) tone.[110] It cannot be assumed that the lodges were hothouses of subversive ideas. Although Helvètius, d'Alembert and

[106] R. Shackleton, 'The *Encyclopédie* and Freemasonry' in the *Age of Enlightenment. Studies presented to Theodor Bestermann*, ed. W. Barber and others (Edinburgh and London, 1967) disposes of this matter. Ramsay had, it may be remarked, spoken of 'a Universal Dictionary of the liberal arts and useful sciences, excepting only theology and politics'. Such an exception was, of course, wholly proper for an orthodox mason.

[107] C'est à répandre les vérités et les connaissances utiles, déjà établies parmi beaucoup de personnes, à les faire parvenir jusqu'à la classe du peuple, qu'ils doivent s'attacher.' (*RF*, iii, 1882, p. 294).

[108] e.g. A. Bouton and M. Lepage, *Histoire de la franc-maçonnerie dans la Mayenne, 1756–1951* (Le Mans, 1951), pp. 76, 82–3.

[109] See Mme R. Robin, pp. 441–3.

[110] C. Mesliand suggests (*AHRF*, 1969, p. 464) that this is one reason why Avignonese freemasons did not feel obliged to conform to the condemnations of the Craft by their Sovereign, the Pope.

C

Voltaire were freemasons, the latter expressed himself scathingly about the Craft and only joined a lodge towards the end of his life, and we should remember that Diderot appears not to have been a freemason at all.[111]

Finally, there are the implicit and sometimes unconscious functions of freemasonry to consider. Any social organism or institution may have a function in society as a whole which may not be recognised consciously by its members or expressed in its stated aims. Clearly freemasonry had an important social role—mere numbers alone ensured that—and this was probably at least as important because of the way it worked in practice as because of the way it was intended to work. It is obvious, for example, that the Craft played a big part in the internal system of communications of a highly stratified and divided society. The most striking examples of its operation in this way are those provided by masons finding through lodges a mechanism which could introduce them into society in countries other than their own. A well-born young man, Casanova wrote, who wished to travel and see the world without being excluded from the pleasures of his social equals, ought to be initiated a freemason.[112] It could be important internally, too. A Bordeaux mason who went to Paris on political business was helped by the Neuf Sœurs.[113] And free masonry sometimes undoubtedly transcended class barriers in doing this, in spite of the limitations on the principle of brotherly equality in most lodges.

At the same time we must not exaggerate the function of masonry as a social tie. In part it simply reflected society's divisions and sometimes made efforts to embody them formally in masonry itself.[114] As a social institution, freemasonry reflects (as might be expected) the duality of the century in which it appeared. It showed both the uneasiness of men increasingly aware of the artificiality of some social institutions which drove them to seek new social ties, and the status-consciousness which was the reaction of those alarmed by signs of a new social mobility. In any case the social functions of freemasonry were many and their significance not easily exhausted. Dining and drinking were not the least important. It was also important that its gossip and suppers provided something like club-life in small towns, while the masquerades of the more recondite, pseudo-chivalrous

---

[111] Although Mornet claims Diderot as a freemason (p. 376), others contest this and seem to have the better case. See the note of Pierre Chevallier, *French Studies*, 1963, p. 118.

[112] Casanova, *Histoire de ma vie* (Paris and Wiesbaden, 1960–2), iii, p. 114.

[113] Doyle, p. 225.

[114] Cf. the religious and social distinctions at Sedan noted by G. Gayot, p. 416.

lodges pleased both noblemen and aspiring 'roturiers'. Grades, titles and the wearing in lodge of insignia and swords seem to have been attractive both to those who already treasured distinction of rank and to those who aspired to it. Perhaps in the last resort the greatest social importance of freemasonry was simply the relief it provided from the triviality, narrowness and rigidity of so much eighteenth-century life.

The emotional satisfactions of masonry are something to which we shall have to return in discussing some of its offshoots. But it is worth remarking its demonstration of how much the appeal of the mysterious and ancient was already being felt long before 1789. It can be seen in the early proliferation of grades and secrets. The movement of thought and sensibility which has been called 'Préromantisme' is already identifiable in the background even of early masonry. In it, many needs were expressed which suggest how rich could be the Craft's social role. Elaborating symbolism, ritual and doctrine, for example, may well have been in some measure a substitute for a traditional religious practice which had come to appear empty and meaningless. In this book, we need not follow up such wide-ranging themes. The point of indicating them here is to touch upon the wide range of responses masonry awoke, and the wide spectrum upon which its functioning should be observed. Its intimate connexion with so much of both the imagination and the vitality of the eighteenth century make it difficult to impose a single formula to express the essence of the free-masons' world, either as they saw it or as they were seen by their contemporaries. In this range of implications lay both the strength of the movement and much of its mystery; by itself, it accounts for at least some of the distrust which the Craft awoke. Whatever its real importance to eighteenth-century civilisation (and much remains to be discovered before we can define this) it was bound sooner or later to be felt to be great, just because it was interlocked with that civilisation at so many points.

Chapter III
Early anti-masonry

THE ORIGINAL ELEMENTS OF ANTI-MASONRY

A VAST and still growing body of specifically anti-masonic literature and legend has made an enormous contribution to the myth of the secret societies. It did not suddenly appear fully formed, with all the associations now clustered about it. For a long time freemasonry attracted only occasional and sporadic hostility; anti-masonry was a historical growth, like masonry itself.[1] Like masonry, too, it has ill-documented origins. The purpose of this chapter is to explore them: to see how far and why freemasons awoke hostility in the eighteenth century.

With this aim must go another: we need not only to identify hostile reactions to the Craft, but to discern those elements in what was known and believed about it which were later to become much more significant. Sometimes, it was only the passing of time that made these elements significant; when they first appeared they were often wholly, or relatively, unremarked. Anti-masonic mythology has always been willing to dispense with any sense of historical context and has ranged back and forth across history and legend, picking up disparate ideas, phrases, images and actions, weaving them into satisfying and insane patterns which suited its varying purposes. Consequently, facts about freemasonry which did not appear significant when they first became public knowledge, could later become part of the mature plot theory.

Until the 1720s there is little evidence of any kind to go on. The idea has been put about that the English government was perturbed by the existence of lodges after 1688 which were subversive because Jacobite and Roman Catholic. This may be plausible but I know of no

[1] A. Mellor, for instance, points out (*Our Separated Brethren*, pp. 253 ff.) that the anti-semitic and satanist themes to be found in the full-blown anti-masonry of the late nineteenth century are not there a century before. (This book is useful on many matters dealt with in this chapter, in spite of an idiosyncratic and sometimes irritating manner of proceeding. An article by the author, 'Pourquoi j'ai écrit "Nos frères séparés"' (*Le Symbolisme*, no. 356, 1962, pp. 256–75) is of interest.)

evidence for it.[2] We know that the seventeenth-century lodges attracted antiquarians, and it also seems likely that people may have been thought attracted to them by hints of alchemical practice, for it was not easy to draw fine distinctions about the motives of all the curious. Beyond that, there was nothing more sinister in the public repute of masonry at that time than the secrecy which led to vague suspicion such as that voiced by the antiquarian, Robert Plot.[3] Secrecy may also have caused criticism and awoken alarm without leaving enduring traces. The secret 'Mason Word' certainly excited comment in the seventeenth century, though only isolated examples of it survive; it was natural that secret signs and methods of recognition should be thought suspicious. One of the first expressions of a new concern in print came, as far as we know, in a London fly-sheet of 1698, addressed 'to all Godly people'. It warned believers that membership of the Craft might endanger their salvation, 'For this devillish sect are Meeters in secret which swear against all without their Following. They are the Anti-Christ which was to come leading them from Fear of God. For how should they meet in secret places and with secret Signs taking care that none observe them to do the Work of God; are not these the Ways of Evil-dom?'[4] It is interesting to find in this first surviving example of anti-masonic writing the charge which was later to loom so large—that the Craft was anti-Christian—but it does not seem to have been plausible enough to wake any response. The transformation of operative into accepted masonry went on unchecked by public hostility.[5]

Such attention as freemasonry may have attracted at so early a date was in any case somewhat diverted and confused by public interest in the new phenomenon of clubs, many of which were springing up at the end of the seventeenth century. There was at that time little to distinguish freemasons clearly from many other gatherings, some of them

[2] It is interesting, however, that according to tradition, in the early French lodges, which were predominantly Jacobite, the 'martyrdom' of Hiram was symbolically used as a reference to the death of Charles I (Mellor, p. 100).

[3] After explaining some of the supposed obligatory undertakings of freemasons (to help one another and so on), Plot said they have some others, 'that none know but themselves, which I have reason to suspect are much worse than these'. *The Natural History of Staffordshire*, p. 317.

[4] See *Early Masonic Pamphlets*, ed. D. Knoop, G. P. Jones and D. Hamer (Manchester, 1945), p. 34.

[5] Perhaps there is a tiny hint of a political suspicion in the 1676 reference to the 'Modern Green-ribbon'd Caball, together with the Ancient Brotherhood of the Rosy Cross; the Hermetick Adepti, and the Company of Accepted Masons' in a fly-sheet (*AQC*, xlv, 1935, p. 312). The Green Ribbon Club, it will be remembered, was an early Whig organisation which played an important part in the Exclusion Crisis.

far more notorious. It was only in the 1720s that the freemasons began to receive much publicity and it was provoked in large measure by the Craft itself. The publication of the *Constitutions* and the speech of the Grand Master in 1726 provided a basis for chatter about them.[6] There followed reports in newspapers, possibly planted by free-masons themselves, advertising the adherence to the Craft of persons of rank and distinction. Beginning with the Grand Feast in 1721, a practice of masonic processions to St John's Day banquets had also grown up. These became spectacles of some scale and even magnifi-cence, many coaches taking part: the procession attending the instal-lation of the Duke of Norfolk as Grand Master in 1730 seems to have been especially sumptuous. Masons also courted publicity by making official and corporate visits to theatres, at which special masonic material would be inserted in the pieces played, both in the form of prologues and epilogues and of special songs. Many of these additions and insertions were subsequently given wider circulation when they appeared in journals, song-books, or as broadsides.[7]

Contemporaneously, in the first decade of masonry's public life, there began that flow of 'exposures' of the Craft which, in coming decades, was to become a flood. Here we face a chicken-and-egg prob-lem. Much early criticism of freemasonry was ephemeral; it disappeared without record. We do not know whether the masonic tendency to court publicity provoked criticism, or whether criticisms called forth the masons' fervent assertions of respectability and virtue. All that we can say is that the two phenomena appear together. By 1730 several out-spoken attacks on freemasons had been published; they have been enumerated by masonic scholars and we need notice only the themes which recur in them.

One was suspicion of the personal behaviour of freemasons in the lodges. *Free Masons; an Hudibrastick Poem* of 1723 [8] admitted them 'very harmless Creatures' with 'nothing plotting in their Natures', but alleged immorality and indecency, hinting at sodomy and flagellation. Since

---

[6] L. Vibert, *The Rare Books of Freemasonry* (London, 1923), p. 33.

[7] See Knoop and Jones, *The Genesis of Freemasonry*, pp. 300–4. One piece which combined crude slapstick and masonic advertisement was the 'tragic-comi-farcical ballad opera' *The Generous Free-Mason* (London, 1731) dedicated to the Grand Master and the brotherhood. Its impossible plot relied on the recognition of a freemason by secret signs. From the start, praises are sung of 'Those Men, whose Lustre spreads from Pole to Pole, Possessing every Virtue of the Soul', and a climax is reached in a final chorus in which Neptune and Tritons praise the 'God-Like Action' and numerous virtues of the brotherhood.

[8] The second edition, in the British Museum, bears this date; Vibert (p. 37) says that none earlier has survived.

no one could be sure what did go on at lodges, and women were excluded, this was to be an enduring theme. It was suggested, for example, by the worried father who strove in *The Free-Masons Accusation and Defence*[9] to dissuade his son from entering the order (though he dropped it in favour of more persuasive arguments later in the pamphlet). In 1730 the charge of sodomy seems still to have been worth rebutting in a masonic song and it was only gradually that growing knowledge of masonic practice led to the allaying of the suspicions aroused by the exclusion of women. What is more surprising in that age is that the charge of drunkenness should so often have been brought especially against masons. *Ebrietatis Encomium* was the first of many attacks on this ground.[10]

Yet none of these attacks seem to have hindered the growth of the Craft which, in any case, quickly replied to them. The 1723 print of the *Constitutions*, it has been suggested, may have been intended as a reply to some newspaper article which has not survived, and in 1726 *A Full Vindication of the Ancient and Honourable Society* replied to such charges as those contained in *The Grand Mystery of the Freemasons Discovered*.[11] Only one literary attack of the period demands any special note. This is Samuel Prichard's publication in October 1730 of *Masonry Dissected*. It stigmatised the Craft as 'pernicious', apparently because some operative masons had been cheated out of their money. It is important for two reasons. It was the first attack on the Craft revealing in detail the ritual of initiation and the words of the oath and it was the first attack on the Craft to enjoy conspicuous success. It ran into thirty editions before 1800, was translated into many languages and enjoyed great renown on the continent of Europe.[12]

There were to be more attacks on freemasonry in English, but none of great importance until attitudes to the Craft had been changed by the outbreak of the French Revolution. In the main, the criticisms levelled against it continued to be quasi-moral and were inflamed by prejudice against its secrecy—a secrecy which, it must be said, was very soon and very evidently reduced in significance by the mild facts brought to light in the 'exposure' literature. Possibly for this reason,

[9] London, 1726.   [10] London, 1723.   [11] London, 1724.

[12] The first three editions are said to have appeared in eleven days (J. T. Thorp, in his edition of parts of *Masonry Dissected*, Leicester, 1907, p. 10). It is said to have been 'reprinted' in October and November 1730 in the *Northampton Mercury* (*AQC*, x, 1897, p. 158). Prichard followed up his success by translating and publishing in 1738 *Masonry further Dissected: or, more Secrets of that Mysterious Society reveal'd*. This suggests cabbalism may be at work in the Craft and speculates on masonic responsibility for the Porteous Riots. There were replies.

anti-masonic writing never reached a high level of intensity in England before 1789. There were other compensating factors, too, which offset the force of attacks on freemasonry. Its respectability was attested by the well-publicised adherence of noblemen and men of station, and many of the acts of the lodges were so public that little suspicion could be felt about them. Their charitable works were praised and, finally, England was a tolerant country, with no legal tradition of prejudice against voluntary association. The country already had a range of voluntary associations for private and social purposes which was astonishing by contemporary European standards. In the circumstances, it is hardly surprising that there is almost no trace of action by the public authorities against the Craft.[13]

Yet the debate on the respectability of freemasonry—if such it can be called—had importance for the future. It already put into circulation ideas which were later to feed the mythology which the society was to attract, especially abroad. This was because some of the facts about it were later to seem more sinister than at the moment of exposure. The difficulty with which future defenders of the Craft would have to grapple was a general one: the impression of impenetrable mystery generated by talk about secrets. Perhaps Dr Anderson himself was chiefly to blame in this respect. The language of his *Constitutions* was assertive and high-flown; it could always be read in a way which promised more than was actually forthcoming, and it encouraged both suspicion among the profane and over-optimism about future revelations among the credulous initiated. Such language thus contributed to a general psychosis of secrecy which gripped those who distrusted the Craft. The line which separated masons from seekers after an esoteric knowledge revealed only to a few was soon irremediably blurred. Finally, Anderson's language also favoured the elaboration of systems of 'higher degrees' whose existence was suspected perhaps even before they were devised.[14]

---

[13] The qualification is needed because of the concern shown by the Mayor and City of Canterbury in 1732 over the possibility that a lodge there might do 'something that may prove of sad Effect'. See S. Pape in *AQC*, lii, 1941, p. 6. It is also alleged (Mellor, p. 104) that Walpole financed *The Free Masons*, a journal of 1733 which satirised the craft.

[14] 'Who knows whether they may not have an higher Order of Cabbalists who keep the Grand Secret of all entirely to themselves?' (*Masonry further Dissected* ..., p. 30). Interestingly, too, the freemasons' replies to criticism also encouraged this idea of inner secrets. See, e.g., *The Perjur'd Free Mason Detected* (London, 1730), a reply to Prichard's earlier attack, whose revelations it discounts on the grounds that Prichard had not penetrated more than the most elementary masonic lore. On later developments, see the following chapter.

Suspicion and distrust were also encouraged by the terms of the free-mason's oath, publicised by Prichard.[15] English masons hastened to attribute to its violence a purely figurative importance, but such language could be taken more seriously then than now. It could also be thought to bear another significance if there indeed existed secrets beyond those of the signs of recognition and the rituals of the lodges themselves. If people believed in such secrets, then, clearly, the more awful the secrets might be, the more likely the infliction of dreadful penalties for their betrayal, the more significant the ritual drawn sword of the door-keeper. Like the Hiram legend, which, by associating the Craft with the idea of revenge, was later to give a footing to both the enemies of masonry and those within the movement who sought to elaborate its symbolic meaning, the secret and the oath were rich in their implications for the future. Like the idea of tolerance embodied in the *Constitutions*, they could come to be given an entirely different significance in countries whose religious and social background was different from that of England and where the traditions of Roman law embodied a much greater distrust of the principle of free voluntary association.

Nevertheless, many of the early continental reactions showed only the same general suspicion of secrecy and alarm about possibly immoral practices which had been shown in England. There was additional reason for the last in that the behaviour of some French noblemen who joined the order was already notorious. The circle of the Prince de Conti or the Duc de Richelieu might impart social éclat but could not be expected to lend respectability to any institution its members patronised.[16] To such information as was already known from English sources were soon added revelations from the hangers-on of French masonry and, finally, the tantalising statements of Ramsay. Like the well-meaning English freemasons, he unwittingly supplied material to the enemies of the Craft and the elements of future alarms: his prattle about Crusaders and chivalrous orders lent plausibility to the picturesque but disastrous association of freemasonry with the Templars, a theme to be richly exploited by later anti-masonic writers.

All this fed an 'exposure' literature which rapidly outran both in volume and sensationalism that already produced in England. Another way in which it was different from its English equivalent was that

[15] It may be remarked in passing that it was moral, theological and practical suspicion of the masonic oath which inspired the Synod of the Presbyterian Church to interest itself in freemasonry in 1745 and, twelve years later, to make an Act requiring purgation of the 'scandal' of taking the oath by sessional rebuke and admonition. See the *Scots Magazine*, August 1757, pp. 432–3.

[16] P. Chevallier, *Les ducs*, pp. 92–3, 100, 168–9.

political themes soon appeared in it and some of them seem to have anticipated important versions of later developments in secret society mythology.[17] This was probably an index of the differences of context in which English and continental masonry were to develop. One important determinant of them was the attitude of the established authorities, both civil and ecclesiastical, towards the Craft.

EARLY OFFICIAL REACTIONS

Chronologically, the first example of official hostility to freemasonry in action occurred in the United Provinces. In 1735 meetings of Dutch lodges were banned. The prohibition seems to have arisen from fears that freemasons were as a group playing a part in politics, though the edict specified that no actual evidence of behaviour contrary to the public peace, or to the duty of good subjects, had been discovered. In the same year there was an attack by a mob on a lodge at Amsterdam composed of Englishmen. The investigation which followed produced a statement that nothing positive had been found against the freemasons but forbade further meetings. Perhaps motives of public order explain this episode. Yet it seems to have been the end of anything that could be called official hostility to freemasonry in the United Provinces. In 1740 we find magistrates forbidding clergy to refuse absolution to freemasons if they are in other ways honest men. In 1744, we are told the lodges at The Hague re-opened. The whole story of the persecuting of freemasonry in the Republic thus appears to come to a swift close. It had remained a matter of particular and local suspicions, had reflected partisan politics, and had ebbed rapidly. It was consciously distinguished from hostility on principled and general grounds but these fine shades of differentiation were not understood elsewhere and soon the fact that the Dutch freemasons had been forbidden to meet was itself being argued to be a reason for harrying the Craft. It was an early example of a snowball effect which was later to prove devastating.

We may pass over the banning of freemasonry in Berne in 1745 and Sweden in 1738; both appear to have arisen from similar local and special causes. Less emphasis was laid on these examples, in any case, by later anti-masonic writers. Nor does action in the Austrian dominions seem very important. The lodge of which Francis of Lorraine

---

[17] I have only been able to trace these themes as far back as their indirect statement (for purposes of refutation) in a pamphlet of 1744, *La Franc-Maçonne ou révélation des francs-maçons par Mme XXX*. See below, p. 86.

was Grand Master, founded at Vienna in 1742, was closed by order of the Empress, his wife, in the following year at the instigation, it is said, of the clergy.[18] This caused no great stir and persecution did not hinder the later development under Francis' patronage of an alchemically-inclined masonry at Vienna. The Empress' efforts to hinder the progress of masonry in the Austrian Netherlands also seem to have been fruitless and when the Rector of the University of Louvain sought governmental support for action against a lodge there, it is note-worthy that he emphasised nothing more serious than that his students might be tempted to run up debts, engage in debauch and neglect their studies.[19]

The action taken against masons in France deserves closer attention. France had the strongest and senior masonic movement on the conti-nent, was a Catholic country, and was the scene of action against freemasons which coincided with the earliest hostility shown by the Papacy towards them. There were, to summarise, two bursts of what might be called 'persecution', one in 1737 and one in 1744–5. They were practically confined to Paris and ceased altogether in 1747.[20]

The official attitudes which lay behind these episodes have been greatly clarified by recent research. Having attracted notice by diarists and journalists, freemasons are first mentioned in police records in March 1737 in a way which suggests that the writer knew very little about them.[21] Later that year, the police interrupted a masonic assembly, fined the inn-keeper on whose premises it was being held and forbade the provision of facilities for such meetings in future. The ground was general: although freemasons were being specially singled out, the authorities based their decision on the assertion that such assemblies broke existing laws against unauthorised associations.[22] In the follow-ing year there were a few more arrests and then police action against freemasons came to a halt until 1744.

In that year another meeting of masons, a dinner at which women were present, was interrupted by the police. The Ordonnance of 1737 was invoked, fines were once again imposed and the ban on un-

---

[18] R. Le Forestier, Les Illuminés de Bavière et la franc-maçonnerie allemande (Paris, 1914), p. 347.

[19] AHRF, 1969, pp. 476–7.

[20] In 1744 two tradesmen were fined at Orléans for allowing masonic assemblies on their premises (AHRF, 1969, p. 426). The assertion, often repeated, that free-masons were officially condemned by the Sorbonne in 1763 seems to be unfounded.

[21] Chevallier, Les ducs, p. 101. The notice is also interesting because it associates them with the Templars.

[22] Chevallier prints the relevant document, pp. 195–7.

authorised assemblies reiterated. This time, freemasons were not specifically mentioned and the inclusion in the charge of an allusion about causing disturbance to the proper solemnity of Whit Sunday suggests that something of a search for excuses for action was going on.[23] A few incidents in the following year then brought this second burst of persecution—pestering might be a better word—to an end.

It has always been difficult to reconcile these events with the large measure of indulgence and support which French freemasonry enjoyed among the great. This difficulty looms even larger if we accept the strong inferential argument that Louis XV had been initiated and if we take account of the large measure of 'penetration' of the whole court circle by the Craft which is known to have occurred.[24] Another difficulty has been the sporadic and ineffectual nature of the persecution: the selectivity applied in the choice of victims is also very striking. There is yet another curious aspect to these events: in 1738, after the first burst of police activity had started, a Papal condemnation of freemasonry was published,[25] but no attempt was made by Cardinal Fleury's officers to invoke religious arguments or sanctions (and, indeed, the Papal Bull of condemnation was never legally received in France and never submitted to the Parlement of Paris for registration). Nor is it clear that the government was impressed by warnings and complaints from bishops, even before the Bull.[26] Finally, the willingness to rest the case against the freemasons on the existing laws regulating assemblies, rather than to have new laws drawn up and promulgated to deal with this problem, suggests uncertainty of touch on the part of the authorities. These curious aspects of the matter seem to be best explained by accepting the argument that this harrying of freemasonry did not spring from any deep and principled opposition of the French state to the Craft, but from the particular, personal and temporary preoccupations of Fleury and his officers. Moreover, these men were acting, it seems clear, against the grain of opinion and against a sympathy which existed towards masonry in court and ministerial circles other than the Cardinal's own. It best makes sense of the evidence to infer that Fleury, well known for his suspiciousness of rivalry and intrigue, feared that a movement under such exalted patronage as freemasonry enjoyed might be turned against him personally. He was

[23] Chevallier, pp. 198–9.

[24] Chevallier, pp. 172–9.

[25] See below, p. 68.

[26] The Bishop of Marseille wrote in alarm to the Intendant of Provence about freemasons at the end of September 1737; his letter is quoted in *AHRF*, 1969, p. 450 fn.

unwilling to provoke a new struggle with the Parlement of Paris by submitting the Papal Bull for registration. A quarrel which had begun in 1713, when the Pope had issued the Bull *Unigenitus* condemning Jansenist doctrines, was still going on because of the refusal of the Parlement to register it as would normally have been expected. The reasons for the attitude of the Parlement need not be expounded here, but the whole area of religious and quasi-religious legislation was extremely sensitive and easily inflamed. A refusal to register even a Bull of canonisation had only recently made it clear that co-operation of Parlement and government could not be hoped for in religious matters.[27] The inadvisability of stirring up enemies at court probably explains why new legislation was not issued. Thus deprived of heavy artillery, Fleury could only fall back on existing police powers and a policy of teasing and irritating, through loyal subordinates, those persons involved in masonic gatherings who were not in a position to hit back. It was the inn-keepers who were fined, not the masons. The harrying lapsed in the early 1740s, when Clermont had just extended his powerful protection to the Order, and, after a brief revival, finally ceased when there was a change in the lieutenancy of police in 1747. Fleury had died in 1743.

There must remain a speculative element in this view. The cross-currents are complicated and still only imperfectly disentangled from one another (there is the possibility, for example, that English diplomacy was somehow involved in the matter). But it is clear that whatever prompted hostility to freemasonry on the part of the French authorities was at least counter-balanced by goodwill in the same circles, that such hostility was neither enduring nor based on serious and settled alarm of any kind, and that it owed nothing to religious fervour or theological principle. When in 1748, the Bishop of Limoges informed the Comte de St Florentin of the existence of lodges in his diocese, the Secretary of State, himself a mason, feeling perhaps that he could not ignore a bishop's appeal, limited himself to asking the Intendant to request the masons concerned to abstain from meeting.[28] Earlier, in 1743, when police activity against the Craft was much more marked, a piece of evidence from Orléans points in this direction, too. When the local 'procureur du roi' asked for severe measures to be taken against the local freemasons, he found little to say against them beyond their secrecy and lack of authorisation. Only one argument appears to have

[27] Mellor, p. 188.
[28] G. H. Luquet, *La Franc-Maçonnerie et l'Etat en France au XVIIIe siècle* (Paris, 1964), pp. 89–90.

gone further and this was the way in which all orders of society mingled in the lodge 'honteusement confondus'. Their lack of religious distinction came a long way after this as cause for alarm in the eyes of the procureur.[29]

It does not seem, therefore, that what was done to freemasons by the public authorities in France (any more than what was done in Holland) was prompted by any general attitude of hostility or fear. Indeed, so far as there was a general reaction in the ruling circles it was favourable. There was, of course, also a snowball effect; persons who had not earlier known or cared about the existence of the freemasons were alarmed by the arrests, raids and publicity. Another factor, nonetheless, may also have helped to create a new public reaction to freemasonry, if such a thing can be postulated. This was the Papal condemnation of the Craft, which we have already touched on, and must now scrutinise more carefully.

THE CHURCH AND EIGHTEENTH-CENTURY FREEMASONRY

If Catholic clergy joined the Craft in the eighteenth century, it is scarcely surprising that Catholic laymen should adhere to it in large numbers. Yet this was in the teeth of formal condemnations of freemasonry in very strong language by two Popes. In 1738, Clement XII published *In eminenti*, a Bull excommunicating all members of the Craft and reserving to the Pope himself the power to absolve them. In 1751, Benedict XIV reissued Clement's Bull in his own *Providas*, in case people should have forgotten it. These, together with a re-issue of *In eminenti* in 1786 by Pius VI, were the only outright Papal condemnations before 1789 (although many more were to follow), but the demands they made on Catholics were unambiguous and explicit. That so many should have ignored them is one symptom of the weakness of the Papal authority in the eighteenth century.

For our purpose, the Bulls are only interesting because of the light they may throw on the growth of hostility to freemasonry and of the mythology connected with it. What were the motives behind them? *In eminenti* stated flatly that the association in the Craft of persons of different religious faiths was in itself bad, a predictable objection. It went on to say that some people of judgment considered the society to be depraved; this is something to which colour is lent by what we

[29] *AHRF*, 1969, p. 426: 'La qualité d'hommes qu'ils envisagent seule, les uns dans les autres, qui les rend tous égaux par la nature, leur fait oublier toute distinction de sang et de naissance, et même de religion . . .'

have already seen of the charges commonly made against freemasons in their early years. In some countries, the Bull pointed out, masonry had already been banned. In this way, therefore, the Bull justified its prohibition on grounds acceptable to many contemporaries, but it went on to give two further grounds for objection. One was the misuse of the oath of secrecy; clearly this threatened the confessional and the authority of the Church. Finally, there was a reference to 'other just and reasonable motives known to us'. *Providas* reprinted the text of the earlier Bull, added a little out of the Digest about illicit association, and invoked the help of the secular arm against the society. It provided no commentary on (or further mention of) the 'other just and reasonable motives'.[30]

If we leave these concealed motives on one side, the other grounds do not amount to anything very new or very frightening. They are prudential and disciplinary; given the ease with which many Catholics demonstrated their ability to reconcile masonry with the acceptance of the faith in the eighteenth century they seem to be exaggerated. It might be inferred that it was the discovery of this fact which explains the failure of the Papacy to reiterate and maintain its condemnation after 1751, when faced by widespread disobedience in this matter. Certainly, very little could be done by the Papacy outside its own territories to enforce the Bulls. But this may also suggest that the hidden motives to which *In eminenti* referred were, in fact, of a temporary nature. Yet the phrase itself was to be glossed in the nineteenth century, when the opposition of the Roman communion and freemasonry was absolute and embittered, as evidence that already, within a few years of the diffusion of the Craft in continental Europe, the Papacy had sagely detected in it a deep and enduring threat to Christendom.

If we try to penetrate the motives which underlay the first Bull, we cannot hope for certainty until we have access to much better documentation than is at present available, above all, to the records of the

---

[30] The French novelist, M. Roger Peyrefitte, has printed (in *Le Symbolisme*, no. 356, 1962, pp. 207–17) an Italian text which he claims (p. 193) to be 'la lettre secrète jointe à la bulle d'excommunication promulguée par le pape Clement XII le 28 avril 1738. Ce texte . . . n'avait jamais été communiqué, même à des auteurs ecclésiastiques, et restait jalousement gardé dans les archives du Vatican.' M. Peyrefitte refuses to say how this document came into his hands and allows (p. 195) that it bears traces of anachronistic amendment, which he attributes to the Holy Office. It is not said to whom it was addressed, nor why it should be written in Italian rather than Latin. It purports to explain the condemnation on the grounds that freemasonry leads to atheism and because it is a secret sect founded by those who, earlier, provoked the Reformation. Until more is known about this text it cannot be taken seriously by historians.

Inquisition. Without such evidence, we do not even know whether the authors of the Bull had read, for example, the *Constitutions*, or whether they relied on other, secondhand reports of masonic theory and discipline. We may accept that there would be good a priori grounds for suspicion: the Pope could hardly be expected to welcome an announced intention to assemble persons of different religious faiths while setting these differences aside as irrelevant to their relationship; he also could not be asked to tolerate a secrecy which endangered the practice of confession and, therefore, the sacrament of absolution; finally, we may assume that the origins of the Craft in Protestant England must have been a ground for misgiving (though we might expect this to be offset by the dominant Catholic and Jacobite influences in early freemasonry at Rome). But none of these grounds for a general caution or even hostility would explain why the condemnation came at one particular moment, why so many Roman catholics took so little notice of it subsequently and why, after 1751, freemasonry seems for a long time to have ceased to interest the Curia itself.

We may recall here two points which may be relevant without being decisive. One is the suggestion that in France there came to a climax in 1737 the process by which the old, Jacobite-tainted wing of the leadership was virtually displaced by men who wished for closer ties with England and English freemasonry. The other is the growing interest shown by English Protestants in the Italian lodges. It has been suggested that these two facts led to an approach by the Old Pretender (who lived at Rome) to the Pope, urging that there was now little for the Catholic and Stuart cause to hope for from freemasonry, and something to fear.[31] Certainly, the accession of Francis of Lorraine, a freemason, to the throne of Tuscany in 1737, and the appearance of an increasingly outspoken anti-Stuart focus for freemasonry at Florence (centred around the English ambassador, Mann), would have lent colour to such an interpretation if we knew any such approach to have been made. But there is no evidence of it. Instead, what facts are known seem to point to a much more particular and local motivation.

What seems to have happened in the later 1730s is that the Holy Office became increasingly concerned about reports of what was going on in individual Italian lodges. At Bologna in 1736, for example, there is said to have been a fruitless but agitated enquiry into masonic

---

[31] Mellor, pp. 90 ff. Another possibility is that events in France influenced the Old Pretender's acquiescence in the Pope's action (see Chevallier, *Les ducs*, p. 119).

activities by the Inquisition. In the following year, just before the succession of Francis of Lorraine, came the first proceedings against masons at Florence and the closure of a Jacobite lodge at Rome.[32] In 1738, it was again Florence that was causing concern; there was evidence of a connexion between freemasonry and free-thinking talk at the University of Pisa.[33] In December that year, the Inquisition raided a bookseller's shop at Florence and carried away prohibited books.[34] In 1739 this concern was to lead to the arrest of a prominent Florentine freemason by the Tuscan Inquisition. In the background was a coolness between Rome and Florence which followed the change of dynasty in 1737 at the death of the last Medici and the accession of Francis of Lorraine. This was intensified in the succeeding years and led at one point to an attempt by the Papal representatives to persuade the new Grand Duke, to dismiss one of his officers whose anticlericalism was, it was alleged, extreme.[35] Nor was this all. Clement XII, Pope from 1730 to 1740, was the descendent of a great Florentine banking family, the Corsini. One of his nephews had hoped to succeed to the Tuscan throne on the death of the last Medici. Another, Cardinal Neri Corsini, was a former diplomat in the service of the Medici who, after the death of his uncle, was to sustain for years at Florence the cause of the Papacy against the Tuscan anti-curialists.[36] In exploring the origins of the Bull we come quickly, therefore, to the need to consider that even personal and family considerations may have operated in shaping it and determining the moment of its promulgation.

It is the special and local, rather than the general and principled nature of the concern that is striking. This was in part admitted by Cardinal Corsini, who remarked of the masons that 'that society was formed in England as a game or innocent amusement but . . . it had degenerated in Italy, where it has become a school of ungodliness'.[37]

[32] It has been suggested by Mellor (p. 129) that the Rome lodge was closed because the Pretender believed it to have been compromised by the admission of Hanoverian sympathisers.

[33] Mellor, pp. 130 ff. In 1738 *Masonry further dissected* . . . quoted (p. 22) a report from Rome of 1730 (?7) that 'the Society of Free Masons, lately detected at Florence, makes a great noise; they pass there for Quietists; but here it is said they are of the Epicurean Sect, and that there are no laws too severe to deal with them. The Pope sent the Father Inquisitor of that office, Post to Florence, in order to prosecute them, at the Request of the Great Duke of Tuscany. . . .'

[34] Venturi, *Settecento riformatore*, p. 308.

[35] In the 1740s relations deteriorated so much that a retiring nuncio was not replaced.

[36] Venturi, pp. 301–2.

[37] Mellor, p. 90. Venturi (pp. 55–8) has some interesting comments and information on the (at first) anti-curial, and, later, anti-clerical tendencies of the Florentine

While it is not possible to be conclusive about the precise motives behind the Bull of 1738, we can say that no evidence has yet appeared that they included any such extravagant assertions about long-maturing and deeply entrenched plots against Christianity, the state and society as were bandied about in the nineteenth century (and were then thought to be corroborated by the dramatic and obscure language of *In eminenti*), but that their background may more plausibly be seen to be a number of local and particular incidents.

If we accept this view, an interesting parallel arises in the case of *Providas*. There was again some concern over events in one of the Italian states. The Bull of Benedict XIV appears, in any case, to require special explanation going beyond a mere wish to ensure the enforcement of his predecessor's legislation, because it accords so ill with the generally tolerant atmosphere of Benedict's pontificate.[38] Circumstantial and direct (though fragmentary) evidence both point to an explanation in terms of the diplomatic and personal relations of the courts at Rome and Naples. Before the publication of Benedict's Bull there was no public mark of the hostility of the Neapolitan government to freemasonry and, indeed, Clement XII's Bull had never been officially received. It seems to have been only at the end of 1750 that the lay authorities became aware of the Craft as a possible danger. This was because of the urgings of a Jesuit, Father Francesco Pepe, influential both at the court and at Rome. Just before Christmas, the Papal nuncio reported to Rome that the archiepiscopal court was receiving denunciations of freemasons, but that it was unlikely to proceed on them for the time being. Only on Boxing Day does another of his letters record that 'il noto padre Pepe, col suo solito zelo, abbia parlato ai ministri regi ed ecclesiastici per l'affare de' liberi muratori'.[39]

---

masonic circle of the 1730s. It is also useful to consult the old book by F. Sbigoli on one of its members, *Tommaso Crudeli e i primi framassoni in Firenze* (Milan, 1884), the only member of the lodge actually to undergo incarceration by the Inquisition.

[38] It should be noted that the often-repeated story that Benedict XIV was himself a freemason only appears in print for the first time in 1752, in a pamphlet criticising the Bull (Mellor, p. 200). His wish to deny this rumour has sometimes been said to explain the Bull (e.g. in *Histoire de la persecution intentée en 1775 aux francsmaçons de Naples*, London, 1780), but if this dating is correct, this explanation is less likely to be true, unless we assume that the rumour was widely current before it appeared in print.

[39] E. Papa, S.J., 'Padre Francesco Pepe S.I. e la sua attività apostolica a Napoli nel giudizio del nunzio Gualtieri', *Archivum Historicum Societatis Iesu*, xxvii, 1958, pp. 307–26, letters of 22 and 26 December 1750. Pepe was in confidential correspondence with Benedict XIV (which irritated the nuncio) for whom he acted as a

At this time, the Grand Master of the Neapolitan lodge was Raimondo di Sangro, Prince of Sansevero, a great Neapolitan nobleman —famous—or notorious—for his advanced, free-thinking views. He was a friend of Genovesi and the author of a book published in 1750 which caused a great stir of disapproval in clerical circles and was placed on the Index. Soon afterwards, in January 1751, a Roman prelate observed confidentially to the alarmed Neapolitan ambassador that the infection of freemasonry at Naples had even gained some persons at court.[40] This was followed by enquiries and governmental action at Naples; the Neapolitans were alarmed and did not wish to act in a way which would put them out of step with Rome.[41] In May, the nuncio was still telling the Cardinal Secretary of State in Rome that it was thought that there were far fewer masons at Naples than the alarm would lead men to suppose, but he admitted that another priest, 'l'impetuoso domenicano padre Rocco', had now sent a memorial to the Queen to excite her influence against masonry.[42]

By this time the Bull had been published at Rome. Pepe had gone there soon afterwards and the nuncio found himself in an embarrassing uncertainty about what he should do. He thought it possible (he wrote early in June) that Benedict had summoned Pepe specifically to talk about freemasons and added, significantly, that if it was true, as rumour at Naples had it, that the Holy See had again condemned freemasonry, then it would be a good idea if he were officially informed of it![43] At the end of the same month the nuncio was still reassuring the Cardinal Secretary of State that the freemasons at Naples were far fewer than Pepe believed but now thought it possible that a royal edict might be issued against the Craft.[44] He had apparently discussed the matter with the Prince of Sansevero who ('lamentandosi apertamente del zelo del padre Pepe') said he would cease to be Grand Master and asserted that he had given up attending even private meetings of masons and

---

direct channel of communication with the King. Papa, in his introduction, rebuts the view of Pepe as an éminence grise, but the references in the correspondence printed by I. Rinieri, *Della rovina di una monarchia*, pp. 601 ff. make the importance of his role clear. See also d'Ayala, 'I liberi muratori di Napoli nel secolo XVIII, pp. 433–4.

[40] d'Ayala, pp. 423–5.

[41] See letter to the ambassador at Rome quoted in d'Ayala, p. 426.

[42] Papa, p. 321, letters of 22 and 29 May 1751.

[43] Papa, p. 321, letter of 5 June. In fact, Pepe communicated the Bull unofficially to Charles before this was done officially (Rinieri, p. 601, Charles' letter of 17 June to Benedict and, p. 605, Benedict's official delivery of the Bull, 10 July).

[44] Proposals for its content had in fact already been communicated to Rome on 17 June, Benedict sending his comments in reply on 29 June (Rinieri, pp. 602–4).

had not in fact celebrated the St John's Day Feast.[45] In fact, the Neapolitan government had been alerted to the possible dangers of freemasonry at least since the previous year, and had already considered arguments for legislation against them.[46] In July, an edict was issued forbidding any further masonic gatherings.[47]

It is still hard to give a satisfactory explanation of this except in terms of a confluence of forces and such an explanation appears also to imply that Bull and Edict form part of a parallel though complex and by no means easy or co-operative process by which the Holy See and the Neapolitan court came to take a similar stand. Clearly, the role of Pepe was important, but the Neapolitan authorities were already alarmed about the sect before their ambassador at Rome reported to them the Papal concern. Beyond this, it has been asserted that the Neapolitan decision was influenced by popular discontent: a scapegoat was being sought for the failure of the miracle of San Gennaio in that year.[48] More generally still, although the Bull seems not to have received the royal Exequatur,[49] there may have been in the background a willingness to act in concert which reflected a desire on both sides to avoid further jurisdictional and legal conflicts such as had dogged Roman–Neapolitan relations in recent years: a common cause would help to erase a troubled diplomatic past. Nor, in those days, did a regalian and anticurial position necessarily connote the kind of anti-clericalism which was later intimately bound up with Italian freemasonry. The greatest of the Neapolitan reformers, Genovesi, seems to have despised the Craft.

[45] Papa, p. 322, letter of 29 June. Sansevero told the nuncio in August (p. 321) that there were only about 200 masons at Naples and among them only four clerics —two religious and two secular priests. He also made a submission in writing which circulated in Naples; the Pope did not reply but directed the nuncio to convey to the Prince his acknowledgement and a recommendation to obey the Bull and the royal edict (Rinieri, p. 609). Presumably it was his blabbing to the nuncio and formal submission which led the Craft to ostracise him as a traitor. For some picturesque details, possibly true, see a memorandum of the history of freemasonry at Naples written in the 1750s, ASPN, XXX, 1905, pp. 251–2.

[46] The memorandum from Orlando referred to below is dated 1 June (see p. 75).

[47] The copy in the Vatican Archives is dated 13 July; Papa dates it 10 July (p. 322), d'Ayala 12 July (p. 431). The relative mildness of this step is striking. The only person punished seems to have been a French merchant, possibly the founder of Neapolitan masonry, who was expelled from the kingdom after a few weeks in prison (d'Ayala, p. 441).

[48] Rinieri, p. 389. This is alleged in his text and it should perhaps be remarked here that his book is a violently clerical and anti-masonic work, valuable chiefly for the documents it prints.

[49] See the report of the Genoese agent quoted in d'Ayala, p. 439. Moreover, no steps seem to have been taken to enforce the royal edict.

It is to a friend of Genovesi's, indeed, that we owe a memorandum which was sent to Rome setting out the reasons for the Neapolitan decree.[50] This was the Celestine monk Orlando. His memorandum is interesting because it shows, presumably, some of the arguments which in the end swayed the Neapolitan court. It begins by setting out an account of the sources Orlando has used. Although not very surprising, it shows the sort of materials which gave a bad impression of the Craft. He refers first to two printed 'fogli' from Holland of 1735 which appear to have been official enactments about the regulation of the Craft. He then says that he has read all that has been written in the dictionaries at his disposal. It seems fair to assume that these included Pivati's. In addition he read two anti-masonic works, *L'Ordre des Francs-Maçons trahis* and *Les Francs-Maçons écrasés*, both of which Pivati acknowledged as his sources.[51] Finally, he has used letters and information from private persons. About these sources he is not uncritical; he declines, for example, to accept the assertions of the author of *Les Francs-Maçons écrasés* that Cromwell founded the Order with secret political aims.

After surveying briefly the rise and spread of the Craft he addresses himself to the question why religious persons, and Roman Catholics in particular, should regard it with suspicion. His first motive is the English origin of freemasonry. The fact that the English are well known as 'per lo piu spiriti forti, e deisti, o sia de niuna religione' means that all lodges must be under grave suspicion on this count.[52] Moreover (he continues) many well-known masons throughout Europe are notoriously despisers of religion and advocates of scepticism and deism. The mason's brotherly solidarity, too, extended as it is between men of all faiths, must also lead insensibly to a consideration of religion as a matter indifferent, and eventually to toleration. Nothing is done at masonic gatherings of a godly nature, and the way is therefore open for their other practices to tend to disorder. The oath itself is

[50] 'Memorie sull'ordine di Liberi Muratori del Padre Abbate D. Giuseppe Orlando della Congregazione Celestina Lector Pubblico di Fisica Sperimentale', dated 1 June 1751, in Vatican Archives, *Benedictus XIV. Bolle Consistorialie XIV*, f. 170–7.

[51] See below, p. 87. The first was singled out by Charles as an unusually useful source of information about freemasonry when he sent the Pope a bundle of documentation about the Craft on 10 August and Benedict's reply a week later agrees that this seems 'il più sincero' (Rinieri, pp. 607–8).

[52] The same point was taken up by the anonymous author (though without the English association) of a *Lettera scritta da Firenze ad un amico in Napoli intorno la setta dei Liberi Muratori* of 1751. 'Questa Adunanza prescindendo dalla Religione, e vale a dire da ogni Religione, vantando solo l'*onesta naturale*, inclina al naturalismo, al Deismo ed all'indifferenza di ogni Religione' (quoted in d'Ayala, p. 421).

offensive and a profanation of the Divine name. All these motives, and perhaps others unknown, says Orlando, prompted the Bull of Clement XII. To them he adds a number of arguments showing why in a purely secular view, too, meetings of freemasons should be regarded apprehensively, as a danger to the state. First comes the fact that the Craft was implanted at Naples by foreigners, who continue to frequent its lodges there. Then there is the secrecy which surrounds the masons' proceedings and the ominous circumstances of a doorkeeping brother with sword in hand. Finally, there are the secret signs.

The language of the Neapolitan edict itself shows traces of this argument. It alleged several of the old charges—secrecy, the guarded meetings, secret signs, sacrilegious oaths, dissolute behaviour—and added to them the general argument that the free practice of the right of association was always pernicious in its consequences. Here, certainly, was an argument likely to be heard with respect by royal counsellors anxious to fortify a royal authority which would need all its strength to combat the entrenched privileges standing in the way of reform in Naples and Sicily. In the other charges, there is nothing very unusual or alarming; and such grounds do little to explain the wilder beliefs which were to come to be held about masonry in the next century. Finally, there is no evidence that the edict was ever enforced and this must at least encourage the supposition that it is best explained as a diplomatic gesture.

Although the question is no longer closely connected with the attitude of the Papacy, it is worthwhile at this point to jump forward nearly twenty-five years to the next crisis of Neapolitan freemasonry. Besides drawing together the story of the public authorities' reactions to the Craft in the Kingdom of the Two Sicilies before 1789, it again demonstrates the negative point that ideology seems always to have counted for very little in official hostility. In fact, whether through deliberate official connivance or simple negligence, the two decades after the 1751 edict gradually revealed themselves as something of a masonic golden age at Naples. Nearly twenty-five years later, freemasonry prospered there as never before. It owed much to the stimulus of French fashion. It was à la mode; it was discussed openly and masons made no secret of their allegiance to the Craft. Soldiers and courtiers belonged to it, and it seems that dislike of the all-powerful minister Tanucci was another fashionable encouragement to membership. An edict of 12 September 1775 suddenly shattered this security. It fell on the masonic society of Naples like a thunderbolt. Recalling the edict of Charles IV and its prohibition on attendance at lodges, it ordered the

Giunta di Stato to proceed at once against offenders who were thereby guilty of lèse-majesté, an offence which carried the death penalty.[53]

The decision to act was attributed by the King to the discovery of a masonic group in the royal cadet regiment earlier in the year. The King who had issued the edict of 1751 had been since 1759 Charles III, King of Spain, and his son and successor at Naples, Ferdinand I, had quickly written to him to ask for advice about what to do. Other evidence that freemasonry was flourishing in the Kingdom of the Two Sicilies had been available for some time, and it is not easy to see why such a discovery should suddenly arouse such concern. The King was undoubtedly moved to act by Tanucci and it is here that the explanation seems to lie, in his personal concern for his position at court. The role of the Queen, Maria Carolina, was decisive. She had long contested Tanucci's authority, was known to favour many of the most prominent freemasons and is believed to have tried to persuade her husband to enter a lodge. Tanucci appealed through his present to his former king. He sought in reality an invocation of paternal authority to coerce the reigning monarch into action against the queen's friends—who were Tanucci's enemies.[54] Charles was only too pleased to interfere in his son's kingdom in support of his former policy and endorsed the policy of a new edict.

The edict required (like its predecessors) the taking of oaths not to attend masonic gatherings; before long a large number of masons had taken such oaths. A notable diminution of masonic activity seems to have been the consequence, but this was not the end of the matter. From Madrid, Charles III urged the intensification of police action. Soon Tanucci was faced with the embarrassing possibility of having to proceed against close friends of the Queen were his police to discover a lodge in flagrante. They might even discover the Queen to be present.

A lodge was 'surprised'[55] in March 1776 which did not cause this embarrassment; it was composed mainly of foreigners and no persons of leading rank in Neapolitan society were found at it. Nonetheless, many such came to visit the prisoners in their detention; far from intimidating the Queen's circle, the prosecution seems to have excited them the more against Tanucci because of its unexpected nature. Tolerance of masonry had for too long been taken for granted. The

[53] d'Ayala, pp. 529–30. The edict was actually published 10 October.
[54] d'Ayala, pp. 533 ff.
[55] The word is hardly appropriate because the meeting was arranged by an agent provocateur. See d'Ayala, *passim.*

Queen's sister herself appeared at the prison. Soon the cause of the masonic martyrs was taken up by a Paris lodge and a pamphlet was published about their woes in London. In court, the defence made much of the innocent nature of the Craft and the general suspicion of official management in the affair. Soon the question of provocation was raised and the trial was turned into a pursuit of the police official concerned. One of the officials of the Giunta itself published a pamphlet defending freemasonry and attacking the prosecution.

There were soon signs that the government—that is to say, Tanucci—felt things were getting out of hand. A hornets' nest had been disturbed. Retreat followed. The French ambassador intervened on behalf of a Frenchman who had been imprisoned because of his suspected connexion with freemasonry. The burning of a pro-masonic pamphlet by the public hangman was a gesture by which Tanucci attempted to show himself still firmly hostile to the freemasons while in fact doing nothing that would further exacerbate relations with the Queen's friends.

At the height of the quarrel, at the end of October 1776, Tanucci resigned from his office, pleading the infirmities of age. There can be little doubt that this was a concealed dismissal, the result of Maria Carolina's harassing of her husband.[56] The setting of this episode must be considered at its widest; the diminution of Spanish influence at Naples would not displease Vienna. But there can be no doubt also that the occasion was provoked by Tanucci's mishandling of the masonic affair. Having begun to attack masonry as a move in the palace politics of Naples, he then showed a lack of resolve in pressing his offensive once it was clear that his enemies were aroused. They, in their turn, seized the occasion to press home their attack on him. The liquidation of the affair of the freemasons followed. In 1777 the Giunta dismissed the case against them and they were released, amid general approval. Tanucci's principal agent in the affair was then prosecuted. Deprived of office and exiled from Naples before the end of the case, he was shabbily treated by Tanucci who failed to protect or to acknowledge his own responsibility for the acts of his former servants. Nevertheless, Maria Carolina eventually relented and in 1782 the episode at last closed with a royal annulment of the proceedings against this unhappy man.[57]

[56] The episode is explored in d'Ayala, pp. 95–110.

[57] These proceedings occupy most of the last four sections of d'Ayala's study, where they are recounted in great detail. It may be remarked that the end of the case was accompanied in January 1782 by another royal gesture at Naples against the Craft, enjoining the Giunta to enforce existing laws against it. Nonetheless, this

This second flurry of anti-masonic activity by the government at Naples demonstrates even more decisively than that of 1751 that the crucial factors promoting it were particular and local, rather than general and ideological. It is not even possible to see whether Tanucci actually believed in the possibility of a general threat to order and authority in the secret meetings which Charles had feared. What was decisive was a political situation in which it seemed that an attack on freemasons might be a profitable manoeuvre. For all their exploitation of publicity and foreign support, the Queen and her friends fought back in the same spirit. Maria Carolina supported freemasons because Tanucci menaced them. Personal and political rivalry determined official attitudes towards the Craft at Naples, as elsewhere.

In 1775 very little was said about religion and nothing that went beyond what had been alleged in 1751. This bears out the general conclusion that the Papal Bulls did not at any time in the eighteenth century evoke wide enthusiasm and support from secular authority. What has been said of their immediate setting and the response to them implies, clearly, two things. In the first place, it does not lend support to the idea that deep and far-reaching beliefs and fears of the Craft provoked Popes gifted with unusual insight into an early recognition of the sweeping dangers and nefarious designs later attributed to the Craft, though this was later to be alleged. Particular, local and personal influences seem to have been decisive in both the formulation and the timing of the Bulls. Secondly, good Catholics were by no means necessarily more ready to follow the Pope's direction in this matter than in many others. Not even the clergy could be bound to obedience to the Bulls. In France, some bishops issued pastoral letters reiterating Papal condemnations of the Craft, but there is overwhelming evidence of the continued participation of clergy in the lodges. Some bishops did nothing to support the policy of the Bulls, and did not seek to enforce discipline in this question even among the clergy, let alone the laity.

An interesting exchange of letters between the Archbishops of Tours and Toulouse took place in 1778 which expresses the divergences of attitudes which the hierarchy could show.[58] Writing of the forthcoming election of a new Provincial of the Cordeliers, the Archbishop of Tours reported that the apparent favourite had been denounced to him by the Bishop of Quimper. 'Il m'a paru plaisant que le grand reproche

---

decree was a dead letter, disavowed by the Neapolitan diplomats within a couple of months (d'Ayala, p. 789). It appears to have been intended as a sop to Charles III.

[58] Printed in RISS, I, pp. 810–11.

du Seigneur St-Luc contre ce Religieux est qu'il est franc maçon. Suivant lui franc maçonnerie et impiété sont une même chose.' A few days later, he wrote again to announce the election of this candidate and said he had been calumniated: 'peut-être n'est il pas très fervent, peut-être même est-il franc maçon ce qui déplait tant à M. de Quimper, mais ce dont je vous réponds, c'est qu'il a de l'esprit, un maintien extérieur bien Religieux, qu'il annonce le désir de rétablir la Règle et que la confiance qu'il a meritée de tous ses confrères lui en facilitera les moyens.' Many bishops would have been as easily satisfied as the Archbishop of Tours in setting aside the obstacle of known masonic attachment in such a case. On the other hand, many would not; a Chambéry lodge in 1787 thought it best not to embarrass its clerical members by inviting them to meetings of the lodge, given the known attitude of the bishop.[59] Even in the same diocese, however, practice need not be consistent. One prince-bishop of Liège was himself a freemason, though a predecessor had issued an interdict against masonic assemblies only twelve years before his accession.[60]

This does not mean, of course, that the absence of a willingness to impose clerical discipline led to disobedience of the Bulls by even a large minority of clergy in countries where the secular arm was not behind the Papal ban. Many were no doubt convinced that the Pope was right. It has been pointed out in one regional study that only eight out of the hundreds of secular priests in Haut Maine can be identified as freemasons, and that only one canon of the chapter at Le Mans belonged to the Craft.[61] There were also important differences between secular and regular clergy. Particularly after the publication of the Papal Bull suppressing the Society of Jesus in 1774 (at which Philosophes and Jansenists exulted) ex-Jesuits and Oratorians were strongly anti-masonic. They were to come round to the view that this, like the earlier expulsion of the Society from France, was the result of long intrigue by Philosophe opponents well represented in the ranks of the Craft. The Jesuits had, therefore, special motives to explain why theirs was the only male religious order whose members consistently do not appear in the lists of clergy who became freemasons. No doubt this strengthened the effect of their oath of loyalty to the Pope which should in any case have been decisive in securing their adherence to the anti-masonic Bulls.

[59] Vermale, La Franc-Maçonnerie savoisienne, p. 6.
[60] AHRF, 1969, p. 477.
[61] A. Bouton, Les Franc-Maçons Manceaux et la Révolution française (1741–1815) (Le Mans, 1958), pp. 28–9.

Nevertheless, whatever the attitudes of individual clergy, in the eighteenth-century climate of opinion, Papal authority could do little to hinder the Craft among the laity without the support of the secular arm and public opinion. This was true even in its own sovereign territories, to judge by the history of freemasonry in the Papal enclave of Avignon.[62] There, though the life of the lodges could be and was disturbed by the activities of the Holy Office, it was increasingly difficult to enforce obedience to the Papal rulings and impossible to eradicate the Craft. The Bull of 1738 apparently had some immediate effect; only towards the end of the 1740s does masonic activity appear again. Yet this resurgence was so strong that an anti-masonic student of Avignonese masonry deplored the hypocrisy with which the best-informed masons there (priests among them) ignored the Papal commands. An amalgamation of lodges in 1749 makes it clear that already more than one lodge had been operating and the new lodge seems to have continued fairly openly until 1751, meeting roughly twice a month. In 1750, warning reached it of what was coming from Rome and after the Bull of the following year the lodge suspended its formal activities. It nonetheless decided that its members should continue to meet from time to time under the guidance of their own elected officers.[63] Meanwhile, the Archbishop of Avignon had followed up the Bull by issuing an allocution of his own in which he demanded the surrender of the manuscript minute-book or register of the local lodge under pain of excommunication. It does not seem that he obtained it. Nor, although there was certainly a slackening in masonic activity, was the Craft much damaged, for from 1774 onwards there is a new resurgence of masonic documentation to attest to its vigour at Avignon. The Inquisitor General issued a new edict against the Craft in 1776 but (a recent scholar suggests) there soon developed a modus vivendi which enabled Avignonese freemasonry to continue its workings practically untroubled providing it did so discreetly.[64] A police raid on one occasion carried off the curtains and furniture from one lodge, but the 'persecution' of which Avignonese freemasons proudly boasted does not seem to have gone much further. The tone of another archepiscopal allocution of 1786, accompanying the publication of Pius VI's Bull, drew attention to the way in which *In eminenti* had been ignored

[62] G. Gautherot, 'La franc-maçonnerie à Avignon', *RISS*, IX, p. 116. This study should be supplemented by C. Mesliand, 'Franc-Maçonnerie et religion à Avignon' (*AHRF*, 1969), which uses new documentary evidence.

[63] 'Au-dessus de leurs obligations de chrétiens, ils plaçaient donc leurs obligations d'initiés' is the bitter comment of Gautherot, p. 122.

[64] Mesliand, p. 459.

and thwarted; it does not suggest great confidence that this could be remedied.[65] Neither the Archbishop nor the Holy Office could check the Craft.

There were doubtless many reasons for the inefficacy of Papal discipline. Special circumstances at Avignon may account for some of them, but it is a striking example of a general phenomenon. It is tempting to assume that, in any case, the Roman Church was by the eighteenth century too weak to exact obedience in such a matter by spiritual sanctions alone. Why this should be so is clearly a very far-reaching question, taking us into the realm where religious belief and practice merge and diverge; it is not possible to pursue it here. Nor would this, in any case, be the whole story. Two other points may be borne in mind. The first is that the authority of a Bull was still nothing like so great as in the next century. It has been pointed out that one individual influence contributing much to the growth of Papal authority was Joseph de Maistre;[66] it is therefore especially interesting to find him in 1782 arguing that freemasons might properly reject the assertion in the Bulls that their oath of secrecy was illicit.[67] This raises a second qualification to be remembered in assessing the meaning of widespread ignoring of the Bulls: arguments could be put forward about their meaning which would leave good Catholics free to give them a sincere but personal interpretation. Moreover, what was a Catholic's duty when the civil authorities did not make the same demand as the Church and did not even formally recognise the Bulls?

The Bulls could only be effective in those Catholic countries where they were officially and legally received and, given the general sensitivity of Church and State relations during the century, it is not surprising that there were few such. France, we have noticed, did not receive the Bulls and this was later to be used by French masons as an argument that obedience to them was not required.[68] It is even possible, because of the anti-curial attitude of the Parlements, that knowledge of the Bulls may have been an additional stimulus to freemasonry among their members. To some of them, who had already taken a violently anti-Papal stand at the time of the Jansenist and *Unigenitus* quarrels, the Bulls must have seemed further evidence of the incorrigible backward-

---

[65] Mesliand, p. 461.

[66] E. Dermenghem, *Joseph de Maistre mystique* (Paris, 1946), p. 76. De Maistre's most celebrated work was *Du Pape* (Paris, 1819).

[67] *Mémoire au duc de Brunswick par J. de Maistre*, ed. E. Dermenghem (Paris, 1925), p. 89.

[68] See, e.g., *Considérations filosofiques sur la francmaçonerie* (Hamburg and Rome, 1776), pp. 209 ff.

ness of Rome. The Bull of 1738 was not published in Tuscany, and the best that the Holy Office was able to achieve there in 1739 had been to impose an uncomfortable imprisonment on one mason while dragging its feet about bringing him to trial (and, even, it is interesting to note, about formulating precise charges against him). It was widely known that the Tuscan government was unsympathetic to the prosecution and some believed it would have connived at the prisoner's escape.[69] Later, in order to get rid of another mysterious figure with masonic connexions, the Papacy had to resort to the extreme threat of threatening to remove its nuncio from Florence. This hardly suggests warm lay co-operation in imposing the Bull. Nor was the Bull received in the Habsburg dominions, perhaps because of the continuing influence of Francis of Lorraine, husband of Maria Theresa and Emperor since 1745, though state action against freemasons was taken independently of it in 1743.[70] In the Austrian Netherlands a pamphlet was published denying the validity of the Bulls.[71]

Benedict's later explicit invocation of the aid of the secular arm is, therefore, a comment on the limited response to his predecessor's Bull. In the Papal States themselves, of course, there was no question of non-enforcement. An ordinance of January 1739 provided for confiscation of goods and the death penalty for belonging to the Craft, and laid on all subjects of the Pope an obligation to denounce meetings of masons which came to their notice.[72] Elsewhere, the Bull's reception and subsequent action were limited. Poland received the Bull of 1738, but nothing seems to have followed. In 1740 the Grand Master of the Knights of St John expelled six members of his order from Malta because they were freemasons. Success was greatest in the Iberian peninsula. In Spain there was a total prohibition in 1740, renewed in 1751. Such action as was taken seems to have been effective; Spanish masonry was slow to grow in comparison with that of other countries. Portugal, too, was a country where the Inquisition could operate and in 1742–4 there took place the notorious torture and trial of John Coustos, a naturalised British subject. This led to diplomatic intervention and did much to draw sympathetic attention to the persecution of the Craft. The Inquisitors are said to have misapprehended its nature and to have treated it as some new religious sect.[73] Among other

---

[69] Venturi, *Settecento riformatore*, p. 57.

[70] Gould, IV, p. 161. [71] *AHRF*, 1969, p. 475.

[72] L. von Pastor, *The History of the Popes*, xxxiv (London, 1941), p. 412. In that year, too, took place the burning of the *Apologie* (see above, p. 36).

[73] Mellor, pp. 175–9. It may be remarked, though, that the persecution of freemasonry was an issue which was only incidental in this case. As contemporary dis-

Catholic countries, it is exaggerated to speak of those in Italy, as one masonic historian does, as the scene of 'une véritable persecution'.[74] Although the freemasons of Savoy were ordered in 1765 to discontinue their assemblies, we know that they did not; subsequently we find the King, Victor Amadeus III, to be a freemason himself.[75] The origins of action against the masons of Leghorn in 1773 have still to be explained. Apart from this, the only important Italian attack on freemasonry took place at Naples and that, it is clear, had origins very different from those beliefs and motives which characterised anti-masonry a century later.

UNOFFICIAL ANTI-MASONRY AT MID-CENTURY

If it is not easy to discern any general principles in such hostility as was shown to freemasonry by the public authorities of the early eighteenth century, it is even less easy to identify any consistency in unofficial reactions beyond a simple distrust of the mysterious and esoteric. Just as the authorities' reactions were rarely simple and never purely ideological, so were those of anti-masonic publicists. And just as the particular causes which had prompted individual governments to harry the Craft ebbed and lost their force, so did reiterated attacks on the Craft once they ceased to be novel. Certainly there was no general response to the Papal criticism of the Craft and hostility on other grounds must have declined as more and more people were initiated and found out what masonry actually was—a harmless amusement. Sometimes special grounds for hostility appeared, but this particularity of reaction, even in anti-masonry, is, it must be recognised, what we should expect a priori (unless we subscribe from the start to the plot and paranoia theories). Freemasonry as a social organism inevitably became involved in the local issues and particular quarrels

---

cussion and exploitation of the case shows, this celebrated case was of more importance in the history of popular anti-Catholicism and the legend of the Inquisition in England, than in that of the debate on freemasonry. The editor of Coustos' account limited himself to saying of the Craft that 'if of no Benefit to the Community, [it] is not prejudicial to it; whereas the Tribunal he suffered under, must be the heaviest curse to every country where it is established'—scarcely a warm endorsement. (*The sufferings of John Coustos, for Free-Masonry, and for his refusing to turn Roman Catholic, in the Inquisition at Lisbon* (London, 1746), p. xxvii.) On the question of the attitude of the Inquisition, Coustos' own account of his indictment (p. 52) says that they stigmatised the 'Sect' as 'a horrid Compound of Sacrilege, Sodomy, and many other abominable Crimes'.

[74] Vermale, p. 6.
[75] Vermale, p. 6.

of the societies where it appeared.[76] The comparative rarity of spontaneous and informal social organisation at that time was bound to
make this more conspicuous than it would be today. The general
secrecy of the Order, however much violated in practice, heightened
suspicions to which this might give rise and was, eventually, to lead to
a much more generalised hostility. Yet this was not to take place until
the end of the eighteenth century and then only under the influence
of much further development. Even then, too, the reassuring bon ton
of aristocratic lodges and a surfeit of 'revelation' had convinced most
members of the European élite that they had nothing to fear in these
mysteries; 'je crois que vous frappez beaucoup trop de la F.M.' wrote
Marie Antoinette to her sister Maria Christina.[77] She may have been
influenced, too, by the knowledge that the French police found it easy
to gain access to the lodges and were satisfied that nothing dangerous
need be feared from them.[78]

Even when, earlier in the century, anti-masonic propaganda had
appeared, it never presented the integrated, political case against the
Craft which was the stock-in-trade of anti-masonry in the next century.
The elements of anti-masonry, though often present together, were
still distinct and political suspicion arose only in special, local circumstances or from a general conservatism, rooted in Roman Law traditions, about the undesirability of private association except under
close public regulation. Except in England, it was always assumed that
specific authorisation was necessary for any but the most informal
assemblies.[79] Even so distinguished a reformer as Genovesi, it is said,
approved the Neapolitan proscription of the Craft because an un-
supervised assembly of men who discussed public affairs was itself

[76] An interesting theme awaiting examination is the relation between freemasonry's attractiveness to the nobility in France and the revivifying of the self-
consciousness and awareness of status of the noblesse in the eighteenth century.
Ramsay's dream of a purified nobility would have interesting implications for the
readers of Boulainvilliers who sought to restore the due role of their order in the
French state and rejected the demands of growing centralisation expressed through
a reforming monarchy and 'ministerial despotism'.

[77] 27 February 1781. Vogt d'Hunolstein, *Correspondance inédite de Marie Antoinette*
(Paris, 1864), p. 95.

[78] See the brief extract from the papers of Lenoir, lieutenant de police 1775–85,
printed by G. Lefebvre, *AHRF*, 1927, p. 301.

[79] 'Even those Assemblies which have nothing in view but what is just and lawful,
cannot be formed without the express approbation of the Sovereign, after he is
fully satisfied of their usefullness, and Tendency to the publick Good' says the
English version of *The Publick Law* of the Frenchman Domat (London, 1722,
vol. ii, p. 310), which bases itself on the Digest. I owe this illustration of the orthodox eighteenth-century view to Mr J. Rogister.

an affront to the normal course of political life.[80] Privately initiated political activity itself was, of course, in most countries indistinguishable from sedition. It seems to have been correspondence with foreign 'Orients', for example, that most worried the government of Sardinia even when the King was himself a mason.[81]

Freemasons themselves at this time contributed most to the suspicion of them by the publicity they increasingly gave to legends about their origins and ancestry (and it was to have even more influence at the end of the century) and, above all, by the Secret and the language of the oath. By mid-century, too, this was becoming more important as masonry ramified and the idea of still higher, hidden degrees, and more important secrets was diffused. On the other hand, allegations of bad character and disorderly personal conduct became less frequent as time passed, though they were always to find a place in attacks on the Craft. As for specifically political criticism of the Craft on grounds of hidden subversive aims, this was uttered at a relatively early date but for a long time won small acceptance. One of its manifestations is nonetheless interesting because it anticipated arguments later to be widely current in the literature attacking the secret societies.

These political accusations can be found not in their original statement, but in a pamphlet refuting them, *La Franc-Maçonne* of 1744.[82] The highly improbable scenario in which its arguments develop displays a lady of fashion, consumed with desire to penetrate the secret of masonry, doing all she can—she only just rejects black magic—to worm the Secret out of her husband. On the way, she tells us of possible interpretations of it which she has considered and rejected: one of them is a political one.[83] It is suggested by the lack of social discrimination in masonic recruitment. Given the indiscriminate mixing of ranks at masonic gatherings, she thinks, and the levelling which results, 'il est donc plus que probable, concluai-je, qu'il n'est question chez eux que d'une Maçonnerie purement symbolique, dont le secret consiste à bâtir insensiblement une République universelle et démocratique, dont la Reine sera la raison, et le Conseil suprême, l'assemblée des sages. Le projet d'une telle République, continuai-je, mérite bien d'être caché dans le sein du mystère; car plus les entreprises sont grandes, plus il est besoin de secret pour les faire réussir: après tout, pourquoi les Franc-Maçons ne feroient-ils pas en grand, ce que jadis les Spartiates ont si bien exécuté en petit, puis réfléchissant sur l'ordre de la nature,

---

[80] A. Broccoli, *Educazione e politica nel Mezzogiorno d'Italia (1767–1860)* (Florence, 1968).

[81] Vermale, p. 6.   [82] See above, p. 64.   [83] *La Franc-Maçonne*, pp. 17–19.

laquelle nous donne en commun l'usage de la lumière, et des élements. Je disois, les Franc-Maçons se proposant l'exemple de cette mère équitable, ont sans doute formé le dessein d'établir un ordre politique, qui mettra aussi en commun tout ce que la terre, et les talens de ses habitans sont capables de produire. Ma conjecture se fortifioit, quand je faisois attention à ces Vers d'un aimable Maçon.

> Nos ouvrages sont toujours bons,
> Dans les plans que nous en traçons,
> Notre regle est sûr,
> Car c'est la nature
> Qui guide et conduit nos crayons.'

Even apart from the light it may throw on the origins of the limerick, this passage is of great interest. Although there is no hint in it of violent subversion, it contains several of the elements which loom very large in the later mythology of the secret societies: republicanism, egalitarianism, the rule of reason, an oligarchy of the enlightened, communism and the ideology of Nature. Nevertheless, this is not all worth noting about it. So far as the registration of early political objections to masonry is concerned it is more important that the lady's theory is easily swept aside by her husband. The pamphlet ends, indeed, much later, with an account of the meeting of a Lodge witnessed by the lady from concealment. It demonstrates emphatically the socially benevolent nature of masonry, and again briefly touches on masonic politics by noticing the drinking of the health of the King and that 'on ne parlait jamais ni de Religion, ni de Politique, ni même de la bagatelle.' [84]

This was a friendly pamphlet. In 1747 appeared a book in which some of these charges were repeated and new ones added. This was Les Franc-Maçons écrasés, which went on to be several times reprinted. [85] It contains the main theme on which all political criticism of the Craft was to rest for the next quarter-century. The author describes the core of the doctrine of the Craft as 'L'Egalité et la Liberté' and ascribes its foundation to Cromwell, who aspired to the reformation of the human race through the extermination of kings and other powers. The historical arguments on which this is based are far from reassuring. We are told, for example, that the Levellers ('leur Chef était le Général Rainsborough, grand ami de Cromwell') conspired against the Protector's

[84] La Franc-Maçonne, p. 58.
[85] Les Francs-Maçons écrasés, suite du livre intitulé, l'Ordre des Francs-Maçons trahi, traduit du latin (Amsterdam, 1747). This work is attributed to the Abbé Larudan, and the earlier book, first published in 1745, is attributed to the Abbé G. L. Calabre Pérau.

D

life because he wished to change their name—to that of freemasons.[86] Nevertheless, they provide the basis from which the author arrives at one of the themes of the argument rejected by *La Franc-Maçonne*: the subordination of mankind to the ordering of natural law and natural distinctions alone, 'le rétablissement de cet âge, nommé par les Poètes l'âge d'Or'.[87] The novel (and for the future, most important) feature of this anti-masonic argument lies in the allegation that not all masons are aware of this design, because of the cloaking of the real purpose of the Order in allegory, that of rebuilding the social order; the true doctrines are revealed only to suitable candidates; others are given only the allegorical interpretation of masonry's aims.[88] This explains why kings and princes have been taken in. He concludes that the charges made against the Craft of a dangerous tolerance in religion and of potentially seditious aim are justified. By way of replacing one scandal about the Order with another, he goes on to allow that the rumours of sodomitical practices are groundless, but provides instead a sensational account of the murder of Prichard, said to have paid for his revelations of the Craft's secrets by having his heart and tongue torn out in open lodge.[89]

It is difficult to know how much effect this had on the public repute of masonry, though a large number of reprintings in several languages may be significant; there was obviously a good market for anti-masonry. It is interesting to see in it at so early a date so many anticipations of later writings; the idea of the initiated hierarchy manipulating the uninstructed grades, the identification of social democracy and libertarian individualism as masonic aims, and the universality of masonic design were all to be given much more attention later on. It is also noteworthy that the whole pamphlet has a strongly anti-rationalist, and, indeed, anti-Enlightenment tone. Its arguments were given more publicity when, in the same year, Pivati drew heavily on it for his encylopaedia article. This must have introduced a wider circle at least of Italians to these ideas. The whole tone of Pivati's account is suspicious and he, too, repeated the story which was to be so important for later fear of the Order, that not all were let in to the Secret; princes, he

[86] Larudan, p. 99. The Levellers, he goes on, finally let themselves be called Fifth Monarchy Men.   [87] Larudan, p. 15.

[88] 'Les Architectes sont les seuls dépositaires du système; on n'en fait part aux autres, qu'à proportion, qu'on les remarque portés à l'adopter, et capables de le soutenir. Peut-être même tous les Ecossais n'en sont-ils pas instruits parfaitement et sans enveloppe' (p. xxvii). For the reference to les Ecossais, already mentioned in the book of 1744, see the next chapter.

[89] Larudan, pp. 57–60, 103.

remarked, following the pamphlet, were kept from knowledge of the full secrets of the Order and their presence was no guarantee of its innocence.

It is nonetheless certain that such attacks did not swing public opinion against the Order. Here, another unfriendly pamphlet of the mid-century is worth remark. *Le Maçon démasqué ou le vrai secret des Francs Maçons mis au jour*[90] mocked the 'jeux enfantins' of the Craft, but declared it innocent of subversive aims: 'les Maçons ne songent n'y à la Réligion, n'y à l'Etat; il ne s'agit entre eux que de plaisirs'.[91] Such confident assertions, together with the relative scarcity of political accusations in the early anti-masonic literature and the evident absence of alarm among wide strata of the European ruling élite of the day, make it clear that the public authorities who had shown hostility to the Order had been unable to communicate their conviction to those they sought to direct. It is much more likely that those who did turn against the Craft responded to the steady and repeated commonsense rational criticisms of it which were to grow in volume as freemasonry emphasised more and more its emotional, irrational content; but this was only to become important as the century went on.[92]

What was emphatically not present in the first fifty years or so of the Craft's life in Europe was *general* ideological or political suspicion. The behaviour of Roman Catholics showed how little readiness there was to take seriously the Papal Bulls as theological or general condemnation. This sort of suspicion was only to appear and become dominant when freemasonry became confused with other movements proliferating in the second half of the eighteenth century. It is to these that we must now turn. Almost all of them—and there were many—got much more lurid publicity than did orthodox freemasonry. Some of them made dramatic and fearsome claims and behaved in a sinister way, thus justifying suspicion. Others were the subject of sensational 'revelations' and allegations. These new arrivals on the scene, by confusing and blurring essential distinctions, were the real creators of the atmosphere of hostility to freemasonry at the end of the century, and in so far as they had not resisted the degeneration of the Craft into sentimental mumbo-jumbo, orthodox freemasons, too, had contributed to it.

[90] London, 1751.

[91] p. 12.

[92] It was in response to this, presumably, that the anonymous but apparently widely-read book *L'étoile flamboyante ou la société des francs-maçons, considerée sous tous les aspects* (Frankfurt, 1766) was written. Its tone is friendly, but derisory, firmly rebutting the graver accusations against the Craft, but urging its members to abandon the inflated pretensions and language which have provoked suspicion.

Chapter IV

Derivation and degeneration: the sects of the later eighteenth century

THE GOLDEN AGE OF MYSTIFICATION

In sheer numbers, there have probably never been so many secret sects and societies in Europe as between 1750 and 1789. They arose in three ways. Some stemmed directly from freemasonry, being degenerate and schismatic offshoots of that parent. They were evidence of that variety and disintegration within the Craft which has already been mentioned briefly and which stemmed, ultimately, from the impulse to the proliferation of new grades and secrets embodied in 'Scottish' masonry. Others were deliberately founded independently from—and sometimes in opposition to—regular freemasonry. These societies, nevertheless, often borrowed from the Craft much of their ritual and organisation. Finally, there were masonic or bastard masonic lodges and chapters which had been, as it were, captured by representatives of other secret associations and perverted or used for their own purposes. This variety makes precise distinctions difficult. In many instances we cannot be positive, and, of course, there is no sharp line at the boundaries where the three classes meet. There is only a vague borderland where unorthodox masonry tails off into fringe activities with no intrinsic connexion with the Craft at all. This confusion was the prime reason why orthodox masons were so often blamed for things for which they were not responsible.

This phenomenon and the impression it produced on the public are what this chapter is about, because that impression was to shape decisively the later mythology about secret societies. They must be seen in perspective against some general features of the history of the eighteenth century. To generalise boldly, three well-known tendencies of the age were particularly important influences on the world of secret societies. The first is the general movement of thought which we customarily sum up as 'The Enlightenment'. This tendency, a rationalising, secularising one, on the whole told in favour of orthodox masonry: men joined lodges because they thought that the Craft embodied the ideals of enlightened men and because they thought that the intercourse they enjoyed in them was culturally and socially beneficial. These motives were also to lead men on to other groups, some of them innocent and open, such as the 'sociétés de pensée' which played so big a part in the diffusion of 'lumières' in provincial France, the reading societies of Germany, or the learned academies of Italy. Others had quasi-political aims and came nearer to effective action; such, perhaps, were the Amis des noirs which took up the anti-slavery cause in France in the 1780s, or the shadowy Société des Trente, important in the early and pre-history of the French National Assembly of 1789. One at least of these bodies, the Illuminati of Bavaria, was later revealed to have subversive aims. What characterised all of them was that they were joined by men who approved of what we call the Enlightenment trend when orthodox masonry, for one reason or another, did not seem appropriate.

The second tendency of the age which affected the growth of secret organisations was the new activity of governments in some countries which is often labelled 'enlightened despotism'. The meaning of this phrase is much disputed and it has been taken to cover a wide variety of facts. Nevertheless, some generalisation from them is possible. What was happening was that states began to interfere, much more than they had done hitherto, with the traditional structure of society. Often the motive was simply that of making the state stronger, but interference was also sometimes justified on novel grounds, whether humanitarian, utilitarian or rationalist. Sometimes the state struggled against established social institutions, sometimes against legal privilege, sometimes against ecclesiastical immunities, sometimes against popular prejudice. It was, therefore, acting in ways which growing numbers of persons found threatening, whether to status and values long accepted, or to material privilege. One result of this was that people began to resent and tried to resist such changes. This was not confined to any particular country or persuasion. German Protestants, for example, who could hardly have been enthusiastic admirers of monasticism, nonetheless criticised the anti-monastic policies of Joseph II in Austria.[1] This could directly and immediately benefit some forms of masonry which emphasised ancient nobility or the transmission of ancient wisdom; some men eagerly joined them because they seemed to promise a chance of united and effective opposition to such innovating tendencies.

[1] K. Epstein, *The Genesis of German Conservatism* (Princeton, 1966), p. 73. This interesting book has much in it which is relevant to this study and I have drawn on it in what follows.

This factor (among many others) fed the third trend of the period which bears on the organisation of secret societies and sects, the last to appear chronologically. It was the growth of irrationalism. In part a reaction against both practical reforming rationalism and the Enlightenment attitude, it had also other, older sources. In thinking of the 'siècle des lumières' we are likely to overlook the power of traditional religious affiliation. At its margins, too, lay religious exaltation, pietism and the enduring fascination of the lingering dream of a mystical—or even magical—approach to nature's secrets. Many people were still drawn to alchemy, a German emperor among them. These irrationalist trends in eighteenth-century society have been largely neglected except in their literary expressions; in the history of literature the peculiar sensibility which has been called 'Préromantisme' has been studied and in it much of a new idea and a new mood becomes most explicit. But more is involved than simply looking forward to a new literary idiom. There was a general revaluation of the emotive, intuitive, affective capacities, and a new distrust of analytical reason, philosophic empiricism and materialism.[2] It has to be understood in terms of cherished tradition and its rediscovery, as well as in terms of innovation.

The best-known expression of this was the Gothick novel and the literature of sentiment, but others were more closely related to the origins of the fear of secret societies. The theosophic movement which was one aspect of the general quickening of religious interests is an example.[3] The curious ritual and ceremonial of some of the sects of the period is another; anyone who has looked into Mrs Radcliffe's novels will at once feel at home amid the paraphernalia of unlit chambers, drawn daggers, cups of blood and skulls which were the stage-props of the cruder rites. The appetite for such things was bound to encourage exploitation by the authors of quackeries and fads of all kinds. The mysticising urge provided them with victims to gull. Among these were many who were striving for personal salvation or transcendence in some specific or unspecific sense. Unflagging, they sought outlets in initiation into hieratic wisdom, recondite sciences, fellowships of the elect, and their enthusiastic but often disappointing pilgrimages from shrine to shrine are half the intellectual biography of the pre-revolutionary genera-

[2] 'Vers 1780, un renversement total s'opère dans les esprits.' A. Viatte, Les sources occultes du romantisme (Paris, 1928), I, p. 184. This remains the fundamental book on the whole pre-romantic phenomenon and makes it unnecessary to produce examples to show the pervasiveness (especially in the upper ranks of society) of the infatuation with the irrational of the late eighteenth century.

[3] Its nature is usefully and lucidly summarised in Viatte's first chapter.

tion.[4] They were often far from being fools; Lavater is an outstanding example of an honest and able, but credulous, man caught up in the pursuit of these possibilities.[5] Nor, as his example shows, was it difficult for many of them to find in Christianity the road to that personal experience of transcendence which they sought. The interest the best of them aroused further ripened the clientèle for new secret sects and mysteries. Adventurers and charlatans profited from them; thus were made further contributions to the emerging myths of secret societies. Cagliostro, for example, posed as the founder of a new 'Egyptian' masonry at a time when the wisdom of the ancient Egyptian kingdoms was much in vogue and was invoked by some 'obediences' as the origin of their secrets. He was astonishingly successful in imposing himself on persons who might have expected to be more sensible, and this success is a testimony to the readiness of the age to swallow something with a flavour of mystery.[6] Occultism rubbed shoulders with pseudo-science. Mesmer was, perhaps, cut from not quite the same cloth, but he exploited the same readiness of the age to fall for the irrational and mysterious (which seems, paradoxically, to have been all the greater when they were wrapped up in the language of science).[7] It was this readiness, above all, which offered the richest

[4] See the words of a nobleman of 1789 seeking admission to an Avignonese sect (quoted in Viatte, I, pp. 21–2): 'Je n'ai trouvé dans les Saintes Ecritures qu'incertitude, même souvent des choses contradictoires et peu dignes de la majesté d'un Dieu que l'on suppose les avoir dictées. Je me suis fait recevoir membre de plusieurs Loges maçonniques, espérant trouver dans les différents grades des lumières qui pouvaient m'amener à des vérités et je n'y ai trouvé que des promesses d'arriver à cette vraie lumière, sans qu'on m'ait tenu de ces promesses. . . . Si je dois en croire ce que l'on me dit de vos vertus, des vérités que vous avez découvertes et des communications que vous avez avec le Très-Haut, vous êtes à même de me tirer de mon incertitude en me donnant des preuves irrévocables de l'immortalité de l'âme.'

[5] Jean Gaspard Lavater, Swiss pastor and writer, living in Zurich, famous for studies in physiognomy. On his ideas, see Viatte, I, pp. 153 ff.

[6] The scandal of the Diamond Necklace, which at last was his undoing, was evidence of his success in imposing himself on aristocratic circles. See, e.g., the sardonic commentary on this in the Marquis de Luchet's pamphlet of 1785, Mémoires authentiques pour servir à l'histoire du Comte de Cagliostro.

[7] 'Si le mesmerisme n'est pas une société secrète, on ne saurait toutefois le séparer de l'ensemble des pouvoirs occultes dans le contexte illuministe de cette epoque,' comments A. Faivre in drawing attention to a Swiss religious enthusiast's interest in magnetism (Kirchberger et l'Illuminisme du dix-huitième siècle (The Hague, 1966), p. 132). Among partisans of Franz Anton Mesmer in France were Lafayette, Brissot, Duport and the Rolands; d'Epresmesnil, leader of parlementaire opposition to the crown and later spokesman of the Right in the National Assembly, was proud to say he was a pupil of Mesmer. For an introduction to the whole phenomenon, see R. Darnton, Mesmerism and the end of the Enlightenment in France (Cambridge, Mass.,

possibilities for the development of new secret societies. Together with its antithesis, the Enlightenment mind itself, and the irritations awoken by rational reform, it explains the continued prosperity of freemasonry, above all in its 'Scottish' and heterodox forms, and the waxing of the new associations in the second half of the eighteenth century.[8]

THE DISINTEGRATION OF FREEMASONRY

Within a few years of Ramsay's discourse, much publicity was already being given in France to the appearance of new degrees, rites and 'obediences' within freemasonry. Soon afterwards, the same trend could be observed in other countries. There was much in the Craft which, from the first, was likely to lead to variety and development, and some things which were always to favour heresy and schism. Even the moral tone of early freemasonry and the conscious rectitude of its English founders, proclaimed in the *Constitutions* and rituals, could tell in this direction. From the start, they inclined people to believe that the Masonic Secret was a matter of arcane, esoteric knowledge connected with some kind of moral regeneration. Another consequence of the secrecy of early masonry was that it imposed a practical problem of discipline (the financial independence of the lodges added to this, of course). It was very difficult to restrain the elaboration of ritual or the speculative fancies of freemasons. Once launched, new obediences which embodied new doctrine quickly acquired the strength of vested interests. Even England had its schism in 1751 when a new (and soon very successful) rite, the 'Ancient Masons', made its appearance. The ensuing quarrel was not healed until 1813;[9] in France, as we have noted, the setting up of Grand Orient did not prevent the continuation of a rival centre of orthodox masonry for another quarter-century. Much more difficult

---

1968). A contemporary exposition is that of J. B. Barbéguière, a Bordelais doctor, *La maçonnerie mesmérienne, ou leçons prononcées . . en Loge Mesmérienne de Bordeaux* (Amsterdam, 1784). It makes the attraction of the cult very difficult to understand.

[8] Mme R. Robin has some brief but suggestive comments on the reflexion of the anti-Enlightenment, irrationalist trend in masonic circles in her paper 'La Loge "La Concorde" de Dijon', *AHRF*, 1969, pp. 442–3.

[9] The essence of the quarrel was the insistence of the Ancient Masons on the regularity of a further masonic grade, the Royal Arch degree. This had become popular in the 1740s, but was not approved by Grand Lodge. The degree was given an emphatically mystical significance and the whole tone and aim of the new rite was opposed to the traditional craft and practical associations of regular freemasonry.

was it, therefore, to restrain local idiosyncrasies which remained confined to individual lodges.

The explicit toleration of a wide range of religious and other views among masons also provided a fertile bed for the growth of variety. The religious and rationalist both sought to develop those implications of the Craft which they found congenial. The vagueness of its formularies gave them great scope. Those with an inclination to do so could easily associate the masonic vows and ceremony of admission with ideas of purification and reintegration with the moral order; this was a natural route for the development of masonry on theosophic lines and is one psychological key to this. Initiation into the means of regeneration was common to all the occult varieties of masonry. That there were traces of quietist and pietist influence in this from the start has also been suggested, and, if this is so, this tendency is even less surprising.[10] Finally, of course, there was the simple urge to elaborate for elaboration's sake. This harmless and innocent activity fitted easily with the idea of higher secrets, transmitted wisdom and an initiated élite.

The whole phenomenon to which such tendencies gave rise is often summed up as 'Scottish masonry'. As early as 1744 the idea was attracting public interest. 'Je n'ignore qu'il court un bruit vague parmi les Francs-Maçons touchant un certain ordre qu'ils appellent les Ecossais, supérieur à ce que l'on prétend aux Francs Maçons ordinaires et qui ont leurs ceremonies et leurs secrets à part,' wrote one critic.[11] He erred only in the notion of an 'ordre', which implied far too great a definition and clarity in the phenomenon. As the most authoritative modern scholar of the breakaways from orthodox masonry in the eighteenth century points out, the term 'Scottish masonry' simply means all the higher grades which were added to the three authorised by English freemasonry.[12] No one knows where the name 'Scottish masonry' first entered masonic usage, nor what it exactly meant at its first appearance. It refers to the whole elaboration beyond the bounds of orthodox masonry which occurred in the eighteenth century and

[10] See, e.g., A. Faivre, *Kirchberger et l'Illuminisme*, esp. p. xvii: 'l'ésprit quiétiste est sensible dans les milieux maçonniques . . . les *collegia pietatis* sont vraiment, en un sens, les prédécesseurs des Loges spéculatives: même distinction entre initiés et profanes, et "catechisation" semblable pour conférer aux candidats la compréhension et la connaissance des degrés de leur symbolisme'. Elsewhere, Faivre also points out that some aspirants to masonry saw in its initiations analogies with alchemical transmutation of elements (in his introduction to Le Forestier, *La franc-maçonnerie Templière et occulte*).

[11] Pérau, in *Les secrets de l'Ordre des Francs-Maçons dévoilés*, q. Ligou, p. 102.

[12] Le Forestier, *La franc-maçonnerie Templière*, p. 51.

after, or, as it was called in France, 'red' masonry in contrast to the orthodox 'blue', which kept the three 'English' grades.

Almost the only definite thing which can be said about Scottish masonry is that it did not come from Scotland.[13] Nor was it, as some have argued, all a Jacobite plot, though many Jacobite masons who did not like the tendencies in official French masonry around the end of the 1730s may have welcomed the appearance of the higher grades which made possible a separation from it.[14] The whole phenomenon is so rich and confused that there is no particular explanation or rationale to be sought within it; it was, rather, a response to a great variety of cultural and ideological stimuli; it manifested itself in many different ways in different places at different moments. Ramsay's address was fundamental to it because it associated the idea of enduring masonic purpose with the superior prestige of masonic practices of Scottish origin. It soon came to be asserted—though in many different and varying forms—that the true inwardness of freemasonry and its adherents' access to the most important secrets of the Order could only be realised through those lodges which retained organic connexion with legendary Scottish origins. The alleged Jacobite connexion, and the opportunites for restricting membership provided by the higher degrees were powerfully appealing, there can be no doubt, to those freemasons who did not find the social equality of the English tradition agreeable and could now recruit lodges entirely from aristocratic circles.

Scottish masonry is everywhere very difficult to deal with as a positive phenomenon not only because of the difficulties of disentangling the truth about it, but because of its fundamental lack of definition. This makes its borders hard to delineate; often, it blurs imperceptibly at its fringe into quite non-masonic activity. Yet this did not prevent those who indulged in these fringe activities from claiming masonic status. The confusion which this caused makes it easy to understand the importance of Scottish masonry in the growth of the later anti-masonic mythology. It contributed to the distrust of the Order as a whole because the claims and behaviour of some of its adherents and practitioners seemed to justify the view that masons themselves might not know the real secrets of their Order, that there might be grades and obediences within it pursuing aims not avowed to the rank and

---

[13] 'Le seul point qui soit définitivement éclairci c'est que la Maçonnerie Ecossaise n'est pas originaire de l'Ecosse' (Le Forestier, p. 5). It should perhaps be noted that, nonetheless, this authority did not have the opportunity of considering a helpful paper with useful references by C. H. Chevalier, 'Maçons écossais au XVIIIe siècle', *AHRF*, 1969.

[14] See the suggestions of P. Chevallier referred to in preceding chapters.

file of the 'blue' lodges, far less to the profane.[15] This was the model of conspiracy which people later came to see in all secret societies. Innocence could never be presumed of the Order as a whole simply because it were proved that individual freemasons were innocent; they had, after all, not got access to the highest secrets, reserved to a small group of hidden directors, the 'supérieurs inconnus'.

France was the home of Scottish masonry and it may be reckoned that country's main contribution to the development of the Craft. Under various designations—chapters, directories, lodges of perfection —the new masonry spread rapidly through the country in the 1740s. By 1750, it was reported in Bordeaux, Arras, Toulouse, Lille and Marseille. It was quickly all but impossible to say which were regular lodges and which were not, and here lies the fundamental explanation of the movement in the 1760s to achieve greater discipline which led to the foundation of the Grand Orient. Many of these associations, too, were already influenced by extraneous religious, alchemical and mystical influences to which we shall return. The details of the new masonic bodies are for the most part irrelevant to this study in any systematic sense. It is only important to note the rate and tendency of expansion. In the 1750s Scottish masonry spread into Germany and Scandinavia, in the 1770s to Savoy and Piedmont. Growth continued in France well into the 1780s, the only important effect on it of the attempt to regularise 'blue' masonry being some degree of consolidation also within 'red' chapters. In 1781 the Grand Orient made a concordat with the Mère-loge écossaise and a year later with the Architectes Africains and L'étoile flamboyante aux trois lys de Bordeaux.[16] Other exotics remained at large, their numbers still growing as new obediences were set up.

Once the Scottish ball had started rolling, in fact, there seemed to be no stopping it. Just as anglomania had made easier the original diffusion of freemasonry, so Scottish masonry benefited from the cultural and linguistic predominance of France at mid-century.[17] Together with

---

[15] Not all 'Scottish' masons made such claims, however. The author of one pamphlet, although rhapsodising at length over the imaginary history of Scotch masonry limits its significance, nonetheless, to its status as 'quatrième grade du F. M. parfait' and only attributes its pre-eminence in the Craft to 'l'ancienneté, la science, la fidélité, et les services importans' (*La société des francs-maçons, soutenue contre les faux préjugés* (Amsterdam, 1772), p. 29). [16] C. H. Chevalier, p. 401.
[17] The names of most German lodges were French and French was for a long time the language normally employed in the lodges. In the Austrian Netherlands, on the other hand, geography to some extent offset linguistic factors and we are told (by J. Bartier, *AHRF*, 1969, p. 470) that the competitive influence of English masonry was important there.

the presence of French soldiers and prisoners, this explains the establishment of the higher grades in Germany in the 1740s. Across the Rhine, deviant and degenerate freemasonry was to flourish as nowhere else. It was important, too, that in Germany even orthodox freemasonry had always been more aristocratic than elsewhere. Moreover, in Germany the influence of hermetic and mystical groups was strong and was to do more than elsewhere to penetrate the Craft. Alchemy was popular there and alchemists were to seek admission to freemasonry in the hope of uncovering alchemical lore in its Secret. It is perhaps hardly surprising that it is said that by the end of the 1770s there was only one lodge in Germany still holding to the tenets of English freemasonry.[18]

There is another point which must be borne in mind in attempting to assess the exuberant development of heterodox masonry and near-masonry in Germany after the introduction of the Scottish rite. This great period of growth was also the period in which Germany began to undergo a major reaction against the Enlightenment. Some similar effects were visible in France, but in Germany this reaction was far more intense and was, also, to some extent a nationalist reaction against France and things French. It deeply affected freemasonry. It is too large a theme for exploration here, but it has to be remembered as the background against which the masonry, pseudo-masonry and near-masonry of the German eighteenth century now evolved. It was also the background which, for some people considering freemasonry from the outside, explained it and gave it meaning; though such thinking might inspire masonic deviations, it also led to distrust of them and of the Craft as a whole.[19]

German masonic developments gave great prominence to two specific features associated with Scottish masonry which merit special notice because of their important effect on later anti-masonic mythology. There were the appearance of 'Grades of Vengeance' and the legend of the Templar connexion.

These came to be connected, but they were distinct in their origins. The creation of grades of vengeance[20] was a step in the proliferation of new degrees which led at extremes to something like a hundred grades. In searching the traditions of freemasonry for elements which might justify new degrees, Scottish masons took up the legend of Hiram,

[18] The 'Union' lodge, Frankfurt (Francovich, p. 55). 'La Maçonnerie, telle qu'elle était pratiquée dans toute l'Europe continentale, était beaucoup plus une création française qu'un produit anglais' (Le Forestier, p. 403).

[19] This background is discussed in the first chapter of Epstein's important study.

[20] They were also sometimes called 'grades d'Elu'.

architect to Solomon, whose self-sacrifice in defence of the Secret stood at the heart of masonic morality. It was alleged that, subsequently, the habitation of his assassins being discovered, certain chosen masters (maîtres élus) were sent by Solomon to kill them or bring them back for punishment. The new grades commemorated these men and the insignia and rituals of their initiation symbolised what had happened. There were various forms, but they usually involved drawn swords, skeletons, horrific oaths and the decapitation or symbolic killing of dolls or images representing the guilty assassins of Hiram.[21] Whatever the moral or psychological value of this innovation, there can be no doubt of its popularity. Grades of vengeance quickly became widespread, the best known and most frequently referred to being the thirtieth degree, that of 'Chevalier Kadosch', which made its appearance in the 1750s.[22]

The legend connecting freemasonry with the medieval Templars can be understood best against two other developments, one internal and one external to freemasonry. The internal one was the interest of many continental masons in finding a more dignified and aristocratic origin for the Craft than the legends inherited from practical, working masons, embodied in the English rituals. Their searches had been given a great fillip by Ramsay's vague invocations of Crusader origins. This was one reason why there soon appeared in Scottish masonry new, knightly and chivalric grades, often with impressive and ornate titles. At the same time there operated an external tendency leading to interest in the Templars and a revival of historical interest in them. This was supported not only by antiquarians, but by sentiment among leaders of the Enlightenment in their favour: they had been, after all, victims of ecclesiastical bigotry and absolute monarchy.[23]

Oddly, it seems that the first printed association of freemasonry

[21] Le Forestier, pp. 52–3. This development soon became known but did not at first attract especial suspicion. King Charles of Naples, for example, in communicating to Rome a document containing details of a 'Grado di Eletto' in 1751, only remarks in this and other grades 'guaste fantasie da per tutto', and is not especially alarmed by signs 'di vendette' (Rinieri, p. 607).

[22] C. H. Chevalier, pp. 400–1.

[23] 'We shall ask ourselves whether, at this period when philosophical proselytism was so formidable, there were not secret societies formed to keep alive a small number of simple truths and to diffuse them clandestinely amongst a few initiates as sure antidotes against the prevalent superstitions. We shall also enquire whether we ought not to number amongst such societies that famous order against which popes and kings conspired so ignobly and which they destroyed so barbarously.' Condorcet, *Sketch for a Historical Picture of the Progress of the Human Mind* (London, 1955), p. 91. This, of course, was not written until the end of the century (it was published in 1794), but is a typical expression of the theme.

with the Templars was made in 1752 by an opponent of the Craft.[24]
The association was by that time beginning to be fairly frequently
asserted in masonic circles and seems to have been due largely to
German Rosicrucians. In the end, it was to take several forms. In some,
the Templars were the originators of freemasonry; in some they were
only the most important transmitters of more ancient lore. One version
linked them to the Argonauts. Shortly before his execution, Jacques de
Molay was said to have passed on the secrets of the Order and the
designation of the hiding-place of their wealth to Templars who had
since passed them on from age to age to successors admitted to the
Order, preserved in the form of freemasonry. Such a legend had a
powerful psychological appeal and, in some versions, held out the
promise of actual monetary gain when the riches of the Templars
would be recovered and distributed to the members of the Order.[25]

The Templar legend was very important in the solidifying of Scottish masonry. It gave a solid historical and above all aristocratic basis
for a new rite. It could be interpreted and reinterpreted in different
ways. Some saw it as the authentication of a Jacobite masonry opposed
to the 'blue'; to some it offered alchemical knowledge (the Templars'
wealth seemed explicable in no other way than by the transmutation
of base metals), to some mere play-acting, to some, perhaps, a mytho-
logised ideal of subversion. It was among these last, and among those
who took a similar view from outside the Craft, that special dangers for
the future lay. The Templar legend soon became conflated with that of
the grades of vengeance and this was to have the most unfortunate
consequences. Hiram's murder came to be understood as the symbolic
representation of the execution of Molay, who had refused to reveal
the secrets of the Templars. The Templars who had escaped to hand
down the secret (some of whom had established themselves, according
to the legend, in Edinburgh) had the task given to the 'Elus', but
the murder they were to avenge was that of Molay. In some versions of
the story this was later to be taken to mean revenge on the heirs of
Philip the Fair and Clement V. This theme was often to recur after
1789, when the Templar mythology was applied to the explanation
of such events as the execution of the French king and the expropria-
tion of the French Church.

[24] Le Forestier, p. 16. For an earlier association in police documents, see above,
p. 82.
[25] Le Forestier, pp. 64–82, has a much fuller discussion. I limit myself to those
essentials of the legend which were important in the growth of anti-masonry.

OCCULT SOURCES OF THE SECRET SOCIETIES

It has always been common for secret societies to claim ancient roots. Such pride in remote and legendary origins has already been remarked in the case of freemasonry itself, and sometimes those making such claims have even been able to convince their critics of their antiquity. In their precise forms such assertions are usually nonsense; the grain of truth in the middle of them has usually lain in their borrowing some details of ritual or doctrine from earlier associations. In some cases, such borrowings can be traced back a long way. It is very rare to find a secret association which starts absolutely from scratch, with no debt to any predecessor.

There was much emphasis on ancient origins during the eighteenth century among sects and associations concerned with the occult and mysterious. Antiquity conferred authority and was indispensable to seekers after the Wisdom of the Ancients. One association which was certainly old-established and came to complicate the story of free-masonic development at many points was that of the Rosicrucians. It was in origin scarcely so much a society as a number of spiritual and intellectual seekers after truth and enlightenment, often directing their attention to alchemical and hermetic lore as a promising subject for investigation. A legendary origin for the sect told of a medieval pilgrim who had gone to the East and brought back its secrets, but it emerges into history with a flurry of publication in Germany and England in the seventeenth century. At that time, the motives of its adepts seem irreproachable. They sought, above all, moral reformation, though by curious means. Some of the first Englishmen who at about the same period interested themselves in masonry certainly appear to have been connected with Rosicrucians and were perhaps drawn to masonry by the belief that the Craft concealed alchemical secrets; it has been suggested that Ramsay, too, held views akin to those of the Rosicrucians.[26] But Rosicrucianism was supposed by some to have had both roots and connexions with freemasonry which were of much greater antiquity than this. It is at least that, although the direct descent to eighteenth-century Rosicrucianism is not always easy to follow, the Rosicrucian contact with masonry can be traced at least as far back as the beginning of the seventeenth century. Later, it was in Germany that the interplay of the two was to be especially influential and important.

[26] Viatte, I, p. 35; Le Forestier, *La franc-maçonnerie Templière*, pp. 35–8; there is a brief summary in Epstein, pp. 104–11.

The core of Rosicrucianism was a tradition of pietism and mysticism, but by the middle of the eighteenth century there had accumulated around this many other characteristics attractive to the unbalanced, the enthusiastic or the merely gullible. It was said that Rosicrucianism could communicate to its adherents the secrets of the Elixir of Life and of communicating with the spirit world. Certainly many people were still being drawn to it by the opportunities it afforded for the pursuit of alchemy. It was thus well suited to appeal to the pre-romantic sensibility and also offered a vehicle for specific action.

Rosicrucians did much to assist the proliferation of Scottish masonry, seeking to explore through it the possibility that masonic symbolism and doctrine concealed the means to universal regeneration. Then, in the 1750s, an unknown group of persons gave masonic Rosicrucianism a new order and form. There was set up a hierarchical 'Order of the Gold and Rosicrucians'. In 1767, this organisation spawned a new rite of Rosicrucian freemasonry, too, influenced by the other masonic proliferations of the period.[27] An elaborate hierarchy of nine degrees was set up, the highest known as that of Magus. Members were organised in circles of nine, and swore oaths of obedience and secrecy. Their statutes and catechisms embodied a deal of unusually high-flown rubbish but seem to have attracted large numbers of members (one among whom was Mesmer).[28] Knowledge of the Order quickly spread as polemical literature about it began to appear. In this way, Rosicrucianism enriched the flow of information and alleged information on the subject of masonic and related rites which rose steadily in the second half of the eighteenth century. It generated yet more confusion among the profane, who tended to mix up all sorts of secret societies in a set of confused impressions. This, in its turn, reinforced a second consequence of the proliferation of quasi-masonic bodies, the growing weakness of orthodox freemasonry when it attempted to rebut the more extravagant charges of improper or illicit conduct which were to be made against it. Not only were the confusions so great that outsiders—and even insiders—could not know what was orthodox masonry and what was not. Still more important was the spreading of an overwhelming impression of secrets and privileged initiates; there were just too many secrets being talked about for anyone to accept any defence of masonry at its face value.

Furthermore, some Rosicrucians were believed before long to have political aims. There is no doubt that the mysticism and pietism of the

---

[27] Le Forestier, *Les Illuminés de Bavière et la franc-maçonnerie allemande*, pp. 187–91.
[28] Epstein's long quotations give the characteristic flavour.

order attracted those who felt alarmed by the tendencies of the Enlightenment, while its political quietism drew to it many alarmed by the questioning of authority in the name of reform. Rosicrucianism embodied, too, a respect for hierarchy and tradition which, together with its aspiration to a universal regeneration based on a revival of religion, made it attractive for the promotion of conservative social and religious policies. This is what happened in Prussia, where, under Frederick William II, it became notorious that Rosicrucian influences were deliberately at work in government. The exact extent of what was achieved remains obscure, but contemporaries were alarmed and saw evidence of this influence embodied in certain persons and policies. The King himself was certainly a Rosicrucian and the work of his advisers, Wöllner and Bischoffswerder, bore fruit in the Edicts on Religion and Censorship of 1788 which marked both the end of 'enlightened' influences in crown policy towards religion in Prussia and an epoch in the debate on 'Aufklärung' throughout Germany. A new censorship of publications was deployed against writing of a rationalistic or enlightened tendency (one author censored was Kant). Both Wöllner and Bischoffswerder had been members of the Gold- und Rosenkreuzer to which they had come after being disillusioned with other branches of Scottish masonry.

Rosicrucianism is a good example of an originally non-masonic influence cutting across the story of masonic variety and development, complicating it still further, and thus arousing more suspicion about it. Throughout the eighteenth century, members of different sects and traditions would, even if they did not wish to modify the organisation or doctrine of one association in the sense of another, yet join others. They thus set up a continual flow of cross-fertilisation between them. We ought not to seek clear definition in what was essentially only a shared general orientation or obsession.

Nor is there much to be gained by looking at all the specific examples of such cross-fertilisations as occurred between the world of the masons and that of the explorers of the occult.[29] Yet one further example, from France, deserves a little more attention than others because it was especially important in its impact on certain varieties of freemasonry. This was the complex of tendencies summed up as 'Martinism'. Although these first attracted widespread public discussion after the publication in 1775 of a book by Louis Claude de Saint-Martin

[29] One which was to be particularly emphasised by later Roman Catholic writers seeking to inculpate freemasonry was the whole complex of tendencies derived from Swedenborg. On his impact, see Viatte, I, pp. 72–103.

(hence the name), *Des erreurs et de la vérité*, they are to be traced back much further. Saint-Martin was the disciple of another speculator, the still mysterious figure, Martinez de Pasqually, half-adventurer, half-seer, who left behind him an incomplete *Traité de Réintégration* which was to be the Bible of his followers.

We cannot even be sure of the correct spelling of Martinez' name and little is known of his origins; hence, in part, his later title, 'le philosophe inconnu'. He was often said to be a Jew, but he seems to have been a Roman Catholic and certainly numbered an Archbishop of Bordeaux among his admirers and patrons. The first organised bodies which were the product of his teaching began to appear in the south of France in the 1750s, under the name of the Juges Ecossais. By 1760, they had spread to Paris and were known under the name of the Elus Cohens. Their doctrinal position seems to have embodied Swedenborgian views about the relationship between this world and that of spiritual beings (though Martinez is said not to have been much impressed when he met Swedenborg in London) and was expressed in a series of rituals whose purpose was to make it possible for spiritual beings to take physical shape and convey messages from the other world. The aim of the cult was the advancement of man's spiritual nature by 'reintegration' with the world of spirits of which he had once formed part. The processes by which this was to be achieved were revealed to initiates after suitable apprenticeship, which fitted them for admission to the ranks of the Elus. This secret brotherhood thus inherited from their ancient predecessors, Eli, Enoch and Melchizidek, the task of safeguarding God's plan for man's salvation through reintegration. Saint-Martin later gave prominence to the idea of the continued historical existence within the everyday world of persons devoted to the secret transmission of a universal religion, coupling this suggestive idea with attacks on the Papacy.[30]

Christian in its origins, theurgic or magical in its implications, Martinism exercised a great attraction. Awkwardly, though in principle distinct from freemasonry, no clear line separating the two can be drawn; Martinist doctrines were quickly carried into freemasonry and individual Martinists founded new sects of their own after Martinez's death.[31] The Philalèthes, for example, originally a masonic system of twelve grades which had as its aim research into the origins

---

[30] Viatte, I, pp. 69–71, 270 ff.

[31] Viatte, I, p. 64. Among those who were Martinists was the young Joseph de Maistre. See F. Vermale, *La Franc-maçonnerie savoisienne* and E. Dermenghem, *Joseph de Maistre mystique*.

and mysteries of freemasonry, soon showed Martinist influences (and, even, perhaps, alchemical ones).[32] Martinism was thus a powerfully confusing force; it also contributed importantly to acceptance of the general classification of the whole group of seekers after revelation as 'illuminés', a term which was to have a major role in the later mythology of the secret societies, where it came to be understood in a sense totally different from and far more specific than that in which it was generally used in the 1770s. De Maistre, looking back on his masonic youth, had found it difficult to distinguish Martinists from what he called 'pietists' and went on to say of the 'illuminés' (among whom he classed Martinists), 'je ne dis pas que tout illuminé soit franc-maçon; je dis seulement que tous ceux que j'ai connus, en France surtout, l'étaient'.[33]

Here were fertile sources of future concern and alarm, suggestive grounds for suspicion of hidden purposes and arcane secrets. Many other examples of occult, quasi-mystical, bogus and even frivolous organisations could be given which further muddied the already opaque waters of Scottish masonry. Mesmer's Order of Universal Harmony, which has been already touched upon, won adherents in masonic lodges, too; Cagliostro's 'Egyptian rite' did the same, as well as setting up its own lodges in south and south-eastern France.[34] The importance of such things for the repute of the secret societies does not lie in the details of their history, but rather in their overall impact. The mystical and occultist movements of continental Europe show a vigour and power of self-delusion which make the imitations of early English freemasonry—the Gormagons, Khibaites and the like —seem very tame. Clearly such sects met a genuine need for a satisfaction undiscoverable either in orthodox masonry or elsewhere. But freemasonry had much to offer them, too. Above all, there were the opportunities of the organisational framework of the lodge system and

---

[32] It specifically excluded officers of the Grand Orient from its meetings. See Le Forestier, *La franc-maçonnerie Templière*, pp. 620 ff.

[33] Quoted in Vermale, p. 2. The word 'illuminé' seems first to appear in a specifically masonic setting as the title of a grade, 'chevalier illustre', in the 'Chapter of Clermont' in the 1750s (Le Forestier, *La franc-maçonnerie Templière*, p. 93). In 1760 a Swedenborgian lodge at Avignon actually took the name, and its system later spread to Paris and Montpellier, where in the 1770s it had adherents in ordinary masonic lodges (Le Forestier, *Les Illuminés*, p. 665). In 1796, the Swiss Kirchberger made some interesting distinctions about the word which are quoted in Viatte, I, pp. 9–10. See also de Maistre's observations, quoted below, p. 296.

[34] Viatte's chapter on 'Les sociétés mystiques' is a helpful survey of the variety of these bodies (I, pp. 104–52) and quotes some interesting contemporary attempts to distinguish among them (pp. 104–5).

the secrecy that went with it. Conversely, occultism had something to offer orthodox freemasonry in the emotional lure of new mysteries to replace the faded ones of the Craft. Confusion was irresistible. The blurring of the line between freemasonry and the new sects was in this way, too, far too easy for the repute of orthodox masons.

One other characteristic of this movement was its debt to German influences and its special prosperity in Germany and Switzerland. France, rather than originating new sects, tended to be a country on which they battened, often with great success and notoriety. It is difficult to believe that much villainy was involved, though there was undoubtedly fraud and charlatanry, but to the outsider they must have seemed suspicious, and perhaps more suspicious when they had foreign origins. Above all, this was true in one instance, in which the history of deviant freemasonry presents a more complete amalgam of all the major hermetic and masonic tendencies than anywhere else and was of German origin. It was also one which was to contribute much to the myths later held against the secret societies. This was the Strict Observance.

THE STRICT OBSERVANCE

German masonry was quick to show eclectic tendencies and reflected the general revival of interest in the occult earlier than that of other countries. In a 'new system of Clermont' foisted on gullible masons in 1758, for example, we find all the influences so far touched upon jumbled up in a hotch-potch of grades and rituals which reflected 'chevaliers de la Rose-Croix', geosophy, alchemy, cabbalist learning, theosophy and a 'central science' transmitted by the original 'Chevaliers Ecossais' to the Templars.[35] It had great success until a sudden access of scepticism among the initiates ended it and the successful career of the adventurer who had thought it up.

One of the grave problems, indeed, with which orthodox freemasonry was specially faced in Germany, was the opportunity the craze for hermetic knowledge, mystery and the Templar legends offered to fakers and adventurers. It was possible to build a career on the credulity of freemasons. This opportunity was best and most successfully exploited by one of the most credulous and influential of eighteenth-century fakers, Karl Gotthelf, Baron Hund. He cannot be dismissed merely as a huckster or a confidence-trickster; there is little doubt that

[35] Le Forestier, *Les Illuminés de Bavière*, pp. 150–1.

he sincerely believed some of the rubbish he talked.[36] In 1755 he introduced a new Scottish rite to Germany, later to become famous and to dominate German masonry for two decades under the name of the 'Strict Observance'.[37] Known at first as 'rectified masonry', it took the name Strict Observance in 1764 when Hund's followers were joined by those of a charlatan who had exploited masonic credulity to the extent of making his followers believe that the English fleet was in his pay but who was exposed by Hund.[38] The name stressed the superior antiquity of the system to the English, denominated the 'Late Observance', and its essence was its claim to direct derivation from the Templars of the original masonic secrets entrusted to them. Hund's original aim had been to establish a Templar rite in Germany which would accumulate funds to repurchase the sequestered property of the Templars. It was supposed to be commanded by the Stuart Pretender and Hund hoped to extend its authority over all masons who would accept 'rectification' by signing an act of submission and obedience. The Order was organised in nine provinces which covered the whole of Europe and had three 'Interior Order' grades superior to the usual three symbolic grades. It was directed by unknown Superiors.[39]

Though its legends were a farrago of nonsense and though it was conducted by a man in whom it is difficult to distinguish conscious deception from sheer exuberant fantasy, the Strict Observance had, it has been remarked, some moral and practical characteristics which assured success. It was well disciplined and its system of grades was more logical than most. Behaviour at its lodges seems to have been better than that generally prevailing in German masonry of the period. An additional appeal to non-nobles was assured when it opened its Interior Order to them. Its ceremonies and official costumes were sumptuous and appealing and it flattered German national pride by claiming for Germany the authentic Templar heritage. It also

[36] Le Forestier remarked in his last book (*La franc-maçonnerie Templière*, p. 108) that 'tandis que l'illusion volontaire des autres ne s'épanouissait que quelques heures par mois derrière les portes closes, il a été dans la vie quotidienne, pendant les vingt dernières années de son existence, une somnambule hypnotisé par son rêve'. Only in 1766 did Hund declare he was no longer able to meet the expense of his office as 'Provincial' entirely out of his own pocket.

[37] His preparations began in 1751, but it is from the later year that the Order began to grow significantly, the first lodge asking for affiliation being one at Dresden. In 1764 it spread outside Saxony and at the beginning of 1766 one of its twenty-five lodges was in Denmark.

[38] It is worth note that the charlatan was pursued by the aggrieved 'Templars' so successfully that they eventually succeeded in getting him locked up for life at their expense (Le Forestier, *La franc-maçonnerie Templière*, pp. 134–5).

[39] Le Forestier, *La franc-maçonnerie Templière*, gives a full account, pp. 103–270.

purported to offer substantial financial benefit to its members.[40] It is not surprising, therefore, that the Strict Observance Order prospered.

Nevertheless, it soon had to face difficulties. One was a chronic shortage of money which led, among other expedients, to the encouragement of alchemical research within the Order. Another was the rapid appearance of divisions within its ranks.

This was largely because of the appearance of a new adventurer, the pastor John Augustus Starck. He was another of those men who, like Hund, confusingly straddle the border between credulousness and conscious deception. By training something of an orientalist, Starck had been admitted to various Scottish degrees while in Paris. Though an ordained Protestant minister, he believed that the Roman church enjoyed over his own and others a superiority in that its liturgy left it closer to ancient magical tradition; he became interested in the reunion of the Christian churches. This was the man who, in 1767, made himself known to Hund as the representative of another branch of the Templar connexion.[41] Starck claimed that its secret directors were at St Petersburg. The distinction of their System, he claimed, was its lineal descent not from the Knights Templar but from the Clerics of that Order, the true custodians of its secrets and lore. Though Hund was at first reluctant to have anything to do with this, he eventually came round to the view that he should co-operate with Starck. He may have been moved by fear of competition (especially when another breakaway Templar order, the System of Zinnendorf, began to make headway). He may also have been influenced by one of the features of Starck's invention which made it attractive, the prospect of alchemical knowledge. It was the claim of Starck's 'Clerks Templar' that they inherited access to esoteric knowledge which might include power over natural processes. This was a reassertion of the elements in the Templar legend which had first so powerfully attracted Rosicrucians. There can be no doubt that the promise of initiation to secrets of this type, of the possibility of direct communication with, perhaps, even the Creator, made a promiscuous appeal to all sorts of dabblers in the occult. Theosophists, Rosicrucians, arithmosophists and cabbalists flocked to Starck's version of the Strict Observance which in this

[40] A tontine for the provision of retirement annuities was at one time envisaged. Le Forestier, pp. 144–5.

[41] Le Forestier (*La franc-maçonnerie Templière*, pp. 157–64) gives a full summary of the history invented by Starck for his Order. Besides claiming the Young Pretender as a Grand Master it includes the novel detail of incorporating into the story at one point the Duke of Monmouth.

respect met a need unsatisfied by Hund's (comparatively) chaste invention.

A union of the two branches or systems was formally concluded in 1772 at Kohlo, in a congress which elected the Duke of Brunswick, the victor of Minden, Grand Master of the 'United Lodges', the name Strict Observance being formally withdrawn in order not to wound the susceptibilities of other freemasons. This might be thought the point at which to take leave of this particular elaboration of Scottish masonry. It is clear that the Strict Observance diffused very widely, both among adepts of its various tendencies and through the 'profane' who did not belong but were aware of an immense and ill-disguised activity, the sense of a great network of secret association. This was undoubtedly of great importance in preparing the ground for the later mythology of the secret societies. Nevertheless, the domestic story of these derivations may be profitably pursued a little further; the subsequent divisions within the Order were to attract even more publicity to it.

Strict Observance (as it was still often termed in the lodges) contined to spread after 1772. Beyond Germany, it could be found as far afield as Bordeaux and Stockholm (where a 'Swedish system' presided over by the Duke of Sudermania, the later Charles XIII, was a cause of difficulty because of its occultist and separatist tendencies), and was established in Hungary, Italy and even Russia. The social success of the new order was great: at a 'Convent' or congress of twenty-one participants at Wiesbaden in 1776 there were present, for example, the Dukes of Nassau-Uringen and Saxe-Gotha, and Prince George and Prince Louis of Hesse-Darmstadt. A huge envelope of fantasy nurtured this success and made the movement seem even more portentous to adepts and outsiders alike. Some of the brothers came even to have misgivings that they might in fact be the dupes of another secret society—the Jesuits. What was happening was the logical working-out of the subtle but crucial change of emphasis registered at Kohlo. At that congress Hund's domination had given way. In terms of hierarchy, princes and grandees were now the directors of the Strict Observance; in terms of ideology, the ideas of Starck had redirected the Order towards the occult and hermetic. Growth and success were to bring out the consequences of this in new dissatisfactions, divisions and weaknesses. This was to give the lie to the appearance of prosperity enjoyed by the Order in the early 1770s. The crucial problem remained of obtaining recognition for one version of the Templar rite when there were others in the field.

It is not necessary to spend time on the elaborate comings and goings, negotiations, confrontations and comments which laboured over this problem.[42] In the next few years the only events in the history of the German Strict Observance which concern us are those which led to publicity and of these by far the most important was Starck's breach with the Order in 1777. Meanwhile an additional source of confusion had appeared in France. In 1774 there joined the Strict Observance Order a figure of much interest and importance in the history both of masonry and of pre-romanticism, Jean-Baptiste Willermoz, a Lyon draper. He had been a mason since he was twenty, soon showing signs of disappointment with what he found when he was initiated; nevertheless, he became a master-mason. Idealistic and disinterested, he was an outstanding example of the eighteenth-century emotional and intellectual pilgrim who roamed eagerly through the occult, cabbalistic world of pre-romanticism searching for the deposit of divine wisdom in which a man could find the means of his liberation.

Willermoz was at one time or another touched by almost every fad and fashion in freemasonry. He founded his own Scottish lodge and, since he could pass by no craze, it is not surprising to find him drawn to the occult. Lyon was, in any case, something of a traditional centre for interest in the occult. In 1763 he founded a Rosicrucian chapter of 'Chevaliers de l'Aigle Noir et Rose-Croix' whose secret grades indicate that it was pursuing alchemical studies. In 1767 he was received by Martinez de Pasqually at Versailles into the lower grades of the Elus Cohens. Becoming Pasqually's representative at Lyon, he there met Saint-Martin, founder of the Martinist Illuminism which Willermoz was to help to diffuse. He had no success in making contact with the spirit world as he had hoped and was still casting about for the secrets which eluded him when in 1772 he entered correspondence with a Strasbourg lodge belonging to the Strict Observance Order. After meeting one of Hund's representatives at Lyon the following year, Willermoz joined the Order, setting up its first Lyon lodge, La Bienfaisance, in 1774 and becoming Chancellor of its new province, the 'directoire d'Auvergne'.[43]

Willermoz was a man of vast ambitions and the new Auvergne Directory soon began to show tendencies to a kind of masonic imperialism. These brought it into conflict with other bodies. Furthermore, Willermoz involved it in the struggles going forward at that time be-

[42] They are discussed at almost excessive length in Le Forestier's work.

[43] On Willermoz see Le Forestier, *La franc-maçonnerie Templière*, pp. 275 ff., and K. Dear's biographical note in *Le Symbolisme*, 1957–8.

tween the Grand Orient and the Scottish rites over which it was trying
to assert its authority.[44] He succeeded in obtaining the Grand Orient's
recognition in a concordat which at once aroused bitter quarrels and
recrimination. The Strict Observance evoked suspicion and hostility
in France because of its German origins and great excitement was
aroused by the implied recognition by the Grand Orient of the authority of the unknown superiors of the Strict Observance over French
freemasons. Even the London freemasons were dragged into the row.

But this was not the only way in which Willermoz complicated the
affairs of the Strict Observance and brought it to the notice of the
profane. He also carried into the Order a new philosophical influence,
that of Saint-Martin; it was to prove a further source of disruption and
confusion—and therefore of publicity. Although he had incurred
Saint-Martin's disapproval, Willermoz had not abandoned the doctrines
he had taken from Pasqually and he sought to embody them in a masonic
form. The result was the 'Réforme de Lyon', from which there emerged
the mystical masonic rite of the 'Chevaliers Bienfaisants de la Cité
Sainte'. It retained the framework of Templar legend, but its essence
appears to have been the secret which was reserved behind the ostensible aims of charity and benevolence: the doctrines of reintegration by
application of the theurgic techniques of Saint-Martin. This was regarded by the adepts as perfectly compatible with Christianity and,
indeed, to be its logical culmination. It avoided the taint of submission
to foreign superiors and although the specific Templar connexion was
asserted, Willermoz avoided the name, which was by now too closely
associated with German masonry. Two new higher grades were introduced in the new rite also, those of 'Chevalier Profès' and 'Grand
Profès'.[45]

Willermoz' creation is, perhaps, of greatest interest to the historian
of ideas because it embodies in a particularly explicit and avowed form
that mysticising, anti-materialist, anti-Enlightenment trend which

---

[44] For details, see Le Forestier, *La franc-maçonnerie Templière*, pp. 392 ff.
[45] In Willermoz' words, 'cette classe est le dernier grade en France du régime
rectifié (écossais), qui était répandue en petit nombre, partout inconnue et dont
l'existence même est soigneusement cachée depuis son origine à tous les chevaliers
qui n'ont pas encore été reconnus dignes et capables d'y être admis avec fruit',
quoted in Vermale, p. 11. But he did not say this when he much later explained the
rectified rite to an enquirer and used rather obscure language which might be taken
to mean that this grade survived—secretly—to form the highest level of the
rectified rite. See P. Chevallier, *Mémoires de la Société Académique de l'Aube*, CIV,
1964–6, pp. 204–5. This is exactly the sort of obscurity and mystification which,
whether intentional or not, was to provoke enduring suspicion of a freemasonry
which included secret and superior grades.

runs through so much of the story of eighteenth-century culture. Interesting though this is, on the other hand, its bearing on the mythology of the secret societies is indirect since the potentially dangerous elements in the Templar legend were already in circulation.[46] What was important was the stimulus provided by the new rite to further disorder; besides being involved in quarrels with orthodox and Scottish freemasons, Willermoz now helped the disintegration of the Strict Observance itself. This was clear from the actual process of creation of the new Order, which emerged from a 'Couvent National des Gaules' summoned by La Bienfaisance at Lyon in 1778. The pretext was the purification of the rectified rite from improper and unhistorical addition to which the 'Provinces de Gaule' of the rite had been unable to object because they were not present at the convents held in Germany. Effectively, the Convent liberated the French rectified lodges from German control by authorising the new rite, dominated as it was by Martinist doctrine.[47]

It is easy to feel out of one's depth in the flood of nonsense which was by now pouring forth in eighteenth-century freemasonry. The masonic world was enormously complicated and very difficult for even an adept to move in it with any certainty of where he was going. On top of the network of orthodox masonic lodges had been built first the higher grades of Scottish rite lodges and then, on them, the Strict Observance, which had now fragmented into what were virtually a number of separate systems. Further individual organisms, often hard to distinguish from one another, lodged in the incoherent fabric of these diffuse structures. Masons and near-masons flowed in and out of one another's lodges, spreading misconception and disorganisation. Their troubles spread disillusionment among the 'rectified' themselves; inevitably, then, the public gained a poor impression of the world of masonry. This state of affairs became even worse as the division of the masonic and pseudo-masonic movements into groups which emphasised mystical and religious aims and those influenced by rationalist ideas became sharper and sharper. Divisions and quarrels led to accusation and innuendo in pamphlets and books which encouraged suspicion and scepticism among the profane about the Craft as a whole. When the Clerks Templar broke with the Strict Observance, there followed an exchange of pamphlets which left the claims of the Strict Observance to a special historical and doctrinal relationship with the

---

[46] Willermoz had in any case rejected grades of vengeance in his new rite.

[47] The presentation of this doctrine at the Convent is described by Le Forestier, *La franc-maçonnerie Templière*, pp. 482–8.

Templars in shreds.[48] This, of course, meant that the Order had little to offer its members; matters were made worse by the revelation also of much of its recent embittered history.

To some extent, attempts had been made ever since the Kohlo Convent to offset this trend by trying to bring some order into the chaos bred of the higher degrees and the Templar legend. But even the Grand Orient in France was finding consolidation very difficult though it enjoyed greater advantages than any of the German connexions; east of the Rhine the new system had little hope of bringing order into their affairs. More gatherings tried, ineffectually, to find the formula of unity, but they rather exacerbated than allayed the growing factionalism. The Convent at Wolfenbüttel in 1777, for example, was not only the occasion of the secession of Starck and his followers. Such apparent improvement of relations between the Swedish and German Templars which it also brought about (and which led to the eventual election of the Duke of Sudermania as Grand Master in succession to the Duke of Brunswick) only masked the real divisions which remained and were to provoke yet more personal irritation.[49] Brunswick, secretly more and more interested in Rosicrucian doctrine, denounced the project of restoring the Templar Order to the representatives of the various 'prefectures' and succeeded in persuading them to circularise the lodges with his views. More uncertainty and recrimination followed and before long the Duke of Brunswick and the Landgrave of Hesse were in interested correspondence with Willermoz, attracted by his mystical and symbolic interpretations of the Templar story.[50] For all the formal geographical extension of the rectified rites, therefore, it was clear

[48] One notable example, *Stein des Anstosses und Fels des Aergerniss* (Berlin, 1780), was long thought to be by Starck, but this seems unlikely.

[49] This Swedish prince, later Charles XIII, was to retire from this office disillusioned in 1781. Among other oddities in the views he held was his tenacious retention of the conviction that the secret Grand Master of the Templars was the Stuart Pretender.

[50] It seems likely that Charles of Hesse was attracted by the idea of alchemical knowledge: 'ce bon prince ne cherche que l'or', noted a French enthusiast in 1780 (quoted in Viatte, I, p. 130). His gullibility (or greed) was such that a notorious alchemist, the Comte de Saint-Germain, found a haven with him when banished from almost every other court and Charles was still pursuing the subject at the age of ninety-three. But he was also an enthusiastic aspirant to religious enlightenment. See the remarkable description by Lavater of the activities of his 'Lodge' at Copenhagen, printed by Viatte (I, pp. 132–5). The same authority suggests that it was no doubt Charles's ideas on reincarnation (he believed himself to be St Peter) which explain his taste for pontificating at religious ceremonies and pronouncing benedictions. In this instance, Charles was again showing a widespread interest; reincarnation was much talked of. Lavater solemnly corrected a Dutchman who discerned in the Duchess of Devonshire a reincarnated Magdalen.

that their divisions and secessions more than outweighed them. The recognition of this at last led to the final attempt to overcome them in the most famous masonic gathering of the century, the Convent of thirty-five representatives of the rectified rites held at Wilhelmsbad from July to September 1782.

One modern masonic writer judges the holding of the Convent an 'act of despair'. Certainly its outcome showed how hopelessly deteriorated the Order's situation had now become. Years later, Joseph de Maistre said it produced 'rien d'utile. Chacun s'en retourna avec ses préjugés.'[51] It was in essence an attempt by the two German princes, Brunswick and Hesse, the leaders of the rectified rite in the land of its origin, to reform the Order and give it doctrinal solidity. This they sought in the currents within the rite which flowed towards mystical and Christian interpretations of its history and secrets and to the disparaging of the Templar heritage and its concomitant, the hopes of a material restoration. This led to their acceptance of proposals set out by Willermoz and defended by him at the Convent; thus, it has been remarked, the Lyon group, ten years previously the disciples of the Germans, now became their preceptors.[52] The Swiss Lavater, who, although not a mason, attended the Convent, was much impressed by a devotion to Christianity which he had not expected to find there.[53]

The main theme of the Convent was the debate between this occult, mysticising party and their opponents, men like Bode and Dittfurth, who have been termed rationalists.[54] Given that Bode, a violent Pro-

---

[51] Quoted by K. Dear (author of the other comment quoted here) in 'Le convent de Wilhelmsbad et son échec' (Le Symbolisme, 1958), p. 117. Willermoz' judgment was more enthusiastic; see Chevallier, pp. 207–9, for a fairly full account by him.

[52] Le Forestier, La franc-maçonnerie Templière, p. 609. The princes had hoped to secure also the support of the young Baron von Haugwitz, later foreign minister of Prussia, and at this time an enthusiastic and pietistic leader of another small quasi-masonic sect, 'the Brothers of the Cross'. Adhering to a more personal and mystical view of the masonic path to Christian revelation, he refused at a late stage to take part and this threw back the princes to a greater degree of reliance on Willermoz than they had wished. One of the most emphatic and developed expressions of the feelings of many of those who sympathised with this tendency is to be found in a long mémoire by Joseph de Maistre, submitted to the Duke of Brunswick. See E. Dermenghem, Mémoire au duc de Brunswick par J. de Maistre.

[53] Viatte, I, 148.

[54] On Bode and Dittfurth, consult Le Forestier, Les Illuminés, pp. 361–2, 664–7 and 637–42. Bode had been an early adherent of the Strict Observance and later made a notorious and unsuccessful visit to Paris, where he had hoped to combat the mystical and theurgic tide in French masonry and turn the French lodges back towards a concern with greater social utility. He went back to Germany very disillusioned, but his visit was subsequently used by anti-masonic writers (see below) as evidence of international masonic conspiracy to bring about the French Revolu-

testant, believed that symbolic masonry as a whole was an invention of the Jesuits, designed to bring about a Stuart restoration in England, and that he urged this view on the Convent, the word seems inappropriate. It is also misleading if we think of other of its senses: it should not be understood in a simple, encyclopaedist sense of opposition to religion or, at least, such a sense would not be true of all the masons who sought to return to the simple, humanitarian ideals of the orthodox English practice. The men who opposed the mystical party were in the main, rather, Protestant masons, gifted with a modicum of critical intelligence and alarmed both by the excesses of the Scottish rites and by what was later to be called 'crypto-Catholicism', which they already thought they discerned in people like Starck. Because of this, the Convent has more than a merely masonic interest: two major themes of German eighteenth-century culture were in conflict at it.

In the end, Willermoz' faction triumphed. The historical legend of the Templar heritage was abandoned and a solemn disavowal of any intention to restore it or reclaim its possessions was passed. The Duke of Brunswick was elected Grand Master of a new rite, the 'Chevaliers Bienfaisants et de la Maçonnerie Rectifiée' whose rituals and codes were left for future discussion. This was a symbolic victory for the Lyon influence but meant little, for the quarrels in print engendered by the Convent accelerated the decline of the reformed Order. Again brought into discredit in 1785 in a pamphlet by Starck, it was soon dead. Meanwhile, it had done nothing to give any new coherence to German freemasonry, for its enemies continued to distrust and dislike the triumph of the Lyonnais and Martinist influences symbolised in its name. The importance of the Convent was as much its effect on public opinion—soon well informed about it—as its organisational achievement.[55]

The Grand Orient was doing better than this in regulating diverging tendencies, but had its difficulties, too, and perhaps no national organisation of freemasonry could have been made a reality once the Scottish system was fairly launched. This was what was important about them for the mythology of the secret societies. By the mid-1780s, the flood

---

tion. Dittfurth was already a member of the Illuminati (see next chapter) before the Convent opened.

[55] Nor did it seem to satisfy the dominant party for long. Still searching for the direct experience of the supernatural, Willermoz went on from his victory to interest himself in Mesmer in the years after Wilhelmsbad (see Darnton, pp. 68–9). More important though, was the relative rapidity with which rumour began to spread of more sinister schemes supposed to have been brought to fruition at the Convent (see below, pp. 124–5).

of argument about sham history and spurious genealogy had (perhaps hopelessly) compromised freemasonry in the eyes of the public at large. To any sensible man, the careers of men like Hund or Starck— to say nothing of less ambiguous adventurers—were evidence that many Scottish masons were charlatans, fools or villains. The internal damage to freemasonry, too, was great. Its proper aims and ideals had been almost wholly lost to sight in the welter of announced aims and new principles publicised by the new rites. That much of the attraction of the new masonry was based on an intensification of what was already drawing people to masonry made confusion easier. The new rites exploited more vigorously the secret, hieratic implications of regular masonry and provided just as attractive a substitute for orthodox religious practice in the combination of symbolic acts and moral principles which they put forward. They sometimes added to this a pseudo-scientific jargon which with some semblance of logic could be tacked to the rationalist architectural symbolism of orthodox freemasonry.

Such confusion was to make it increasingly plausible to attribute sinister designs indiscriminately to masons. After the abolition of the Jesuits, members of that Society sometimes attributed their woes to masonic influence. Preaching by ex-Jesuits and by Franciscans against the Order had begun to be common in the heavily clerical state of Bavaria by the early 1780s.[56] Though all the indications point to the conclusion that orthodox lodges remained obedient to the non-political injunctions of the original Constitutions and that most of the new rites had non-political esoteric and mystical interests, this was not to be believed when people later came to look around for scapegoats for revolution. Then, the confused windiness of some of the language of the fringe masons and the remoter implications of symbols innocent in their first adumbrations would be remembered.

This evolution was to take some time. In the immediate aftermath of the Wilhelmsbad Convent all that can at first be discerned is a growing public awareness of masonry and attention to it in novels, plays and art. A steady flow of information and assertion, true and false, had already prepared the German and European public mind for more sensational tales. Nor, when masons themselves found distinctions so hard to draw between valid and invalid claims, is it surprising that there should exist confusion among the profane about what was and what was not attributable to the Craft. Many elements existed, ready for crystallisation into a simple and dramatic view which would formally articu-

[56] Le Forestier, *Les Illuminés*, pp. 438–9.

late the theory that a great social danger existed in the long-tolerated eighteenth-century underworld of the secret society. The catalyst for this change came suddenly, in the middle of the pre-revolutionary decade, with the exposure of a conspiracy which was to be the most important single source of all the nonsense which was to mould the paranoiac view of history embodied in the myths of the next century. This was the exposure of the Illuminati of Bavaria.

Chapter V
The Illuminati panic and after

WEISHAUPT'S ACHIEVEMENT

IN the early summer of 1776, a young professor at the Bavarian university of Ingolstadt conceived a new secret society.[1] He was Adam Weishaupt, born there in 1748, himself the son of a professor who had died while Adam was still young and he owed his subsequent education to the patronage of his godfather, the powerful Baron von Ickstatt, member of the Electoral privy council. Thanks to this support he received a scholarship at a Jesuit college. He seems to have found the Jesuits' instruction uncongenial; he later spoke of it with contempt, though he was powerfully impressed by other achievements of the Society. Certainly his considerable native powers only began to exercise themselves in a more congenial way when he came up to the university at the age of fifteen. He read widely in the 'enlightened' French authors and had already won a reputation for brilliance and scepticism when, after graduation, he began to teach there himself in 1772.

Like his father he belonged to the Faculty of Law, but this subject by no means exhausted his emotional and mental energies. He was much more interested in the resolution of doubts raised in him by the mechanical processes of the Jesuits' religious instruction. Weishaupt also soon showed a wish to proselytise; he began to gather admirers and disciples. His career was assured, in that his patron could advance him, but this, like his speculative cast of thought, brought Weishaupt into abrasive relationships with his colleagues. Ickstatt had been, thirty years before, the initiator and prime mover of a quarrel within the university over teaching methods and the employment of books by non-Catholics. This had led him into fierce conflict with the Jesuits, then the dominant academic influence in Bavaria. Ickstatt had triumphed, but when Weishaupt took up his first post, the embers of controversy and hostility were still glowing. When the young man was

---

[1] Le Forestier, *Les Illuminés de Bavière et la franc-maçonnerie allemande*, remains the fundamental and most useful study of this subject and I have drawn freely on it in this section. The same author's book on *La franc-maçonnerie Templière*, already cited, is also relevant.

pushed rapidly ahead, and in his first published work praised the work of such Protestant authors as Grotius, new rows erupted. They reached a climax at the news that Weishaupt was promised the chair of canon law held for ninety years by Jesuits but then, after their dissolution in 1773, vacant.

In these quarrels Weishaupt became known as an able academic intriguer. He acquired a new patron in Ickstatt's co-director of the university[2] and, reasonably irritated by refusals to pay him his salary after he had been appointed to the chair of canon law, was soon telling tales about his colleagues and intriguing on a great scale, meddling in the affairs of faculties other than his own. He kept in touch, however, both with anti-clericals and with ex-Jesuits. All the evidence of this period of his career reveals him as a familiar hazard of academic and collegiate life: the clever, cantankerous, self-absorbed and self-deceiving bore. It was always to be difficult—and it remains difficult— to distinguish in him the sincere, if exalted and headstrong, apostle of a new revelation, and the cynical and unscrupulous careerist and liar. He rapidly became an isolated figure, distrusted and disliked by all sides. Yet there was more to him than this suggests. Weishaupt was also a specimen of a very rare type, for he was one of the few convinced egalitarians of his day. He was convinced in the fullest sense, in that he sought to put his ideas into practice, but controversy has gone on since the eighteenth century about how far he intended to go.

This was to appear later. Weishaupt's next psychological development after the stormy opening of his professional career was the crystallising of his taste for disciples and will to dominate. He conceived the idea of a band of proselytes who would struggle with him against the forces of religious obscurantism at Ingolstadt. Memories of early reading about the Eleusinian mysteries and the secret association of the Pythagoreans played a part in this; even as an undergraduate he had drawn up draft statutes for a society on similar principles.[3] His eventual creation also shows that he was influenced deeply—even if sometimes by repulsion—by the organisational and disciplinary achievements of the Jesuits, which he saw as a true secret society, seeking the advancement of its own ideals at the expense of society as a whole. Then there were the freemasons. It is said to have been a meeting with a Hanoverian Protestant in 1774 which led him to try to join a lodge. He was soon disillusioned; the fees demanded were high

---

[2] He quarrelled with Ickstatt and went so far as to decry him before his students, whose applause he always seems to have courted (Le Forestier, *Les Illuminés*, pp. 22–3).   [3] Le Forestier, pp. 26–7.

E

and the much-promised secrets of the Craft seemed to be known to all the world. With its mystery, the appeal of masonry to Weishaupt also vanished. Nevertheless, he had gone a little further into the world of secret societies and his thinking about them had been enriched by experience.

Weishaupt now decided to form his own sect. It came into existence on 1 May 1776. His specific original impulse may have been a desire to combat the clandestine and enduring influence of former Jesuits within the university; he rapidly rationalised difficulties growing out of his own rashness and taste for intrigue as the product of obscurantism and soon envisaged wider purposes for his society. An oppressive clerical-ism, it is true, somewhat isolated Bavaria from the cultural life of the rest of Germany;[4] elsewhere fringe masonic and other secret organisa-tions were flourishing and Weishaupt soon found he had a small but keen clientèle of cultivated men for a society with an 'enlightened' flavour. Moreover, he seems to have had the advantage of building on an existing student secret society.[5]

Weishaupt's plan was to provide an organisation to promote his concealed egalitarian aims, in the first place by the study of letters and the useful arts. A formidable programme of instruction in them was devised with a double purpose: they were to be studied both for their own sake and because the exercise of reason in them would train the mind to strip off the trammels of obscurantism and tradition. From this, thought Weishaupt (who seems to have combined an unshakeable belief in the power of reason to penetrate confusion and ignorance with an obsessive need to confuse those around him with lies and decep-tions), would emerge an understanding of man's true nature, rooted in equality and rationality.[6] On this the enlightened man could found his hopes of an amelioration of society.

The principles of egalitarianism and rationalism were to be revealed only slowly in the explicit teaching of the new Order. Here Weishaupt drew on masonic technique; the initiate was to be led gradually towards the secret doctrines, first by reading the classical moralists, and only eventually through the works of Holbach and above all, the materialist

[4] Le Forestier speaks of an 'entente cordiale entre la papauté et les Wittelsbach' (*Les Illuminés*, p. 101). The anti-Enlightenment ascendancy retained its hold on Bavaria right down to the French Revolution.

[5] Le Forestier, p. 29.

[6] Weishaupt's emphasis on the evocation of an existing good human nature rather than on the imparting of a secret doctrine of transcendence is an important distin-guishing characteristic linking him clearly to the Philosophes and distinguishing him from the mystics and theosophists. See Le Forestier, p. 81.

Helvétius. In this he would be supervised by a senior initiate to whom he undertook to be completely and unquestioningly obedient. The gravest obligations of secrecy and pledges to set aside the ties and claims of family and friendship were laid upon the novice; it was, in some measure, the extent to which these went beyond the traditional masonic obligations that later made the Order seem so frightening and formidable. These obligations undertaken, the novice might hope to proceed through the other grades of initiation, his instruction and character being scrutinised in a series of regular self-examinations in the form of written replies to questionnaires; from the self-knowledge thus achieved would spring, Weishaupt hoped, the moral improvement on which the Order was to base the regeneration of the world. Initiates would then know that there lay ahead of them two further grades: 'Minervale' and 'Minervale Illuminato'.

They would not know that most of what they were told was nonsense, nor that Weishaupt had also provided for another, supreme level of direction above these grades. This was the Areopagus, a secret, withdrawn circle of directors of the whole Order, alone cognisant of its founder's true identity, of the history of the Order, and of its secret aims. Here Weishaupt's social idealism, nurtured on Rousseau, Morelly and Mably, culminated in a subversive purpose, the revolutionary education of the members of the Order for the transformation of existing society. The means to be adopted was the insinuation of members into positions of authority and influence, because, for all his high-flown revolutionary language, it was towards a peaceful transformation of public attitudes and morals that Weishaupt aspired.[7]

This was why he urged his first adepts to seek recruits among the socially distinguished, the rich and the able.[8] The Illuminati began as a meeting of only five members; in 1779 it had 'colonies' in four Bavarian cities other than Ingolstadt and numbered fifty-four, among them young noblemen and clergymen.[9] The gatherings of the Order

---

[7] See Le Forestier, Les Illuminés, pp. 328–9.

[8] See passages from his letters quoted by Le Forestier, especially pp. 31–2. It is interesting to compare these with the views of Mirabeau who, in his 1776 proposals for a new 'association intime' within freemasonry noted that 'les gens de qualité, pourvu qu'ils aient vaincu les préjugés qu'on impute à leur état, sont des membres précieux de l'association, parce que le point d'honneur de fidelité à leurs engagements les y rendra plus attachés; la crainte de perdre l'estime de leurs amis les rendra plus exacts à en pratiquer les devoirs; enfin, la certitude que leur donne leur naissance de parvenir aux postes les plus éminents, les met le mieux en état de travailler efficacement aux grandes vues proposées. . . .' RF, iii, 1882, pp. 299–300.

[9] Le Forestier, Les Illuminés, p. 44. See also p. 95 for the special provisions drawn up to ease the passage into the Order of the well-to-do.

were marked by an anti-clerical and, even, sometimes, anti-religious spirit which explains its special attraction in a country where the clergy still exercised so much control of education, publishing and social life. In the library of the Order—to whose enrichment, among other means by theft, Weishaupt gave much thought[10]—would be found 'advanced' literature unavailable publicly because of the censorship. The rest of Germany resounded with debate on questions of politics in the second half of the eighteenth century, as well as on religion and philosophy. Republicanism and natural rights were in vogue and the ideas of Rousseau were eagerly discussed. The American War of Independence greatly stimulated this tendency. The Illuminati were thus providing something for their members which, though not easily available in Bavaria, was common enough elsewhere. The Order was both an agency for the transmission of the commonplaces of Enlightenment ideas and attitudes and a quasi-religious sect, meeting the needs of men dissatisfied with the traditional sources of faith and contemplating an ultimate utopian regeneration of society.

The carefully generated mystery which surrounded the Order must also, at first, have been attractive. Its business was conducted under false names which were a characteristic expression of Weishaupt's love of subterfuge. He himself took that of 'Spartacus' and most of the others' pseudonyms were classical, too, though one of the original five called himself 'Shaftesbury', and 'Tamburlane' and 'Confucius' later made their appearance. Such devices may have helped to preserve secrecy. They did not protect the Order from the financial troubles and personal quarrels which soon overtook it. No doubt Weishaupt's own vanity and passion for double-dealing made this almost inevitable, but it is difficult to believe that the Order could have survived long in its original form in spite of the enormous effort (to judge by his correspondence) which Weishaupt gave to it. It was highly unlikely that its members could have long sustained their loyalty—and therefore their discipline—once the initial enthusiasm had worn off, the ceremonies had lost their novelty and the lack of real achievement was apparent. Soon, the Areopagites were quarrelling with the founder; they had, after all, to deal with the pressing demands of the novices for further enlightenment while he withdrew into a vast correspondence on forms, grades and doctrines. Besides having their own ideas on these matters, some of the senior members of the Order were by 1780

[10] A preliminary strategy envisaged the accumulation of materials on the history of monasticism and the great monastic orders, in particular of works written in a hostile spirit.

beginning to show signs of wishing to abandon it or of converting Weishaupt's dictatorship into an oligarchy.[11]

There does not seem much likelihood that the Order would have survived this crisis had not it been given a new lease of life by Weishaupt's decision to infiltrate freemasonry and recruit fresh members in its lodges. This decision was not arrived at in one step. Weishaupt's early disillusionment with masonry was succeeded by fear and distrust; the Craft seemed to threaten his own order by the attraction it exerted through its promise of secrets and ulterior grades. One motive for him to apply again to join a lodge (which he did in 1777) was to place himself in a position to be able to communicate masonic secrets to them himself. The lodge to which he was admitted was a Strict Observance lodge.

The idea of doing more than tapping masonic lore for the benefit of the Illuminati seems to have originated with a pupil of Weishaupt, Xavier Zwack. He took the pseudonym of 'Cato' and had been the moving spirit in the recruitment of the Order at Munich. Weishaupt cautiously came round to agree that some of the Areopagites should become freemasons in order to link the two systems and to make possible the subsequent transmission of masonic grades to other Illuminati. It was some time before this developed into the idea of full union with the freemasons, in which the Illuminati would become another masonic system, like the Strict Observance. This was a scheme with great prospects. In the first place, it would give access under conditions of secrecy to orthodox lodges for recruiting purposes and for the diffusion of anti-clerical propaganda. It would make possible the shunting-off of Illuminati who proved incapable of full revelation into Illuminati masonic lodges which would provide them with amusement and diversion to take their minds off their dissatisfaction with their own progress. Finally, it could provide a ceremonial and ritual which many Illuminati would find attractive.

The advantages to the secret and conspiratorial aims of the Illuminati are also obvious. Once the Craft had been penetrated by them, they could use the lodge structure to pass from place to place seeking proselytes and receiving help. The secrecy of the Craft would hinder detection and the technique of gradual revelation was one which masons

[11] Other matters also bothered the Order. The elaboration of new grades as always in the world of masonic and quasi-masonic societies gave rise to much discussion and even the name of the Order was a source of dispute. Weishaupt had begun by naming its members 'Perfectionists', before hitting on Illuminati. Even this was not wholly satisfying: in 1779 he was thinking of renaming it the 'Society of Bees', a suggestion which was not pressed. Le Forestier, *Les Illuminés*, pp. 134–5.

would find familiar and congenial. The Illuminati were the first society to seek to use for political subversion the machinery of secret organisation offered by freemasonry and through the Craft they began again to spread. The first masonic lodge dominated was one at Munich, which succumbed to Illuminati control in 1779. An emissary was then sent to Frankfurt to obtain (from the only lodge in Germany faithful to English masonry) authority to set up daughter lodges. This was successful. From Bavaria, the Order then ramified throughout central and southern Germany and Austria. It has been traced as far afield as Italy, Grenoble, Lyon and Strasbourg. It attracted intellectuals; Sonnenfels, Goethe, Schiller, Mozart, Wieland and Herder are all said to have belonged to it. So did men of affairs, Kolowrat, Cobenzl and Hardenberg among them.[12] By mid-1782, it seems to have had about three hundred members, mainly men of some position. At Vienna, there was even talk that Joseph II might become a member.[13] The Bavarian lodges were prosperous and owned or leased homes and apartments where they met. In 1783 the Order spread to Bohemia and Milan, and the following year to Hungary.

The grip of the new order on masonic lodges grew steadily. A big effort was said to have been made to recruit discontented freemasons at the Wilhelmsbad Convent, though with little immediate success.[14] The demoralised and chaotic state of German freemasonry at the time of this abortive gathering tempted some Illuminati to contemplate taking over the direction of the whole of it, through the creation of a confederation of lodges under the direction of so-called 'Ancient Scots Superiors' who did not, in fact, exist, but whose instructions would be transmitted by the Illuminati. (An interesting detail of this scheme was its propagation of an old plot myth in its own interests. This was the story that the Jesuits were behind all the extravagances which had corrupted freemasonry, from the Templar legend to the activities of Hund.[15]) This intrigue was to extend as far as the lodges

[12] Francovich, p. 57; Epstein, pp. 92–3. Another member was Metternich's father. On the other hand, the Berlin publicist Christoph Friedrich Nicolai, firmly identified with the rationalist, anti-clerical movement, treated the approaches of the Illuminati with grave reserve, and Lavater, more predictably perhaps, refused his adhesion when approached by Knigge in 1783 (Le Forestier, *Les Illuminés*, pp. 402–5).

[13] Le Forestier, p. 347.

[14] The main Illuminati representative at the congress was Dietrich von Dittfurth. He recruited Bode who, soon after, recruited Prince Charles of Hesse, who had succeeded the Duke of Sudermania in the direction of the Strict Observance. See Le Forestier, *La franc-maçonnerie Templière*, pp. 646 ff.

[15] Le Forestier, *La franc-maçonnerie Templière*, pp. 637–42, gives an account of Bode's launching of this story on his fellow-masons at the Wilhelmsbad Convent.

of Poland (and in the process yet another masonic system was spawned, the 'Eclectic Alliance'). Only in France did the Illuminati meet with no success; the Grand Orient was wary of the mysterious new order, as it had been of the Strict Observance, and if, as was later alleged, an attempt was made to penetrate it, it certainly failed. Yet the Illuminati were to achieve no enduring success in Germany, either.

Most of what is known and has so far been said about the Illuminati derives from evidence which became available about them when they were exposed. We owe it, paradoxically, largely to the defection of a member who was perhaps of greater importance in spreading the order in the early 1780s than anyone else, Adolf Francis, Baron Knigge. He was born in Hanover in 1752, into a distinguished family, and grew up a man of talent and address. He was another of those curious, morally amphibious eighteenth-century Germans whose lives blur the line between the charlatan and the fanatic, and who found escape and satisfaction in the pullulating secret societies of the masonic underworld. He had already been a mason, had joined other secret societies and had attempted to enter a Rosicrucian lodge before being recruited to the Illuminati by the emissary sent to Frankfurt in 1779. In searches for philosophic and theosophic instruction, Knigge was drawn to the Illuminati by the promise of its 'secrets'.

Knigge quickly brought in a number of recruits in his turn. But he was a man who wanted results and soon became sceptical about an order into which he seemed to penetrate only a little way. To avoid a rupture, Weishaupt took Knigge completely into his confidence and at one stroke Knigge found himself co-adjutor to the founder and in a position of the greatest influence. This was shown by the new impetus he gave to amplifying the masonic affiliations of the Order and in the elaboration of new grades. This reflected, in part, Knigge's temperamental attraction towards the mysterious and mystical, a sympathy opposed to Weishaupt's early rationalist idealism.[16] Soon, he found the Areopagites' views too narrowly anti-religious and too intolerant and he began to press for the reform of the Order. He wished it to abandon the egalitarian educational scheme devised by Weishaupt and the sectarian rationalism of its founder. These could be tolerated as an expression of a natural reaction to circumstance in priest-ridden Bavaria, but would cripple the Order when it sought

[16] Nonetheless, among Knigge's services to the Illuminati was the writing and publishing of some anti-Jesuit articles in an 'enlightened' vein. See Le Forestier, *Les Illuminés*, p. 223.

to spread in Protestant Germany, where religious sentiment was respected. He also seems to have believed in the reconciliation of religious belief and 'enlightened' philosophy at the highest level; the utility of traditional religion for most men seemed to him evident and was incorporated by him in Illuminati doctrine. There was an element of conscious tactics in this.[17] Nevertheless, Knigge's ideas had been accepted at an assembly of the Areopagites in July 1781.[18] This opened a new phase in the history of the Order: oligarchy replaced the personal despotism of Weishaupt. Soon Knigge was given powers to initiate new Areopagites. The Order was re-shaped to give priority to the scientific investigation of nature and humanity which was its main task in Knigge's eyes. It was also to commit itself wholeheartedly to the masonic framework, hiding its true aims and identity under whatever name seemed appropriate.[19]

The grades already existing became the subdivisions of a new pre-paratory class of initiates.[20] Above them came a masonic class, itself subdivided into two levels, one of three symbolic grades (the apprentice, companion and master of ordinary masonry) and one of the two Scots grades—novice and cavalier—which were higher. Above this, in turn, came the third class, of 'mysteries'. This had four sub-divisions: priest, reigning priest, grand magus and the Man-King. From the second, masonic class, the initiator of the class of 'mysteries' selected suitable candidates for admission to his own grade. No one, therefore, could now progress beyond the original grade of 'Illuminatus Minor' without first becoming a mason. This was the structure with which the Order achieved its great expansion in the early 1780s, and which carried it to its peak in 1784.[21]

At this stage, new dissensions were already troubling the Order. The roots of a quarrel between Knigge and Weishaupt lay, doubtless, in temperamental differences which could be ignored or surmounted only briefly. The decisive occasions of quarrel seem to have been the drafting of the ceremonial directions for admission to the higher

---

[17] Knigge once said that the true doctrine of Jesus Christ had been the establishment of liberty and equality, but that it did not matter if not everyone understood this, providing they could agree not to quarrel as sects. Le Forestier, Les Illuminés, p. 336.

[18] Le Forestier, p. 240.

[19] Knigge recommended the Illuminati also to disguise themselves as learned societies. Le Forestier, p. 304.

[20] For the new scheme of grades see the table in Le Forestier, p. 230, and the chapter which follows for the ceremonies associated with them.

[21] Le Forestier, p. 399, says that about 650 adepts can be identified, but that this is certainly less than the total actually achieved.

grades.[22] Weishaupt deplored the use of quasi-religious forms and Roman Catholic models for this purpose and found Knigge's proposals both too elaborate and too mystical. This led to accusations that Knigge was falsifying the intentions of the Order and at last to an outright split. Soon Knigge was threatening to reveal the secrets of the Order to its enemies. In July 1784 it was agreed that Knigge should leave the Illuminati.

By this time, the Order had other worries. Some of its members had been garrulous. Suspicion had been aroused among members of the Strict Observance as early as 1782 at Wilhelmsbad; Willermoz had quickly gone into print against his opponents and had alluded (though not by name) to Dittfurth's attempts to subvert the Strict Observance for revolutionary ends.[23] Alarming rumours about the Order were circulating in Bavaria by 1784. Hard things were said in public by members of the lower grades about kings and priests. The public became interested, and so did the ruling élite of Bavaria. The hand of the Order was believed to be operating within the administration. In the previous year, a Minervale Illuminato had left the Order and revealed its secrets (with horrific exaggerations) to his employer, a duchess of the Bavarian royal family. His revelations soon became public. Suspicions had already also been awoken that the Illuminati were connected with an Austrian plot to subvert Bavaria in order to make possible the long-coveted annexation of the Electorate to the possessions of the House of Habsburg; they were reinforced by these revelations.[24] Whatever the precise truth of them, the state was alarmed; journalistic, clerical and academic outcry against the Order and police

[22] It is interesting to note that one of the doctrines which Weishaupt sought to impart to the aspirant to the priestly grade included the assertion that secret societies had, from the earliest times, kept alive the true doctrine of human nature in spite of the race's degeneration under the rule of kings and princes (Le Forestier, Les Illuminés, p. 283). This is another instance in which there can be detected the generation of evidence which later feeds the myth of a plot of the secret societies not only universal, but timeless.

[23] See passage quoted in Viatte, I, pp. 148–9. This had been the launching of a story thereafter central to the myth. Contemporaries who endorsed it were Charles of Hesse and Haugwitz; much later, too, it was said that one of the French participants, Virieu, had confirmed the story immediately on returning from the Convent (Le Forestier, La franc-maçonnerie Templière, pp. 861–3).

[24] Le Forestier, Les Illuminés, pp. 440–4. The reverberations of such an accusation were significant. Joseph II of Austria was, of course, admired by those who held 'enlightened' views and by anti-clericals. Prussia—also involved in the Bavarian question—stood not only for Bavaria's territorial integrity, but was already the focus, in many people's view, of a religious reaction. Whether any support was actually given to the Illuminati in Bavaria by Joseph II is not established but seems improbable.

action began at the same time. On 23 June 1784 the Bavarian Elector published an edict forbidding his subjects to be members of secret or unauthorised associations; it spoke of fears aroused among the public. This was not specifically directed against the Illuminati, but they consequentially suspended their meetings. Soon, a contest of publication and counter-publication on the object of the edict began, but the first actual attack on the Illuminati had preceded this, it seems.[25] There began a steady flow of publication, much of it citing documentary evidence and naming the Order. Soon, this material was added to by official action, when a drive (said to be encouraged by the ex-Jesuits) was launched to bring to light incriminating literature. Pamphlets began to appear which sought to distinguish between innocent conventional freemasons and the inculpated Illuminati. Increasingly charges were made against them of irreligion, disloyalty to the dynasty, political intrigue and moral corruption; it was alleged, moreover, that whatever the edicts might say, the Illuminati were still at work in the Bavarian court. Preachers reiterated these charges in their pulpits. So alarmed did Weishaupt become that he decided to make a direct approach to the Elector, declaring the innocence of the Order, and demonstrating it by revealing to him most of its secrets. He was too late. On 2 March 1785 appeared another edict, this time condemning freemasons and Illuminati explicitly. It spoke of legitimate suspicion based on religious, social and political considerations.

This seems to have been the deathblow to the Illuminati in Bavaria. Weishaupt had already fled when the edict appeared. A row at the university which had begun over the selection of books for the library and had ended in his removal from his chair had provided him with some of the éclat needed for a convincing withdrawal as a victim of clerical persecution. He thus just escaped the interrogation and investigations which now began. Ludicrous statements were made by witnesses anxious to ingratiate themselves with the authorities. Arrests and formal charges of holding illegal assemblies soon followed. Documents were searched for. Soon, this provided the biggest single body of evidence ever added at one time to the secret society mythology when, in 1786, the lodgings of Zwack were raided (he had already left

---

[25] Wolfstieg cites a novel, J. M. Babo's *Gemälde aus dem menschlichen Leben* (1784), which contained incidental criticism of the Illuminati whom the author saw as a danger to his own hopes of the adoption of physiocratic (?) agrarian policies in Bavaria. Charles of Hesse, drawn briefly into the Illuminati after the Wilhelmsbad Convent, soon broke with it under the influence of Frederick William, then heir to the throne of Prussia; this, too, preceded Bavarian action. Le Forestier, *La franc-maçonnerie Templière*, pp. 714–15.

Bavaria). Hundreds of papers were seized and were published in a sensational volume in the following year.[26] A mass of Weishaupt's letters thus found its way into print. There had been found with them even more alarming and compromising material, from notes on the admission of aspirants which appeared to show the Order's rights of life and death over them, to prescriptions for procuring abortions and making secret ink and poisons. Those who wished to authenticate the printed collection at the Electoral archives were invited to do so. Arrests followed.

After this explosion of material, confessions, self-justifications, letters and protocols poured into print. The scandal had, indeed, already before this turned a torrent of publication into a flood. Together with several other Illuminati Weishaupt had defended himself in print in 1786; his *Apologie der Illuminaten* was followed by two more works by him the following year. Soon a further collection of confiscated documents appeared.[27] Knigge brought out a defensive account of his role in 1788.[28]

There is no need to trace the detailed development of this exposure literature or the action taken by the authorities.[29] Wolfstieg lists more than fifty items published about the Illuminati before 1790, most of them in Germany, but others from Copenhagen, Paris, London and even Boston. By the time that the French Revolution broke out there was, therefore, a rich body of detailed and circumstantial evidence on which to base suspicions about secret societies which were far deeper and far wider-ranging than any so far aroused by the freemasons. That there was much rubbish mixed up with the hard facts did not matter.[30] Moreover, much of it seemed to compromise freemasonry, too, and to justify earlier suspicions of the Craft.

Freemasons and other secret societies themselves sometimes assisted this process. The revelations were, for example, exploited by the Rosicrucian masons. Particularly well entrenched in the lodges of Prussian freemasonry, they had long sought to set their fellow-masons

[26] *Einige Originalschriften des Illuminaten Ordens, Welche bei dem gewesenen Regierungsrath Zwack durch vorgenommene Hausvisitation zu Landshut den 11 und 12 Oktober 1786 vorefunden warden* (Munich, 1787).

[27] *Nachtrag von Weiteren Originalschriften* (Munich, 1787). This contained, among other things, a letter of Weishaupt of 1783 which was the basis of later accusations against him of incest and infanticide.

[28] *Philo's endliche Erklärung und Antwort* (Hanover, 1788).

[29] A further Bavarian electoral edict of 16 August 1787 prescribed the death penalty for anyone recruiting a new member to the Order.

[30] e.g. 'revelations' that the Illuminati had poisoned the heir presumptive of the Duke of Zweibrucken, that they encouraged sodomy, onanism and prostitution.

on their guard against the deistical and nationalist tendencies of the Illuminati before these revelations were made. They now asserted that the Order had simply gone underground, but still continued at work.[31] The continued activity of lodges known to have been infiltrated by the Illuminati lent colour to such assertions; there had indeed been also an attempt to anticipate the collapse of the Order in Bavaria by ordering the lodges there to cease their activity and turn themselves at once into reading societies in order to keep their membership in being.[32] Yet, though it has importance in the positive history of the next generation of secret societies, the question of the survival of the Illuminati is for our purpose less significant than the effect the revelations had on the myth of the secret societies by making such assertions plausible. The tendency of Weishaupt's work was, after all, impossible to conceal. He was, we may think, naïve: his social philosophy was based on an optimistic primitivism which had little to offer the future. He believed that the recovery of man's original nature was all that was needed to create the good society and that this demanded essentially only that men should understand the weight of prejudice and error which encumbered them. But he was an authentic revolutionary, if only in an intellectual sense.[33] He tried to give the social ideals of the Enlightenment realisation by conspiratorial means. As such, he was a startling irruption into eighteenth-century political and cultural life, and revelations about his work attracted much attention. The effects of this were manifold.

In the first place, there was the further damage the Illuminati revelations inflicted on freemasonry. If the most indulgent view of freemasonry's own innocence were taken, it still must have seemed unlikely after the revelations that all the Illuminati who had penetrated the lodges had been subsequently eradicated; there must still be some at work. People were bound to conclude that at least a danger existed that some lodges were perverted in their aims. Most people were not likely to be as indulgent as this, though. Some limited themselves to seeing in Templar lodges the perverted masonry they had always struggled against, reinforced now by the Illuminati infusion.[34] But for many of them, the suspicion of freemasonry as a whole which had been

---

[31] Le Forestier, *Les Illuminés*, pp. 410–11; some of the Illuminati themselves thought the dispersal of the organisation not necessarily a bad blow.

[32] Francovich, pp. 64–5.

[33] Le Forestier (*Les Illuminés*, pp. 327 ff.) argues strongly that the practical revolutionary *intention* behind Weishaupt's words was small and that he never envisaged the concrete realisation of his ideals.

[34] See reference in Francovich, p. 17 fn.

intensified by the emergence of the many new sects in the late eighteenth century now seemed justified; here was real evidence of the disreputable nature of what went on in that mysterious world and in the Craft itself. No one could be sure how many masons shared the Illuminati views.

Evidence of a new credulity and alarm was soon provided from France, where the story of Illuminati attempts to penetrate the Grand Orient got about after Mirabeau's visits to Berlin. He had made three between January 1786 and September 1786, on quasi-official business by which he hoped to gain a footing in the world of diplomacy. While there he frequented circles where rationalist influences were dominant and formed a favourable view of the Illuminati, whom he praised for struggling against the Jesuits. One of them, of some notoriety, became his friend; this was Mauvillon. This was to lead to accusations from anti-Illuminati publicists that Mauvillon had in fact initiated Mirabeau into the secret Illuminati plans for the subversion of French freemasonry and that this had led to the recruitment of the Grand Master, the Duke of Orléans, by Mirabeau after his return. Verisimilitude was given to these charges by the favourable comments which Mirabeau made about the Illuminati in his *Monarchie Prussienne*—yet he does not seem to have understood the situation in Germany very well, even confusing the Illuminati with the Prussian Rosicrucians. Nonetheless, the story was to prove enduring and to seem more than ever convincing after 1789. As late as 1803, a German publicist could assert that Mirabeau had been initiated an Illuminato under the pseudonym of Leonidas.[35]

By the late 1780s enormous confusion existed about the whole world of masonry, secret societies and sects; everything was by then so muddled up that the uninitiated could not be expected to make distinctions where even adepts often found themselves at sea. The discredit which might be won by any particular body therefore tended to contaminate all others. Nonetheless, the full impact of the Illuminati revelations was not to come until after the shock of the French Revolution had reinforced it.[36] Paradoxically, in the excitement over the major figures of the exposure of the 1780s, people lost sight of some Illuminati

[35] J. A. Starck, *Triumph der Philosophie im 18 Jahrhundert* (Frankfurt, 1803), II, p. 350. On the whole Mirabeau episode see Le Forestier, *Les Illuminés*, pp. 662–4. No doubt some of his own confusions were terminological (see comments on the word 'illuminé' elsewhere in this book), but in 1819 an anonymous and seemingly well-informed author suggested they were deliberate. See *La vérité sur les sociétés secrètes en l'Allemagne . . . par un ancien Illuminé* (Paris, 1819), p. 7.

[36] See below pp. 146 ff.

who, as individuals, actually did contribute to the positive leadership and organisation of secret political societies in the next few years. On the whole, the movement everywhere ebbed; some Illuminati, nevertheless, continued to spread the doctrine. At the time those among them who attracted attention were publicists who, above all in Germany, were especially identified with attitudes and beliefs of the Enlightenment. There were fears that their work went on, and that the Illuminati were still at work in secret; this was shown, for example, in the violent reaction to the advertising of Bahrdt's Deutsche Union in 1788.[37] This proposal for the circulation of 'enlightened' literature to reading clubs all over Germany was taken to be a device for the adepts of the Illuminati to get control of the Frankfurt press. Far from this in fact, Bahrdt's proposal was attacked by the Illuminatus Bode. Yet the affair reverberated for years while Bahrdt went on to confirm the suspicions of many people by satirising the Prussian Religionsedikt in 1789 and replying to Zimmermann, who was now attacking the Aufklärung to which he had once adhered.[38]

It has been powerfully argued that it is in this sort of context that the Illuminati revelations must be placed to understand them fully, and that the major importance of the scare they produced was their crystallisation, or precipitation, of a long-implicit intellectual reaction.[39] Perhaps this discounts a little too readily other factors in German intellectual development in this period, but undoubtedly the anti-Illuminati literature which soon appeared in great quantities forged and anticipated the arguments later used by German Romantics against the ideas of the French Revolution. It harped on the association of Enlightenment principles with political and social sedition which has so often been looked at only as a product of the reaction after 1789.

This literature could and did exploit the very large body of original documentation now provided by the correspondence and papers of the leading Illuminati. Such revelations as those of the instructions for recruiting, or the emphasis on the immense potential of men united in secret to act in concert which had been made so much of it Weishaupt's writings, inflamed a general alarm. The generally cynical treatment of religion as a useful fraud also shocked people, the more,

[37] Karl Friedrich Bahrdt, a freemason notorious as a rationalising theologian, can be approached via the references in Epstein, pp. 118–20.

[38] J. G. Zimmermann was a fashionable Swiss doctor who attended many crowned beds of Europe.

[39] See the important article by J. Droz, 'Le légende du complot illuministe et les origines du romantisme politique en Allemagne', RH, ccxxvi, 1961, which should, nevertheless, be considered in the light of the wider-ranging discussion by Epstein.

perhaps, because so many of them had been taken in by the assertions of Illuminati masonry. And among the papers published in the later 1780s was also plenty of specific assertion and allusion which fitted well into existing suspicions and fears. One such example was the claim made by one of the Illuminati to Knigge, at the moment of his recruitment to the Order, that the enlightened reforms of Joseph II had been made possible by the activity of the Illuminati.[40] Another was Knigge's recommendation that the Illuminati should disguise themselves as members of learned societies. Such evidence fitted perfectly the preconceptions of the men who already formed a latent opposition to 'Philosophy' and who were to have their fears confirmed after 1789. Other, similarly alarming and useful, information could also be found in voluminous documentation provided by the correspondence of the leading Illuminati.

In fact, opposition to 'Philosophy' was already swelling in Germany. It was part of a movement which was also an opposition to the secular, reforming state which so often justified its policies in rational and utilitarian terms. Already in 1765 the alarmed Duke of Wurtemberg had proposed to Lavater the creation of a vast, benevolent secret society to combat rationalism and irreligion.[41] Opposition to rationalism and reform was noisy even in the 1770s; the activity of the former Jesuits was often very important in giving it expression. There was already talk of a plot against Christianity.[42] Certain trends at work in Protestantism told in this direction, too. One consequence was the foundation at Basle in 1780 of a secret 'Deutsche Christumsgesellschaft' to bring together men of different denominations in defence of Christian truths: such ideas were being increasingly well received and a secret society structure seemed appropriate to their promotion. In Prussia especially, religion prepared the ground for acceptance of the startling revelations about the Illuminati. *Die Wahre Reformation*, a book of 1785, already set out the scheme of a conspiracy among enlightened writers to attack the truths of religion before the scandals broke.[43] With the Illuminati revelations this could be coupled to the myth of political and social subversion. This more complex and dangerous

[40] Francovich, p. 55.

[41] Viatte, I, p. 301; Faivre, p. 15. The proposal of the secret society form is significant of the fascination this idea exercised.

[42] See the letter of 1772 of the Swiss Kirchberger, quoted in Faivre, p. 43, fn. 2. 'Aus zuverlässigem Bericht, und Vergleichung eterelcher Umstände schliesse ich, es nege schon reit etwas Zeit in Deutschland ein Komplott worden, der nichts weniger zum Vorwurf bat ab die christliche Religion um zusturzen.'

[43] It was, of course, an argument set out in France ever since the dissolution of the Jesuits.

legend was set out in a much discussed book, *Enthüllung des Systems der Weltbürger-Republik* in 1786.[44] The purposes of the Illuminati in seeking to dominate freemasonry were there succinctly summarised: 'To emancipate all of mankind from religious and political slavery. Put specifically, to advance deism and cosmopolitanism.'

This was one example of the general pattern in Germany, where attitudes and tendencies implicit in pre-romantic culture were put into a new focus and given a new dramatic content by the Illuminati crisis. The result was the appearance of virtually all the elements of the conspiracy theories to be put forward so vigorously in the next few years. Before the Illuminati came to the surface, even those who had attacked freemasonry had not asserted that a great and universal plot was to be found at its core. This now became an idea of common currency and was to be an essential key for the interpretation of many other things— such as the Templar legend—soon to be fitted into the complete secret society myth.

DEEPENING CONFUSION

Religious reaction and the rising tide of Illuminati and anti-Illuminati revelations precipitated not only alarm but even greater confusion. This meant that there were still obstacles to be removed before there could emerge the simple views which were eventually to produce something like a conservative preponderance in conspiracy theories. The greatest solvent of these confusions would be the French Revolution: but just before it began they were very widespread and important indeed. In part, they arose from the contradictory and conflicting claims made by Weishaupt and his followers. In part, they were a reflexion of the disorder of freemasonry at the end of the eighteenth century, and the existence within it of groups of very different philosophical and ideological tendency. The resultant bandying about of labels and accusations not only brought the freemasons even more into the public eye, but also soon almost deprived the terminology of the subject of such hard meaning as it possessed. The consequent difficulties have already been touched on in the case of the word 'illuminé'. This word—already in circulation in French masonry before the days of the Illuminati—was soon being used by people in diametrically opposed ways which must trouble the historian. Nevertheless, such facts do not obscure the general trend, the growing willingness to use

[44] Anon [Ernst Anton von Göchhausen], Rome [=Leipzig], 1786. I have not examined this book and rely on Epstein's summary, pp. 96–100.

a conspiracy framework of explanation in interpreting recent and current events. The very confusion of the debates which arose in the late 1780s is an expression of this.

In one way, writers who might be classified as men of the Enlightenment had always been susceptible to such an interpretation. Many of them had said that it was the wickedness of kings and priests which bogged men down in misery and folly. More specific views within this general tendency now began to be expressed which matched views put forward on the anti-Enlightenment side. Weishaupt and his colleagues, for example, had been quick to denounce Jesuit influence among their critics and opponents. This further complicates the problem of tracing a clear genealogy for the secret society mythology; yet at the moment when the main structure of ideas which underlay the myth was taking shape it was a general willingness to listen to views which presupposed conspiracy of some sort—from whatever quarter—which was important in preparing public opinion for what was to come, rather than any response to a particular version. Thus, on the eve of the great Revolution itself, the French public was given an alarming account of a reactionary conspiracy threatening Europe in 1788, by the publication of an *Essai sur la secte des Illuminés* by a well-known man of letters, the Marquis de Luchet.[45]

Luchet had for years been writing about the world—and underworld—of letters and culture. He had written, for example, about Cagliostro at the time of the affair of the Diamond Necklace, dealing ruthlessly with the mystifying claims of that charlatan and the gullibility of those who patronised him. In part the *Essai* was another exercise in his prolonged examination 'du penchant des hommes aux choses extraordinaires'.[46] But he was also at this time in the service of Prince Henry of Prussia, the brother of Frederick the Great. His purpose was to combat Rosicrucian influences at the Prussian court.[47] This led him to address himself in his book to the important theme of the irrationalist threat to the Enlightenment itself. He approached it in

[45] J. P. L. de la Roche du Maine, Marquis de Luchet, was a friend of Mirabeau, who was sometimes said to have been the author of the *Essai*. My references are to the third edition, 1792. Its republication showed its success. The first edition is according to Wolfstieg only the second publication on the Illuminati in a language other than German.

[46] The title of the first chapter of the *Essai*.

[47] Le Forestier, *Les Illuminés*, p. 621. It may have been from Luchet that Mirabeau drew the confused ideas about German secret societies which he embodied in his book on the Prussian monarchy, but this whole question remains obscure and more than one explanation is possible. See for one discreditable to Mirabeau the accusations of the author of *La vérité sur les sociétés secrètes en Allemagne*, pp. 35–6.

shocked amazement at its success. 'Aurait-on prévu,' he asked, 'que la fin déshonorée de ce siècle serait témoin encore des fruits honteux de la crédulité; que le flambeau de la philosophie pâlirait devant les torches du Fanatisme; que la Patrie des Fontenelle, des Montesquieu, des Voltaire, des Diderot, des Helvétius, des d'Alembert, accueillerait un S——, un W——, un Cagliostro, un Lavater, un d'E——, et vingt autres Théosophes, dont les noms devraient avoir le sort de leurs talents, c'est-à-dire demeurer à jamais inconnus ?' [48]

The 'Illuminés' of Luchet's title turn out to be, therefore, not Illuminati, but the protagonists both of the mystical, cabbalistic derivations of Scottish masonry of the late eighteenth century and also of the theosophic, religious revival already mentioned which played so big a part in German romantic origins. Specifically, he had in mind the Berlin Rosicrucians. Luchet not unreasonably from his point of view as a defender of Enlightenment and rationalism, lumps these together in their general tendency. The public was already well informed about them in gossip and scandal about the masonic derivations and the mystical crazes which had been going on for years—and Luchet provided a framework of interpretation into which they could all be fitted, the whole thing made more palatable by horrific descriptions of initiation rituals. How, asked Luchet despairingly, could it ever have been expected that Frederick's Prussia would be the cradle of such nonsense?

He recognised a partial explanation in the well-known propensity of the human race to folly. In France, fashion counted, too; 'des femmes, jadis aimables, au lieu de donner dans la dévotion, se jettent dans la Théosophie. . . .' [49] But this was not the whole story, he thought. There also existed even in France a new disposition to credulity such as had not existed even in the last years of Louis XIV. Even those who did not pretend to new beliefs at least showed 'un éloignement marqué pour tout ce qui tient au progrès de la raison'. [50] This could be seen, for example, in the cold reception given to the admirable reforming law on the civic status of non-Catholics. [51] In Germany, of course, the situation was far worse. Prone to error because of their national history ('la servitude y frappe tous les esprits'), the unhappy Germans were also bowed under the intellectual burdens of an educational system dominated by theology. 'Que peut-on dire sur un sujet si rebattu? Des

[48] He was, of course, here taking broadly the same line as Bode and Nicolai, defenders of rationalist enlightenment in Germany. His references presumably, are to S[aint-Martin], W[illermoz], d'E[spremesnil].

[49] Luchet, p. 20.

[50] p. 21.   [51] For the significance of this, see below.

analyses ou des interprétations; des critiques ou de prétendues découvertes; tout cela conduit à des systèmes. Des systèmes aux erreurs,
des erreurs aux sectes, il n'est qu'un pas.'[52] And so Germany had
become the great theatre of theosophy.

This had provided a conspiratorial opportunity. The sect of the
Illuminés had only needed to exploit this situation, said Luchet. They
had done so all the more ably because they had drawn on the experience
and the methods both of the Jesuits and the freemasons. While no
friend of the former, Luchet was careful to exonerate the Craft from
conscious collaboration: 'cette Institution, respectable par son
antiquité et par ses deux bases premières, l'égalité et la charité, a tour-
à-tour essuyé des proscriptions et l'appui le plus déclaré; mais toujours
les respects de la multitude, l'indifférence du sage, et la tolérance des
Gouvernemens raisonnables.'[53] What the Illuminés took from the
freemasons was the practice of submitting candidates to ordeal and
some of the mystical mumbo-jumbo into which deviant masons had
fallen away from orthodoxy.[54] On this basis the Illuminés had erected
a plot to combat universally the progress of reason and science through
the agency of the princes they could convert. 'Peuples séduits, ou qui
pouvez l'être, apprenez qu'il existe une conjuration en faveur du
despotisme contre la liberté, de l'incapacité contre le talent, du vice
contre la vertu, de l'ignorance contre la lumière.'

The techniques of the Illuminés, as Luchet describes them, seem
disproportionate to their far-ranging ambitions. It is true, he does not
provide his readers with much information about them at all beyond
saying that they are organised in circles of nine members, communicating with one another by hieroglyph. They also, he alleges, practice
the techniques of gradual revelation of secrets—'on n'en tenait pas
moins les cathecumènes à une distance incommensurable du sanctuaire
des perfides'[55]—and of exploiting the ignorant goodwill of masons
whose probity is well known so as to use them to insinuate their
opinions among other masons. The insinuation of notions of 'reform'
within masonry, the promotion of such derivations as the Strict
Observance and Eclectic lodges, all helps in the gradual ripening of
men's minds for fanaticism, and the overthrow of talent, effort and
knowledge.

[52] p. 23.   [53] p. 40.
[54] The sect, says Luchet, 'adopte du régime jesuitique, l'obéissance aveugle et les
principes régicides du dix-septième siècle; de la franc-maçonnerie, les épreuves et
les cérémonies extérieurs des Templiers, les évocations souterraines et l'incroyable
audace', p. 46.
[55] p. 61.

Luchet did not believe the remedy for this disease to be a difficult one. The essential was that men of goodwill should rally openly to the banner of reason and enlightenment. Above all, philosophical authors should come together to denounce the theosophic trend. 'Il n'est pas d'abus capables de résister à la force, à la raison, l'éloquence combinées.'[56] Wider reading and better education would reveal the follies of predecessors of the Illuminés, but it is interesting to see that Luchet also had a specific recommendation to make to freemasons: they needed, he thought, to carry out a real internal reform of their own order. 'Il s'agirait de conserver cette société bienfaisante, d'en prévenir les abus, et d'imiter plutôt l'Empereur qui la garde avec des modifications, que Naples qui la chasse avec ignominie.'[57] For freemasons this means the abolition of 'chapters' and the mysterious assemblies of higher grades. The Scots lodges should suppress the Reformed and Eclectic lodges. Orators of lodges should be chosen among men known 'pour avoir un peu de philosophie dans les principes'.[58]

The main interest to us of Luchet's long pamphlet lies in the evidence it provides of the diffusion of conspiracy theories on both sides of one of the great ideological and cultural divisions of the eighteenth century. The Philosophes had always been ready to talk of religion as a plot of priests against the interests of mankind. This basic assumption was now taken a step further; it was now alleged that there existed a special secret conspiracy whose anti-Enlightenment aims were the mirror-image of those beginning to be imputed to freemasonry in Germany after the Illuminati exposures. Luchet thought there were many princes already infected with illuminé ideas and, as his reference to Jesuit teaching on regicide shows, the supporters of Enlightenment were no less prone than its opponents to be quite uncritical in sweeping into the same argument very diverse and disparate evidence.

This was also illustrated by other authors who took up anti-Jesuit themes and who shared Luchet's general viewpoint. Traditional suspicions of the Society as a subversive and anti-monarchical force went back far beyond the polemics of the 1760s which had preceded and

---

[56] p. 123.
[57] p. 164. Joseph II had in 1781 forbidden any association to have foreign superiors, a regulation primarily affecting religious orders, but one also leading to the reorganisation of 'rectified' masonry in a system confined to the Empire. Then, in 1785, a 'Patent concerning Freemasons' empowered police to supervise lodges and required them to be officially registered. Luchet may also be reflecting here something of the tendency shown by the intelligentsia to desert freemasonry in the years just before 1789 which is remarked elsewhere.   [58] p. 165.

accompanied its dissolution.[59] The Jesuits' formal disappearance was soon followed by assertions that they continued to assert their influence in hidden ways. This was not wholly untrue (as Weishaupt's career showed), but some widely believed versions of this story were ludicrous. Some said they had resuscitated the Rosicrucian Order (and it is this which Luchet seems to imply) while others alleged that the Society had adopted Templar masonry as its cover. Views of this sort had been given much publicity before the Wilhelmsbad Convent, notably by Bode, who circularised his colleagues on the matter, and undoubtedly contributed to the distrust of the mystical Martinist group felt by the more Protestant and rationalist members of the Strict Observance on that occasion.[60] The Illuminati upheaval gave these accusations new vigour; it was soon even alleged that the Jesuits had probably infiltrated the Illuminati too.[61] More important, though, was the publicity Weishaupt's sympathisers gave to the opposing view that 'crypto-Catholicism', Rosicrucianism and mystical freemasonry had Jesuit support in their attacks on the Illuminati. The decade of the 1780s saw, therefore, a great reinforcement of one special version of secret society theory which was in essence absolutely opposed to the one which was to gain greatest currency after the Revolution. Were not the terminology anachronistic, we might say that the skeleton of the conspiratorial mythology of the Left, as well as that of the Right, can already be discerned.

There were, we are told, no fewer than six different theories of Jesuit complicity in masonry put forward in the 1780s (one in a work by Knigge).[62] In 1788 a Frenchman, Nicolas de Bonneville, having been initiated (he claimed) as a freemason, provided for his countrymen a version of Bode's ideas which reflected concerns similar to those of Luchet.[63] Bode had been in Paris in 1787 and had met Bonneville, possibly through the Loge des Amis Réunis. Certainly the parallel was close between Bode's earlier statements and Bonneville's *Les Jésuites*

---

[59] See M. Défourneaux, 'Complot maçonnique et complot jésuitique', *AHRF*, 1965, pp. 180–6, on the prophecy made by the Chevalier Folard in 1729 (which was later turned round and put to use by anti-masonic writers). Le Forestier draws attention (*La franc-maçonnerie Templière*, p. 635) to a Bohemian pamphlet of 1680 identifying the Jesuits with the Rosicrucians.

[60] Le Forestier, *La Franc-maçonnerie Templière*, pp. 636–41. On rationalists' fears of Jesuits see also Viatte, I, p. 301.

[61] By Göchhausen, says Epstein, p. 99.

[62] Le Forestier, *La franc-maçonnerie Templière*, p. 719, fn.

[63] Of Bonneville, an interesting figure, there is no adequate study. P. Le Harivel, *Nicolas de Bonneville pré-romantique et révolutionnaire* (Strasbourg, 1923) may be consulted. See also below, Ch. VI.

chassés de la Maçonnerie et leur poignard brisé par les Maçons, of which the thesis was that Jesuits had tried successfully to take over the direction of freemasonry and that in doing so they had perverted its true nature and diverted it from its true humanitarian and scientific tasks. Bonneville's tone was strongly anti-clerical and libertarian; his arguments were as unscientific and inferential as those of most other writers who have sought to uncover the key to masonic activities in the work of conspirators ('Voltaire lui-même est mort jésuite. En avait-il le moindre soupçon?').[64] Nevertheless, the book is interesting. Like Luchet's it shows how conspiratorial theory was usable by polemicists attached to the ideals of the Enlightenment and even to the aspirations of traditional and orthodox freemasonry. Such observers were now sometimes beginning to turn against freemasonry itself—or, at least, some of its varieties—and to criticise it from a flank where, in general, it had found support. This fed still further the growing public taste for the revelation of conspiracy which was about to be stimulated as never before by the outbreak of the French Revolution. Like the anti-Illuminati writers, Luchet and Bonneville not only promoted their own special points of view and sought to defend the ideals of the Enlightenment, but helped to reinforce a general notion that malevolent and secret human agencies could be discerned behind complicated and disturbing social facts.[65]

One episode which showed how deeply such convictions about long-maturing plots could infect political issues was the debate in France in the late 1780s over the proposal (later implemented by a royal edict) to extend limited civic rights to non-Catholics, which meant, substantially, to Protestants. This was bitterly resisted by the French clergy in their corporate capacity (they published their Remonstrances to the King) and by ecclesiastical polemicists among whom were, it was believed, ex-Jesuits continuing to conspire against toleration and enlightenment.[66] A conspiratorial interpretation of the episode was, however, much more prominent on the other side.[67] The act of a

[64] Bonneville, *Les Jésuites chassés*, II, p. 74 (quoted in Viatte, I, p. 307).

[65] More publicity was given to alarm about the Jesuits by Mirabeau in his book on the Prussian monarchy. The story rolled on into the Revolution; Le Forestier (*La franc-maçonnerie Templière*, p. 814) quotes from a pamphlet of 1790 a statement attributed to a Jesuit that 'depuis que le monde est monde, notre société existe sur la terre; nous nous sommes alternativement appelés Mages, Prêtres, Druides, Templars, Rose-Croix, Jésuites, Francs-maçons . . .'

[66] One such was the Abbé Barruel, on whom see below (p. 188).

[67] For an amplification of the abbreviated account which follows, see J. M. Roberts, 'The origins of a Mythology. Protestants, Freemasons and the French Revolution', *BIHR*, 1971, pp. 78–97.

reforming government was interpreted as the triumph of a long-matured plan to subvert the essentially religious foundations of the French monarchy. Two versions were put forward of the fundamental conspiracy and they were sometimes combined in varying mixtures. One attributed the whole business to the beneficiaries, the Protestants whose role throughout French history was a continuous demonstration of the inseparable connexion of their principles with republicanism, anarchy, violence, disloyalty and foreign interference in French affairs. In the other version, the Protestants were excuses, catspaws, or in some other way the instruments of a great Philosophe conspiracy, whose last great triumph had been the dissolution of the Jesuits and whose catchphrase of toleration was the carrier of the diseases of infidelity, immorality and presumption which would destroy State, Church and Society if left to rage unchecked.[68]

In the debate which raged in 1787 and 1788 on this issue, much was said which was later to be resurrected and incorporated in new versions of the secret society mythology in other contexts. Here, it is necessary only to note three of its features. The first is that it was in the debate which raged on this that we first encounter controversialists who were later to contribute importantly to conspiratorial literature after the outbreak of the Revolution. The second is the readiness of polemicists to interpret in terms of plots a discussion over a political issue which raised strong feelings. This readiness was present well before the meeting of the States-General and the colossal events which were to make such interpretations even more attractive. The final significant feature of this debate was its occasion. The royal edict was one of those novel, irritating extensions of state intervention with vested interest which, in part because of their novelty, could be interpreted almost as interventions with a divinely-ordained order. Men who advocated and engineered such changes were bound to be very wicked men indeed.

No doubt this is why, even before the Revolution and in spite of

---

[68] The theme of the intellectual conspiracy of the enlightened Philosophes was already central in French intellectual life, though perhaps its implications were more sharply defined and less pervasive than the concern over rationalism in Germany, where more than one established religious denomination existed. Its great stimulus was the publication of the correspondence of the Philosophes. Already freemasonry was said to be connected with the Enlightenment tendency. The earliest example I have come across is Belgian; the author of the *Lettre d'un Docteur en Théologie de l'Université de Louvain, à un Etudiant en Droit dans la même Université, touchant la Franc-maçonnerie* (Louvain, 1775) says that Christians should have nothing to do with the Craft, 'à moins qu'ils n'aient déjà déposé le personnage de Chrétien, et pris parti parmi la Secte philosophique qu'on remarque depuis quelque temps être très étroitement liée avec la Franc-Maçonnerie'.

traditional suspicions of the Jesuits, most examples of conspiratorial interpretations of history are already to be found taking the anti-Enlightenment line, using that term in a wide sense. This could appear even when writers might show some sympathy and understanding of what they attacked. Even a respect for the allegedly benevolent aims of Weishaupt could be combined with a concern showing the deep nature of the alarm he had produced. One such example was a Count Windischgrätz, who published in 1788 his views on the subject.[69] This was after Weishaupt had attempted a justification of the activities of the Illuminati which masked his early atheistical and materialist position, and set out a more spiritual justification of the Illuminati teachings and symbolism.[70] This work was to be followed, over the next few years, by a long series of philosophical works (the earliest of which Windischgrätz may have read) which suggest that more than a tactical change was eventually involved. Weishaupt had a confused scheme of re-interpreting his original materialist position in a much more idealist way.[71] Windischgrätz apparently accepted this as sincere and acquitted Weishaupt of subversive intentions in the usual sense. Nevertheless, he addressed himself to the undoubted fact that Weishaupt had adumbrated a theory of secret societies as institutions of educational and moral reform.[72] With this, Windischgrätz took issue. He believed that it was of the nature of secret societies to be dangerous whatever the intentions of those who directed them. This was the theme of his long pamphlet.

Windischgrätz was interested seriously in moral and philosophical problems, and much of what he says is taken up with long arguments about free will and determinism, but the gist of what he has to say

[69] *Objections aux sociétés secrètes*, London, 1788.

[70] *Das verbesserte System der Illuminaten mit allen seinen Graden und Einrichtungen.*

[71] The list of the relevant publications appears at the beginning of Le Forestier's discussion of 'le testament philosophique' in *Les Illuminés*, p. 557. During the 1790s Weishaupt seems to have established himself as a serious philosopher, if we are to accept the statement of one of the earliest proponents of Kantian philosophy in England, A. F. M. Willick: 'without entering upon an enquiry into Mr Weishaupt's *moral* character I can safely aver, that his *literary* works have been received, upon the Continent, with almost universal approbation. In this assertion, I am supported by the Conductors of the first German Reviews in general, and particularly by the respectable evidence of Prof. Staeudlin himself, as well as by that of the celebrated Prof. Eberhard of Halle, both of whom have ranked Mr Weishaupt's writings among the first philosophical compositions of Germany' (*Elements of the Critical Philosophy* (London, 1798), p. ii).

[72] Le Forestier, *Les Illuminés*, pp. 595–612. Windischgrätz recommends Weishaupt's book 'à tout homme, dont le cœur est droit et pur ... il se persuadera, que toute cette Société probablement a été indignement calomniée. . . .' (p. 1).

about secret societies is that they are likely to encourage habits of mind and behaviour destructive of attention to the ordinary moral and social duties. The danger of degeneration from the high ideals of a secret brotherhood will always be present because of the difficulty of reconciling the secret obligations to the society with those of the outside world. Claims to use the opportunities of secret organisation for the preparation of the regeneration of the world are always to be regarded as dubious, given men's ordinary weaknesses. This is particularly true, suggests Windischgrätz, of the techniques for selection and instruction of members which Weishaupt recommends. These certainly had something of a Moral Rearmament flavour about them; Weishaupt had made much of the need for a close scrutiny of a man's character in order to appreciate its strength and weakness with a view to its manipulation.[73] Windischgrätz felt that it was unlikely that the directors of the Illuminati could have been sure that the men they would recruit would always themselves have sufficient strength of character not to abuse the techniques of control made available to them: 'l'Homme qui se fait une Etude de gouverner les Esprits, est rarement un Homme dont les vues sont droites, et presque toujours un Esprit médiocre.'[74]

Windischgrätz also went on to argue that Weishaupt's understanding of the basis of the morality he was preaching was defective[75] and to utter a general warning about the dangers of recommending a universal and indiscriminate benevolence which, in some ways, anticipates Burke. He recalls those who sought the good of mankind at large to their immediate and personal duties. 'Commencez par vous convaincre, que vous n'avez pas le droit; que vous n'êtes pas les Envoyés du Ciel; que vous ne pouvez, en aucun cas, vous livrer à ce désir aux dépens de votre devoir.'[76] Even if there are despots on the thrones of Europe, some of them are enlightened and they will respond to argument which points out their errors; this will be a more efficacious way of reform than the forming of secret societies. 'Si vous voulez former des sociétés secrètes, formez-en, mais bornez-vous à rechercher, dans le

---

[73] See, e.g., Le Forestier, *Les Illuminés*, p. 57.

[74] p. 11. Windischgrätz may have had in mind not only Weishaupt's statements, but Knigge's *Uber dem Umgang mit Menschen*.

[75] He has an interesting pro-Enlightenment argument here which shows the extent to which Weishaupt had already swung round to a new position. He argues that since atheists have been able to arrive at it and sustain it, the idea of justice is independent of the idea of God. It is, in fact, the same as the idea of human happiness; morality need not, therefore, be established, as Weishaupt has asserted, on the principles of the spirituality of the soul and the existence of God.

[76] p. 54.

silence de vos Cabinets, ce qu'il faudroit enseigner aux hommes, pour les rendre heureux.'[77]

Windischgrätz, it is clear, was not an uncharitable or obsessed critic. Far from it; his pamphlet is refreshingly sensible and one of the first to show some commonsense in dealing with the Illuminati. His considered judgment against secret societies as instruments of social regeneration is, therefore, important as a demonstration of the depth of misgiving which secret societies were likely to arouse after the exposure of the Illuminati.[78] If a balanced and not unfriendly judge could be so unsure of the bona fides of the movement, what was to be expected of the easily excited and alarmed public at large? There was plenty of dangerous material lying about by 1789 from which to derive a real hysteria against secret societies. The Illuminati was only the most recent expression of the danger which many were beginning to feel. It was the one verified example of a secret society working with subversive purposes, but it confirmed and revivified older suspicions of secret sects and societies, above all of freemasonry. The curious and disreputable people who had been prominent in the great elaboration of such bodies which marked the second half of the century were to be remembered and taken seriously because of it. It was recalled that the masons had always proudly stressed the secret and remote origins of their rites and doctrines. The Templar legend had recently been given great publicity, in all its Jacobite, Rosicrucian, occultist variations. People began to read again pamphlets like *Les Francs-maçons écrasés*. Some people may even have remembered the Papal condemnations, though they do not seem to have been much mentioned in contemporary literature. Above all, since the Illuminati had tried, perhaps with more success than had been discovered, to make use of the masonic lodges, it was coming to be feared that the nature of masonic organisation and its secrecy would prevent further detection of subversive aims in their midst. Even freemasons had revealed their alarm that, unbeknown, their Craft might perhaps have been subverted by the Jesuits.

Such thinking may have contributed to an observed feature in French freemasonry in the 1780s which, in the light of subsequent events and allegations, seems ironic. This is the incontestable fact of decline, which seems to have affected lodges of both aristocratic and middle-class composition; many 'lodges' seem to have had no more

[77] p. 55.
[78] It is worthwhile to recall that the Illuminati were not the only secret society of the period to claim to foster moral regeneration. See Le Forestier, *Les Illuminés*, p. 612, fn.

than a paper existence in 1789.[79] Yet this was hardly noticed and, when the Revolution began, a reviving suspicion of freemasonry was to take its place among the other elements of the later myth of the secret societies which were assembled and available. The masons were much in people's minds at a moment when decades of reforming activity had disturbed and irritated vested interests. All that was needed was a great crisis and one was about to burst. With that, the transformation of the eighteenth-century theories of intellectual and spiritual plots into the paranoiac political vision of the nineteenth would be achieved.

[79] Le Forestier, *La franc-maçonnerie Templière*, pp. 820–3, summarises the evidence.

Chapter VI

The Secret Societies and the French Revolution

THE CHALLENGE TO EXPLANATION

I⊤ is very easy today to underrate the emotional shock of the French Revolution. Because it opened an era of revolution in which we still live, we are used to the idea of revolution in a way in which the men of the eighteenth century were not. The unrolling after 1789 of a seemingly endless series of events not only novel and surprising, but shocking and terrible, quickly led men to see what happened in France as a unique, sometimes glorious, sometimes frightening phenomenon, and later to speak of *The* Revolution as if it were a living, personal force, whether malevolent or benign.

The special character of the events in France appeared very rapidly. What had begun by looking like an old-fashioned 'Fronde' of self-interested noblemen was transformed by the meeting of the States-General in May 1789 and the people's entry on the stage. The capture of the Bastille and the peasant risings which flared up in the summer made it impossible for the Crown to dismiss the National Assembly, as the States-General soon proclaimed themselves. There followed a mass of legislation, which, whatever the qualifications historians have detected in its motives, effectiveness and enforcement, transformed Frenchmen's formal relations to one another, regulated property afresh and provided a new frame for the government of the country. This was an unprecedented revolution. By 1791, feudalism had been abolished, the Church had lost its lands and its juridical independence of the State, and the attempt to recast the traditional polity as a constitutional monarchy was well under way. The attempt failed; in 1792 the monarchy was overthrown after a bloody coup. Soon afterwards the notorious September massacres horrified Europe and Louis XVI went to the scaffold in January 1793. The Revolution then seemed to turn on its own children. Revolutionaries fell out; the Girondins were proscribed and when Charlotte Corday assassinated Marat she sealed their fate. Their execution or flight took place during a civil war all the more terrible because its background was a foreign invasion. Great efforts and much bloodshed—the system of the Terror—

brought France through the crisis of 1793, but, as further purges showed, the success of the Committee of Public Safety was to lead only to the intensification of violence. Hundreds were guillotined. Danton and his followers followed those of Hébert to the scaffold. In his turn, Robespierre, the bogyman of the counter-revolution, followed them. With further executions and the last spasms of popular revolution in the 'journées' of 1795, the Revolution at last reached the slightly less stormy but still choppy waters of the Directory; from 1796, although plots, coups and purges continued, they were less bloody (the 'dry guillotine' of exile to Guyane was more frequently used than the blade in the Place Nationale). They ended, at last, in another revolution, the coup d'état of Brumaire which brought the young General Bonaparte to power.

These events were astonishing and terrifying enough, even without the exaggeration and distortion which they soon received. Their impact was greatly increased by the propaganda of the emigration. The fright that they gave to Europe, nevertheless, was based on something more actual than the mere demonology of the counter-revolution. From 1792 France was at war. After early setbacks, she more than once triumphantly carried the war into her enemies' territories; given the inherent strength of France, this was itself hardly surprising. Yet it seemed so, because it had been assumed that she was too much weakened by revolution to play her traditional part as a great power. Further and more alarming surprises were to follow. Where her armies went, revolutionary institutions and revolutionary ideas had followed them, whether the governments of France wanted it or not. A new element of ideology had entered international life. Since 1792, when the Republic announced in a famous decree that it offered friendship to oppressed peoples everywhere, the discontented of all lands had been able to look to an avenging and protecting power. From 1793 onwards, that power was exporting revolution. First in Belgium and the prince-bishopric of Liège, the legislation of the Republic carried forward everywhere the benefits of secularisation and the Rights of Man. When the French armies broke into the Rhineland and Holland and, later, Italy and Switzerland, they found sympathisers there who eagerly helped in setting up new satellite republics with constitutions on the French model, and social and legal institutions to suit. The example of these republics was chilling to the authorities of what was already called the Ancien Régime. Two world orders seemed to be in confrontation. And if the experience of the first decade of the Revolution meant anything, it was that there were in every country, openly or secretly, sympathisers with the Revolution waiting the day when they might transform their countries as France had been transformed.

This was the unfolding pattern which explains the near-hysterical state of shock of the European monarchies by the end of the first decade of the Revolution. Their initial reaction to the Revolution had been one of realpolitik; the States-General would embarrass the French monarchy and weaken it as a European power for some time. This might offer opportunities for dabbling in intrigues such as those which had already presented themselves in the complicated domestic troubles of the United Provinces, where British, French and Prussian statesmen had been hard at work stirring the pot in 1789. Catherine the Great and Joseph II could not find the weakening of French influence regrettable at a moment when they had their own pre-occupations in Eastern Europe and a new partition of Poland was approaching, though they were a little surprised at the swiftness with which events moved in the first year of the Revolution. What was startlingly to change foreigners' views was the revelation that a more fundamental change was on foot. The sweeping away of the dynastic state might not be unprecedented, in that Great Britain had lived under a contractual monarchy since 1688. But the English constitution never embodied a universal threat; it was, as Englishmen proudly proclaimed, peculiar and local. And although English legal institutions embodied the principle of legal equality of status to a greater degree than those of any other state, English society did not reject in practice the organising principle of a hierarchy of birth which was now proclaimed to be swept away in France. Any American advance towards democracy could be discounted; everyone expected that infant federation to succumb to internal divisions (only the France of the Terror caused Europeans to revise their views of the inherent weakness of Republics as governments of anything other than small city-states). With dynasticism, too, went established Christianity; nowhere in Western Europe had it ever been asserted since their appearance that rulers should not support and urge formal adherence to the Christian religion. Beyond these great changes, when confiscation of property began, and when the doctrine of popular sovereignty as a solvent of vested and prescriptive right was advanced, the horrified spectators became aware, like Louis XVI on the morning when he was told of the fall of the Bastille, that they witnessed not a revolt but a revolution.

This background, above all, must be kept in mind if we are to understand the sudden, sweeping success of the myth of the secret societies. The scale and violence of the changes that men were called upon to account for soon seemed to exhaust all conventional and familiar categories of explanation.[1] Some new dimension of understanding was needed. There was, too, a certain unity of principle and a certain recurrence of pattern in so many of the things that were occurring: this made men look for general and overall explanations. The changes of 1789, for example, were breathtakingly swift for many Frenchmen; they deplored them and it was tempting to see in them the marks of careful orchestration and planning.[2] This is a frame of mind which is easy to understand; historians and politicians have always been prone to it. Even now, we still speak of *the* French Revolution though we refer to an immensely complicated process; this is because we feel that there was a sense in which it was a unity. Clemenceau once said that the Revolution was a bloc; he meant that there was little point in discriminating about what to accept or reject in its legacy and many people have shared that view. From such a position, which is justifiable, it is easy to slip into the fallacy that to identify the Revolution as a general process permits the inference that there must be a single general cause which explains it.

Simple explanations in terms of single causes are easy to grasp and have often been accepted by people who had enough information to know better—many Marxist historians, for example. For the layman, unused to historical analysis, and above all for the frightened layman, the appeal of such an idea requires no elaboration. It seems to unify all the complicated data which is otherwise so difficult to understand. 'Communism' and 'capitalism' are simple ideas which have made it possible for many people to grapple with the complexities of the world since 1945 or 1917. They seem to make simple sense of very involved processes and, above all, provide an explanation which still attributes responsibility to human agents and can therefore provide a release for fear, indignation and moral outrage.[3] Plot theories of history prosper

[1] Not, of course, that older ones ceased to be employed. People were always to attribute much to the simple working of personal ambition. Eighteen months after the summoning of the States-General, the author of an émigré pamphlet, *Les conspirateurs démasqués* (Turin, 1790), the parlementaire Ferrand (Antoine François Claude) still interpreted all that had happened in terms of the work of two rival plotters, Necker and the Duke of Orléans.

[2] D'Antraigues, for example, seems to have been much affected by what he thought were clear signs of careful planning and preparation of the 'abolition' of feudal rights and dues on the night of 4 August by hidden manipulation of the Assembly. See his *Lettre de Louis d'Antraigues à M. des . . . sur le compte qu'il doit à ses Commettans de sa conduite aux Etats-Généraux* (Paris, 1790), pp. 63–73.

[3] Not all contemporaries, of course, needed this release. Cf. the sensible Malouet (*Mémoires de Malouet*, 2nd edn. (Paris, 1874), I, p. 292), 'Je n'ai point vu de faction

because of the need for such release. That this need was for a long time especially acute provided the fundamental support of the myth of the secret societies in its heyday. The importance of the French Revolution was that it was the first event of such importance that could awake such a response throughout the civilised world. It provided facts of universal significance which needed to be explained and for which quite extra-ordinary explanations alone seemed to be appropriate. Moreover, the seeds of such explanations were to hand in the masonic legacy of the eighteenth century and in the rich confusion of ideas and rumour which its derivations had generated by 1789.

Such explanations were not, of course, the only ones available, nor the first. Others, much older, could be brought forward which also went far beyond the simple traditional explanations which relied on personal ambition as a source of conspiracy. The French Revolution was, for example, interpreted by many people in terms of millenarian expectation, providential design or divine retribution. Many confident prophecies had been made during the eighteenth century of some great coming calamity; they were eagerly recalled after 1789 when the Revolution appeared to justify them.[4] Long before that, too, Sweden-borgian illuminés had seen in gathering signs of storm the fulfilment of their expectations of the end of the age; others predicted the Second Coming. Yet others eagerly awaited the coming catastrophe because it appeared to portend moral and social regeneration (a view sometimes later given a sinister significance by those looking for contrivance and conspiracy).[5] When the storm had broken, much more emphatic assertions of the providential nature of the Revolution were made.[6]

---

dirigeante, pas même le club des Jacobins, qui vivait au jour le jour, comme le parti de la cour.'

[4] For a gathering of some texts, see *Prophetic Conjecture on the French Revolution and other recent and shortly expected events* (London, 1793).

[5] For examples of this apocalyptic mood, which persisted well into the nineteenth century, see Viatte, esp. I, pp. 98–9, 128, 232–8; II, pp. 16–18.

[6] The best known is de Maistre's *Considérations sur la France* of 1796, but in this genre it is not always easy to separate a legitimate heightening of language from a true conviction that a single providential influence is at work. See, e.g., Saint-Martin's *Lettre à un ami ou considérations politiques, philosophiques et religieuses sur la Révolution française*, Paris, An III (esp. p. 12). Viatte (II, pp. 69, 93) suggests that the similarity of tone in de Maistre's book and that of Saint-Martin is explained by the association of both with Willermoz. An earlier example of the providential interpretation of the Revolution is the anonymous pamphlet *La véritable politique à l'usage des Emigrés Français* (Cologne, 1794) whose theme is summed up in a sentence: 'Dieu dirige les événemens: il a voulu par la révolution nous châtier, parce que nous étions des enfans coupables et nous rappeler nos devoirs que nous avions perdus de vue' (p. 6).

Soon there were to be assertions of diabolical intervention, too, which in the nineteenth century were to blur into some versions of the secret society mythology and anti-masonry. Quite soon, also, the stories of a Protestant or Philosophe plot which had been formulated before 1789 were given a new application. There was, therefore, plenty to add to the legacy of anti-masonic suspicion and the recent scare about the Illuminati which prepared men to accept ideas of malevolent agency and of extraordinary significance as explanations of what was happening to them after 1789.

Finally, the fact of development has to be recalled from the outset. We have to take into account the way in which the actual unrolling of the Revolution produced important changes in thinking and feeling which disposed more and more people to accept general, monolithic explanations. As the years passed, both revolution and counter-revolution generated excitements and fears which could very quickly erode any firm grasp of reality or even of probability.[7] One widespread and well-known example was the way in which the xenophobia—and, in particular, anglophobia—came out in stories of Pitt's gold as a corrupting agent.[8] Another example was the readiness to assume that there existed a much greater degree of unanimity and hostility to the Revolution than in fact could ever have been achieved by those who feared it; already in September 1789 it was said that the repercussions of French events in Liège and Switzerland were leading to the forming of a secret confederation of princes against the Revolution, in league with the Austrian queen, Marie Antoinette.[9] Such exaggerations and

[7] In what immediately follows I deliberately select some examples current in pro-revolutionary circles: the readiness to accept stories of plots on the other side has been given due attention already by other scholars (e.g. F. Baldensperger, *Le mouvement des idées dans l'émigration française (1789–1815)* (Paris, 1924), II, pp. 12–15) and will in any case be amply illustrated later in this chapter.

[8] By no means only among revolutionaries. See the comments of the émigré Vaudreuil, to the King's brother, Artois, at the end of 1789: 'je ne mets pas en doute (*quoi qu'on vous ait dit*) que l'argent des Anglais ne soit le principal moteur de la révolution que nous avons éprouvée et celle du Brabant. Ils ne nous ont pas pardonné la guerre d'Amérique, et je sais que le marquis de Lansdowne, autrefois Lord Shelburne, avait une correspondance très-suivie avec l'abbé Morellet et plusieurs autres chefs de la démocratie; que son fils, Lord Wycombe, a été à Paris pendant tout le temps de la révolution et animait tous nos jeunes gens. . . .' It was said, too, that Lansdowne was about to enter the English government. (*Correspondance Intime du Comte de Vaudreuil et du Comte d'Artois pendant l'émigration*, ed. L. Pingaud (Paris, 1889), I, p. 74. See also pp. 96, 99–100.) See, also, below, p. 185, for the connexion of distrust of foreigners with another theme, the dislike of Protestantism.

[9] Buchez and Roux, *Histoire parlementaire de la Révolution française* (Paris, 1834–8), II, pp. 424–5.

F

misinterpretations are easy to understand. Much more confusing and significant is the quickly evident readiness of people to see the hidden hands of plotters in facts which now seem to have obvious and simple explanations. Memories of the rumours of the 'pacte de famine', for example, spilled over into stories of plots to starve Paris by cutting off its food supplies.[10] When the Commune of Paris reported to the representatives of the city the activities of its 'comité de recherches' in November 1789, it distinguished no fewer than three major groups of plots, whose aims ran from the kidnapping of the King to attempts to spread seditious rumours.[11] An incident such as the discovery of concealed arms carried by courtiers led to further suspicion;[12] soon people were generally talking of assassination threats and plots against the lives of individuals (and this was long before the murder of Marat). As the temperature rose, such language became habitual on both wings of the political spectrum. The extreme revolutionaries gloried in the danger they supposed themselves to run and exploited it to gain popularity.[13] One collective response was the brutal madness of the September Massacres. With the civil war and Terror, the obsession with plots and personal danger became even more intense. In Robespierre the line between illusion and reality can hardly be drawn, so intense was his conviction that obstacles to the revolutionary government of France could only originate in the schemings of malevolent plotters. His example may be special, in that few hated and feared with such intensity, but it was fed by and contributed to the atmosphere.[14]

[10] For examples, see J. Godechot, *The Taking of the Bastille* (London, 1970), esp. pp. 170–1.

[11] *Archives Parlementaires*, X, 339.

[12] See the crucial instance of the searching of courtiers by Lafayette's men, 28 February 1791.

[13] See, for example, Collot d'Herbois' assertion (25 April 1792) that 'depuis six mois je marche au milieu des assassins' (Buchez and Roux, XIV, p. 133), or, on the other side, the vanity of the conclusion of Guadet's speech of the same day (*ibid.*, p. 141).

[14] For an example, see Robespierre's reference (5 December 1792, quoted in J. M. Thompson, *Robespierre*, I, 294) to Mirabeau. His witch-hunting mentality leads him confidently (his sincerity cannot be doubted) to the view that Mirabeau *would have been* a counter-revolutionary, had he lived! His language is always full of exploitations of the suggestibility of his audience and never more than when his own angry, persecuted sense of innocence blurs into his public concern: 'je développerai un système suivi de conspirations. C'est par des rapprochements que j'y parviendrai; car des discours, des phrases lâchées à propos, de sourdes intrigues, sont les moyens employés pour détruire l'opinion publique, et miner la liberté. Je vous ferai voir par quelles trames on me rend l'objet des plus affreuses persecutions.' (from his indentification of the Girondin 'conspiracy' against him, at the Jacobin Club, 25 April 1792. Buchez and Roux, XIV, p. 143).

It is very difficult in such matters to separate the role of the individua who gives shape and definition to collective fears from the collective readiness to believe him. Fortunately, for our purpose, this does not much matter. Both elements register the fact that French political culture—and this affected equally what came later to be called Left and Right—had evolved to the point at which explanation in terms of plots would find an eager audience, just as they had done in English politics a hundred years before. As the Revolution progressed, more violent and more and more destructive, so these ideas tended to generate action which, in turn, lent colour to the exaggerations of the other side. Finally, we should remember that besides excitement, fear and hatred, millions of Frenchmen in these years also experienced hunger, deprivation and hardship, with all the psychological stress that accompanied them. The Great Fear of 1789 was only the last and biggest of many mass panics in town and countryside and the terrible conditions of that year were essential to its explosion. Once it had taken place, it, too, fed into the political atmosphere not only yet more evidence of the existence of hidden hands, but yet greater needs of extraordinary explanations in malevolent contrivance.

It did not matter that although 'plotters' were proclaimed to have been exposed the misfortunes they had been charged with still continued. The logic of the plot theory is open-ended and its psychology always satisfying: the punished few are shown by the continuation of misfortune itself not to have been the real directors of the plot after all, but only its instruments. Somewhere, still to be uncovered, there remain the 'supérieurs inconnus', the secret managers of everything that happens, from the execution of the King to the invasion of the Papal States, from the famine of 1789 to the coup of Thermidor. A Lafayette or a Robespierre, though culpable, is at last only a puppet at the end of strings pulled by invisible managers; his very failure and personal disaster are evidence of this. This is the fully developed plot logic, deeply satisfactory: heads I win, tails you lose. Nothing may not be fitted into it. Once accepted in form, then any particular version identifying particular villains can be filled in as necessary and the French Revolution was to provoke many versions before it was done. That of the secret societies of masonic origin was the most successful and was to have most influence on the shape of later political irrationalism. It became the most popular of the many monolithic, simple explanations of the French Revolution which were available. Rich with legendary detail which could be plausibly fitted into the pattern of later events, it was mysterious and splendidly unverifiable. It was already associated with great persons who were to be conspicuous in the Revolution. Above all, it could be plausibly linked to many other versions of the conspiracy theory of the Revolution. But it is just this potential which makes it so hard to trace the growth of the anti-masonic myth of the Revolution in its pure form; almost always it is mixed up with something else.

FREEMASONS AND THE REVOLUTION

It is useful in reading the nonsense written and talked about plots during the revolutionary decade to have some impression of what the actual history of freemasonry was in those years, and of what freemasons actually did to attract notice as a serious political influence. This is by no means as easy to achieve as might appear and this is not merely because of the secrecy which ought to have surrounded masonic activity (in practice, it often did not). There is, if anything, too much information, and it is best to recall at the outset a simple point, though one all too easy to overlook: that, long before questions of interpretation arise, the 'facts' have to be scrutinised with the greatest care. They are thickly studded with plain error, arising from misinformation and misconception. It was well known, for example, that the Duke of Brunswick was head of the Strict Observance; when, therefore, the Duke of Brunswick accepted defeat at Valmy in 1792 and so readily withdrew the allied army under his command, thus sparing a revolutionary France an almost certain defeat, the inference seemed to many people clear that a masonic understanding was at work between the two sides. The basic flaw in this inference lay in its premise, never questioned, that the duke was in each case the same great Germanic masonic dignitary; unfortunately, he was not. The two were uncle and nephew. This level of elementary confusion and inaccuracy is typical and must constantly be borne in mind. From the start it vitiates many of the 'facts' alleged about freemasonry's part in the Revolution.

Another difficulty which soon appears is that no clear line can be drawn between organised and individual masonic activity; this was both overlooked and exploited by the anti-masonic propagandists. They should have been more scrupulous, but it is bound to be difficult to separate men's actions as masons from their actions in other roles. It should have been clear, too, that whatever the Craft was by 1789, it could not present a united front. French lodges enjoyed almost complete individual freedom to conduct their own affairs and many of them did not acknowledge the Grand Orient. Apart from its regulation of grades, that body had little in the way of doctrine to impose even on those lodges accepting its authority. And outside this obedience and that of Grande Loge, there further stretched the ramifying exotic and breakaway tendencies and obediences.

In fact, when we find evidence of group activity in the Revolution by masons forming part of one of the two great obediences in France, it nearly always turns out to be explicable on grounds other than masonic, even when making use of masonic organisation. Usually it is a matter of a lodge or a few lodges providing opportunities for people interested in the agitation of certain political questions to get together. De Maistre was a freemason and, although he was always willing to defend the Craft against the nonsensical charges levelled at it, he seems to have been willing to concede at least this much when he acknowledged that if masonry had served the Revolution, it had done so as an 'association de clubs'.[15] It should not seem surprising or sinister; it simply means that both the lodge organisation and the familiarity which it created meant that freemasonry was in principle helpful to collective action. Moreover, this was at a moment when the traditional forms of collective action—corporations, orders of society—seemed less satisfactory than hitherto for this purpose, and when few other such nuclei had yet come into being outside England.[16] This should be by itself sufficient to explain why some lodges appeared to be foci of discussion and propaganda during the crisis of 1787-9. Some may also have influenced the drawing-up of cahiers for representatives to the States-General; it would certainly be surprising if these documents, usually reflecting the interests and concerns of local notables, should never have been influenced by discussion in the lodge, one of the few places where such men were likely to come together socially. As informal electoral organisations, too, we may assume without inferring a sinister purpose that the lodges had a part to play; certainly a large number of masons were elected to the States-General.[17] Those men who stood out in local communities as possible deputies were likely also to be voted for by fellow masons who had seen them in the lodge. There were few social institutions which could have competed with lodges

[15] Quoted by Baldensperger, II, p. 17. De Maistre was writing in 1793. See also below, p. 295.

[16] One which had, of course, was the Amis des Noirs, which was suspect to those who feared secret societies.

[17] G. Martin suggests that nearly five-sixths of the Third Estate were masons, but he wrote as a mason proud to accept the charge of masonic responsibility for the Revolution and exaggerated manifestations of it. See the review by A. Mathiez, AHRF, 1926.

as informal organisers of electoral support, and for the bourgeoisie this was specially important. This, however, by no means implies that all freemasons, even if they favoured the Revolution, approved of its effect on the life of the lodges. In Mayenne, for example, a lodge at Laval listened to one of its members pronouncing a eulogy of the States-General in early July 1789. Afterwards, another mason who was present opposed the reception of the text in the archives on the grounds that such a speech was a political act and therefore foreign to the principles of freemasonry. His view was taken sufficiently seriously for the matter to be referred to the Grand Orient for adjudication—and the objector's point of view was subsequently upheld.[18]

A few years later, such masonic reactions would be overlooked or forgotten, just as, in retrospect, it was also to be forgotten by many Frenchmen how widespread had been enthusiasm and pleasure over the events of 1789. It was not sinister that the excitement of that year should sometimes have found expression in masonic gatherings, if only because the sort of men who were masons were typical of the élite of France and had few other regular gatherings—except the clubs which quickly appeared—where they could express their enthusiasm. There was nothing specially significant about this, but some masons were no doubt on occasion carried away into language which associated them more strongly and particularly with the Revolution than was afterwards to prove agreeable. A specimen of such rhetoric has been recorded from a Breton lodge where, just after the fall of the Bastille, a mason asserted that 'c'est de nos temples et de ceux élevés à la saine philosophie que sont parties les premières étincelles du feu sacré qui, s'étandant rapidement de l'Orient à l'Occident, du Midi au septentrion de la France, a embrasé les cœurs de tous les citoyens'. This sort of imagery was later to be much quoted against freemasons and the speaker continued, equally rashly, with an eulogy of 'le jour un roi citoyen vient annoncer qu'il veut commander à un peuple libre et former de son superbe empire une vaste loge dans laquelle tous les bons Français vont véritablement être frères'.[19] Such exaltation may have been natural, given the temper of the times, but such rhetoric, a sort of moral takeover bid for the Revolution, was later only too easily to be used against freemasons. Indeed, a whole anti-masonic

[18] Bouton and Lepage, p. 92.
[19] Quoted in RISS, V, p. 2653. I do not know whether these words were published in 1789, though possibly the reference (L. Maître, in L'Humanité nouvelle, October 1903, pp. 611–21) would reveal this. Do they imply some special appreciation of the esoteric, mysticising tendencies in masonry which the Grand Orient had resisted? The evidence is too slight to say, but the possibility is intriguing.

literature was to rest on misinterpretations made possible by the figurative language of some masons.

The Grand Orient was always cautious, as its judgment to the Laval lodge has already suggested. The circulars it sent to provincial lodges show an interesting evolution. On the eve of the Revolution they only pointed out the danger to the Craft which lay in disorderly conduct—such as gambling—or the holding of lodges in 'profane' settings. From the early winter of 1789–90 there comes a change of tone which might be termed 'political', but limited to an urging of the importance of teaching the new duties of the citizen and of subscribing to patriotic donations. Soon the circulars of the Grand Orient were asserting that the conduct of masonry in the Revolution had convinced the profane that the calumnies of the past were baseless. By 1791 the tone changed again; they were pointing out that the duties of the citizen and the freemason were perfectly coherent—a striking assertion, since it implied, apparently, that some masons had found this difficult to believe. By this time, the lodges were beginning to crumble and there are complaints of empty coffers at the Grand Orient. But before the circulars came to an end, one of January 1792 said that masons could congratulate themselves in contributing to the dissipation of the clouds which had so long concealed the torch of philosophy and reason.[20] The most significant point about such an evolution of language and material seems to be its continuation under the Revolution of the usual masonic caution in public affairs and debate. The Grand Orient moved with opinion, rather than ahead of it.

One well-known area of masonic activity which was bound to attract suspicion was to be found in the army. It has often been suggested that it explains the poor support given by the army to the authorities in 1789.[21] This is, to say the least, not proven. The Gardes françaises, a notoriously badly behaved regiment, certainly proved inadequate support for the régime in the crisis, but this need not be attributed to the existence of a lodge among them before the Revolution.[22] It probably owes as much to their contamination by civilian contact during a long period when they were stationed in the capital. There is no evidence that freemasons did anything to provoke the even more alarming signs of indiscipline in the army which appeared in 1790,

[20] These circulars are discussed in E. Lesueur, 'Le G. O. de France et la loge La Fidelité d'Hesdin (1788–92)', AR, 1913.

[21] e.g. by G. Martin, quoted in H. Soanen, 'La Franc-maçonnerie et l'armée pendant la Révolution et l'Empire', AHRF, 1928, p. 531.

[22] Soanen. The author of Les conspirateurs démasqués had drawn attention to them, 'corrompus depuis si longtems' (p. 33) but without blaming freemasonry for this.

when, indeed, mutinies often occurred against officers known to be freemasons. Nor did regimental lodges prosper any better than civilian as the Revolution went on; during the Terror they disappeared, and did not revive until after Brumaire.

In the States-General and National Assembly, the circumstantial evidence of masonic activity found by those who cared to look for it is always inconclusive and ambiguous. The presence of many well-known freemasons among deputies—Sieyes, Orléans, Lafayette—was, of course, soon remarked. But it seems certain that these men would have been prominent in the affairs of the Assembly anyway. Their association—and that of other, less well known, but active and effective, masons—with particular measures and proposals is also inconclusive. Even concerted action by groups in which freemasons were prominent does not take us far. The Comité de Trente, for example, whose role in the Assembly's abolition of feudalism on the night of 4 August 1789 was so important, was not itself a masonic body, although its membership included several members of two celebrated lodges, the Neuf Sœurs and that of the Rue du Coq-Heron.[23] Yet this example shows very clearly how circumstantial evidence could be scraped up about masonic participation in the Revolution of sufficient plausibility to satisfy people who sought to discern conspiracy, for some went so far as to say that the name itself of the Comité de Trente referred to the thirtieth degree of Scottish masonry, the so-called Knights of Kadosch. In part this was because the idea of collective political action by persons not otherwise linked to one another was at that time new and unfamiliar, natural as it may seem to us today. The eighteenth-century mind, outside England and North America, found it very difficult to grapple with the new world of political organisation whose most striking expression was the new invention of the political 'club'. People saw in the very existence of these new and unfamiliar bodies a sinister pattern. The Club Breton, for example, the source of the later and more famous Jacobin Club, was originally built (as its name suggests) around the Breton deputies who came to the States-General. Later, this fact seemed much less interesting to some people than the parallel fact that its original membership had been almost entirely masonic. One of its outstanding early leaders, Le Chapelier, was a well-known freemason. It was recalled later that many of the Breton deputies had played an outstanding part in the pre-revolutionary struggles of the Breton Provincial Estates which in some ways had pre-figured, as if in rehearsal, the troubles of the States-General. It was de Kerengal,

[23] Michon, *passim*.

a freemason and a member of this group, who in the night of 4 August joined with d'Aiguillon (another freemason), to propose the abolition of feudalism.

Another body about which even greater alarm was felt and in which the hand of freemasonry was discerned was the Cercle Social. This was not a club; it had no formal membership and any citizen might address its meetings. The words of its founders show its comprehensiveness: 'nous invitons . . . tous les clubs, *toutes les loges,* toutes les sociétés nationales et étrangères à s'unir à nous pour déliberer . . . Nous declarons reconnaître pour membres de la Conféderation Universelle, les Electeurs de 1789 dans tout l'Empire, les Amis de la Liberté de la Presse, *tous les Francs-Maçons de l'Univers, quel que soit leur système particulier,* les Amis de la Constitution, Gardes Nationales, et tous ceux qui ont été élus par le Peuple à quelque charge publique.' [24] Associated with the Cercle, too, was a press which produced various periodicals, of which the most famous was the *Bouche de Fer* of 1790–1. At the Cercle Social and in the pages of the *Bouche de Fer* strong egalitarian and revolutionary views were expressed; the name of the periodical itself arose from the suggestion that a 'bouche de fer' or sealed letter-box should be installed in each commune to receive denunciations of abuses and suggestions for action which would be considered by an elected body, La Censure, in each department. The Cercle Social itself appears to have ceased to meet after July 1791, but its founders continued to play a conspicuous part in the journalism of the Revolution.

One of them we have already met: Nicolas de Bonneville, the author of *Les Jésuites chassés de la Maçonnerie.* [25] His colleague, the Abbé Fauchet, a freemason and co-founder with him of the Cercle Social, is also an interesting figure in the history of the Revolution, but fell out with Bonneville. Neither of them, of course, concealed their masonic connexions which were soon exploited by the denouncers of the Cercle Social. Nevertheless, these were to be found as much among revolutionaries as among reactionaries. It was the journal of the Jacobins that sneered at Fauchet and Bonneville because their system 'paraît être un mélange de ceux des anabaptistes, des martinistes et des rose-croix'. [26] Fauchet had in the pages of the *Bouche de Fer* condemned Voltaire, the

[24] Quoted in Le Harivel, *Nicolas de Bonneville,* p. 52 (my italics).

[25] See above, p. 139.

[26] *Journal des Amis de la Constitution,* 21 November 1790, quoted in Le Harivel, p. 147. Bonneville had, perhaps, been provocative; he had said that the Jacobins were really directed by the Jesuits and on another occasion, that they were directed by a masonic sect of which Orléans and Artois were the Grand Masters! (J. Charrier, *Claude Fauchet,* i(Paris, 1909), p. 168).

patron saint of rationalist and progressive 'lumières'.[27] Certainly it is not easy to draw clearly from the *Bouche de Fer* a coherent doctrine and it may be that differences of view over masonry and its significance helped to bring on the eventual quarrel between its two directors. Bonneville was Saint-Martin's publisher and friend, but Fauchet, addressing (through the *Bouche de Fer*) another frequenter of the mysticising sects of the masonic underworld, Anarcharsis Clootz, assured him that he had 'autant d'éloignement que vous pouvez en avoir pour les illuminés d'Allemagne, de Prusse et d'ailleurs. Mais je suis convaincu qu'ils dénaturent la maçonnerie.'[28] It may also be that the novelist Restif de la Bretonne wrote in the journal; he was Bonneville's friend and certainly it contained the sort of semi-Mesmerist nonsense which can be found elsewhere in his writing.[29] This may speak for Bonneville's own leanings in this direction. Whatever its sources, this doctrinal incoherence embodied something of the clashes of view in late eighteenth-century culture which had already revealed themselves in, say, the troubles of the Strict Observance, or Luchet's worries about illuminés. They explain why such a journal should find itself under attack from Left as well as Right, though other, more deviously political, factors were at work, too. A different sort of charge (which was no doubt thought by Jacobins a more serious one than that of Martinism) was that the *Bouche de Fer* advocated the 'loi agraire' which was the bogy of the French Revolution (roughly, it meant the confiscation and egalitarian redistribution of land); this was, in fact, a slander, though Bonneville himself advocated an egalitarian distribution of inherited property and on several occasions inveighed against the accumulation of excessive wealth.[30]

No doubt the most important consequence of the publicity given to Bonneville's views was that many people who knew of his connexion with freemasonry felt that, in a vague sort of way, it was now more suspect because of him and Fauchet. He was, after all, nearly always in advance of his time; he toyed with feminism and at the time of the Varennes crisis the *Bouche de Fer* printed the Cordelier petitions not

[27] Charrier, p. 170.

[28] Quoted in Viatte, I, p. 263. We may here have an example of the confusion already noted over the word 'illuminé'. Fauchet may have meant both Illuminati and the mysticising sects, both of whom could be said to denature freemasonry.

[29] Darnton, pp. 132–4.

[30] Le Harivel, pp. 35, 52. Viatte (I, p. 266) points out that the institution of property was questioned by some notable and celebrated theosophists. Later, of course, the spectre of the 'loi agraire' was to be revived in the aftermath of the Babeuf conspiracy.

accepted by the Jacobins. But also, much that was precisely relevant to freemasonry got into print because of Bonneville. He himself, it has been said, marks the transition from religious to revolutionary freemasonry; [31] certainly he was outspoken about the uncompromisingly revolutionary stance freemasonry should take. In a book on religions in 1792 he said that 'de tous les systèmes religieux ou fédératifs, celui connu sous le nom de *franc-maçonnerie* est le plus général: comme rien ne doit être secret chez un peuple libre, *et que leur objet est rempli en France*, que leurs temples s'ouvrent!' [32] This sort of language inevitably led to replies from freemasons alarmed by the implications it might have for the public repute of the Craft. La Harpe, for example, attacked him for mixing up freemasonry with constitutional principles, [33] and no doubt it was not only non-masons who were alarmed when the *Bouche de Fer* advocated the restriction of public office to freemasons.

Masonic alarm about the Cercle Social can be seen in an anonymous pamphlet, *La profession de foi des francs-maçons*, [34] which attacked Fauchet and Bonneville for attempting to draw freemasons into their gatherings; 'Bonneville n'est point franc-maçon,' it asserted. Although the author claimed that masons would not, in fact, be led astray by the Cercle he urged them not to be in language which suggests that he felt a real danger to exist. His words also suggest the threat of guilt by association with which Bonneville's reputation faced the Craft. 'Hâtez-vous de désavouer cet audacieux et dur novateur. Hâtez-vous de répéter à l'univers que vous ne fûtes jamais les ennemis d'aucun gouvernement; d'aucune religion; que vous ne voulez dicter de loix à personne; que, satisfaits de celles que vous avez reçues, vous n'aspirez qu'à l'union, qu'à la paix, qu'à tous les sentimens affectueux qui honorent et font chérir l'humanité . . . que vous avez quelquefois gémi sur les abus du despotisme, mais que vous eûtes toujours en horreur le fer qu'on portait dans le sein du despote.' [35] These were, obviously, the words of a moderate constitutionalist, and probably typical of the views of

---

[31] Viatte, I, p. 266.

[32] Quoted in Viatte (my italics).

[33] La Harpe found the journal of 'un fou nommé Bonneville, et une autre éspèce de fou, l'Abbé Fauchet' one in which 'se trouvent pêle-mêle toutes les rêveries des illuminés avec des discussions politiques, le jargon de la mysticité avec l'emphases des predicateurs, où l'on remonte jusqu'à la tour de Babel et l'Arche de Noé, pour redescendre aux sections et aux districts, où l'on ne projette rien moins qu'une religion universelle, une régénération universelle, etc.' Quoted in Le Harivel, pp. 155–6. See, too, the charge of mysticising the political principles of the Revolution which Chénier levels at Bonneville (quoted in Viatte, I, p. 308).

[34] 1791?

[35] Tyrannicide was, of course, traditionally associated with the Jesuits.

many of his brothers in the early stages of the Revolution. His advice to his colleagues is unambiguous: 'Bannissons de nos temples les aristocrates et les démocrates, et les charlatans. Continuons de marcher sur la ligne droite et perpendiculaire tracée par nos ancêtres; méprisons les cris d'une vaine cabale et soyons soumis aux loix.'

In retrospect, although Fauchet went to the guillotine with the leaders of the Gironde in October 1793, Bonneville's associations and aims were to be remembered as sinister mainly by critics and myth-makers on the Right. When that happened, such attacks on him and on the Cercle Social as were made by the Jacobins were to provide much of their ammunition.[36] Bonneville's part in the Cercle Social and the journals linked with it would then be put together with other of his earlier, but also well-publicised, assertions. He was, after all, a self-proclaimed mason when he wrote about the Jesuits. He was the friend of Mesmerists. He was said to have been in touch with Bode, the Illuminatus, who had gone to Paris in 1787 for a congress of the Philalèthes; the inference was clearer than ever after 1789 that Bonne-ville was an initiate of the Illuminati.[37] At the beginning of the Revolu-tion—as Bonneville was himself at pains to point out—he had been one of the Electors of Paris; he gloried in his role during the turbulent days of June and July. He had been the first proposer of a Garde bourgeoise which was the seed of the National Guard which effectively removed the power to coerce from the hands of the royalists.[38] He even claimed to have urged his fellow-citizens to insurrection in defence of the National Assembly at Versailles. In his non-political and literary works, too, scraps of evidence could be found of his continuing, if ill-defined and idealistic, attachment to freemasonry.[39]

Yet all this, sifted and discussed as it was to be by those anti-masonic writers who later attacked Bonneville, is in some ways in flagrant contradiction with other of their assertions (for example, that the

[36] For some later evocations of Bonneville and the Cercle Social, see the follow-ing chapter.

[37] Le Forestier, Les Illuminés, p. 664. This story became a key-piece in the demon-strations of the plot theorists.

[38] Le Harivel, pp. 4–6.

[39] In De l'Esprit des Religions (Paris, 1792), we are told by Le Harivel (pp. 43, 45), he concludes that the symbol of the Cross, which he detects among the Druids, was essentially composed of the set-square and compass, and that Jesus Christ was 'un initié, qui, comme Moïse, Brahma et autres est venu apporter la vraie doctrine, laquelle n'est point du tout le religion chrétienne'. It was presumably this book which attracted the attention of the Abbé Lefranc, who seems to have been the first polemicist to attack Bonneville for his views on Christian origins (in Conjuration contre la religion catholique, see below, p. 177). Much later Bonneville translated into French Tom Paine's Essay on the origin of Free Masonry (London, 1818).

Jacobin club was masonic), is certainly inconclusive, and, even if the full case against Bonneville is conceded, would only amount to saying that we have in him another individual whose masonic background may have influenced his political attitudes. This did not deter those who sought a wider significance in such 'facts'. Alarm arising on such grounds and from such sources about the participation of individual freemasons in the Revolution was from the start confused with, and likely to transform itself into, accusation of masonic responsibility for the whole thing. By itself, the participation and even the prominence of many French freemasons in the Revolution either in Paris or the provinces is meaningless. Since freemasons were still very numerous in 1789 (and ex-freemasons possibly even more numerous), they were bound to be well represented among the deputies. Once they were in the Assembly, too, they were more likely to co-operate with old friends and acquaintances than with men of whom they knew nothing. They may even also have sometimes found joint activity easier than would non-masons because the life of the lodge had familiarised them with the idea of collective action and the conduct of business.[40]

The feeble evidence which has been adduced for conscious masonic conspiracy at the centre of the Revolution is in any case almost always drawn from 1789 or shortly before. As we go further into the Revolution, even such 'facts' as are then available crumble away, and the actual history of masonry and of many masons cannot be fitted into any reasonable statement of the conspiracy theory. Freemasonry, inevitably, reflected the concerns and ideas of the society which had produced it. It therefore also reflected its divisions as soon as the moment of seeming unanimity and euphoria which caught so many

[40] D. Ligou makes some shrewd remarks on the possibilities in this area in 'Structures et symbolisme maçonniques sous la Révolution', *AHRF*, 1969, pp. 511–16. It is, of course, one side of the case put forward by Augustin Cochin in, above all, *Les Sociétés de pensée et la Révolution en Bretagne (1788–1789)* (Paris, 1925), and earlier in a letter of 1904 to Charles Maurras in which he explained that he had said nothing about masonry in a study just completed by him on the 1789 election in Brittany because 'ce n'est même pas elle, précisément, qui nous intéresse; mais cette idée générale si bien mise en lumière par Ostrogorski que dans un pays où les anciens corps indépendants, provinces, ordres ou corporations, tombent en poussière, un parti organisé d'une certaine manière s'empare fatalement de l'opinion, la dirige artificiellement, par le seul fait de son jeu mécanique, sans rien devoir ni à des causes naturelles, économiques ou autres, ni à l'action légitime de ses idées, ni même au nombre de ses affiliés ou au talent de ses chefs'. A. de Meaux, *Augustin Cochin et la genèse de la Révolution* (Paris, 1928), p. 267. He went on to say, wisely, that 'il n'est pas facile de se rendre lisible sur un pareil sujet: la marche de la Maçonnerie n'a rien d'héroïque' (p. 269). As has been pointed out by E. Dermenghem (*Joseph de Maistre mystique*, pp. 89–90) there is a parallel here with a view expressed by de Maistre in a phrase already quoted (above, p. 155).

Frenchmen up in 1789 had passed. Masonic lodges then began to show the same divisions about the course of the Revolution as the world of the profane. On the whole, masons were moderates, willing to go some way and not too far or too fast towards the goals of reform held up to them, though some took sides more decisively. But when this happens, the evidence is that there was no *masonic* commitment to one side or the other. The freemasons of Maine, it seems, produced one terrorist, two regicides who voted for Louis XVI's death, and a fair number of functionaries and officials in the revolutionary régime at the local level. On the other side, six of them were guillotined and over fifty noble freemasons emigrated.[41]

The history of notorious individual freemasons who were prominent in the National Assembly is equally unhelpful in supporting the theory of planned masonic activity. For all the fame of his Grand Mastership, Orléans' motives are much more easily and simply explained by personal ambition than by his masonic affiliation.[42] He was soon spurning his masonic loyalties and resigned his Grand Mastership at the beginning of 1793. He finished on the scaffold, too, a victim of the Revolution which, according to some plot theorists, he had engineered. Lafayette, another prominent mason, must also have been a singularly inept plotter, if we are to judge by his incapacity for keeping in step with the Revolution after Varennes. Mirabeau at first sight looks more promising; he was, after all, suspected of an Illuminati taint when he returned from Germany to France even before the Revolution. But the nineteenth-century publication of his Notes to the Court reveal him to have been a King's Man at heart, and, whatever else, not a masonic plotter—and now it is thought possible that he was not a mason at all. Brissot seems to have been a member of a Chartres lodge,[43] but the fate of the Girondins hardly bears out the theory of successful conspiracy.

Individual examples could be endlessly multiplied—the former founder of the Philalèthes, Savalette de Langes, was an ADC of Lafayette[44]—but there is nothing that can seem sinister in the instances unless all explanations of participation in the Revolution except the

[41] A. Bouton, 'Dispersion politique des francs-maçons du Maine au printemps 1792', *AHRF*, 1969, pp. 496–9. Another paper in the same collection, P. Barral's 'Les francs-maçons grenoblois et la Révolution française', mentions, en passant, a number of émigré freemasons from Grenoble, too (pp. 508–9). The phenomenon was very common and a complete list of émigré freemasons would be headed by Artois, the King's brother.

[42] His masonic connexion is not thought especially significant, for example, by the royalist author of *Les conspirateurs démasqués*.

[43] Le Bihan, *Loges*, p. 65.

[44] Le Forestier, *La franc-maçonnerie Templière*, p. 621.

masonic are excluded a priori. Perhaps the only evidence worth taking seriously about the relationship of the freemasons to the revolution is general, indirect and inferential. They can hardly have failed to contribute to the short-lived atmosphere of philanthropic, libertarian, egalitarian and constitutional progressiveness which inspired much of the early work of the National Assembly. They no doubt served to generalise and disseminate the basic ideals of the humanitarian élite of eighteenth-century France. They must also have contributed to the rhetoric and the symbolism of the revolution, though this, too, was an informal and casual contribution and other sources were just as important. This language (and even the symbolism) was very general and reflected a mental world which was the patrimony of many progressive-minded Frenchmen. All that can be said is that some of the masonic symbols—the plumb-line, the set-square—recur in the official documentation of the Revolution and that this was later to attract attention and suspicion.[45]

On the other side of the argument the factual evidence is overwhelming that the overall effect of the Revolution on the Craft in France was disastrous. If there was a masonic plot, then it backfired terribly. The Craft was already showing signs of weakness before 1789 and a loss of interest and enthusiasm was marked among the aristocracy. Their attendance was waning from the mid-1780s. This decline was sharply accentuated as many freemasons came to feel threatened in their own privileges and as the emigration began to drain off the membership of many of the most important lodges.[46] The Grand Orient may have suffered much more than Grande Loge in this respect because it was more fashionable.[47] (This revelation of the degree of freemasonry's dependence on the aristocracy is itself significant.) The situation worsened steadily and by 1792 very few lodges were still active. Freemasons were, on the whole, constitutionalists and they were by then finding themselves labelled reactionary and unpatriotic. In due course, the terrorists turned on the Craft as aristocratic; a former Grand Master of the Templars, the Duc de Cossé-Brissac, was lynched at Versailles in 1792. Regarded in a hostile way by all those who were firmly on the side of revolutionary government, masonry was suspect because it was a private association and all private associations were destructive of the General Will and revolutionary solidarity and

[45] D. Ligou, *AHRF*, 1969, *passim*. See also M. Dommanget, *AHRF*, 1928, and F. E. Brunot, *Histoire de la langue française* (repr. Paris, 1966), IX (2), pp. 630–4.

[46] See, e.g., *AHRF*, 1969, pp. 444–6, 491–9, 508–9. On the whole question, see the figures cited in Le Forestier, *La franc-maçonnerie Templière*, p. 823.

[47] Chevallier, 'Les Origines de la Franc-maçonnerie à Nogent-sur-Seine', p. 183.

purity. Like other corporations (which had been abolished), said a letter of September 1794 to the Société Populaire of Toulouse, the freemasons were aristocratic and secret; they might sow seeds of disaffection. Furthermore, they were extravagant; 'ne contribuent-ils pas, par ce moyen de débauche superflue, à priver la classe indigente des Sans-Culottes du pain nécessaire?'[48] In another important provincial town, Orléans, things went even worse for the Craft; in 1793 its lodges were sacked by sans-culottes.[49]

The class composition of French freemasonry no doubt does much to explain such facts. But popular pressure arising from this motive was reinforced by others. Any self-proclaimed secret organisation was bound to be suspect at a time when so much was said and feared of plots. Gradually, the lodges, irrespective of their obediences and tendencies, succumbed to their unpopularity, or, perhaps, to the unwillingness of their members to court it. This was happening from 1789 onwards and it is not a process which can easily be followed. The lodges of Grenoble appear to have ceased to meet in 1792, though there is evidence of individual admissions to one of them after this.[50] Until 1794 the Grand Orient was still constituting new lodges, but what happened to them is hard to discover. Occasional evidence such as the letter from Toulouse is evidence of what people believed to be going on at particular dates. Masonic records add a few more scraps—for instance, the piquant information that the last manifestation of masonic activity in Paris for over a year appears to have been on the day of the Feast of the Supreme Being in 1794.[51] From Thermidor until the beginning of the Directory, however, there is a silence which suggests a virtually total cessation of masonic activity. Lodges survived, their workings suspended, in both the Grande Loge and Grand Orient connexions, but this is about all that can be said of the effect of the Revolution on the organised activity of masons until the coming of the Directory.[52]

There is in this matter a problem of distinction, it is true, and it is

[48] *RISS*, II, pp. 678–9. Two years before, a petition from Lyon asking for a watch to be kept on the freemasons also drew attention to 'leurs orgies, dites banquets', thus reviving, of course, one of the oldest slanders against freemasonry (quoted in Le Forestier, *La franc-maçonnerie Templière*, p. 843).

[49] *AHRF*, 1969, p. 432. This had been the fate of the mother lodge of the Rite Ecossais Philosophique even in 1789, we are told (Le Forestier, *La franc-maçonnerie Templière*, p. 824).

[50] *AHRF*, 1969, p. 510.

[51] *AHRF*, 1969, p. 500.

[52] M. Le Bihan has however suggested that some lodges met *throughout* the Revolution (e.g., *Loges*, p. 96).

one which, again, goes some way towards explaining the conviction with which the theory of the masonic plot was to be upheld in the teeth of strong negative evidence. The formal history of the freemasons is, it is said, only a part of the story. Some lodges, when they ceased to meet, nevertheless continued in effective existence (it was soon claimed) because of the virtual identity of their membership with that of local sociétés populaires which sprang up in many towns. Some freemasons found in these a satisfactory realisation, or, at least, continuation, of the ideals and ideological principles of freemasonry. Modern research has confirmed that, in some places, a société populaire could well seem to be the local lodge operating under a new name because of the large coincidence of personnel. In other places, too, a revolutionary municipality sometimes looked very much like an old masonic lodge.[53] Yet there are many contrary instances.[54]

In such circumstances, nonetheless, it need not surprise us that few people thought that the actual and unhappy fate of masonry and its condemnation by the Jacobins acquitted it of the charge of conspiring to bring about the Revolution. These could, in any case, be accounted for by the theory of reserved secrets and degrees of initiation. From almost the start of the Revolution, the idea was put about that the freemasons were uniquely to blame for the ills that were falling on France and it soon took root in the literate class. Enough publicity had been given to the revolutionary activity of some prominent masons at that stage for the actual fate of freemasonry to be ignored. Yet though attacks on masons began early in the Revolution and were to provide the most continuous threads in the conspiracy theories, they were not the only ones. Anti-masonry was always mixed up with other themes, though it provided the core about which they could be synthesised and transmitted to the next century. At first sight this seems extraordinary; after all, so many freemasons and ex-freemasons were alive and the grosser stories must have been known by them to be untrue. The destruction of their certificate of respectability had, nonetheless, been achieved by the growth of Scottish masonry and all the mumbo-jumbo of illuminism. After this, no one could be sure what to believe, even from his own experience; the way was open for the myth-makers to fish among the slanders of anti-masonic propaganda old and new for material that suited their book.

[53] E. Lesueur, AR, 1913; H. Labroue, 'Les origines maçonniques du club jacobin de Bergerac', L'Acacia, 1913, p. 81, and 'Les origines maçonniques du club jacobin de Bergerac', RF, 1913.
[54] Ligou, AHRF, 1969, p. 514.

SOME VERSIONS OF THE PLOT MYTH

On 17 August 1790, Marie Antoinette wrote to her brother, Leopold II, 'J'embrasse ma belle-sœur et vos enfants; prenez bien garde là-bas à toute association de franc-maçons. On doit déjà vous avoir averti; c'est par cette voie que tous les monstres d'ici comptent d'arriver dans tous les pays au meme but. Oh! Dieu garde ma patrie et vous de pareils malheurs!' This was a long way from her view of a few years before. Then she had written to one of her sisters to defend the Craft: 'tout le monde en est; on sait ainsi tout ce qui s'y passe: où donc est le danger?'[55] We do not know how she came to change her mind, whether she listened to the gossip of courtiers, whether she read about masonry or whether she attempted some serious analysis of what she saw going on in terms of what she knew of men's masonic connexions. What is certain is that she was not alone in changing her mind; she may even have been typical. Many people came to suspect masonry, though it is difficult to know how soon after the outbreak of the Revolution this happened. At the beginning of 1790, Montmorin, then Foreign Minister, was still assuring the French ambassador at Rome who had alarmedly reported the arrest of Cagliostro there under the Papal laws against freemasonry, that 'il ne paraît pas qu'en France les mystères nés de la franc-maçonnerie aient produit d'autre effect que de ruiner quelques dupes'.[56] No doubt sensible men long agreed with him. But there was a readiness to do otherwise and the first attack on the Craft to be made after the Revolution began seems to have been in 1790.

This was a pamphlet by the Abbé Baissie,[57] whose opening words echoed the eighteenth-century Bulls of condemnation: 'la Société des Francs-Maçons est illegitime et contraire à la loi de Dieu, aux lois de l'Eglise, et à celles de l'Etat.'[58] Nor, in much of what followed, did the Abbé go beyond them. He deplored, as had many others, the sweeping, impious nature of the masonic oath and recalled the legendary condemnation of the Order by the Sorbonne. When he turned to more original arguments, he came nearer to politics, but it is striking that

[55] The first quotation is from Von Arneth, p. 136. The second comes from the letter of 27 February 1781 (already quoted above, p. 85 and printed in Vogt d'Hunolstein, p. 95).

[56] Quoted in Baldensperger, II, p. 13.

[57] *L'esprit de la Franc-maçonnerie dévoilé, relativement au danger qu'elle renferme* (Rome, 1790). I have used the second edition (Paris, 1816); the British Museum does not have the first, said to be 'introuvable' (*Dictionnaire de biographie française*, 1948, s.v. 'Baissie'). Antoine Estève Baissie was a secular priest.

[58] Baissie, p. 3.

he did not go so far as to accuse the freemasons directly of engineering what was happening in France. 'S'ils avaient la force en main, o Dieu! quel ravage ne causeraient-ils pas sur toute la face de la terre.' Their secret lay in the Cromwellian, anti-monarchical origins of the Order: the aims of liberty and equality.[59] In France, only the grades of 'Ecossais' and 'architecte' knew this secret, but they cherished the masonic aim until the Craft should find 'un Prince favorable à leurs pretentions, et à leur système de tolérance'; then, says Baissie, 'ils en profiteront'.[60] They will demand, with force of arms if necessary, 'l'affranchissement des lois assujettissantes, et l'exemption de tous les droits de péages, et de tout impôt'. This is as near as Baissie comes to an allusion to the events of 1789–90. He then goes on only to say they share the aims of the Philosophes ('ils tendent plus ou moins sourdement à la ruine du genre humain') and that the powers should unite to suppress them. Their political cunning is underlined in a comment which anticipates arguments which might be used to defend masons on the basis of their actual role in the Revolution: 'ils ne prennent toujours part aux petites révolutions particulières d'une contrée, parce qu'ils méditent pour l'avenir une révolution générale, et leurs vertus pacifique en apparence, qu'ils nous donnent pour une preuve de leur innocence, ne sont fondés que sur la crainte d'échouer.'[61] Baissie had much more to say, in a somewhat rambling way, about the grades and ceremonies of freemasonry, but except for providing more circulation for such exotic details he had nothing to say on this that had not been said before and there is nothing in this which concerns our theme. His interest lies in the general arguments already cited. Although they do not go so far as to attribute direct responsibility for the Revolution to the Craft, they open the way implicitly to such a charge by the parallels Baissie suggests. He was also the first writer to reaffirm the old Cromwellian legend and its concomitant, the secret aims of Liberty and Equality, at a moment when those words had begun to have national significance. One other of his points is also of interest, because it anticipated later writers. This is the linking of freemasonry with the Philosophes, whose 'plot' against Christianity and the Church had been talked about by clerical polemicists ever since the dissolution of the Jesuit order. It had already been connected with their preaching of that 'tolerance' to which Baissie also refers, and in the debate on the rights of Protestants which had taken up so much attention during the last years of the ancien régime it had been asserted that 'philosophy' and Protestantism were working hand in hand to subvert Church and

[59] pp. 36–42.   [60] p. 59.   [61] p. 62.

State. It is significant that before there is any charge that the Craft has a specific and sinister role in what is going forward in France it is thus linked to other plot themes already familiar to Baissie's readers. Much more such conflation of myths was to follow.[62]

In the same year a mason was moved to a defence of the Craft which suggests that it by then knew itself to be under attack. It is anonymous, but comes from a lodge at St-Brieuc to which the orator belonged.[63] Masonry, he says, has suffered from the secrecy it has thrown over its own ceremonies. It has led 'êtres superstitieux' to think that 'les seules maximes de la Maçonnerie ont préparé, produit et dirigé notre fameuse révolution, admirée par l'univers étonné, tandis qu'il est évident et incontestable que les progrès de la raison longtemps concentrés par la crainte des verges toujours agissantes du despotisme eussent suffi pour lui donner naissance'. When however, he went on from these rather sensible remarks to enthuse about masonry's role he was, in fact, to provide just the sort of ammunition which was to be used against the Craft in the next few years. 'Qu'il est flatteur pour nous, mes frères, d'avoir fourni à ce sénat régénérateur le frère [the grand master of the Lodge] que nous avons choisi pour diriger nos travaux.' This was exactly the kind of circumstantial point on which the critics of masonry were to build to great effect.

In spite of such disclaimers as this, it has been suggested that it was in the work of an Eudiste priest, the Abbé Lefranc, that there first appears the story of explicit identification of freemasons as the heart of a conspiracy behind the Revolution.[64] This may not be so, and it has not been proved to be so, but it is clear that his short book, *Le voile levé pour les curieux ou les secrets de la Révolution révelés à l'aide de la franc-*

---

[62] It is also true that they could be and were kept distinct. A book attributed to d'Antraigues, *Dénonciation aux Français catholiques, Des moyens employés par l'Assemblée Nationale, pour détruire en France, la religion catholique* (London and Paris, 1791) attacked Philosophes and Protestants bitterly but did not mention freemasons.

[63] Passages from it are quoted in G. Martin, La *Franc-Maçonnerie française et la préparation de la Révolution*, 2nd edn. (Paris, 1926), pp. 51–2.

[64] M. Défourneaux, 'Complot maçonnique et complot jésuitique', *AHRF*, 1965, pp. 170–86. François Lefranc was vicar-general at Coutances and then Superior of his Order's house at Caen until it, like others, was dissolved. After refusing to take the civic oath he went to Paris, where he seems to have co-operated in literary work with Barruel. He died in the September Massacres of 1792. It is interesting that the Eudistes, or Congregation of Jesus and Mary, had within a relatively short time after their foundation become already in the seventeenth century conspicuous for their opposition to Jansenism, a movement which was, of course, frequently to be evoked by anti-masonic writers as associated in the work of subversion. In the following century, his murder was attributed by enthusiasts to deliberate planning by irritated freemasons.

maçonnerie, published in 1791, anticipates some comments by a royalist paper in the following year which were long thought to be the first major attack on masonry from this point of view.[65]

Into Lefranc's book many tributaries may have flowed, to judge by the list of eighteenth-century anti-masonic writings which he said in his Introduction that he had read.[66] He approaches the question of masons' involvement in the Revolution by a long discussion of their origins and history, and in the process rejects a number of implausible theories only to replace them with another, that the Protestant sects of the Reformation era, and, in particular, the Socinians, lie at the root of the Craft.[67] It is interesting (and important, as we shall see) that so early an example of an anti-masonic interpretation of the Revolution should start here. Again, at the outset of revolutionary polemics on masonry, we find the masonic myth blended with another, more familiar because of the recent publicity given to it, the anti-Protestant myth. It is to be explained, of course, by the personal experience of Lefranc and many other priests. In 1791, whatever might be alleged—as was already being alleged—about the fundamentally republican tendencies of the revolutionary politician, their most striking (and, to some, atrocious) acts had so far been against the Church. The secularisation of Church lands, the tolerance of non-Catholic public worship and, finally, the schismatic (as it seemed to many) Civil Constitution of the Clergy were accomplished facts. From them could be inferred a plot, fundamentally anti-religious if also, incidentally, anti-monarchical, and it was one whose roots could and would be traced back into the depths of French history, back as far as the Wars of Religion.

This, subsequently, after discussing masonic organisation and ritual, is Lefranc's argument. The principles of the freemasons, he points out, are like those of the organisation of republics. The fundamentals are liberty and equality. In a chapter on 'ce que l'Assemblée nationale doit à la Franc-maçonnerie' he goes on to demonstrate what this has meant in practice. In the first place, it has affected the composition of the Assembly for, even before the States-General met, freemasons were doing all they could to lift their Grand Master, the Duke of Orléans, to some great position, 'qui le mit à même de figurer au premier

[65] A 'second', revised, edition of *Le voile levé* appeared the following year, together with English and Italian versions. The bibliography of this work is very obscure and complicated. See Roberts, *BIHR*, 1971, p. 82, fn. 2. For the royalist paper of 1792, see below, p. 179.

[66] This list does not appear in the Introduction to all editions.

[67] 'La franc-maçonnerie est la quintessence de toutes les hérésies qui ont divisé l'Allemagne, dans le seizième siècle', *Le voile levé*, p. 31.

rang'. Subsequently, the Assembly once formed, it in all things followed a masonic lead. The reconstruction of France shows this; it has been reorganised on masonic principles and even with masonic terminology into departments, districts, cantons, arrondissements. The oath required of the clergy under the Civil Constitution strikes him as similar to that required of freemasons.[68] Even the sashes of municipal officers correspond to the first decoration awarded the apprentice-masters. As for policing, the 'fonctions du frère terrible, le grand inquisiteur des loges maçonnes, sont remplis parmi nous par la comité des recherches, qui est présidé par le terrible frère Voidel'.[69]

The inaccuracies and implausibilities of Lefranc's account (of which much more could be cited) need not trouble us. What is significant here is the falling into place of many details later to be repeated by the demonologists of the next century and a half. Lefranc even went on to argue that, like masonry itself, 'l'assemblée nationale n'a-t-elle pas aussi une double doctrine, l'une qui n'est connue que de ce qu'on appelle les faiseurs, et une autre qui est publique, dont chacun s'imagine pénétrer le sens? Un doctrine dont les comités ont la clef et quelques membres du côté gauche; et une autre doctrine qui est faite pour ceux dont le suffrage est nécessaire, mais qu'on ne cherche pas à instruire à fond des desseins de l'assemblée?'[70] This evoked a very old anti-masonic fear, that of the incompletely revealed Secret, for, Lefranc asserts, only the highest grades, the Scottish Masters and Grand Architects, know it completely.

Lefranc goes on to make other points by analogy, and to blame masonry for having deliberately changed the character of Frenchmen, making them cruel and vindictive by its frightening ceremonies, but in his final chapters he returns to the theme of masonry's anti-religious aims as fundamental. The Craft seeks, he asserts, to whittle away the central dogmas of Christianity by introducing men to symbols and ideas which implicitly conflict with them. Naturally, the Church is the main obstacle to this and they design to overthrow it. Protestant co-operation is to be expected: 'le comité secret du club des Jacobins était presque en entier composé de protestans.'[71] The ritual of the higher degrees shows, clearly enough, the nature of these far-reaching anti-religious aims; it is Lefranc's strength, throughout, that he makes great

[68] *Le voile levé*, p. 63.
[69] p. 60; The 'frère terrible' is an officer of a masonic lodge who had certain ceremonial duties as a guard to its ceremonies.
[70] p. 62.
[71] p. 90. Here we have a good example of the straightforward factual error which looms so large in this literature.

use of the materials publicised in the previous half-century which gave details of ceremonies and symbolism which at last, after the events of 1789–91, could be made to seem full of a sinister significance apparently justified by the Civil Constitution of the Clergy.[72]

At this point, Lefranc takes the argument further. 'La franc-maçonnerie veut renverser le trône comme elle a renversé l'Autel' is the title of his eighth chapter. In this design, he thinks, great progress has been made. 'Voulant détruire la royauté, ils ont cassé tous les corps qui paraissent en être l'appui . . .' and have left only a removable func-tionary, 'un roi de théâtre.'[73] Here he plunges, briefly, into the story of the Knights of Kadosch, whose ceremony of admission includes an assault on a crowned image. Here, too, he associates the Templars with the story, the Kadosch grade proving that they had infiltrated freemasonry with the idea of revenge. The story of the Baron de Menou's seals, bearing the legend 'ennemis du culte et des rois' is told,[74] the principle of popular sovereignty is stated and said to be a Protestant principle, and the 'mot' of a Philosophe about strangling the last priest with the entrails of the last king is again repeated (though without a precise attribution).

It is not exaggerating to say that all the essential elements of the myth are laid out here, but Lefranc cannot be given special credit for priority because a much shorter pamphlet of the same year, *Causes et Agens des révolutions en France*, also contains many of them and adds some others of its own.[75] In this brief work, as in Lefranc's, Protestant-ism lies at the roots of the masonic plot; though freemasonry is not mentioned by name, references to 'loges' make it clear that it is the Craft which the anonymous writer has in mind. These lodges have secret doctrines, he continues, which are revealed only to those who survived tests of reliability, but the basic principles are well known— the dogmas of equality and popular sovereignty (drawn from Calvin), the assertion that all revealed religion is an imposture, and the under-

---

[72] 'Il est donc évident que c'est à la franc-maçonnerie que l'église de France doit imputer la désolation ou elle est reduite, qui est telle qu'elle n'en a jamais éprouvé de pareille' (pp. 151–2).

[73] p. 155.

[74] Jacques François, Baron de Menou (1750–1810), became a famous figure in plot literature because of his seals. He was one of the liberal minority among the noble deputies in the States-General. For another reference see the next pamphlet cited as well as the works of Sourdat de Troyes and Montjoie cited below.

[75] No place or date of publication, but almost certainly Paris, and certainly 1791. It is the date which makes it impossible to be sure that Lefranc's book precedes it. Their relation can be explored further, but nothing conclusive emerges. See Roberts, *BIHR*, 1971, pp. 80–3.

taking to overturn thrones and the Roman religion everywhere. Louis XVI and Monsieur, his brother, are on a list of those who have offended the 'ligue'—a richly-evocative word—of conspirators and will suffer for it, but this will only be the latest step in a struggle against throne and altar which has gone on for the whole of the eighteenth century.[76] Its directing centre and bureau of correspondence at the moment of writing is the Jacobin Club; the members who are deputies form the core of the sect. They have engineered the diversion of public funds to the great network of clubs which now covers France. To this argument the pamphleteer adds lists of members of committees of the National Assembly and Jacobin Club which he regarded as especially sinister, and, finally, a classified list of some four hundred deputies with indications of their various degrees of complicity in the abominable grand design.

It was also in 1791 that there appeared in French the first allegation of an Illuminati connexion with what was happening in France. This came by a roundabout route, from Italy. In December 1789, the celebrated charlatan Cagliostro had been arrested at Rome by the Inquisition.[77] He sought to exonerate himself under interrogation by pretended revelations about his masonic past. Among other things, he spoke of the Templars, the Strict Observance and the Illuminati, of whose secrets he professed to know much more than had hitherto been revealed, alleging that they had plans to extend their organisation to France and had deposited huge sums subscribed by masons in banks in Holland, England and Italy, to enable them to do this. After overthrowing the Bourbons, they planned to turn on the Papacy. In 1791, publicity was given to these and other assertions in the *Vie de Joseph Balsamo, connu sous le nom de comte Cagliostro, Extraite de la Procédure instruite contre lui à Rome, en 1790.*[78]

[76] A reference to 'le départ du roi' (for Varennes) gives us almost the only indication of the date of this pamphlet (p. 6). For other reasons, it cannot have been written after October 1791.

[77] E. Petraccone, *Cagliostro nella storia e nella leggenda* (Milan, 1914), pp. 163 ff.

[78] Paris and Strasbourg, 1791. It almost at once reappeared in a second edition. It was a translation of the work of the same year published officially at Rome: *Compendio della vita e delle geste di Giuseppe Balsamo denominato il conte Cagliostro che si è estratto del Processo contro di lui formato in Roma l'anno 1790 e Che può servire di scorta per conoscere l'indole della Setta dei liberi muratori.* This also went into a second edition in the same year. Although Lefranc mentions Cagliostro in *Le voile levé*, he does not mention the Illuminati and it seems likely that he had not by then read the 1791 book. Le Forestier says it was at once translated into German (*Les Illuminés*, p. 660). An English version, *The Life of Joseph Balsamo, commonly called Count Cagliostro* (Dublin, 1792) made a point in an 'advertisement' by the translator, that 'whatever motive may have influenced the court of Rome, it will be a lasting reproach on the reign of

Cagliostro had long been notorious. Almost anything about him would be likely to sell well. In the light of this, it is interesting to see how the story was presented in France. It would of course have been possible to publish a pamphlet which concentrated on his sensational career and came to a climax in his condemnation. Yet this was not done. Instead, the French version provided a simple translation of the Italian book (enlarged slightly by an unfriendly foreword and some critical notes) which was as much an anti-masonic tract as an exploitation of Cagliostro's news value. Of the four chapters into which it is divided, only the first is truly biographical; there follow a chapter on free-masonry in general, another on Cagliostro's attempt to propagate his 'Egyptian' masonry, and a last about a lodge of freemasons discovered at Rome. The author of the Italian preface (translated with the rest of the work for French readers) explained this argument and explicitly subordinated the story of Cagliostro to wider issues. For him, it was another example of the follies and wickednesses of a credulous age which prided itself on its 'lumières'. Among these wickednesses, masonry and its derivatives were pre-eminent and the Papal condemnations were triumphantly justified by what had followed them.[79]

This emphasis on masonry rather than the man can be seen also in the translator's avertissement and notes. Here, though he stigmatises the injustice of Cagliostro's condemnation under 'cette inique loi' which made membership of the Craft a capital crime in the Papal States, there is also plenty of evidence of suspiciousness towards the latest developments of freemasonry.[80] The translator cited Luchet's view that normal masonry was innocent, but thought it likely that Cagliostro's 'Egyptian' rite could have become dangerous. Doubts were expressed about 'les maçonneries connues sous le nom de *rectifiées, de la haute, de la stricte observance*' and (the translator continues) 'celle de Cagliostro, avec sa vision béatifique, ses évocations des esprits supérieurs, sa régéneration physique et morale, détruisait, dans les esprits,

---

Pius VI to have detained, tried and inflicted the punishment of perpetual imprisonment on a man, against whom he could only prove the crime—of being a free mason!' (pp. viii–ix). In notes elsewhere in the book, it may be remarked, this translator expresses warm sympathy for the renovating work of the Revolution in France (e.g. pp. 77, 99).

[79] *Vie de Joseph Balsamo*, pp. xvii–xxvi. It is true that on the subject of Cagliostro's revelations about the supposed revolutionary plans of the Illuminati (see above) the author comments that 'nous n'avons pas de traces suffisantes pour décider absolument de la vérité de cette histoire' (p. 132).

[80] pp. v–vi. He makes the interesting point that Cagliostro's sentence had been condemned by both wings of the French press. The footnotes to the text several times again defend the innocence of orthodox masonry.

les lumières de raison, et les portait au fanatisme, qui, dirigé par des fourbes habiles, leur obéit en aveugle, et devient capable de tous les crimes'.[81] This charge by analogy was essentially that already made more generally by Luchet. It rested on Luchet's essential confusion of the non-rational phenomenon of 'illuminisme' with the activities of the Illuminati as, indeed, the closing section of the *avertissement* shows. Here, Cagliostro's rite was said to have 'rapports avec la sombre folie des *Illuminés* d'Allemagne, sur laquelle on peut lire des détails curieux dans le livre de M. de Luchet . . . Cette secte de maniaques environne aujourd'hui plusieurs trônes, tient la bandeau de l'erreur sur les yeux de plusieurs souverains, écarte loin d'eux les talens et les vertus, distribue les emplois civils et militaires, et ménace de leur ruine les états dont elle tient les rênes. Elle enveloppe dans sa haine, et la religion qui la condamne, et la philosophie qui la combat: elle appelle les philosophes, *les ennemis.* Cagliostro fut introduit à Francfort-sur-le-Mein, dans l'antre de ces forcenés.'[82] There follows an account of an illuminé reception of a novice, filled out with the familiar machinery of subterranean vigils, altars of bones, masked emissaries, horrific oaths.[83] In countries where such associations exist, the translator concludes, 'L'on vit au milieu d'un ramas d'hommes inconnus qui ont abjuré l'humanité, sont devenus étrangers à tous les liens qui unissent les hommes, et ont banni de la terre, la confiance, la concorde et la sûreté.'

It is possible that this book influenced opinion against freemasons at two different levels. The pure Papal condemnation of the original Italian author's preface would be welcomed by those indisposed to make distinctions over degrees of guilt and wickedness inside the Craft. They were likely to swallow Cagliostro's revelations of revolutionary designs by the Illuminati (and sustained by masonic funds) without qualification.[84] More cautious judges, who knew something of orthodox masonry, could limit their agreement to the standpoint of the translator. The important facts were not new except for the details of Cagliostro's success at Lyon and Paris. Apart from what was said of Cagliostro's answers to interrogation the book contained virtually nothing not already familiar to readers of almost any of the anti-masonic literature of the last ten years. But the moment was propitious; the events of the

[81] p. viii.
[82] pp. viii–ix.
[83] 'De ce moment, vous êtes affranchi du prétendu serment fait à la patrie et aux lois', the candidate is told (p. xiii).
[84] Cagliostro's allegations of his discoveries about this appear on pp. 130–2 of the *Vie de Joseph Balsamo*, and on pp. 107–9 of the first edition of the *Compendio*.

Revolution had confirmed the suspicions of some and awoken them in others. The book could expect wide attention both from those who accepted the judgments that the Craft was essentially and originally pernicious and by those who were thoroughly confused by late eighteenth-century developments and felt vaguely that something was wrong somewhere.

It seems likely that the Cagliostro book may have provided Lefranc with some encouragement and information for his return to the conspiracy theme, in his *Conjuration contre la religion catholique* of 1792.[85] It is evident from it that he had been widening his reading (he mentions Luchet and Mirabeau and discusses Bonneville's *Esprit des Religions*) and he refers to a much wider range of secret sects than the freemasons, finishing with the Martinists. Unfortunately, he does not know much about them and confuses very opposed points of view.[86] The Illuminati of Bavaria are mentioned mainly for their adoption of Jesuit techniques and principles; the Rosicrucians are supposed to be a subversive sect. On those whom he calls 'illuminés' he is wholly unhelpful. This registers, no doubt, the general confusion which reigned at the time on these topics and is, perhaps, for that reason the most significant and interesting feature of the book. It shows not only the confusion and alarm which were eventually to give such force to the conspiracy mythologies, but how it had now become difficult, whatever its fundamental aims, for any secret association to avoid the stigma of guilt by association. The other general point of interest in the book is Lefranc's emphasis—wholly consonant with his anti-Protestant bias—on the debt of the last wave of the secret associations to Germany.[87]

It is impossible to know the effect of individual statements such as

[85] *Conjuration contre la religion et les souverains; dont le projet, conçu en France, doit s'exécuter dans l'univers entier* (Paris, 1792). There are also a number of interesting details in its attacks on Bonneville. Lefranc denounces his views on Christian origins (presumably those in *De l'Esprit des Religions*), alludes to a nasty anti-monarchical remark Bonneville made about Philip the Fair (the allusion to the persecutor of the Templars would not have been lost on his readers) and throughout assumes that Bonneville and Fauchet are part of the general plot—in association with the Jacobins. There is also an identification of 'Robertspierre' as one of the plotters. The Incorruptible was later much singled out in this way, but no evidence exists that he was a freemason, in spite of frequent allegation to that effect. All that can be shown is that his grandfather was. See H[ector] F[leischmann], 'Le grand-père de Robespierre franc-maçon', *AR*, 1911, pp. 112–14.

[86] It is interesting, for example, that Willermoz' group at Lyon used their influence *against* the constitutional clergy (Le Forestier, *La franc-maçonnerie Templière*, p. 841).

[87] 'Le flegme allemand, pouvait lutter longtemps sans s'enflammer, contre la mysticité. . . . Mais la legèreté française n'a pu resister aux préparations magiques' (Lefranc, *Conjuration*, p. 255).

these on public opinion. All that can be done is to recognise that none of these authors achieved the fame or were to have anything like the long-range influence of some of their successors.[88] Moreover, wild as the views already expressed might be, they are still a long way from showing widespread acceptance of stories about conspiracies going back to primitive antiquity. People might jump to wildly erroneous conclusions, but except in so far as they involved Protestants they still tended to be conclusions only about the few years preceding the Revolution. Other evidence seems to confirm this, too. 'La secte des illuminés est la cause et l'instigateur de tous nos troubles,' wrote an émigré leader in 1790;[89] but to go back to the Bavarian revelations was not to go very far or, even, by the standards of what was to be thought acceptable later, to be very unreasonable. Three years later, evidence that extreme views were still far from dominant even among émigré clergy can be found in a memorandum written for the Pope by the former leader of the intransigent clergy in the National Assembly, Maury, then Archbishop of Nicea. He wrote to recommend the Pope to help the counter-revolution by issuing a Brief that might be sent to the King's representatives. It was to contain a section on free-masonry, whose terms seem almost surprisingly mild at first sight, for it was to assert that although the leaders of freemasonry were culpable, not all freemasons shared their guilt; there were, after all, too many former freemasons among the émigrés not to make this concession prudent. The Pope should ask that the hitherto ignored Bulls against freemasonry be enforced in France after the restoration of royal authority and should issue a new one to reinforce them.[90] This was not a very radical demand and it does not demonstrate much more than that Maury believed some freemasons to have been revolutionaries. It did not even show continuing belief in an enduring danger of sub-version for Maury said that he thought the leaders had abandoned the

---

[88] On the other hand, it may be that this has something to do with the circumstances of publication. Right-wing pamphlets disappeared quickly from circulation after 10 August and Lefranc's seem to have been printed in small editions. This led, for example, to the Abbé Hesmivy d'Auribeau printing a fairly full analysis of both Lefranc's works in his *Mémoires pour servir à l'histoire de la persecution française*, (Rome, 1794), I (only vol. pub.), pp. 900 ff. He seems to have relied on this for his arguments against the 'Secte abominable et sanguinaire'.

[89] Vaudreuil, I, p. 342. 21 October 1790. Clearly he did not understand them, though, for he goes on to blame the king of Prussia, 'imbu de ce pernicieux système' and with an illuminé (Bischoffswerder) as his principal confidant. He sees the hand of Protestant interests at work.

[90] A. Theiner, *Documents inédits relatifs aux affaires religieuses de la France 1790 à 1800* (Paris, 1857), I, pp. 396–7.

Order once their purposes were achieved: his aims, therefore, were presumably only to assure the reassertion of the wise provisions of Papal authority in this matter.

Nor can anything be legitimately inferred from the publication about the effectiveness of the earliest arguments that secret societies were responsible for the Revolution. Presumably a market for them existed, but there was too much information about, in any case, for such accounts to be considered the only source of the new mythology. The first attacks on freemasons, too, came from clergy who tended to tag them on to earlier issues—the Philosophe onslaught and the Protestant peril—which had already aroused their alarm and suspicions before the Revolution. The clergy were, of course, the first big group of Frenchmen to be faced also with a major crisis of conscience, the oath imposed by the Civil Constitution which was bound to force them to decide for or against the Revolution.[91] This no doubt also explains in part their early prominence in this debate.

Time was needed both for the maturing of the fullest and richest statements of the secret society theme and for the development of a collective mentality of counter-revolution among laymen which would find these acceptable. Eventually, in the best versions of the great drama of subversion, virtually the whole of human history would be

[91] It used to be said that a royalist journal, *L'Ami du Roi, des français, de l'ordre et surtout de la vérité*, four volumes of which appeared in 1791 and 1792, contained the first formulation of the masonic plot theory, but we have seen that this is not so. Its author, Galart de Montjoie, though a layman, relied in any case for what he had to say on the two books of Lefranc, and referred his readers to them (*L'Ami du Roi*, iv, p. 101). He was also more interested in Philosophes and Protestants, about whom he has much more to say, and this, too, suggests he is only following the clergy's lead. He deals with the first in a general historical introduction and has a second chapter entitled 'De l'influence qu'ont eu les calvinistes sur la révolution'. Their turbulent and seditious history leads him to argue by inference: 'la conduite qu'ont tenue les calvinistes depuis l'origine de leur secte, n'est-elle pas la même que celle que tiennent aujourd'hui ceux qu'on appelle révolutionnaires?' Later, he says 'je ne dis pas que cette secte a seule et immédiatement opéré la destruction de notre monarchie, mais je dis que les calvinistes l'ont toujours en vue, qu'ils l'ont préparée, et que des hommes dont la tête est imprégnée d'idées républicaines, ne pouvaient manquer de l'opérer.' (i, p. 10). The place of Calvinism in the pre-history of Revolution is confirmed, he thinks, by Mirabeau's later arrival in Paris with a clear plan of revolution; 'tout me porte à croire que ce plan conçu d'abord et rédigé par des calvinistes, saisi ensuite avec avidité par quelques philosophes qui y ajoutèrent leurs idées, fut perfectionné dans la société du feu baron d'Olbach, ou on ne le confiait qu'aux prosélytes que plusieurs épreuves avaient fait juger dignes d'être initiés.' (i, p. 56). Though not very precise, as an attempt to weave together very disparate elements, this would probably have convinced those predisposed to dislike Protestants. In much of the rest of the work Montjoie is dealing with plots too, but mostly those of individuals.

exploited for evidence of a conspiracy sometimes seen as almost coeval with man himself.[92] Even the most violent of émigrés became even more committed against the Revolution as it went on and would not usually have been ready to swallow the more extreme views about its origins until some time after its outbreak; bitter experiences were necessary to prepare men to accept them. These came for many only after the fall of the Monarchy. 1793 was the crucial year; it was the execution of the King, the civil war and the Terror which drove the unbridgeable gulf between the Revolution and many of its opponents. After this, the battle-lines were much more clearly drawn and on the anti-revolutionary side the general swing to reaction led to greater readiness to accept extreme statements about the origins of the Revolution.[93]

When this happened, much deeper explanations of masonic culpability were produced. The first important one appeared in 1796, *Le tombeau de Jacques Molay*.[94] The author took as the core of his case the old legend of Templar vengeance. Round this he built a comprehensive accusation 'des Adeptes, des Initiés, des Franc-maçons, des Illuminés', all agents of a great plot whose origins were to be sought in the work of Jacques de Molay as he lay in prison awaiting execution. This was the first big exploitation of the Templar legend so much prized by eighteenth-century masons; it was presented now, surprisingly, in an anti-Jesuit version. It drew also on some details which seemed to lend great plausibility to the plot theory.

From his prison—on the site of the Bastille—Jacques de Molay was supposed to have founded four lodges, one of them at Edinburgh. These were to transmit the task of avenging his death and the Order's dispersal to their successors; the instrument which bound them was an oath 'd'exterminer tous les rois et la race des Bourbons; de détruire la puissance du Pape, de prêcher la liberté des peuples, et de fonder une république universelle'. These lodges of inner plotters were eventually surrounded by other lodges, of freemasons not admitted to the Secret.

[92] It may be interjected here that the fancies of the anti-masons could be matched by masons themselves; it was an English freemason who is said to have stated that freemasonry dated from *before* the Creation.

[93] Baldensperger (II, pp. 35–44) points out that it is only in 1793 that there begins in the emigration the total rejection of Enlightenment ideas and flight to obscurantism often thought to characterise it. Earlier, clerical émigrés had difficulty in combating an atmosphere of aristocratic scepticism (pp. 219–25).

[94] Charles Louis Cadet-Gassicour, *Le tombeau de Jacques Molay ou le secret des conspirateurs, à ceux qui veulent tout savoir* . . . (Paris, An IV). This was later reprinted as the first part of *Les Francs-Maçons ou les Jacobins Démasqués: fragmens pour l'histoire* (Paris, n.d., but not before 1800).

Throughout the centuries since this work of vengeance had begun, the 'initiés' (this is the term Cadet-Gassicour favours) have been involved in all the great subversive movements. They formed connexions, we are told, with the Assassins and the Old Man of the Mountain; they supported Masaniello and Cromwell; they were among the Superiors of the Society of Jesus and supplied the Jesuits who assassinated Henry IV and attempted the life of Louis XV; through the Jesuits again, they educated the revolutionary leaders of 1789; they were behind Cagliostro and Swedenborg. The assassination of Gustavus III of Sweden and the revolution there had been their work, leading to his replacement on the throne by the initiated adept, Charles of Sudermania; they had begun the French Revolution with the storming of the Bastille because that had been Molay's prison.[95] Orléans had been one of the conspirators; his hoarding and export of corn on the eve of the Revolution had been a deliberate attempt to foment distress and disorder. Another of the things of which he is accused adds the nuance of anglophobia: 'après avoir fait les journées des 5 et 6 octobre, Philippe se rend luimême à Londres pour conspirer avec Fox, Stanhope, Sheridan, les docteurs Price et Priestly.'[96] Subsequent divisions among the initiés have not altered the general direction of their work; Orléans has been destroyed by Robespierre but Terrorism is a part of the plot, too. In spite of a setback to Thermidor, when Robespierre was overthrown, the plot is still going forward. 'Babeuf, Amar, Antonelle, Vadier . . . le massacre, l'incendie, le viol, la famine . . . rien n'est oublié dans leur complot anarchique.' Moreover, there is the danger of yet worse to come: the dissolution of the Jesuits has not, in fact, shaken their power. 'La bulle de Ganganelli n'a supprimé que leur habit, leur grand chapeau; mais leurs doctrines, leurs liaisons subsistent; il y a des Jésuites partout, dans les conseils et près du Directoire, dans les tribunaux, dans les administrations, à la tête des armées; il y en a dans le Parlement d'Angleterre, au Vatican, dans l'Escurial . . . Les gouvernements les reconnaîtront un jour . . . peut-être trop tard.'

This was much more comprehensive and articulated than any earlier attack on the secret societies. Already in it can be seen the blind, obsessive ingenuity with which men were to express their fears of the secret societies in the next century. Some of those were to be more

---

[95] The death of Derwentwater on the scaffold is also adduced as evidence for the masonic tendency to general subversion; it fits, of course, into the story of a Jesuit–Stuart plot operating through freemasonry.

[96] *Le tombeau*, p. 20.

selective than Cadet-Gassicour—particularly in rejecting what he said about the Jesuits—but were to share just the same credulousness and lack of judgment in piecing together similar jumbles of the most diverse scraps of information, libels and half-baked inferences. Cadet-Gassicour had drawn on a wide range of sources for his. Anglophobia was in the air and, in any case, traditional; it went back almost to the first coming of freemasonry into France. Much had already been said also of Orléans' personal ambitions, long suspect to loyalists; here it was linked with echoes of the 'pacte de famine'. Folard and anti-Jesuit prejudices alleging regicide are put into line alongside the old anti-masonic stories about Cromwell's masonry as evidence of republicanism. The idea of the few, inner initiates may come from the Illuminati revelations or simply from the higher grades of Scottish masonry. Bang up-to-date was the reference to Babeuf (and it was not to be taken up by other writers for some time). The explanation which could link all the diverse phenomena thus assembled was the persistence of a long-matured, well-guarded Templar plot.[97] Within it, orthodox masonry had an important part, but was not itself the mainspring. It had two roles. The first was to provide cover through the existence of its ordinary, harmless and respectable lodges. 'Il y a donc en Europe une foule de loges maçonniques; mais elles ne signifient rien. Les vrais Maçons Templiers ne sont que cent huit sur la terre; ce sont eux qui, par vengeance, par ambition, et par système ont juré le massacre des rois et l'indépendance de l'univers.' It was these initiates, 'les vrais Franc-Maçons, les Jacobins, ligués sur la tombe de Jacobus Molay', who were everywhere amassing wealth and seizing control of government.

In a later pamphlet of the same year, *Les initiés anciens et modernes*, Cadet-Gassicour was in the main concerned to reply to critics of his argument,[98] but he also went into a little more detail about the managing

[97] 'Si les étrangers, les anti-religionnaires, les anarchistes ont sans cesse troublé la tranquillité publique, ils n'étaient que les instruments d'une faction conspiratrice, celle des initiés, qui, parlant toujours des grands interêts du peuple, n'est occupée que des siens. C'est dans cette faction que se confondent les Orléanistes, les Dantonistes, les Girondins, les terroristes, et tous ces noms inventés pour tromper les gens credules. Les grands troubles politiques se sont opérés près des points de réunion des chapitres des Templiers. C'est en Suède, en Angleterre, en Italie, en France que les trônes sont attaqués, chancellent ou tombent, que la puissance ecclésiastique sé detruit.' *Le tombeau*, p. 23.

[98] He observes that critics of his views should try to explain on other grounds the frequent predictions of the revolution which had been made in the eighteenth century, the simultaneity of outbreaks when it began and the fact that Jacobins and initiés advocate similar policies, such as a 'loi agraire'. This last example, of course, was very misleading. Although some extreme revolutionaries did advocate such a

of the plot. Relying in considerable degree (as he acknowledged) on Luchet, he drew attention to the way in which the followers of Jacques de Molay had exploited men's taste for the marvellous and fantastic. The Rosicrucians had a similar scheme, and the Illuminati had pulled together their work, together with that of the Templars, the Somnambulists and the followers of Swedenborg and Schoepffer. This seems to be an admission that the track the plot follows is really too tangled and complicated for precise distinctions to be drawn. This was indeed so; already many who were themselves illuminés were adopting explanations of events which condemned the plots of rationalist freemasonry.[99] But it is also interesting because it shows how the mounting evidence of the existence of mysterious and cabbalistic sects at the end of the eighteenth century provided rich, if confusing, corroboration for plot theories for those who wished to believe them.

Cadet-Gassicour's attack was more comprehensive and generalised than any earlier one. Its appearance may mean that people were beginning to consider more favourably patterns of explanation of the Revolution which could account for all the confusing twists and turns of events since 1789 with a simple formula. The reference to Babeuf is interesting in this connexion; Cadet-Gassicour seems to have been first in the field with the suggestion that this, too, could be accommodated within a general conspiracy theory. But many other authors were also exploiting themes which could be incorporated into his comprehensive myth. One obvious starting-point was the notorious masonic connexion of the Duke of Orléans. Ferrand's anonymous pamphlet of 1790, *les conspirateurs démasqués*, had already exploited the fact of his Grand Mastership. By the time a three-volume history of the supposed conspiracies of the Duke appeared five years later, the emphasis of the story had passed away from the Duke's own efforts to exploit masonry to promote his personal and dynastic interests to the use of him by masonry for its own ends.[100] Montjoie, the author of

---

law—in effect the term stood for communising and then redistribution of land in small parcels—the Convention (in which, however the term is construed, 'Jacobins' were dominant) decreed the death penalty for anyone proposing such a law. Perhaps Cadet-Gassicour was thinking of the allegations about Bonneville, who seems to have favoured distribution of property at death. The anti-Jesuit allegations in *Le tombeau de Jacques Molay* (see above) may also derive from this source.

[99] See Viatte, I, pp. 293–6.

[100] Galart de Montjoie (alias Christophe Félix Louis Ventre de la Touloubre, under which name the book is sometimes catalogued) author of *L'Ami du Roi*, already noticed, was the author of the *Histoire de la conjuration de Louis-Philippe-Josèphe d'Orléans* (Paris, 1796). In it, he does not assert a general and universal conspiracy, only a coincidence of general aim among the conspirators: 'notre patrie

the book, spends comparatively little time on the subject, but what he has to say is at a number of points interesting because of its exploitation of individual pieces of gossip bandied about in connexion with Orléans. He acknowledges that there is a mystery about the origins of Orléans' involvement with the freemasons; though not personally engaged in the attack on the Parlements launched by 'le despotique Maupeou' the Duke protected those who praised that subversive reform and perhaps, thinks Montjoie, this is where the story should begin.[101] Once Grand Master of the Grand Orient, however, he was admitted to all the secrets of the Order and must have known that it was anti-monarchical.[102] It became known (says Montjoie) early in the Revolution that his responsibility was in fact even deeper; he had been admitted to the grade Kadosch in a ceremony held in the presence of the bones of Jacques de Molay, during which the aspirant to the grade cut off the head of a crowned figure, thus presumably symbolising the fate of the Bourbons.[103] Nevertheless, concludes Montjoie, the culpability of Orléans lay not in his wholehearted participation in the plot, but in the attempt to use so wicked a sect for his own purposes. He was rewarded by the support of freemasons, both in 1789 and later in the Jacobin Club. He was then to abandon the Craft when he found it working too slowly for his interests to prosper.[104]

n'a cessé depuis deux siècles, de nourrir dans son sein, des partis ennemis de l'ordre politique qui réglait parmi nous autrefois la hiérarchie sociale. Les calvinistes d'abord, les jansénistes, les encyclopédistes, les économistes, toutes les sectes, sans en excepter celle dont les membres prenaient le nom burlesque de francs-maçons, ont marché par des routes diverses, vers une forme de gouvernement, autre que celle qu'ils trouvaient établie.'

[101] The illusion to this episode is a small but significant instance of the growing tendency to fit more and more of the eighteenth century into a pattern of continuing subversion, without regard to the true origins of the events concerned. Others found Choiseul's ministry the beginning of the time of troubles, e.g. the Abbé Proyart, in Louis XVI détroné avant d'être roi, a work also placing much emphasis on Italian Jansenists.

[102] p. 53. Another nobleman writing in 1797, La Tocnaye, is more sensible, merely remarking that Orléans sought to exploit the masonic organisation. In a note on freemasonry (Les causes de la révolution de France (Edinburgh, 1797), pp. 35–8) he asks good freemasons to excuse him; he knows that only a few have evil aims but points out that their secrecy, discipline and intercommunication are bound to arouse suspicion. There has been talk, too, he adds, of dreadful ordeals and of the secret being the swearing of enmity to the Pope, the King of France and the Grand Master of the Knights of Malta. From his own observation—he was formerly a regular officer—he only asserts that masonic connexions were in 1789–90 certainly bad for military discipline. On La Tocnaye, see the references cited in Baldensperger, p. 47.   [103] Montjoie, p. 57.

[104] A point reiterated in a later work of Montjoie, L'école des factieux (Paris, 1800), p. xiii.

In his book on Orléans, Montjoie also referred in passing to a theme which had occupied him five years before, the role of Protestants in the Revolution.[105] This theme had by 1797 lost its distinction through being mixed with others, and, in any case, much larger issues than the establishment of religious toleration had come to dominate thinking about the Revolution since the days when Lefranc traced the evil of the day to the sects of the Reformation. Nonetheless, it was still a theme attractive to some, and in 1797 a much more detailed and concentrated attack on Protestantism than any earlier one appeared and showed, in an elaborate argument, that primacy might be restored to the traditional villains even if full account were taken of recent revelations about the secret societies. This was the long chronological history by Sourdat de Troyes, *Les véritables auteurs de la Révolution de France de 1789*.[106] It purported to demonstrate the common parentage of Jansenism, Calvinism and the Philosophes. After quoting the Chevalier Folard's prediction of 1729, Sourdat continues the story into the eighteenth century with the creation under English auspices of a Protestant seminary at Lausanne during the war of the Austrian Succession. This assimilates fresh elements to the myth; fear of English plots was a recurrent demagogic theme in the Revolution and here was the hand of England at work against France under the ancien régime.[107] Dutch money also was at work in this operation, says Sourdat, and its result was the infiltration of Protestant emissaries into France and the revolt of 1743 at Montbéliard.[108] The same alliance was at work in 1789, but then took a new and far more sinister form, involving the freemasons. A new villain appears, the Swiss Necker. 'Dans l'intervalle de ses deux ministères, M. Necker avait assisté (s'il n'avait pas convoquée) à une assemblée tenue à Nîmes, et qui scella l'union de la triple alliance. Il ne s'y étoit pas rendu seul: Lafayette, Dumouriez,

---

[105] See above, p. 179.

[106] Neufchatel, 1797.

[107] It is interesting to see this appearing later in the last book of Montjoie, too, *L'école des factieux*. After saying that the freemasons were only a symptom of revolutionary disorder and not its cause, Montjoie fell back on a ragbag of explanations, among them the anglophobe's: 'la haine pour les Bourbons dont Pitt a hérité du Lord Chatan [*sic*], l'interèt incontestable de l'Angleterre à détruire la France, le désir de la vengeance et l'ambition du duc d'Orléans, et surtout le caractère faible de Louis XVI, sont les seules causes de la Révolution.' p. xi. After this, anglophobia was always a recurrent theme in anti-masonic propaganda. It flourished especially about the end of the nineteenth century (around the Fashoda crisis) and under Vichy.

[108] The seminary existed. I have not been able to uncover any English connexions, but on those with Dutch Protestantism see *Bull. Soc. Hist. Prot. Fr.*, 1877, pp. 257–79.

Clavières, l'abbé Raynal, et autres chefs d'émeute, encyclopédistes, philosophes, etc, franc-maçons, calvinistes. Là fut repris le plan tant de fois conçu et avorté . . . de mettre la France en république . . . La conjuration, enfin, y reçut sa dernière perfection, elle fut annoncée presqu'aussitôt par l'allégorie ingénieuse qui ne fut entendue que de peu de personnes: de la bête du Gevaudan, dont les gravures d'abord fort multipliées dans le royaume, furent promptement retirées par le parti, afin de ne pas laisser au peuple le temps d'en pénétrer le sens.'[109]

Soon, according to Sourdat, because of the work of Rabaut du Puy (brother of the more celebrated Protestant who sat in the National Assembly, Rabaut de Saint-Etienne), Nîmes became the organising and communications centre for the 'adeptes de tous les pays' and, especially, 'le centre de la cabale *franc-maçonnique*. Cette institution, puérile en elle-même, avait adopté tous les attributs de la mysticité, dans un assemblage de rites et de pratiques, aussi méprisables que ridicules. Dès 1783, Rabaut du Puy, secondé des principaux Calvinistes, fondait trois loges à Nîmes, la loge *Philanthropique*, la loge de *Bienfaisance*, la loge de *Henri IV et Sully*. On y attirait tous les hommes dont l'ésprit de credulité ou d'effervescence pouvait profiter aux vues du parti.'[110] With the affiliation of the Nîmes lodges to the Parisian Grand Orient the network was complete for the subversive work of masonry in 1789.[111] Then, rumours of brigands were put about by the lodges, correspondence was maintained to co-ordinate activity, funds were raised to set disorder in motion and to hoard grain. Nîmes was the headquarters; 'de là, on insurgeoit tous les Calvinistes du royaume et ceux du Faubourg St Antoine, qui, au nombre de plus de 30 mille,

[109] Sourdat, p. 448. Another of his denunciations by name is that of Bonneville (p. 460).

[110] p. 451.

[111] There is an interesting detail: 'le duc *d'Orléans* fut reconnu chef des loges; on en prit l'occasion de mettre sur le croix emblematique de ces loges, les trois lettres L.P.D., qui, pour le public et les confrères non-initiés, semblent être les initiales de Louis-Philippe d'Orléans; mais leur veritable sens était, *Lilium pedibus destrue*.' (p. 452). Unfortunately, these letters are one of those symbolic elements which dog the student of the bizarre world of the secret societies and are given different interpretations at different times. Although the order of the letters is changed we find, for example, that four Italian masonic rites of the Restoration interpret L.D.P. as signifying 'Liberté de Passage', and another, omitting the D, interprets L.P. as 'Libertas Populi' (Francovich, p. 19). Baissie (*op. cit.*) says L.D.P. stands for 'Liberté de passer' (p. 59). Le Forestier (*Les Illuminés*, p. 660), recognising the claim of the order L.D.P. (which he says is one of the symbols of a particular grade of Scots masonry, that of Chevalier d'Orient or Chevalier L'Epée) and the meaning Liberté de Passage, does so in connexion with yet another version of the letters' origin; they are reported to have occurred on a cross said to have belonged to Cagliostro and to signify 'Lilia Destrue Pedibus'.

suffisaient pour entrainer le peuple parisien.'[112] At about the same time a Europe-wide masonic propaganda was begun. 'À cette époque, la franc-maçonnerie, qui jusqu'alors n'avait eu pour objet apparent, qu'une association ou confrairie de plaisir et de oisiveté; qui se faisait maxime de ne se mêler de rien, et même de bannir scrupuleusement de ses assemblées, toute espèce de discussion ni politique, ni sur le gouvernement, prit une toute autre attitude, une autre importance; elle devint une coalition sérieuse, et elle engendra la *propagande*, dont la devise, gravée sur un des cachets de M. de Menou, était, *ennemi du culte et des rois*; et cette propagande embrassa et empoisonna en un instant toutes les nations de l'Europe, que d'elles-mêmes, sans le savoir, fournirent des fonds à la révolution française.'[113]

In this version of the plot theory, masonry is again the vehicle of other organisations with more sinister purposes of their own. The selection of Protestantism for the role of villain and motor is no more difficult to understand in 1797 than in 1791, for their gains in civil status still made the argument 'Cui bono?' attractive. At a time when a monarchist restoration could be hoped for, the historical association of Protestantism and republicanism was worth recall. And even the war with England may have contributed to public receptiveness for a plot story with an anglophobe colour to it. It was at least within the range of experience of more people, too, than any version of the Templar plot.[114]

Nonetheless, this is only to distinguish degrees in the bizarre. Even in a Protestant version, with some specious history to lean on, we are with this sort of argument already on the high seas of confusion and error. By the mid-1790s, indeed, it seems likely that most people who were sympathetic to conspiracy theories were happy to jumble up together fragments of information and scandal which they forced into

---

[112] Sourdat, p. 453.

[113] Sourdat, p. 456. See also *L'Ami du Roi*, i, p. 101, for this story which turns up first in 1791, and below, p. 207, fn. 6.

[114] Sourdat goes out of his way (pp. 457–9) to deal with Cadet-Gassicour's story, and to reject it as being without scholarly foundation. Moreover, he asks, as the Bourbons were not on the throne of France in 1314, when Jacques de Molay was burnt, why should they be exterminated to avenge him? 'Tant que l'auteur n'expliquera pas cette enigme, nous sommes autorisés à regarder cette histoire comme un de ces drames-romans assis sur un fait simple, et décoré de tous les embellisemens, de tous les ornemens de l'imagination. Peut-être, et c'est que nous sommes portés à croire jusqu'à demonstration contraire, sont-ce les véritables auteurs de la mort de Louis XVI, qui pour détourner les regards et l'opinion qui les accusent, ont bâti cette fable, et, profitant de ce que le Duc d'Orléans était franc-maçon rejettent le crime sur les Franc-maçons.' This is an interesting example of the almost limitless possibilities of argument in these matters.

unreal but wholly satisfying syntheses.[115] It was this confusion, and the gullibility which underlay it, which explain the success of the most famous of all attempts to provide a conspiracy theory. It was the book of the Abbé de Barruel which did more than any other, thanks to its success, to shape the next century's idée fixe about secret societies.

BARRUEL AND HIS BOOK

Augustin de Barruel was born in 1741, of an ancient and noble family, at Villeneuve-de-Berg, in the Vivarais.[116] He began his long association with the Jesuits as a boy at one of their schools and then entered the Society as a novice in 1756. Until the crisis of their dissolution he taught classics for them at Toulouse but then went into exile. The date when he left France is not certainly known, but he lived first in Prague and then elsewhere abroad for some years, continuing to teach and on at least one occasion travelling with a pupil as far as Rome. During this time he was ordained priest. He eventually returned to France in 1773. Soon afterwards, he took a post as tutor to the children of a great aristocratic family; his employer was the Prince François Xavier de Saxe, the nephew of the great Marshal de Saxe and son of Augustus III, King of Poland. Although the Prince's relations with his uncle-in-law, Louis XV, were not good, this appointment must have given Barruel a very intimate view of the life of the high aristocracy; it says much for him that although, naturally, he later sought to enlist the influence of the Prince (who was, after all, brother to the Dauphine and therefore uncle to Louis XVI) he never seems to have tempered his religious principles to please his employer.

[115] See, for one example only, the letter to Kirchberger of 1796 quoted by Viatte, I, pp. 310–11.

[116] His father held the 'charge' of 'lieutenant général de baillage' of Villeneuve-de-Berg. No full biography of Barruel has appeared and in what follows I have drawn on the Abbé Fillet's *Notice biographique, littéraire et critique sur le révérend père Augustin de Barruel* (Paris, 1894), on the article in Michaud's *Biographie universelle*, and on a memoir by J. J. Dussault which prefaces an edition of one of Barruel's own works, *Les Helviennes ou lettres provinciales philosophiques,* 7th edn. (Paris, 1830). Thanks to Father Joseph Lehergne, SJ, archivist of the Paris province of the Society of Jesus, I was able to consult some of the Barruel papers conserved in the provincial archives (cited below as ASJP) and also to read at a late stage in the preparation of this study the typescript of an unpublished work deposited there by the late Father Abel Dechêne, SJ, *La vie combative de l'abbé Barruel (1741–1820)*. This is at present being made ready for publication by Father Michel Riquet, SJ; its appearance will at last give Barruel discussion on the scale he merits, a hundred and fifty years after his death. I am most grateful to Father Lehergne for his helpfulness and generosity in allowing me to consult these materials.

This period of Barruel's life, which he spent mainly at the château of Chaumont, came to an end in a quarrel and Barruel found himself without a job. By then he had already published his first printed work, an ode in which, like many of his countrymen, he celebrated the accession of Louis XVI. It does not make inspiriting reading today, and the verdict of his nineteenth-century editor seems just: 'pièce qui n'est pas d'un poète, mais ouvrage d'un bon Français.'[117] Nonetheless, it seems to have sold well. He had been appointed almoner to the Princesse de Conti and it may have been this which procured for him a pension in 1783. On this he subsisted while continuing to interest himself in the world of letters, collaborating in the production of the conservatively-inclined *Année littéraire* which strove to fight off the attacks of the Philosophes on religion, and publishing in 1779 a French prose translation of a long Latin poem on eclipses, the work of another much more celebrated Jesuit, the savant Boscovich.[118] Not surprisingly, given the fate of his Society, he soon began to play off his own bat against the Philosophes. With this aim he published his first major work, *Les Helviennes*, in two parts in 1781 and 1788; it brought him his first wide repute and was translated into German, Spanish, Italian and Polish.[119]

This was a work of some intellectual pretension and a contribution to an important argument. Many authors, especially after the dissolution of the Jesuits, sought to provide literary refutation of the prevailing ideological tendency towards Enlightenment. There was something of a wave of apologetic which sought to sustain the Church against the attacks of the Philosophes and *Les Helviennes* was a part of it.[120] Barruel thus plunged into the major debate of the day and also into the role of clerical controversialist which he was never to relinquish. *Les Helviennes* prefigured many of his later ideas and attitudes, for his target was one at which he was to continue to shoot all his life. Barruel was one of the most persistent of the conservative critics of Enlightenment, that is to say, of those who attacked the movement and its

---

[117] *Ode sur le glorieux avènement de Louis-Auguste au trône, présentée à la Reine* (Paris, 1774).

[118] *Les éclipses, poème en six chants dédié à sa Majesté, par M. l'abbé Boscovich* (Paris, 1779).

[119] The name is taken from the Latin name of the people of the Vivarais, the Helvii.

[120] It is interesting that this led him into another bitter debate (and legal proceedings) with a fellow countryman from the Vivarais, whose cosmological and geological views seemed to him to deny the evidence of the Bible. See A. Mazon, 'Les démêlés de Soulavie avec l'abbé de Barruel,' *Revue du Lyonnais*, XIV, 1892, pp. 30–55.

teaching from the point of view of traditional religious teaching. (This was a standpoint which was with time to become confused with that of the newer, idealist and spiritualist criticism of Enlightenment emanating from Germany.) In *Les Helviennes* Barruel was unabashedly polemical. For the most part he based his case on the excellent opportunities which the texts of the Philosophes offered for contradicting one another, or at least for illustrating one another's inconsistencies. He also showed in this work another characteristic he was often later to display by writing in a lively, truculent manner, but sometimes showing real humour. *Les Helviennes* was much praised by sympathetic readers.

Barruel had now found his role and was hereafter in the front rank of ecclesiastical journalists. He continued to attack the Philosophes, 'cette secte, depuis quarante ans acharnée à saper dans les ténèbres les fondemens du temple', as he called them, in the monthly *Journal Ecclé-siastique*, which he edited from 1788 to 1792.[121] In its pages he fully discovered his skill and temperamental suitability for polemical journalism. His subject-matter was, for the most part, the religious questions which were raised by the reforming decree granting civil status to Protestants and then, much more decisively, by the Revolution.

The *Journal Ecclésiastique* contains much from Barruel's own pen and thus provides plenty of evidence about his response to the Revolution. In 1789 he took part in the electoral assembly of the clergy of St-Sulpice and seems to have spoken there in a conservative sense. On the other hand, he was not then unaware of the need for domestic reform within the Church.[122] Soon, any moderation in these matters faded away and the volumes of the *Journal Ecclésiastique* are increasingly marked by angry denunciation of the philosophic 'secte' and its teachings—which, Barruel insisted, would rebound on its supporters themselves.[123] Later, as the issue of the Civil Constitution more and more

---

[121] The quotation is from the January number of 1789 (I), p. 3. *Les Helviennes* had been summarised and highly praised in the *Journal* in 1787 (II), June (pp. 51–71) and July (pp. 79–96) numbers. But it is interesting evidence of the confused state of much argument of the time that the *Journal* was to be in 1791 the subject of an anathema provoked by the Grand Inquisitor, which was, however, later withdrawn (Theiner, I, pp. 241–2).

[122] 'Barruel était réformiste, mais nullement révolutionnaire' is the indulgent verdict of his biographer (A. Dechêne, *La vie combattive*, typescript, p. 108).

[123] 'Votre évangile était Voltaire, Rousseau, Helvétius, et cent autres productions ennemies de Jésus Christ. Vos anti-chambres ont bientôt répété les blasphêmes de vos convives; de vos anti-chambres ils sont passés dans les carrefours, et des carrefours jusque dans les chaumières. Le peuple a imité vos mœurs, et s'est trouvé impie; dissolu comme vous, il devient inquiet et jaloux, remuant et séditieux.' *Journ. Eccl.*, 1789 (I), January, p. 40. Among those who at one time told Barruel that they believed the revolutionary Church settlement to be 'une horrible

defined the lines of debate, Barruel showed greater and greater intransigence and he was one of the foremost opponents of the oath which became the crucial issue.[124]

As Barruel was an ecclesiastic and had been involved in controversy on ecclesiastical questions before 1789, it is hardly surprising to find him much exercised on these matters, but he had also a more general hostility to the Revolution, and suspicion of its origins which he expressed in 1789 in a short pamphlet called *Le patriote véridique*.[125] It consisted in the main of material already printed in the *Journal Ecclésiastique* and summed up the causes of the Revolution as 'dépravation des mœurs publiques, et . . . les progrés du philosophisme'. These had already before 1789 provoked God's anger in drought, hunger and poverty, he said. Both of them, it is interesting to read, rested, in Barruel's view at this stage, on an anterior condition, the abuses within the body of the clergy. 'C'est vous, prêtres sans zèle, qui donnez au sophismes de l'impie le poids et le crédit de la raison,' he admonished his colleagues.[126] At this stage, therefore, he had nothing to say about plots beyond what he had already asserted for years about the intellectual subversion sought by the Philosophes, a theme to which he later returned at length in *Histoire du clergé*. Nor was there anything about secret societies in a discussion of the principle of popular sovereignty which he published in 1791.[127] Later, he asserted that he was early in the Revolution gathering material for the pamphlet of Lefranc.[128] Whether true or not, it may have been Lefranc's work which suggested to him

---

conspiration du philosophisme la plus impie contre la religion' was the 'constitutional' Bishop Gobel, who was talking of giving up his new mitre in the early months of 1792. He did not, in the end. See Theiner, I, p. 353, and the letters of Barruel on the following pages.

[124] There is a mass of writing on this topic. For an admirably concise summary, see J. McManners, *The French Revolution and the Church* (London, 1969).

[125] *Le patriote véridique ou discours sur les vraies causes de la révolution actuelle* (Paris, 1789).

[126] *Le patriote véridique*, p. 58. His experience at Chaumont may explain some of Barruel's disgust at the inadequacies of the French clergy, at least in its higher ranks, before 1789. He remarks in a letter about one of his charges that 'l'almanack marque de grands revenus pour les évêques, surtout pour celui de Paris, car Monsieur Louis vise toujours un peu haut. L'archevêché de Paris lui plairait beaucoup, dit-il, quoi que cependant il ne soit pas si riche que l'évêché de Strasbourg . . . Personne n'est plus intéressé que moi à l'accomplaisement de ses voeux.' Quoted in Dechêne, p. 38.

[127] *Question nationale sur l'autorité et sur les droits du peuple dans le gouvernement* (Paris, 1791).

[128] Mellor, p. 250. Barruel was later to write somewhat critically of Lefranc's observations on masonic grades.

first a topic he had not previously interested himself in, freemasonry, and to carry the search for plotters beyond the Philosophes.

Soon after the September Massacres, Barruel emigrated, to be welcomed in London by, among others, Burke. The history of the French clergy which he now published was heavily impregnated with allegations of plots (to destroy the monarchy and the non-juring clergy), but contained no general allegations about conspiracies behind the Revolution beyond what might be inferred from the hotch-potch of accusation brought against outstanding revolutionary figures such as Orléans.[129] The history showed, nonetheless, that any residual goodwill from his hopes of reform in 1789 had long since evaporated. It also showed, in its ready acceptance of atrocity stories about the fate of priests and aristocrats, a credulousness which was to be much more evident in his greatest work. In 1797, the first two volumes of this book, which was to bring him and the conspiracy theory world-wide renown, *Mémoires pour servir à l'histoire du jacobinisme*, appeared. Thereafter, Barruel enjoyed fame, notoriety, admiration and enmity. The way to his return to France was opened by Bonaparte's coup. In 1800 he published *L'Evangile et le clergé français, sur la soumission des pasteurs dans la révolution des empires*, which dealt with the duty of submitting to the powers that be. To judge by another pamphlet of the same year, he was not attracted to the new régime, but felt that it should be accepted because of the opportunities it offered to the Church.[130] In 1802 he returned to France and soon wrote in favour of the Concordat.[131] He was given an honorary canonry of Notre-Dame and it has been said that Pius VII wished to make him a cardinal but that Barruel declined.[132]

He seems to have had powerful friends in the régime and was possibly given information about conspiracies by Fouché.[133] He was certainly on good terms with Desmarest who was for many years the director of the secret police and was a former priest himself. He was once out of favour and briefly arrested on the suspicion that he had helped to spread the Papal brief ordering Cardinal Maury, who had

[129] *Histoire du clergé pendant la révolution française* (London, 1793). Burke recommended it (*Correspondence of Edmund Burke* (London, 1968), VII, p. 426). There were English, German, Italian, Spanish and Portuguese translations.

[130] *A l'anonyme auteur du soi-disant véritable Etat de la Question de la Promesse de Fidelité* (London, 1800).

[131] *Du Pape et de ses droits religieux à l'occasion du Concordat* (Paris, 1803).

[132] 'Les souvenirs du P. Grivel sur les PP. Barruel et Feller,' *Le Contemporain*, July 1878, pp. 54–5.

[133] The Abbé Fillet remarks in his *Notice* that Fouché gave Barruel material for the *Mémoires* (p. 17), yet the dates alone make this improbable.

been appointed to the archbishopric of Paris by Napoleon, to withdraw from his see. At the Restoration he was assured of favour. He at once identified himself with the restored régime and engaged in controversy with Grégoire, the former constitutional bishop, over the location of sovereignty in post-Napoleonic France.[134] He died on 5 October 1821, while engaged on a refutation of the doctrines of Kant (which was destroyed at his orders) and he left also incomplete a work on the origins of secret societies.[135]

Barruel's busy life would by itself assure him a minor but lasting place in the history of the revolutionary era, but his fame rests on the *Mémoires pour servir à l'histoire du jacobinisme*. His historic celebrity rests solely on this book, which caught the public's attention at once when the first volumes appeared in 1797.[136] They were soon translated into English, German, Italian, Spanish, Portuguese and Dutch. An *Abregé* was published by the author in 1798; it and the original were widely cribbed, abstracted and commented. It became the bible of the secret society mythology and the indispensable foundation of future anti-masonic writing. 'Toute la politique anti-maçonnique du XIXe siècle a ses sources dans le livre de l'abbé Barruel,' remarks a standard authority on French eighteenth-century thought.[137] Its enduring influence can still be seen in twentieth-century writers on secret societies; it is a small but interesting symptom of its enduring importance that in the *Revue Internationale des Sociétés secrètes* which began to appear in 1912, three out of the first four references of the opening volume are to Barruel's book. It is notable, too, that it was still being reprinted in Paris the same year (and had been in 1911).

Barruel provided a remarkably clear and well-ordered historical account, heavily and plausibly documented, which wove together almost all the existing plot theories and all the well-known events of the Revolution into one great synthesis. Most people, says Barruel,

[134] *Du Principe et de l'obstination des Jacobins en réponse au Sénateur Grégoire* (Paris, 1814).

[135] Fillet, p. 21; 'Les souvenirs du P. Grivel', p. 65. In the late 1790s he was already receiving warnings about Kant's dangerous doctrines from his German correspondents; he seems to have been engaged intermittently on his refutation from about 1800.

[136] There seems to be some obscurity about the first edition of this famous book. J. Droz (RH, ccxxvi, 1961, p. 314) seems to imply that the first was at Hamburg. This would be the edition in French of which three volumes appeared in 1798 and two in 1799, to which I refer in what follows. But these were preceded, it seems, both by the original French edition published in London 1797–8 and by the translation of it into English (by R. Clifford) of the same years and, possibly, by a second edition of the translation which was published in 1798.

[137] Mornet, *Les origines intellectuelles*, p. 362.

recognise the terrible things done by the Jacobins during the Revolution in France. Yet few understand their meaning, that, in the Revolution 'tout a été prévu, médité, combiné, résolu, statué: tout a été l'effet de la plus profond scélératesse, puisque tout a été préparé, amené par des hommes qui avaient seuls le fil des conspirations longtemps ourdies dans des sociétés secrètes, et qui ont su choisir et hâter les moments propices aux complots'.[138] Few see that the disasters which followed were not the result of well-intentioned error but of deliberate mischief. Few see that the Jacobins themselves are only the last and most obvious villains in a great plot whose authors and agents have been far longer at work and are far more widespread, and whose aim is not merely the destruction of the French monarchy but universal dissolution, the overthrow of society and religion itself. The predecessors of the Jacobins were the Philosophes, the freemasons and, above all, the Illuminati. These last have conspired not merely against Christianity but against any religion; not merely against monarchy but against all government. They seek not only revolution but anarchy.

Barruel spent five volumes in analysing not only the Jacobins who are the confluence of these plotters' efforts, but the three main conspiracies which lie behind them. In his first volume, an account of the Philosophes, he is returning to his earliest interests in the field. He provides very little evidence of revolutionary activity by them beyond quoting their language and pressing its figurative and literal significance as far as it will go in favour of a subversive interpretation. His aim here is to demonstrate the existence of an anti-Christian conspiracy. On the freemasons he has more to say. Whereas the Philosophe had been fundamentally anti-religious and later developed anti-monarchist views,[139] the mason, says Barruel, is fundamentally anti-monarchical. Freemasons attempted to introduce into France republican institutions under the guise of reform; this was the purpose, for example, of the attempt by Necker to introduce changes in local administration which prefigured the later revolutionary Departments.[140] Nor were these first efforts limited to France; peasant risings in Bohemia and Transylvania were also evidence of a far-flung conspiracy.[141] Nonetheless, Barruel allows qualifications of masonic guilt. He had himself once been initiated at the conclusion of a lively dinner party and perhaps thought it only fair to exonerate freemasons especially from charges of indecent behaviour in their lodges,[142] and no doubt his exile in England explains his wish to exculpate English masons from his strictures. They fell

[138] *Mémoires*, I, p. xi.   [139] II, pp. 1-24.   [140] *Mémoires*, II, pp. 39-40.
[141] II, pp. 251 ff.   [142] II, p. 325.

among the innocent whose presence in the masonic ranks he acknowledged; nonetheless, he was firm in his assertion that the Craft was
fundamentally vicious. This he sustained by the old argument of inner
secrets. It is those whom he calls 'arrière-maçons' who horrify Barruel,
not the crowd of honest but deluded masons to whom the secrets of
the 'arrière-loges' were not revealed.[143] These secrets were communicated to the true villains in ceremonies whose terrible brutalities already
foreshadow the excesses of the Revolution. The core of the secret was
the two words made famous by the Revolution: Liberty and Equality.[144]
Not every mason construes them in the same sense, but they are even
in their most innocent acceptance the first links of a chain binding even
the innocent and well-intentioned freemason. They are linked directly
to other symbols and rituals. Barruel traces their origins in the Mani-
chean heresy (transmitted via the Templars) and reveals the horrifying
details of the ritual of admission to the grade Kadosch. In the eighteenth
century, he claims, freemasonry has proceeded by using the initiation
of the great to establish its respectability. Powerful social protection
has forwarded the work of the occult adepts; societies with apparently
unimpeachable aims have in fact served as 'front' organisations to
conceal the plotters' true intentions. At least six hundred thousand
masons have been organised in a great conspiracy led by, among
others, Lafayette. In 1789 there stood at the controls of the machine
one supreme villain, the Duke of Orléans, ambitious to possess the
French throne.

With his third volume Barruel comes at last to the core of his book,
the long and violent denunciation of the Illuminati, the most wicked
of the conspiracies. In support of his views he drew rich and lurid
detail from the 'revelations' which had poured out since 1786, and on
informants who supplied him with written memoranda. One charge
soon made against him was that he relied too much on one publication,
the *Originalschriften*, but he cites several others and in any case such
refined criticism missed the point. What he did was to weld together
for good the interpretation of the Revolution as a masonic plot with
the suspicions aroused about the Illuminati. Besides this, his many
errors and confusions were irrelevant. Thereafter, they were always
inseparably mixed up in the thinking of those who accepted the secret
society mythology. Even in the twentieth century this association was
to be taken for granted.[145]

---

[143] II, p. vi.   [144] II, pp. 271-2.
[145] See, for example, the writings of Nesta H. Webster. The attention which
Barruel gives to the Illuminati and Germany in general is not only to be explained

Barruel began by distinguishing two 'Illuminisms', that of 'Atheism' and that of 'Theosophy'.[146] Weishaupt's society was in the first category; its aims had been the conquest of opinion and the effecting of political and social change. Barruel expressed regret that his investigations had failed him in so far as he had been unable to obtain an account of the ritual and doctrine which surrounded the admission ceremonies to the highest grades of Magus and the Man King, but given the enormous length of his discussion of the details he could discover, this is perhaps fortunate. The essence of the matter was clear to him: the secrets of the sect had as their kernel atheism, universal anarchy and the destruction of property. All this was developed in great detail and many familiar themes reappear. Wilhelmsbad was depicted as a great Illuminati success, Swedenborg attacked and Bode very roughly handled.[147] In his fourth and fifth volumes Barruel concludes his work with an account of the seizure and domination of the masonic structure by the Illuminati. This gives occasion for a discussion of the Deutsche Union scheme and the persecution which Zimmermann was supposed to have undergone. Finally, allying with the faction of the Orleanists, the true aims of the conspirators are at last disclosed in the cataclysm of the Revolution and the emergence of the Jacobins. This terrible climax had, of course, been plotted in its final details in 1787, when Bode came to Paris for his famous meeting with Bonneville at the Philalèthe congress at which, according to Barruel, the Comte de Saint-Germain, Cagliostro and Condorcet all assisted in the instruction of the 'chefs de conspiration'.[148] The subsequent identity of form in Jacobin and masonic organisation was clear to Barruel's eye, but he succeeded in bringing the story successfully down to a very late date. The papers

---

by the abundance of polemical and revelatory material available in German free-masonry and its troubles. Barruel's pre-revolutionary career may have given him some familiarity with the German language and there is evidence in his papers which suggests that as early as July 1794 he was translating a work by Göschausen which touched on the Illuminati. (On the other hand, one of Mme Zimmermann's letters to him which survives shows that she thought he did not know German. Perhaps he could read it but preferred not to write it.) He was also at that date consulting other German materials on this subject and was aware of the great controversy about the Deutsche Union scheme. Baldensperger hinted darkly in language so obscure that it is difficult to be quite sure what he means (Le mouvement des idées, II, pp. 21–2), that the interest Barruel shows in Germany may be explained by direct encouragement from Vienna. In fact, J. A. Starck corresponded at length with Barruel between the publication of his second and third volumes, supplying him with a mass of information and correction. Starck's letters are to be found among the Barruel papers, ASJP. See also below, pp. 197–8.

[146] Mémoires, III, p. xiv.   [147] III, pp. 124 ff., 160, 191–4.

[148] V, pp. 65 ff.

found in Babeuf's possession and subsequently published showed, by their references to a 'loi agraire', that that conspiracy, too, was part of the subversion of property.[149] Further, even the success of Bonaparte's Italian campaign was attributed to the preparations made for it there by the Illuminati (many of whom had been converted to the sect by Zimmermann).[150] Last of all, Kant was dubbed guilty by analogy; his philosophy was essentially that of Weishaupt.[151]

It is now difficult to grasp, let alone understand, the success—and the enduring success—of this farrago of nonsense. Even an admirer, writing soon after his death, said of his last three volumes that 'quand il vient aux *francs-maçons* et aux *illuminés*, il ne paraît plus consulter que son désir de donner à des effets terribles des causes non moins effroyables: il suppose, il conjecture, il imagine beaucoup plus qu'il ne prouve; il a l'air de composer le roman du *Jacobinisme* beaucoup plus que son histoire. . . .' He concluded that 'en général, il fut trop séduit'.[152] There was some point in drawing distinctions between two parts of the work, too, as is shown by the interest taken in its progress by a figure we have already encountered, the German theologian-adventurer, J. A. Starck. His assistance was acknowledged by Barruel himself but in terms which to a reader of the letters must seem to understate its importance. Starck was put in touch with Barruel by a Frenchman, De Luc, reader to Queen Charlotte, who took the view that Barruel was in danger of compromising his argument and weakening the effect of his book if, as in the two volumes which first appeared, he continued in the third to blur the distinction between innocent and guilty freemasons by insisting that the Craft was ab initio vicious. Starck agreed. He sent Barruel a long set of 'remarques' on the first two volumes by way of correcting their emphasis, expressing admiration but also the hope that there would be a revised edition, and promised to supply Barruel with further materials demonstrating the wickedness of the Illuminati. He subsequently did so in great profusion: the later volumes draw heavily on his information and, in particular, on a mémoire of over a hundred pages.[153] This material contains much self-justificatory matter, for Starck was, inter alia, providing a satisfactory and blameless account of his own part, but it also contained an implicit criticism of Barruel's thesis and that criticism contained an important general truth. This was the fact that freemasonry, in so

[149] V, pp. 172–5.   [150] V, pp. 206–9.
[151] V, pp. 245–50.   [152] Dussault, p. xvi.
[153] Like the letters, now among the Barruel papers, 6, ASJP. He was not, of course, Barruel's only informant on this topic. Another was the widow of Zimmermann.

far as it was uncontaminated by the Illuminati, was in no general or doctrinal sense a guilty body. As Starck wrote to Barruel, 'si on voulait se donner la peine d'étudier tous ces degrés, toutes ces explications des hiéroglyphes, on y trouverait en vérité et facilement le Déisme, le Matérialisme, le Spinozisme et même tous les horreurs et folies des Cabbalistes juifs, des Gnostiques et autres hérésies des premiers siècles de l'Eglise. Je sais aussi que les maçons ont quelquefois eu bien de part aux révolutions, comme par exemple en Russie ou en Suède, ou la déthronisation de Pierre III et le rétablissement de la souvereinté par Gustave III est originairement concerté dans une Loge. Je connais même un grade d'Elu où le récipiendiaire jurait haine à la tyrannie, le poignard à la main. Mais vous ne trouveré pas une loge dans laquelle ces explications dont j'ai parlé auraient été regardés comme système de la maçonnerie soit dangereuse dans ses principes. Les explications étaient un abus aussi bien que la part des quelques uns ont pris aux révolutions.' As for the relations with other sects such as the Rosicrucians, Martinists, Illuminati, he went on, 'on ne peut pas dire que ce soient des maçons; ils ne sont que des griffes nouvelles entées sur la maçonnerie'.[154]

Starck soon sensed that he was not making headway and later restated his case in much weaker terms in the hope of getting Barruel to modify his argument. 'Je suis très persuadé' (he wrote at the end of August 1797) 'qu'on ne peut pas damner tous les maçons sans exception, je suis même convaincu qu'il y a entre eux dont le système est entièrement orthodoxe sans le moindre atteinte de fanatisme: mais je suis aussi persuadé que ce nombre est si petit, qu'on ne doit plus y réfléchir, et peut être ont-ils déjà abandonnés entièrement cette société pervertie.' But Barruel would not listen. Starck was to be disappointed—and even angered—by the last three volumes of the *Mémoires*. Copiously documented as they were on the subject of the Illuminati, they did not show that Barruel had taken any notice of Starck's main point in extending his assistance, the assertion that freemasonry was in itself innocent until the Illuminati had got to work on it. Barruel stuck to his over-simplification; freemasonry was a whole and it was wholly and fundamentally bad, innocent though a few of its dupes might be.

Barruel's gullibility and anger may perhaps be sufficiently explained as much by his experiences as a Jesuit, the target par excellence of enlightened persecution, as by his own lack of critical acumen.[155] But

---

[154] Letter of 21 April 1797. Barruel papers, ASJP.

[155] But not all would agree. See Rivarol (quoted in Baldensperger, II, p. 20): 'la nature en a fait un sot, la vanité en a fait un monstre.'

the defects in his work should also have been apparent to all readers as they were readily apparent to some. He does not even use his material to his own best advantage. It was soon pointed out, for example, that he did not appear to know that Amar, member of the notorious Comité de Surêté Général, was a freemason—and a Martinist, to boot. He overlooks evidence about distinctions within freemasonry which would in fact have strengthened his case by drawing attention to consciously different degrees of masonic participation in the Secret. He was, for a theologian, careless about ideological and doctrinal distinctions and wrote nonsense about Swedenborg and the Martinists.[156] He mistranscribes and misreports. He cribs, uncritically, stories which must weaken his case in the eyes of anyone who had some acquaintance with the world of which he was writing (Montjoie's horror story of the initiation ceremony of the Duke of Orléans is one example). He relied a great deal on private information from many informants, but seems never to have rejected it if unconfirmed. Sometimes, he is simply comic: an instance is his detection of the masonic triangle in the blade of the invention attributed to Dr Guillotin (Guillotin was, of course, a freemason). He is clearly ignorant of many important facts which were well known; such, for example, was the resistance of the Grand Orient to penetration by the Illuminati. He has nothing specifically new to say and only draws together the slanders and commonplaces of scores of attacks (some by him) on Philosophes, freemasons and Illuminati.

Moreover, even admirers soon recognised his shortcomings. De Maistre, who was to come round to a much more favourable view, wrote a lengthy and detailed refutation.[157] One author even claimed Barruel had not gone far enough. This was the Abbé Fiard, who was something of a specialist in magic. He had since the 1770s been warning France of the dangers of tolerating and even encouraging magicians and wizards (as, for instance, Mesmer and Cagliostro had been taken up by fashionable society) and after reading Barruel deplored his failure to see (particularly in the case of Weishaupt who, thought Fiard, showed obvious magical powers) that 'la France a été horriblement *trompée*'.[158] Certainly her misfortunes were contrived—but not in the same Barruel thought. 'Les vrais factieux, les véritables conjurés contre toute société sainte ou profane, il ne faut pas les chercher dans ceux que l'on appelle *illuminés, jacobins, arrière-maçons* . . . Si [ils] ne

---

[156] See de Maistre's comments, below, p. 297.

[157] See below, p. 296; also see Viatte, I, pp. 318 ff.

[158] *La France trompée par les magiciens et demonolâtres du dix-huitième siècle* (Paris, 1803), p. 3. Fiard had republished earlier writings on the subject in *Lettres magiques ou lettres sur le diable* ('En France', 1791).

communiquent pas réellement avec les démons . . . quelques nombreux qu'on les suppose, leur rage est impuissante contre la totalité du genre humain.' Wizardry, not philosophy or masonry, explained the Revolution. To say otherwise might even be itself a sign of the devilish skill of the true plotters. Necromancers had once put it about that Turgot or the encyclopédistes had caused the Revolution: this was a subterfuge, because the 'Démons' probably never dictated their plans to these men at all.[159]

This criticism appears to be unique in its direction. Most were more conventional. The *Monthly Review* soon pointed out that 'of the Abbé Barruel's *three* conspiracies, Anti-Christian, Anti-monarchical, Anti-social, each successive one has been brought forward with diminished evidence and decreasing plausibility'.[160] Refutations soon began to appear for there were many alive who could testify personally about his assertions.[161] But the flood of works by admirers began steadily to rise, and so did the number of translations, abridgments and re-editions. How can this startling success, given Barruel's weaknesses, be explained?

One element in the explanation must be the order in which he developed his argument. The publication of the first two volumes on their own was important because it presented to the public the most familiar parts of his case first. This was especially true of the attack on the Philosophes, which had been begun in France in the decades of the 1770s and 1780s and now coalesced with the anti-rationalist wave in Germany. By the mid-1790s it could point to an enormous body of statements by the Philosophes whose dramatic and figurative language gave apparent confirmation of anti-Enlightenment fears.[162] It is significant that the *Monthly Review* noticed all the volumes of the *Mémoires* as they were published and did so in an increasingly hostile manner, but allowed Barruel to have a point over the Philosophes. 'That, in the opinion of many, the author will be thought, in some instances, to indulge his imagination too much, and to have been hasty in his conclusions, it is easy to foresee;—but, after every deduction is made on

[159] *La France trompée*, pp. 187–8, 125.

[160] *Monthly Review*, January–April 1798, p. 510.

[161] The most celebrated is that by J. J. Mounier, *De l'influence attribuée aux Philosophes, aux francs-maçons et aux illuminés sur la Révolution de France* (Tübingen, 1801).

[162] By 1790 all the main literary works of the Enlightenment were in print, above all its correspondence. They were quickly turned against their authors. Cf. D'Antraigues (pseud. H. A. Audainel): 'Je ne connais . . . aucun ouvrage plus intéressant à lire avec attention, que les lettres du roi de Prusse à Voltaire et d'Alembert, et leurs lettres au roi de Prusse. Je supplie tout catholique de les lire avec attention.' (*Dénonciation aux Français catholiques* (Paris and London, 1791), pp. 28–9).

this account, more than sufficient both of his fact and argument will remain, to establish his assertion of the existence of an anti-Christian conspiracy.' [163] If this was to be the verdict of an unfriendly critic, it can be understood how well-prepared was Barruel's audience for this part of his argument. It was another of Barruel's advantages that he was in a large measure preaching to the converted, though, in this connexion, it is especially interesting to note the qualified response of Burke. Though deeply sympathetic both to the plight of the émigré clergy and to the general tenor of Barruel's views, Burke only endorsed their expression in the *Mémoires* in a guarded and precise manner. When he wrote to Barruel in 1797 on the publication of the first volume of the *Mémoires* he expressed warm and friendly feelings, but, although the letter was to be used subsequently for purposes of advertisement, his endorsement of the doctrine of the book was limited. 'I have known myself, personally,' he wrote, 'five of your principle conspirators; and I can undertake to say from my own certain knowledge, that so far back as the year 1773, they were busy in the plot you have so well described, and in the manner, and on the principle you have so truly represented —to this I can speak as a witness.' [164] This was, perhaps, unusually limited agreement. Many thousands of people found in Barruel's book confirmation and elucidation of what they had already experienced and expected, rather than novelty. [165] This was true even of those who were fascinated by the material Barruel used while, as Shelley put it, rejecting the 'poetic aristocracy of an expatriated Jesuit'. 'Although it is half filled with the vilest and most unsupported falsehood,' he wrote to Elizabeth Hitchener, 'it is a book worth reading.' [166]

---

[163] *Monthly Review*, September–December 1797, p. 532. Dussault (p. xv) makes a similar point: 'lorsque M. l'abbé de Barruel, dans la première division de son plan, attribue en partie la révolution aux écrits et aux intrigues de la secte philosophique, il ne dit rien qui ne soit clair et palpable; chacun peut apprécier ce qu'il avance; les pièces du procès sont entre les mains de tout le monde . . .'

[164] Letter dated 1 May 1797, printed at the beginning of R. Clifford, *Application of Barruel's Memoirs of Jacobinism to the Secret Societies of Ireland and Great Britain* (London, 1798). Clifford was the translator of the *Mémoires*.

[165] Not everyone found their own pet version of the plot theory within Barruel's pages, of course. Windischgrätz published in 1801 another pamphlet (*Dissertation sur l'opinion que l'on doit avoir des auteurs de la Révolution Française et des sectes intrigantes de nos jours*) in which he is said to have reproached Barruel for failing to identify the Jesuits as among the authors of the Revolution!

[166] Both quotations are from 1812, the first from *Proposals for an Association* (repr. in *The Complete Works of Percy Bysshe Shelley*, ed. R. Ingpen and W. E. Peck (London and New York, 1928), V, p. 263), the other from a letter of 27 February (*The Letters of Percy Bysshe Shelley*, ed. F. J. Jones (Oxford, 1964) i, p. 173). These clarify the picture suggested by Hogg (*The Life of Percy Bysshe Shelley* (London, 1906), p. 379) who speaks of his 'eager credulity' in reading Barruel, a 'favourite book at

In this lay one explanation of the success of Barruel's work as a whole; it was exhaustive and compendious. His skill lay not in the plausibility with which he drew attention to specific facts or alleged facts, but in his setting out of a comprehensive scheme which knitted together a mass of fascinating information. It coincided splendidly with the emotions and needs of the moment. After a pause while France had been on the defensive, the armies of revolutionary France seemed to be on the march again. The invasions of Italy and Switzerland produced new examples of subversive factionaries—'patriots'—ready to emerge to aid their liberators. The emigration had by then diffused widely the ideas and superstitions of a counter-revolution only too ready to grasp a conspiratorial interpretation of its failures. The mythology of the secret societies was ready to hand, fed for decades by the revelation literature about the freemasons and recently by the great Illuminati scare. What the Revolution had brought about in men's minds was the conviction that there was almost no institution, no traditional value, no social landmark which was not threatened in some way, and a ready audience was available to someone who could link together in an ordered scheme the various plot theories which were lying about and provide with their aid a rationale for the colossal psychological and political changes which men felt they were undergoing. This was Barruel's opportunity. He was all the better qualified to seize it, of course, because, as the victim of one of the first changes which announced the revolutionary era—the suppression of the Jesuits—he was himself utterly convinced of the truth of what he was saying and it required no abrupt transition but only development in his long-settled habits of mind. So convincing did what he produced seem to his readers, that he, more than any other person, defined the terms in which freemasonry's connexion with the Revolution is still discussed. Few objective scholars have dictated the shape of their subject for so long as this unbalanced and undiscriminating priest. As an outstanding French student of masonry remarked only recently, 'nous sommes tous plus ou moins victimes—bien souvent plus que moins—de la légende barruellienne. . . .' [167]

---

college', but does not make it clear that this does not apply to Barruel's conclusions but only his evidence. It seems to have suggested to Shelley the 'methodical society' for the defence of 'rational liberty' on as firm a basis as that which would have supported the visionary schemes of a 'completely-equalised community' which he proposed to Leigh Hunt a year earlier (letter of 2 March 1811, *Letters*, i, p. 54). Mary Shelley records in her Journal in 1814 that he was again reading bits about the Illuminati to them from Barruel—as he had done to Hogg years earlier.

[167] Ligou, *AHRF*, 1969, p. 511.

Chapter VII

The seedtime of the political secret societies

THE REACTIONARY MOOD

A MAN who had been lieutenant de police of Paris for ten years under the ancien régime was well placed to judge the real extent of any danger which might have been presented by freemasons before the Revolution. Yet, looking back on those days, Lenoir could only bring himself to reflect during the 1790s that 'sans doute ce qu'on a imprimé en faveur de la franc-maçonnerie n'est pas très exact; mais dans ce qu'on a imprimé contre, n'y a-t-il pas aussi beaucoup d'exagération?'[1] Even such limited caution soon became rare. Besides the operation of the events already remarked, the startled men of the eighteenth century had been forced to grapple (even before Barruel wrote) with what it is no exaggeration to call a new political universe. This new political universe and the forms in which it expressed itself are essential to the explanation of the mounting appeal of the plot mythology Barruel exploited. Its essence was a view of politics whose roots lay in Enlightenment itself and sometimes proclaimed by the revolutionaries; it rested on the assumption of one great and general antithesis, Good versus Evil, Right versus Wrong. Practically, it was expressed in the rapid crystallisation of the day-to-day politics of the Revolution into a straight two-sided confrontation and the appearance of the Left-versus-Right convention. This confrontation was soon expanded to become an ideological antithesis which could find room for any piece of historical data which people wished to fit into it; it was this disembodied conflict which provided the origin of the historical dialectic of first Hegel and then Marx, and it has haunted the philosophical and historical consciousness of Europe ever since. At once, such a polarisation hardened men's attitudes and blunted their discrimination. The idea of the struggle between Revolution and ancien régime, reason and religion, rich and poor, talent and birth (or whatever other translation

[1] Quoted in Lefebvre, *AHRF*, 1927, p. 301. The note is not dated, but is probably from the later 1790s. Lenoir was himself a mason, but also employed police spies who went into the lodges. He said they brought him no reports 'des évènements capables de troubler l'ordre public ou qui indiquassent qu'il s'y tramait des complots contre les gouvernements des souverains'.

was given to the idea from time to time), helped to create behaviour exemplifying its own reality.

Theories of plots and secret organisations could easily be fitted to such a simplification by men prepared by the Illuminati revelations and a general cultural bias in favour of historical explanations resting on human volition and contrivance. Nor was the primary antithesis itself the only thing in the new politics which translated easily into conspiratorial terms. Specific innovations also suggested them. Attempts gave reality to a sovereignty which could traverse any settled custom and overthrow any established constitution; the practice of association in order to carry to success political programmes of universal applicability; the invention of clubs and parties; the launching of unrestricted debate on ethical, religious and social principles through the press; the idea that the activity of struggling for power by appeals to public opinion was legitimate—in short, the whole emerging world of modern politics: these were disorienting and frightening facts whose total impact was so great that only colossal and portentous explanations such as those of Barruel seemed adequate to explain it.

It was not, therefore, just the specific horrors and upheavals which the Revolution brought with it which set the wind in Barruel's favour. This is not to dispute his significance, or that of his school. Undoubtedly he was the major literary influence helping to spread the conspiratorial theory of the Revolution and the myth of the secret societies outside France. But the story of that spread is always a counterpoint of particular personal and literary influences and some elements of hard fact, even when only a grain or two was available. Even as he wrote, more facts were being added. By 1799—a date which is convenient not merely because it sees Bonaparte's accession to power in France, but also because it brought the victories of the Second Coalition which seemed to betoken the end of the revolutionary danger—many Europeans had actually experienced secret organisations at work in politics, and some of these consciously strove to be more than mere conspiracies and to take some enduring form. Many more believed in such bodies. This announced an era; Barruel's book in fact appeared on the eve of what was to be the only important period of activity in Western Europe by secret societies with political aims. Some of those who joined them no doubt expected much—too much—of them, just because of the persuasiveness of the secret society mythology; the legend which had purported to interpret reality was thus now to obtain corroboration and reinforcement by helping to create it. A true process of feedback was at work and soon gave publicity to fresh facts.

Growing bitterness in the political struggles of the era (and a cor-responding heightening of the stakes for those who took part in them) can by itself explain why people should turn to conspiratorial means to bring about the changes they desired. The most striking example of this in France was the Babeuf conspiracy.[2] It not only subsequently led to a diffusion of techniques and personnel throughout France and Italy which fed other conspiratorial organisations, but it associated a certain social egalitarianism with the political ideas already at the centre of the European revolutionary movement.[3] For European, or at least Europe-wide, it was to become, thanks to the movements of the French armies. Of course, once conspiracies tainted with these ideas made their appearance the similarities and interconnexions which were detected between them by those who believed in secret societies confirmed the existence of a general and deep-rooted conspiracy, of which all the individual manifestations were simply shoots and branches. Not all the policemen and soldiers who pursued the subversive organisations believed this; indeed, probably most of them did not. But the evidence they produced accumulated; it fed a public mind which, after Barruel, was always ready for more sensational revelations. And even when they did not swallow the full nonsense themselves, the co-operation of police in different countries—especially after 1815—was to lead to coopera-tion among their opponents. From this, in turn, was to spring the brief appearance during the first half of the nineteenth century of something like an International of revolutionary movements which had spiritual and ideological, if not organisational, solidity. But this is to look too far ahead for the present. In the developments of the revolutionary decade we have now to consider how the first true political secret societies came into being. The starting-point is the general nature of the reaction of European governments to the danger they thought faced them from France.

The first responses of foreign governments to the Revolution in France had generally shown indifference or self-interested optimism; perhaps, they thought, they might get something out of a period of French paralysis or weakness. In most countries, this soon changed to alarm. The publication of Burke's *Reflections* and its rapid subsequent success demonstrate a change of mood in the directing classes of Europe which readily influenced governments. The mechanisms of

[2] See below, p. 233.
[3] Dr Francovich, of course, has claimed (in his *Albori Socialisti*) that this had already happened thanks to the Illuminati. The case remains worthy of considera-tion, if not decisively proven. In this connexion, see the alleged deathbed deposition in 1812 of an Italian nobleman printed by Rinieri, pp. 616–18.

the changes which followed—what governments actually did, and how fast they did it—have not yet been studied in all European countries in the same detail. Usually, nonetheless, they mounted police action against anything that looked like a secret society, a conspiratorial gathering, and against open 'clubs' analogous to those which so rapidly became notorious in France. In most cases this meant action against free-masons, who thus tended to be driven by the action of their oppressors into hostility to the government of their own country and sympathy with the Revolution and France. But the pace was not everywhere the same, nor the results.

In Great Britain, for example, there was great outcry against 'Jaco-bins' (a term rapidly spread through Europe as a synonym for 'revo-lutionary'), some notorious trials took place and some much vilified legislation was introduced. There was enormous bitterness towards the Revolution on both patriotic and social grounds and Englishmen found themselves fighting an ideological war for the first time since the seventeenth century (a fact soon reflected in the divisions of domestic politics). Yet in spite of this, though Barruel's book was well received, the mythology of the secret societies did not win wide ac-ceptance. People did not seem to require it. The comparative sanity of the English educated classes in this matter is only an outstanding example of a continuing coolness towards the myth which has meant that very little has to be said about this country in the course of this book.

If the myth was not popular in the 1790s in England it was never likely to be, for that was the moment above all when emotion favoured it. No one could have shown a more comprehensive and embittered ideological opposition to the Revolution, for example, than Burke, yet he seems not to have feared the secret societies and, though he knew what was alleged of them, virtually ignored the topic. As early as 1790, in the *Reflections*, he detected a 'confused movement' which threatened a 'general earthquake in the political world' and, as evidence that this was so, pointed out that 'already confederacies and correspondences of the most extraordinary nature are forming in several countries'.[4] His footnote shows that he had in mind the Illuminati, but this is all that he ever seems to have said about them. When Barruel's book came out six years later, he gave it, as we have seen, only a guarded welcome.[5]

It is almost surprising that the theme did not attract him more, but

---

[4] *Reflections on the Revolution in France* (Cambridge, 1912), p. 58.
[5] See above, p. 20.

in this he was typical of his countrymen who were much against Jacobinism and the French, feared what the United Irishmen might be up to, and saw the hand of conspiracy in the mutinies in the fleet, but seem to have felt no need at all to fit these reasonable, if exaggerated, fears into a framework of universal subversion and legendary history. When in 1799 the Committee of Secrecy reported to the House of Commons, it was sure that systematic conspiracy resting on political societies was to be feared. It therefore recommended restraints on the 'licentiousness' of the press and extraordinary powers for the government, but made no mention of Philosophes, Illuminati or freemasons.[6]

No doubt resistance to this particular mythology is one reason why freemasonry remained unpersecuted on this side of the Channel. Had the islands ever been successfully invaded by the French, this might have changed, but, even admitting this remote possibility, the impeccable respectability of the British freemasons must be recognised as uniquely successful in resisting the taint of treason. This was true even when other societies were under heavy legal and public pressure and others besides Barruel were exploiting the conspiracy fears of the decade in print. The freemasons did not go uncriticised, it is true; in June 1794, the *Gentleman's Magazine* carried as its leading article a summary of Lefranc's *Le voile levé* with comments. The tone was suspicious, but the author's enquiry about the 'tendency' of freemasonry soon provoked a brief and angry reply the following month from 'Rusticus', and in August a 'P.M. of the lodge of Antiquity' developed a much longer refutation of Lefranc, whose work was dismissed as 'fabulous'. No doubt, said the writer, 'imposters' had introduced 'modern fanatical innovations', but this was not to say that freemasonry was in itself vicious, indeed, the opposite was true: it was a school of morality and decorum. 'Had the example of Masons, or the influence of their tenets, a proper weight in the scale of government, we should not so frequently witness scenes of dissension and discord.'[7]

[6] Report of the Committee of Secrecy of the House of Commons, 15 March 1799. It is also worth remark that no excitement at all seems to have been aroused early in the Revolution by the communication to Grenville by Lord Auckland, then at The Hague, of a note given him by the Grand Pensionary which asserted the existence of a secret club, la Propagande, aiming at universal subversion by winning over public opinion. The note is printed in Hist. Mss. Comm. XIV Report, Appendix, v; *The manuscripts of J. B. Fortescue, Esq., preserved at Dropmore* (London, 1894), ii, p. 69. For the response of a French counter-revolutionary to reports about la Propagande, see J. Chaumié, *Le réseau d'Antraigues et la contre-révolution 1791–1793* (Paris, 1965), pp. 82–5.

[7] *Gentleman's Magazine*, pp. 491, 612 and 697.

Possibly the best argument of such apologists was that anyone could become a mason and see for himself what went on, for it was one likely to carry much more weight than in continental countries where derivations and heresies made the counter-argument of reserved secrets much more effective. One British writer who attempted to use it was himself a freemason. In 1797, a little after Barruel's first volumes appeared, the Scotsman Robison produced a version of the conspiracy theory with the specific aim of protecting the reputation of orthodox English freemasonry by throwing the blame on the Illuminati and other now traditional villains (among other things he repeated the story that the Jesuits invented Scots masonry and the Templar legend). He asserted that Jacobites among whom 'the celebrated Chevalier Ramsay had a great share in all this business' had striven to subvert orthodox freemasonry towards the mystical and occultist rites (singling out Willermoz' Lyon circle as a special example) and condemned mystical writings as productive of impiety and destructive of faith. His book was attacked, but it enjoyed great success, as its reprinting quickly showed.[8]

Yet though the atmosphere made such a success possible, the mythology in Great Britain never became strong enough to threaten the entrenched respectability of English freemasonry after seventy years of life and Robison's pleading can hardly be said to have been necessary. A bill of 1799 against the freemasons made no headway in Parliament; the Craft was, indeed, specifically exempted from the Unlawful Societies Act of the same year which did not extend to regular lodges of freemasons in being before the passing of the Act.[9] The ostentatious loyalty of English freemasonry was guaranteed by the succession of three princes of the blood royal to the Grand Mastership between 1782 and 1813, the Duke of Cumberland, the Prince of Wales and the Duke of Sussex and, in 1793, at a particularly bad moment in the Revolution because of the violence of events in France, the *Freemasons'*

---

[8] *Proofs of a Conspiracy against all the Religions and Governments of Europe, carried on in the secret meetings of Free Masons, Illuminati and Reading Societies* (London, 1797) with further editions in Edinburgh (1797), Dublin (1798), London and New York (1798), was severely handled in the *Monthly Review* (January–April 1798, p. 303, for a notice of the second edition), and the *Freemasons' Magazine*, X. Another masonic reply was W. Preston, *The misrepresentation of Barruel and Robison exposed* (London, 1799) who also draws attention to a translation of *The Life of J. G. Zimmermann* by Tissot (London, 1797) as one of the first places in which alarm over the Illuminati was raised in England. Barruel himself criticised Robison.

[9] 39 Geo. III c. 79 which thereby became the first statutory acknowledgment of the existence of freemasonry. Lord Liverpool in 1814 tried again to legislate against masons, but his bill had no success.

Magazine printed a picture of the Prince of Wales as its frontispiece and mingled his feathers with masonic symbols in its title page. This would not in itself have been sufficiently reassuring, perhaps (Orléans, after all, had been a Bourbon), had it not been for the fidelity of the Craft in England to its original apolitical ideals. This, together with its relative freedom from the taint of the esoteric breakaway obediences of European masonry, placed it in a very strong position.[10] Masons improved it whenever possible, by their own efforts. They printed loyal addresses to the King in the *Freemasons' Magazine*. They piously recorded the execution of the Duke of Orléans as 'the forfeit of his crimes'.[11] Later, the same magazine denounced him strongly and was at pains to explain away his association with the Prince of Wales. The Craft seems, it is true, not to have been entirely freed from apprehension that masonic conduct might still attract hostility. In 1800 Grand Lodge made a public protest against the charge of disloyalty and recalled the standing inhibition on political discussion, but such signs of concern do not imply very grave danger.[12]

The freemasons, then, did not suffer much from the reaction to the revolutionary shock in Great Britain, though this can hardly be taken as evidence that the conspiracy theory had not won some acceptance there in so far as it relied on other villains. Even the most level-headed and liberal-minded Englishmen were bound to pause to reflect that there did exist in the United Kingdom at least one major conspiratorial threat. In so far as this country has ever faced a true revolutionary danger since the seventeenth century, it has always been in Ireland. The danger there was pointed out by the writer Clifford in a book whose title explicitly drew attention to the need to fill a gap in Barruel's information.[13] On Ireland, where the United Irishmen conspiracy had just been detected, Clifford was more plausible than in his attempt to weave his account of the English Corresponding Societies and the mutinies of the fleet into the same scheme. In the case of the United Irishmen there was, too, the masonic connexion of some members and their use of masonic symbolism and language to draw on for those who did not feel convinced of English masonry's respectability. Nonetheless, events on the other side of St George's Channel did not change the

[10] Willermoz later alleged (Chevallier, *Barral*, p. 206) that the Duke of Gloucester had shown interest in the Strict Observance Order, but this seems unconfirmed.

[11] Issues of July and November 1793.

[12] This is quoted by G. Oliver, in *The golden remains of the early masonic writers* (London, 1847), ii, pp. 3–4.

[13] *Application of Barruel's Memoirs of Jacobinism to the Secret Societies of Ireland and Great Britain* (London, 1798).

general impression given by English masonry of respectability and loyalty.

In continental Europe outside France, the greatest concern about secret societies was from the first shown in Germany and the Habsburg dominions. Its origins have already been touched upon; they are to be sought before 1789, in the reaction against Enlightenment in the 1780s and in the special provocation given to this reaction by the work of Joseph II. By 1789 this had led to a confused and ambiguous situation, but there already existed a widespread acceptance of the 'plot' theory—thanks to the Illuminati revelations—which the events of the French Revolution were likely to confirm. When it came, there were swift reactions. As early as October 1789, Frederick William II was writing to the Elector of Saxony to point out that what was known of Illuminati penetration of masonic lodges suggested that there was a danger that the disorders of France might be repeated in Germany.[14] In the following year the Austrian government received the first warnings from one of its diplomats (Metternich's father) that French agents and propaganda, organised from a Parisian centre, might be expected to undertake subversive activity.[15] Already, in the same year, a Hamburg newspaper announced a plot to spread anarchy from France and there was widespread concern over the existence of a 'propaganda club' supposedly set up to bring about subversion in the French interest.[16] These alarms all met with a ready response; the threat of subversion could now be linked to the threat to traditional religion already felt to be inherent in the Aufklärung and the threat to the traditional social order discerned in such 'enlightened' reforms as those carried out in Austria. The first political impact of this mood had been Rosicrucian conservative successes in Prussia and a mass of pietistic and philosophic publication which embodied anti-masonic themes as well as anti-rationalist themes.[17] The growth of the plot psychosis in Germany depended more than anywhere else on a general anti-Enlightenment and anti-rationalist attitude which carried over into political thought important elements of mysticism, irrationalism and reaction. In 1791 came what seems to have been the first published statement outside France of the link between intellectual and political

[14] Le Forestier, Les Illuminés, p. 616.

[15] E. Wangermann, From Joseph II to the Jacobin Trials, 2nd edn. (Oxford, 1969), p. 62.

[16] Le Forestier, Les Illuminés, p. 634 and K. Julku, Die revolutionäre Bewegung in Rheinland am Ende des achtzehnten Jahrhunderts, II (Helsinki, 1969), p. 33, where there are newspaper references.

[17] See Faivre, passim (but esp. p. 50) on the work of such writers as Zimmermann.

revolution and secret societies, a pamphlet by the former Illuminatus, Eckartshausen.[18] It was reprinted two years later. Soon, too, the necessary personal connexions were being alleged in the repetition of the story that Bode had corrupted Bonneville to Illuminati doctrines in 1787.[19]

In the circumstances, it is not surprising that much of the early sympathy felt in Germany as elsewhere for the attempts of the French to put their house in order should soon have begun to dissipate. Times were hard; a few examples of popular disorder in town and countryside alarmed people who had seen what followed such troubles in France.[20] Soon, the proximity of the Rhineland to the Revolution began to produce a special alarm there. Some of the German lay rulers of the region had feudal territories in Alsace which were affected by French legislation on feudal rights, and some ecclesiastical rulers had jurisdictions which extended to territory soon subjected to the French laws confiscating ecclesiastical property and to the Civil Constitution of the Clergy. This gave the Rhineland a special political sensitivity. Finally, it also produced the first German Jacobins. Germans elsewhere were especially appalled when French invasion brought the collapse of the traditional authorities in the Rhineland and the appearance of vociferous French sympathisers and collaborators.

It may be that some of these groups had origins in masonic lodges; at any rate masonic influence was soon said to be at work among them.[21]

---

[18] *Über die Gefahr, die dem Thronen, dem Staaten und dem Christenthume dem gänzlichen Verfall drohet, durch das falsche Sistem der Leutigen Aufklärung und die kechen Anmasoungen sogennanter Philosophen, geheimer Gesellschaften und Sekten* (Munich, 1791).

[19] This story seems to have circulated in Germany just as quickly as in France. See *Wiener Zeitschrift*, 1793, p. 245. On the other hand it does not get mentioned in C. Girtaner's enormous and tedious compilation, *Historischen Nachrichten über die Französischen Revolution* (Berlin, 1792–1803), 17 vols., one of the main channels by which Germans obtained information about the Revolution, although Bonneville is described in it (iii, p. 25) with special reference to his masonic connexions and his aims 'die Freimaurer Logen zu Seminarien der Anarchie und des Aufruhrs zu machen'.

[20] Epstein, *Genesis*, pp. 441–6.

[21] A few years later, the Mainz Jacobin Club was satirised on the stage for being under Illuminati influence (Epstein, pp. 461–2). Evidence has been found (*AR*, 1913, pp. 101–2) of the Mayor of Strasbourg printing in German a message from the French mother-lodge of the Scots Rite for distribution across the Rhine. Of the importance of the Jacobin club there, among whose members exiles from the German states were prominent, there can be no doubt. Its activity is noted, *passim*, by K. Julku, *Die revolutionäre Bewegung*, already cited. The same author has also discussed a German 'Jacobin' who had been a freemason and involved with Rosicrucianism in his article 'La conception de la Révolution chez Georg Forster' (*AHRF*, 1968).

Certainly, as in many other countries, sympathisers with France could be found easily among freemasons. But a difficulty remains: did freemasons turn to France because they were always revolutionary at heart, or did they serve the French in anger after being persecuted by their own governments? Though the question is not relevant to our purpose it should have occurred to contemporaries. What is clear is that, however the process worked, the result was a situation which strengthened the belief that freemasons were ipso facto subversive and prompted many freemasons to do things which then reinforced this view. Whatever the truth of the matter, they were, in the state of the public mind, an obvious target for the many governments in Germany which now began to put new vigour into their policies of repression. What has been called a 'rain of repressive edicts' fell upon Germany.[22] The Bavarian government in 1790 actually decreed the death penalty for some offences in connexion with Illuminati activity and went so far as to banish a number of suspects.[23]

Such reactions were very disproportionate to the danger, in so far as it can be estimated. In retrospect, the impressive feature of Germany's history in the decade after 1789 is the lack of revolutionary potential displayed. But this, of course, could always be attributed to the efficacy of repression and, therefore, used as an argument for further repression. The fear was great and contributed powerfully to the building-up of even greater credibility about the secret societies.

How little danger there was can be seen in the famous 'conspiracy' brought to light in the Austrian and Hungarian Jacobin trials of 1794. The background to this was particularly complicated, because the last year of Joseph's life had already presented the Vienna government with a real internal threat that was in origin wholly unconnected with events in France. This was the opposition—which became outright rebellion—in Belgium and Hungary to the reforming legislation of the 'enlightened' monarch. But this was not all that alarmed the Emperor and some of his advisers. However strong his wish to exercise a jurisdictional supremacy over the clergy, for example, and to control education, Joseph deplored the development of atheism and scepticism which accompanied freedom of publication and religious toleration. To this extent, he was himself sympathetic to the intellectual reaction.[24] Yet this reaction cut in other ways across Joseph's

[22] Epstein, p. 459.

[23] Worry persisted; as late as 1801 an Austrian spy reported that the Illuminati were at work in Bavaria (Le Forestier, Les Illuminés, p. 700).

[24] In 1788, the police action against a Viennese associate of Bahrdt's German Union was evidence of the changing mood. See Wangermann, pp. 41–3.

policies, for it seemed to imply a recrudescence of clerical authority and a reinforcement of the feudal structure. Given the divisions among his advisers and civil servants, it is not surprising that some uncertainty marks the relation of government and Enlightenment on the eve of 1789. It is perhaps too much to speak of an internal crisis in the Josephine system in 1788–9, but there is a sense of internal dislocation and confusion of purposes and of an awareness that demands were now being made by the unprivileged too which indicated that obedience could no longer be unquestionedly assumed. Yet on that assumption had been based the policies directed against privilege.

One of the responses of authority was the improvement of repressive machinery by the creation of a new centralised secret police, with far-reaching powers.[25] This was one sign on the eve of the Revolution that it would find the Austrian government especially aware of the dangers of subversion. Another important fact was that because of its supporters in the anti-clerical campaigns, this government already had more than a nodding acquaintance with the way in which some free-masons and Illuminati had taken opportunities to influence government.[26] There were, therefore, several influences inclining the Habsburg government towards a more reactionary stance even before the events in France provided fresh grounds for fearing the effect of conspiracy. Those events strengthened a tendency to reaction already implicit in Joseph's new awareness of the difficulties facing him. His own sister's humiliations now provided fresh arguments for the unwisdom of concession to popular demands. The danger of uncaging forces in his own dominions which could not be controlled, were he to persist in the campaign against privilege, must have become more apparent. 1789 was, moreover, a bad year for popular discontent at home. The war with Turkey and Joseph's economic policies both caused widespread hardship; the ruling classes became fearful when their own peasants began to carry out attacks on their landlords like those of the summer in France. The sails were therefore being set for reaction before Joseph's death.

Yet the speed with which it came and the contribution of fears of secret societies must not be exaggerated. The instructions drawn up

[25] Wangermann, pp. 36–43. Under Leopold, these powers were restricted, but they were later enlarged again. Eventually, they provided a security organisation with wide responsibilities for the control of public opinion and the repression of subversive activity throughout the entire Habsburg dominions. See also D. E. Emerson, *Metternich and the Political Police* (The Hague, 1968).

[26] In retrospect, such examples as those from Hungary cited by Wangermann, p. 11, must have seemed sinister. See also p. 48.

in March 1790 for the secret police were very full, and ranged over the whole field of responsibility for subversion, but they did not specifically mention secret societies.[27] Leopold then continued the tendency announced under Joseph. Alarm over events in France grew stronger as war came nearer. By 1792, Zimmermann, the anti-rationalist polemicist of the 1780s, felt able to urge Leopold to lead a league of German princes against the disciples of Weishaupt.[28] This hope was dashed by the death of the Emperor in 1792, but he had by then already given some encouragement to the intellectual reaction. He patronised a periodical founded at the end of 1791 by L. A. Hoffmann, self-appointed defender of German civilisation against Aufklärung and Illuminati. Hoffmann had once been on the other side; he had worked for Joseph II in the operation of his anti-clerical policies and had been a freemason while still too young for formal initiation. Nevertheless, he had refused to become an Illuminatus and was even before 1789 urging good freemasons that grave danger lay in the misleading approaches made to them by the new Order. At about the same time he had begun to attack such rationalist writers as Nicolai. When the Revolution came, he quickly interpreted it as a manifestation of the Illuminati conspiracy.

The new periodical which he edited was the *Wiener Zeitschrift*, the most important of those in German providing regular space for anti-Illuminati propaganda.[29] A leading authority has singled it out as the first avowedly conservative periodical in Germany.[30] It associated German patriotism, anti-rationalism and the usual suspicions of secret societies. From the start it closely followed events in France (one article in the first number was a denunciation of the Amis des noirs). One of its features was a controversy between Zimmermann (who advised Hoffmann) and Knigge, in which the Swiss insisted that the Illuminati were still at work in places of influence. Letters of encouragement from Frederick William II appeared in the third number; it also contained a prologue denouncing the 'horde of cosmopolitan and philanthropic writers' and the 'terrifying impotence' of secret societies. It asserted the need to turn public opinion against the principles of what it termed 'Aufklärungsbarberei'.[31] This the *Wiener Zeitschrift*

[27] Wangermann, p. 37.
[28] For Zimmermann, Faivre, pp. 46–8; Epstein, p. 488; above, p. 147.
[29] *Wiener Zeitschrift* (Vienna, 1792–3). There were three parts each year.
[30] Epstein, p. 517.
[31] I (1792), pp. 3–6, 'Diese Schriftsteller . . . sie führen das grosse Wort bei den meisten Nationen, und zumal in ganz Deutschland. Die offentliche Meinung ist in ihren handen. Ihre meistens berühmten oder vielmeher berüchtigen Namen, ihr Hunger und ihre Habsricht, ihre unverschämte und zugellose Schwatzhaftig-

strove to do by steady, if undistinguished, propaganda in the conservative interest. Selections of 'Aufklärung-Sottisen' were included in most issues and much was made of the horrid example of the Illuminati. Particularly violent attacks were made on Knigge, whom Hoffmann still believed to be an active conspirator. That the Illuminati had made a deep impression on Hoffmann is clear, for its influence appears also in a curious body called 'The Association' which he had conceived as a reply to the great Jacobin conspiracy. Leopold had given him encouragement in this, too. It was in fact to have been a conservative secret society, whose aims were 'to counteract French propaganda, demagogic principles, the heady wine of philanthropic libertarianism, irreligion and false Aufklärung as well as all secret orders, factions and societies devoted to these goals. Furthermore, to define and spread true principles. . . .'[32] This is an interesting example of the power of the secret society craze to generate bodies which themselves give the mythology greater substance. Hoffmann's confidence in the secret society technique extended, too, to the borrowing of specific practical and organisational details from the Illuminati.[33]

This scheme crumbled with Leopold's death and the *Wiener Zeitschrift* survived only until September 1793.[34] Its contribution to the atmosphere of reaction was made by then and it had been an important one. Moreover, Austria had gone to war. The need to close ranks made conciliation of the conservatives alienated by reform even more important. It also made the use of police against supposedly subversive elements seem much more urgent. It was early in February 1793 that an instruction was given to the police that all secret 'conventicles',

---

keit, alle ihre Ranke und Kniffe, verbunden mit der fürchterlichen Allmacht der geheimen Orden, geben ihren verderblichen Grundsätzen überall Genricht, Einfluss und die traurigste Wirksamkeit.'

[32] Quoted in Epstein, p. 522.

[33] For other examples of Leopold's patronage of Hoffmann, see Wangermann, pp. 86–7, where it is suggested that the Emperor's main aim was to use his arguments to bring the recalcitrant Hungarians to heel by emphasising dangers in the policies of opposition to the crown which they might have overlooked.

[34] Hoffmann thereafter fell out of the public eye, but continued to write, publishing, among other things, an attack on Bode in 1795 based on the familiar story of his promotion of the French Revolution by his 1787 visit to Paris. It was suggested in the following century that Hoffmann was the original of the villainous Monostatos, in *The Magic Flute*, but this seems improbable, though the pervasiveness of masonic influence and symbolism in the opera have often been remarked (see E. J. Dent, *Mozart's Operas. A Critical Study*, 2nd edn. (Oxford, 1947), p. 223, and, for a closer examination of Mozart's masonic affiliations, H. Bradley, 'Bro. Mozart and some of his masonic friends', *AQC*, xxvi, 1913).

H

whatever their pretext, were to be forbidden.[35] By the end of the year all masonic lodges had ceased to meet. Little could be done against this current. Those who had previously had the ear of the administration in the heyday of Josephine reform and still had some access to it can hardly have helped matters if, like one of their number, they urged the government back to reform with the threat that if it were not resumed the Illuminati would provoke revolution.[36] This was the background against which there came in 1794 the discovery of a 'plot' which was to be used as striking confirmation of the fears of those who saw the hand of secret societies at work in everything.

In spite of the way in which the discovery and trials were subsequently presented, no general and co-ordinated conspiracy seems to have existed.[37] In the Habsburg dominions there were a number of discontented persons. Four groups of them have been distinguished, of which the most important were those in Hungary and Vienna. The business of co-ordination of their activities was only starting when the arrests were made. All that had been achieved by them was a certain amount of discussion and some dissemination of printed propaganda for reform. Nevertheless, this was serious enough, and in both the Viennese and Hungarian groups there was also evidence of Illuminati influence. In Hungary the most important conspirator, Martinovics (who later turned out to be the most useful informant for the police), had actually organised two secret societies which embodied both the classical device of reserved secrets and the socially revolutionary concern of the Illuminati. One of his societies was designed to recruit the Hungarian gentry to launch a revolution with the aim of national independence; the other, unknown to members of the first, was to be ready to exploit the success of the first by, in due course, overthrowing the Hungarian feudal structure. Members of the Viennese group showed masonic influence, too, in the nature of their ceremonies and had taken an oath said to show Illuminati tendencies to 'promote virtue, and to hate despotism and the hierarchy of the triple-crowned monster'—that is, the Roman communion.

From 1793, the police had known about the Viennese circle. The worsening international situation and bad domestic circumstances of 1794 seemed to make an exposure desirable in order to rally public opinion. An 'agent provocateur' was employed to provide the evidence for arrests. These arrests brought in, among others, Martinovics;

[35] Wangermann, p. 129.
[36] Wangermann, p. 117.
[37] For what follows, Wangermann, pp. 137–73.

until then, the Hungarian secret societies had not been known to the police, but he now told them all about them. Soon, arrests were extended to Styria as further traces were uncovered.

The authorities now set out deliberately to exploit the possibilities of influencing public opinion which the discoveries offered. A special commission was set up to try the Austrian prisoners, others went before Hungarian courts or military tribunals. Most of the accused were found guilty. There were two executions in Austria (one of a dead man) and seven in Hungary. Heavy sentences of imprisonment were also imposed. But the most important result was the confirmation which the conspiracy provided of all that had been feared of the pernicious impact of enlightened ideas. It was the decisive moment in the swing to complete reaction in the Habsburg dominions.

After the Jacobin trials, fear of secret societies was an ineradicable element of German conservatism.[38] The dismay felt earlier by those who deplored the blindness of the age in failing to see their importance was now dissipated.[39] Practically, the pursuit of suspected conspirators by the police and the imposition of censorship on periodicals and authors believed to express seditious and subversive views went to extraordinary lengths. Sometimes the results were very odd. This was the case with an impeccably conservative journal, *Eudämonia*, founded with the support of the Margrave of Baden and the Landgrave of Hesse-Cassel in 1795.[40]

Its prospectus pointed out the enormous importance of French authors in preparing the way for the French Revolution and announced that its aim would be to provide news and commentary which would enable people to meet the common danger. Information would be given about revolutionary and anti-revolutionary writings and about the worthy deeds of Germany's rulers and the merits of the German polity (Verfassung) would be demonstrated.[41] Each number contained several articles, and there were six numbers to a volume. One of the

[38] It may be remarked that 1794 was something of a turning-point elsewhere, too; discoveries of conspiracy also took place in Naples and Piedmont (see below).

[39] See Faivre, *Kirchberger*, pp. 48–9, on the disappointment felt at Leopold's death.

[40] *Eudämonia, oder deutsches Volksglück, ein Journal für Freunde von Wahrheit und Recht,* 6 vols. (Leipzig (I), Frankfurt (II–V) and Nuremberg (VI), 1795–8). Barruel made use of it.

[41] 'Nachrichten, wodurch schädliche Entwürfe, Unternehmungen, Gesellschaften etc., welche zum Umsturz der christlichen Religion und der gesetz mässigen Verfassung der Staaten, Länder, Provinzen, Republiken, etc. abzwecken, ausgedekt und dem Publikum in ihrer Blösse und Verwerflichkeit dargestellt werden.' (I, iv). One foreign writer to whom considerable publicity was given was Montjoie, whose book on the Duke of Orléans was discussed in two articles (IV, pp. 53, 97 ff.).

editors was the stormy petrel of the Strict Observance and opponent
of Baron von Hund, J. A. Starck. In 1782 he was still encouraging
brother masons to forget their differences and divisions.[42] Soon he was
disillusioned and broke with freemasonry, his touchy and quarrelsome
nature expressing it in a novel in which he exposed his former masonic
brothers. This provoked even more bitterness and rancour than his
earlier divisive activity in the Strict Observance. At about the same
time he appears to have undergone a decisive theological evolution.
Even in Paris in 1765 he had somehow managed to reconcile his status
as a Protestant pastor with a clandestine 'conversion' to Catholicism,
but this had not prevented him in the following decade from making
contributions to the rationalist reinterpretation of Lutheran theology.
In the 1780s he finally changed direction again. He began to advocate a
much more Catholic position and was soon attacked in the great debate
on 'crypto-Catholicism'; his behaviour was said to be the result of a
Jesuit plot to undermine Protestantism.

In 1787 Starck had published a twelve-hundred-page reply to his
critics in which he took up the theme of the secret societies.[43] The outbreak of the French Revolution found him ready to discern in it at
once the stigmata of the Illuminati conspiracy. His presumed contributions to *Eudämonia* took the same line.[44] Starck's old King Charles's
Head, Knigge, appears many times in its pages and is the object of
violent abuse and attack.[45] Kant was a more distinguished object of
attack and was handled more cautiously, with sneers and innuendo
rather than outright abuse. Mauvillon and Fichte were other victims.
All the time, too, *Eudämonia* hammered away at the theme that the
Illuminati were still at work; they were even supposed to be engaged
in a plot to stifle the sale of Barruel's book in Germany.[46] Nonetheless,
the editors' touch was not always happy; when they denounced the
chief Viennese censor as a secret Illuminatus, several of their issues were

[42] *Ueber die alten und neuen Mysterien* (Berlin, 1782), in which, nonetheless, he does
suggest that schism may by then be irreparable (p. 372).

[43] *Über Kryptokatholicismus, Proselytenmacherey, Jesuitismus, geheime Gesellschaften*
Frankfurt and Leipzig).

[44] Presumed because the articles are anonymous and have not been properly
distinguished. Another contributor was L. A. Hoffmann.

[45] Starck shared the view that Knigge, rather than Weishaupt, was the source of
the wickedness of the Illuminati and the demon of the sect. He described him once
to Barruel as 'le Mirabeau, le Robespierre, le Sieyès des Illuminés, unis dans une
seule personne'. Letter of 22 March 1798, Barruel papers, ASJP.

[46] *Eudämonia*, VI, p. 425. The fear of a conspiracy controlling publishing went
back, of course, to the Deutsche Union scare of 1788 (see above, p. 132). Bode and
Bahrdt were denounced in the first issue of *Eudämonia* for this (pp. 5–9).

prohibited in Austria. In 1797 an imperial decree imposed a total suppression of this and similar journals.

It is worthwhile to follow Starck's career just a little further, before leaving the story of Germany's growing susceptibility to the secret society legend in the revolutionary decade. Immediately after the closing down of the paper he was offering advice to Barruel, hoping, as we have seen, to get him to take up a less indiscriminate attitude towards freemasonry, but failing. In part because of this failure he published six years after the end of *Eudämonia* the most complete and coherent account of the conspiracy theory to appear in German in the *Triumph der Philosophie im 18 Jahrhundert*.[47] It has long been thought to have been prompted by a wish to answer Mounier's refutation of Barruel, which had been published in Germany, but, in fact, he was thinking about it before that work appeared.[48] In it, Starck provided a discussion on the scale of Barruel's and it had a comparable success in Germany, though it never made the same impact elsewhere.

Starck took his story back to the Greek philosophers and proceeded from them via the medieval heresies. In many details his account differs from that of Barruel, whom he had advised, but on the general importance of the philosophes, their connexion with more ancient intellectual perversions and their wicked methods the two authors substantially agree. Important differences of emphasis emerge only in the discussion of the immediate origins of the French Revolution, where Starck lays much more stress than could Barruel on the development of the German Aufklärung and its implications. He knew enough to be unable to go as far as Barruel in condemning freemasonry and restricts himself rather to the charge that many lodges had allowed themselves to be penetrated by the Illuminati who then exploited them. It was the Illuminati who were the keystone of his version of the plot theory and it was the Illuminati, of course, who embodied most evidently the views of the Enlightenment.

Here Starck showed the greatest credulousness, believing not only the worst and most exaggerated interpretations of such evidence as had come to light, but that the Order had survived persecution and continued to exist and act in a clandestine manner. He insisted that Bahrdt's Deutsche Union scheme was an attempt to spread its principles and that it was in the 1787 mission of Bode to Paris that there was

---

[47] Germantown [Frankfurt]. Much of it had appeared in *Eudämonia*.

[48] ASJP, Starck to Barruel, 16 January 1800: 'Je travaille à un livre qui pourra servir de compagnon de votre ouvrage. C'est le *triomphe de philosophie* avec le motto anglais: *Havock and spoil and ruin are my gain*.'

to be found the origin of the Revolution of 1789. He said that French freemasons had not become Illuminati as a result of this, but had formed secret committees—with, inevitably, the Duke of Orléans at their head, though Orléans had not grasped the republican purposes of the plotters. These committees became the reading circles and clubs of the revolution, of which the most famous was the Jacobin Club.

In defence of this thesis Starck considered and, to his satisfaction, disposed of the claims of other theories about the causes of the Revolution. Once the Revolution had begun, its religious policy seemed to him a sufficient further proof of its Illuminatist nature. After this, it is hardly surprising that he believed two million persons to have died in the Terror and that sixty thousand people were employed in propaganda for distribution among France's neighbours. (That in Germany he supposed to be directed from Strasburg, under the direction of the Illuminatus mayor of its revolutionary municipality, Dietrich.) Faced with this threat, given the demoralised nature of established religion and the omnipresence of the Illuminati the outlook for Germany was, he thought, gloomy. The only hope was firm, determined action of the princes by educational reform, police control and censorship, to end the influence of the radicals in their states.

By 1803 many sources had thus flowed together into a plot obsession which was to have a central place in German romanticism. Starck had earlier helped Barruel to rectify some of his factual errors; he himself took the view that orthodox freemasonry was innocent, only becoming dangerous because of Illuminati infiltration. Yet such distinctions were by this time almost insignificant; what matters is the general acceptance of a conspiracy framework which his success implies.[49] He was, after all, trying to do properly a job he believed Barruel and Robison to have botched. He provided the literary and philosophical expression of a view of the danger facing civilisation from secret societies which had been ominously put in an administrative form by the founder of the Austrian secret police a year before. As his retiring advice, this official warned the Emperor that the danger of the secret societies was such that the police would have to extend his service's operations to survey not only public spirit in the Habsburg lands, but throughout all Europe.[50] In this advice, the police ideal of the Restoration was already crystallised.

German-speaking Europe is so important in this phase of the myth-

---

[49] J. Droz, 'La légende du complot illuministe et les origines du romantisme politique en Allemagne', *RH*, 1961, pp. 335–8.
[50] Emerson, p. 29.

ology of reaction that not much need be said about other countries. In Portugal the Craft had always had a rough passage and in 1792 it was ordered that freemasons should be handed over to the Inquisition. In Spain, too, their suppression was the duty of the Inquisition. Even where reaction was not violent, official concern could bring quiet suppression. In 1790 we find the members of the Sincerité lodge of Savoy voluntarily suspending their activities, and undertaking not to meet again. This was not the whole story in Savoy; lodges owing obedience to the Grand Orient in Paris continued their activities down to July 1792 in spite of police surveillance.[51] This division in Savoyard masonry seems to have reflected in some degree a division between largely aristocratic lodges and those containing a more middle-class membership; it was certainly remarked later that among the membership of the sociétés populaires at Chambéry, which appeared after the French occupation in 1793, were former freemasons from the bourgeois circles whose ranks, unlike those of the aristocracy, were not depleted by emigration. Possibly this fact, together with the enrolling of former freemasons in the new administration set up by the French, contributed to the royal edict of May 1794 closing all masonic lodges in Sardinia. But alarm over discovery of an insurrectionary plot seems also to have played a part.[52]

This example, nevertheless, introduces a new element. Savoy was actually occupied by French forces. Here, as in the Rhineland and many other places later, the welcome given to the invaders by persons who had once been freemasons and later served the French as Quislings seemed the most powerful evidence of all of international conspiracy and the strongest justification of harsh measures against them.[53] In this way above all, the events of the Revolution provided others than Frenchmen with what seemed to be irrefutable evidence of conspiracy. As the French armies entered the territory of their neighbours sympathisers sprang up around them to give this evidence all the more convincing an aspect. This was nowhere more true than in Italy, where,

[51] Vermale, pp. 20, 37. See also R. Sòriga, Le Società segrete, l'emigrazione politica e i primi moti per l'indipendenza (Modena, 1942), pp. 5–6, for evidence of the ending of the contributions paid to the Grand Orient by the Savoy lodges, in which the Governor of Savoy commented favourably on the Chambéry lodge as 'composée de personnes honnêtes de toutes les classes et sans mauvaises intentions'.

[52] It is perhaps worth remark that even in the United States the matter of secret societies attracted enough attention for Congress to debate freemasonry.

[53] It is interesting, though, that Belgian freemasonry seems to have had more success in resisting slanders of revolutionary sympathies than that of other countries. Even Barruel found it hard to make a case against them. See the interesting observations of J. Bartier, AHRF, 1969, pp. 478–85.

for nearly three years, the presence of French occupation forces was to stimulate political effervescence as nowhere else. This was also the country in which the first purely political secret societies appeared, thus providing yet more confirmation of what was suspected by alarmed reactionaries and was soon to be feared by revolutionaries. Finally, it was from Italy in these years that there came the man who more than any other came himself to embody the myth of the secret societies, Buonarroti.

BUONARROTI

If the history and mythology of the secret societies have a personal focus, it is Buonarroti, for forty-odd years a pest to European policemen. He was to do more than anyone to give reality to the spectre of the universal conspiracy although he achieved nothing. Not unjustifiably, he has been called the first professional revolutionary; in him we can begin to trace a thread of revolutionary practice and theory which reaches as far as the twentieth century and may even go back to the Illuminati. He appeared first on stage in the disturbance brought to Italy by the French Revolution. At that time, too, there emerged there the first important political secret societies and many of the men who would spread the techniques and principles of these societies all over Europe in the next two or three decades. The reaction of Italy to the French Revolution is, therefore, of special importance to the mythology of the secret societies. Whatever conspiracies existed elsewhere, they first achieved in Italy a consistency and organisation which gave them more than temporary significance.

Although Illuminati influences were already at work in Italy before 1789, there is no reason to believe that without the Revolution they would have prospered any better there than anywhere else. The decisive influence in the shaping of Italian secret societies was the Revolution itself, the major force making for change in Italian life between 1789 and 1799. It made itself felt in two clearly defined phases. Down to 1796, the Revolution influenced Italians through propaganda, personal contact, cultural interconnexions and diplomacy; after that year, when the French armies broke into the peninsula, the direct influence of the French soldiers and administrators on the spot and their interpretation of the orders they received from Paris was what mattered most. The young Buonarroti's entry into conspiratorial and subversive activity took place during the first phase.

Italy then presented a wide variety of political and social circumstance on which the Revolution was to operate. Unlike France, she was not united before 1789. Her thirteen major political divisions were importantly different from one another in government and administration. Their economies, too, varied greatly. Although there was everywhere an overwhelming predominance of agriculture, sharp contrasts existed in the conditions of rural life from region to region. The peninsula's great seaports (Naples was the third largest city in Europe), old urban centres and pockets of long-established industry introduced further variety. The nobilities and directing élites were distinct from one another, some largely urban and patrician in origin, some feudal and landed. Their privileges varied, too, for in some states (notably Tuscany and the Austrian-ruled provinces of Lombardy and Mantua) governments had put into practice some of the rationalising and reforming measures associated with 'Enlightened Despotism'. The States of the Church were unique. Although the clergy everywhere exercised great authority, they there ruled directly; the eighteenth-century Papacy was not highly regarded by other governments. In its own territories it had already begun to arouse the turbulent anti-clericalism which later tr oubled the Legations.

Nevertheless, the Roman Church was the dominant cultural and ideological force. Tiny Protestant and Jewish communities hardly mattered. The predominance of the Church was accepted by the educated minority, who did not usually go so far in enlightened scepticism as their equivalents in France. Feeling against the Church tended to take traditional regalian or Jansenist and anti-curial forms rather than to run to outright attacks on religion or the Catholic church per se. In any case, those interested in such matters were few. For the most part, literate Italians lived in the straitened isolations of their local capitals. Like their inferiors, they were divided from one another by tradition, economics, government and even language. Italian nationalism did not exist; at best it was a cultural ideal, a generalisation from literature and history. The influence of the French Revolution had to play, therefore, on a collection of diverse and sluggish societies.

Official Italian reactions to the Revolution and to the development of a new French foreign policy were varied. Sardinia, of course, as a neighbour of France, had to face a more direct threat than other states. Emigrés had quickly appeared at Turin with tales of horror and insult which alarmed the French-speaking nobility of Piedmont; the House of Savoy ruled a feudal monarchy which felt itself especially threatened by the propaganda assaults of republicanism and egalitarianism. This combined with the danger which was felt over Savoy, exposed on the other side of the Alps to French attack, to produce hostility to the Revolution in Turin earlier than anywhere except Rome. War did not actually begin between the two states until July 1792, but was quickly followed in November by the French annexation of Savoy. The Papacy, the other early Italian antagonist of the Revolution, had been the first territorial power to suffer despoliation, when the French annexed Avignon. Other Italian states were less directly disturbed. Naples had a special interest in French affairs because of family ties. Venice, remote from the immediate impact of the Revolution, was not disposed to, or provoked into, formal hostilities. Genoa, like Tuscany, had to walk uneasily between the pressures of British and French diplomacy. There were, therefore, important differences in governmental attitudes. Only Sardinia among the Italian states committed itself to war with France and persisted in it until 1796.

Nevertheless, there was a general and gradual tendency for the Italian governments to harden their attitudes to France when they dared to do so. This was partly because there seemed to be a growing subversive danger from France, even for neutrals. The general diffusion of the ideals of 1789 was actively promoted by French diplomatic agents in the peninsula, and the line between propaganda and subversion was impossible to draw. The decree of 19 November 1792, promising help to peoples anywhere who wished to throw off the chains of oppression, was just as much of an affront to Italian governments as to others. Finally, the French government came eventually to patronise and protect Italian malcontents who had fled from their own states in increasing numbers to assemble in France with the aim to returning one day to the peninsula to carry out a revolution there. Some of these exiles had fled to avoid persecution, and such persecution was likely to be further provoked by their flight and by the growing threat the French patronage of them was felt to embody. Gradually, almost all Italian governments became more repressive. Censorship of publications was tightened up; known French sympathisers were kept under surveillance; potential centres of subversive organisation—such as masonic lodges—were harried. This, of course, made some of the victims of these methods feel even more pro-French.

The sharpest change of front occurred at Naples. Maria Carolina had patronised the Craft since its 1777 victory. It flourished and all the major deviant forms seem to have taken root there in lodges sometimes in rivalry with one another. Then, just as family ties with the French court had in the past helped the Neapolitan masons, so they began to tell against them as Maria Carolina learnt of her sister's troubles. On 3 November, soon after news of the October days reached Naples, a royal decree was issued confirming those of 1751 and 1775 with respect to freemasonry (and making illicit any other privately organised association).[54] After this there was a lull; no further action followed until 1792. Then the transformation of a lodge into a patriotic 'club' on the French model suddenly shocked the authorities and opened an era of rapidly worsening relations with masonry. The presence of a French squadron delayed action, but as soon as it had left arrests began. Not all freemasons were immediately pursued, but by 1794 the government was no longer prepared to make distinctions between freemasons and Jacobins.[55] Carlo Lauberg, a mason and founder of the patriotic society at Naples, made use of the lodges to further the revolutionary propaganda in which he had been encouraged by French diplomatic representatives at Naples, trying to infiltrate them with his adherents. He seems to have gone so far as to make plans for a violent coup. Learning that this had come to the ears of the authorities, Lauberg left Naples in January 1794, and in his absence a storm of repression fell on his fellow-plotters, many of whom were known freemasons. In October, three minor figures said to be ringleaders were executed, a riot followed and a major exodus of French sympathisers and would-be revolutionaries who wished to overthrow the Bourbons began. Most of them went first to Liguria or Lombardy, thus initiating the first of a growing number of contacts between Italian radicals from different states.

None of the other states saw anything quite as alarming as this. The Neapolitan conspiracy had a similar impact to the Austrian; it seemed to show that Italy, too, faced a real revolutionary threat from within and that the French would be warmly welcomed when they arrived. This certainly alarmed the rulers of other states, too, but nowhere was there detected anything quite so dangerous as in Naples. In the Papal States, there was no change of policy. As the circum-

---

[54] It is an interesting detail that, apparently, the disfavour of the court for the earlier two decrees had been so effective than no copy of either could easily be found for reference in 1789 (d'Ayala. *ASPN*, 1898, p. 803).

[55] d'Ayala, pp. 807–9. In Sicily the story was a little different. A hunt for freemasons was under way there by 1792, when the Viceroy was informed of the existence of lodges at Syracuse and Catania holding feasts and circulating seditious books. In 1795, a series of condemnations seem virtually to have ended masonic activity in the island for the time being. E. Librino, *Arch. stor. siciliano*, 1924, p. 384.

stances of Cagliostro's arrest showed, the authorities there were anxious to enforce even in 1789 legislation against freemasonry which was fifty years old. There can be no doubt of the genuine alarm the Papal authorities already felt at what was described by the Inquisition as 'una scuola di faziosi rivolta a danno della Religione e del Principato'.[56] Yet no real political danger came to the notice of the authorities except a conspiracy in Bologna in 1794. (The conspirators were defended at their trial by Aldini, a freemason who was later to hold office under the French satellite régimes.) Venice, a byword for decadence, hardly saw any stirrings, but produced a large number of émigré sympathisers with the French. In Lombardy, there was little to trouble the government. Only in Piedmont did the discovery of a plot in 1794 seem to offer grounds for alarm comparable to that at Naples.

Yet, all this time, the number of discontented and militant exiles grew. More and more, such men went to France. In 1793 the Neapolitan Aurora, an associate of Lauberg, turned up in Paris to offer the Convention his services in raising an Italian legion to be used for the liberation of the peninsula when it should take place. This was an important symptom. The protection of a common ally against what were increasingly seen as common enemies was for the first time to make Italians out of Neapolitans, Romans, Venetians, Romagnols and Lombards. A special fillip was given to them when the French government set up at Oneglia, a small town of the Piedmontese Riviera, the first Italian civil administration. The man in charge of it was Buonarroti. Oneglia was for him one of the seminal events of his life, launching him on a lifelong career of revolution.

Filippo Giuseppe Maria Ludovico Buonarroti was born at Pisa in 1761.[57] His mother was from a noble family of Siena, his father a Florentine patrician; it is not surprising, therefore, to find him a page at the court of the Grand Duke in 1773. This was not the only sign that his

---

[56] E. Petraccone quotes this from one of the documents in the Cagliostro prosecution in his book, p. 175. Another document (pp. 177–8) alleged that five thousand masons had planned a rising in Rome.

[57] His brother, Michelangelo, bore the same name as the great painter, an ancestor, but it has often been mistakenly attributed to Filippo, even by associates. For his life, see E. L. Eisenstein, *The first professional Revolutionist* (Cambridge, Mass., 1959), an admirably succinct and sane assessment of the flood of scholarship, antiquarianism and speculation devoted to Buonarroti since 1945 (for reasons discussed in Miss Eisenstein's bibliographical essay). This book indicates all the important earlier work, but since its publication a little additional biographical material has appeared. See, especially, M. A. Morelli, 'Note biografiche su Filippo Buonarroti', *CS*, 1965, pp. 521–64, which I have drawn on in what immediately follows.

family, although not rich,[58] enjoyed influence which would have assured him a safe, if not outstanding career; the Grand Duke also acceded to his father's request for help in advancing him in the Tuscan military Order of St Stephen, whence he acquired his own title of 'cavaliere'. In his studies at Pisa he showed ability rather than assiduity and was soon marked out as a headstrong boy. In 1780 he ran off to Marseille where poverty led him in despair to join the French army. Once again the help of the Grand Duke was solicited; the Tuscan consul at Marseille was ordered to act, the young man was bought out and shipped back to Leghorn. His teachers continued to deplore his wildness and lack of self-control.[59]

Buonarroti's temperament may have contributed to a row which blew up in 1781 between his own family and that of a Genoese girl whom he wished to marry. Once again, the intervention of the ducal administration was sought and his teachers were by now expressing many more reserves on his character and conduct. The Grand Duke ordered him to obey his father, with whom he was at loggerheads. Nonetheless, stormy though it might be, there was little in his career down to 1782, when he graduated, to suggest that he was not likely to remain a somewhat wild but not very untypical member of Tuscan upper-class society. In the same year he married the girl of his choice.

Soon, the young husband was clearly suffering from poverty. His family began to increase. As late as 1789 he was pleading (successfully) to be discharged from a debt to the state. That he should obtain this concession was all the more surprising because he had already fallen foul of the authorities in a more serious matter. In 1786, books of an irreligious and seditious character were confiscated from his library. He was, it appears, already something of a Rousseauian fundamentalist and may also have studied the works of Mably. Also among the books confiscated in the same raid were some masonic works and it appears that he was already a freemason. It has also been suggested that he may have joined an Illuminati-influenced lodge in 1786; certainly the views he was soon to express were not inconsistent with the egalitarian emphasis of Weishaupt's teaching. They may well have appealed to a young nobleman conscious of his déclassé standing and poverty. On the other hand, he also expressed views strongly critical

[58] 'Ma famille n'était pas riche et j'y jouissais, longtemps avant la Révolution, de l'exécration des esclaves décorés de Léopold,' said Buonarroti in 1793 (quoted in Robiquet, RF, liv, p. 491). See also Morelli on his family's means. Further light has been thrown on his schooling by Armando Saitta in CS, 1965, pp. 840–2.

[59] 'Le passione in questo giovane non hanno confine, e sarà sempre la vittima delle medesime' reported one (quoted in Morelli, p. 542).

of the Illuminati in 1787. This was in a French newspaper, the *Journal Politique*, which he published at Florence. Then he went to Corsica in October 1789 to be a journalist there.[60]

Corsica had a disturbed history in the eighteenth century and the outbreak of the French Revolution brought yet another phase of excitement to the island. Buonarroti may have met in Tuscany many of the numerous Corsican exiles who made their way there and he had also probably read Rousseau's work on the island. In April 1790 he began to publish the *Giornale Patriottico di Corsica*, which became the first newspaper in the Italian language to support the French Revolution. When Paoli, the hero of the islanders' earlier rebellion against Corsica, returned to the island in June 1790, Buonarroti was one of those who warmly welcomed him.[61] Meanwhile, he continued to publish articles urging the local authorities to press forward with revolutionary measures (his newspaper ceased to appear towards the end of 1790), to address them personally, and to keep up a correspondence with many people on the mainland. In the prospectus of the *Giornale Patriottico* he had noted approvingly that the disparity of fortunes in Corsica was not great; soon he was urging legislation by the National Assembly at Paris (Corsica had become a Departement of the new France) to make the comparative egalitarianism of the island's society even more complete. It was not this, however, which now landed him in fresh trouble, but the much more sensitive question of religion.[62]

Buonarroti's vigorous urging of radical measures and canvassing of the sympathies of the Corsican democrats led by the end of 1790 to his appointment to the direction of the island's administration of ecclesiastical affairs and national lands appropriated from the Church. This was just before the island—like metropolitan France—was bitterly divided by the new Civil Constitution of the Clergy. In June 1791, nearly a year after the enactment of the new laws at Paris, discontent led to a meeting claiming to be a majority of the inhabitants in the parish church at Bastia on Ascension Day; it passed a series of resolutions restoring the arrangements which obtained before the Civil

[60] See on what follows E. Michel, 'Vicende di Filippo Buonarroti in Corsica (1789–94)', *Archivio Storico di Corsica*, IX, 1933, pp. 481 ff. Light has been thrown on the *Journal Politique* he published at Florence by Morelli, and L. Basso, 'Il "Journal Politique" di Filippo Buonarroti', *CS*, 1967, pp. 862–4, and the one known surviving issue has been printed in the same review (pp. 865–72) by Leo Neppi Modona. The reference to the Illuminati is on pp. 869–70.

[61] E. Michel, p. 485.

[62] On what follows, see also P. Robiquet, 'Buonarroti, une émeute cléricale à Bastia', *RF*, liv, 1908, p. 490.

Constitution, asking the exiled bishop to return, and demanding that 'M. Buonarroti, toscan, qui a fait le métier de gazatier en Corse et qui y a répondu des maximes contraires à la religion et tendantes à inspirer du mépris pour les ministres des autels, serait chassé sur-le-champ de la ville'.[63] This assembly had been preceded by a procession of women which restored the arms of the former bishop to the cathedral, attacked the home of a constitutional priest and tore up the trees of liberty planted by patriots in front of the residence of the constitutional bishop. After the meeting, events took a still worse turn, for, the same evening, the local officials were besieged by an angry crowd. Two of the functionaries were escorted to the harbour by soldiers and left the island amid the booing of the mob. Buonarroti, meanwhile, had taken refuge in the dungeons of the castle. Eventually, he was discovered, hustled down to the quayside barefoot and abused, and thrust aboard a ship for Leghorn with orders that he should be handed over to the Tuscan authorities there.

The Tuscan government had already warned him that he would be imprisoned if he returned to Tuscany without its permission; the Governor of Leghorn now locked him up, though, as a nobleman, he was not incarcerated in the dungeons of the fortress. This may, in any case, have saved his life from the angry Livornese mob. Shortly afterwards, he made a solemn abjuration of his revolutionary principles and appealed to the Grand Duke for mercy on the grounds that his return to Tuscany was involuntary. When the French minister at Florence spoke in his favour, he was released after about a week in prison. Thus ended his first brush with authority arising directly from political activity.[64] In July he was back again in Corsica, once more in the revolutionary swim. The local authorities urged the National Assembly in Paris to grant him the naturalisation as a French subject for which he had applied in the preceding September.

A visit to Tuscany in the following April, ostensibly to take his family to Corsica, led to another brush with the authorities. This time, compromising letters were found in Buonarroti's effects which convinced the authorities that he was in touch with a network of sympathisers on the mainland. Confusion over his national status seems to have saved him and enabled him to return to Corsica, where he stayed until September. He then went to Paris with Corsica's deputies to the

[63] Quoted in Robiquet, p. 496.
[64] Buonarroti's plea is printed by Michel, *Arch. Stor. Corsica*, pp. 515–19. It is dated 6 June 1791. He was released on 12 June (misprinted 22 June in Michel, p. 491).

Convention, one of whom, Saliceti, was his particular friend and patron. He was sent back to a judicial office and identified himself with the extreme revolutionary wing, now anti-Paolist.

In December, an expedition mounted against Sardinia from Toulon again brought him together with the young Bonaparte.[65] It was in all respects a failure. But it may be that it was this brief experience which led him to envisage the revolutionary organisation of Italy. Whether or not this is true, he seems to have framed a republican constitution— of which no copy has survived—for the tiny island of San Pietro, just off Sardinia, and he returned to France in April as its special deputy to ask for its annexation.[66] In Paris, he denounced Paoli to the Convention and was at last rewarded for his long revolutionary services by a special decree of naturalisation as a French citizen on 25 May 1793.

A new phase of his life now opened. He had gravitated towards the admirers of Robespierre and was now identified as a member of that group. It is not surprising, therefore, that he should have been sent 'en mission' first to Lyon, then in the hands of rebels against the Convention, and then to Nice on a mission with Robespierre's brother, Augustin. While in the south, it was intended, in 1794, that he should go back to the island, but the expedition he was to have accompanied never sailed. Instead, he received his posting to Oneglia.

In the early months of 1794, the 'guerre des alpes' between the Sardinian and French forces underwent an important development when the French Army of Italy moved down the coast, taking a series of small Sardinian towns. Oneglia, one of them, was occupied on 10 April. It was decided to make it a centre of government; it contained, with its surrounding territory, about thirty-five thousand people. The French army was accompanied by three 'représentants en mission', Augustin Robespierre, Buonarroti's old friend Saliceti, and François Ricard. Buonarroti was attached to them as an 'agent révolutionnaire' and was appointed by them 'commissaire national' at Oneglia, the appointment being confirmed on 22 April.

Buonarroti was by then already installed at Oneglia and had taken in

---

[65] Michel, p. 502. There is a story, told later by Buonarroti, of an exchange between the two friends in which he promised to play Brutus if the young Bonaparte's Caesarean ambitions should be realised. G. La Cecilia, *Memorie Storicopolitiche dal 1820 al 1876* (Rome, 1876), I, pp. 137–8.

[66] For some details and references on this episode, see A. Saitta, *Filippo Buonarroti. Contributi alla storia della sua vita e del suo pensiero* (Rome, 1950), i, p. 9, and also Buonarroti's *mémoire* of 8 May 1793, printed by Saitta (*CS*, 1965, pp. 835–9), which asks for naval and political support for the island.

hand its administration, calming and reassuring the inhabitants, the first need. Yet some of Buonarroti's early decrees can hardly have helped to do this. Revolutionary tribunals were introduced, the sequestration of the property of exiles and the sale of belongings of former 'agenti della tirannia' were all announced. There was also an ominous circular about a census of wealth. The decree authorising the distribution of grain to the poor may have been more acceptable, but cannot have pleased the rich peasant.

All Buonarroti's early decisons were authorised by the représentant Ricard, and did not go beyond the elastic limits of revolutionary extemporisation, but they also clearly matched the general egalitarian tenor of Buonarroti's views. One of his proclamations launched a virtual class-war against the possessors of property and is clear evidence that Buonarroti's notion of revolution already contained a large element of economic egalitarianism. Nevertheless, the practical needs of the war and the economy seem to have restrained any radical social transformation at Oneglia; in this way, of course, what happened there mirrored on a small scale what happened elsewhere in France. Italy's first taste of revolutionary institutions, therefore, was perhaps less sharp than Buonarroti would have wished.

Administrative experience was the first important acquisition by Buonarroti at Oneglia; it does not seem to have tempered his revolutionary zeal as it has often tempered that of others. More important still was the opportunity his post offered him because of the presence of large numbers of Italian refugees. To Oneglia came exiles from all over Italy; Buonarroti's predominantly social politics began to be affected by the experience of these men. Their plight directed attention to their oppressors, the numerous governments under which Italy was divided. Meanwhile, the refugees courted him. He was not only the man on the spot to whom they had to turn for daily assistance and counsel, but he was their best access to Paris and the ear of the government, now dominated by the brother of his friend, Augustin Robespierre.

Soon Buonarroti was talking of using Oneglia as a revolutionary centre from which to mount revolution in Italy. 'Oneille pourra devenir le foyer d'inspiration pour les superstitieux italiens,' he wrote.[67] He wanted to print copies of the Declaration of the Rights of Man in Italian for distribution in Italy, but no printing-press existed at Oneglia, and the Genoese government (Oneglia was a little enclave in Genoese

[67] E. Pia Onnis, 'Filippo Buonarroti, Commissario Rivoluzionario a Oneglia nel 1794–95', NRS, 1939, p. 359.

territory) would not allow them to be printed at Finale, the nearest. The Genoese indeed went further, protesting at Paris about Buonarroti's subversive activity. It seems that his own proclamation of May, too, may have circulated in Italy.[68]

He was also by this time beginning to stir up local opposition, when there suddenly came the news of Thermidor. This was a bad setback; Buonarroti's friends in Paris were now out of office. It did not immediately affect him in that he continued to work at Oneglia with official approval for several months; perhaps he was too unimportant to be noticed. In December he resigned, but when he was recalled to Paris in March 1795 it was not for political reasons but to face a criminal charge of illegally confiscating land belonging to a Genoese nobleman. He had not achieved a great deal at Oneglia, except in one enormously important respect. This was the building-up of his acquaintance among many of the outstanding Italian Jacobins shortly to be elevated to the first rank of revolutionary politics in Italy. The first connexions of many of them with the man who was to be the most legendary of all the secret society organisers had been forged and a tie between social and national revolution established which was to be one of the great spectres of nineteenth-century conservatives. The next important connexion he had still to make awaited him at Paris. After his condemnation he was locked up in the Plessis prison there; his fellow-prisoner was 'Gracchus' Babeuf.

Largely on ideological grounds, a great deal of attention has been given to Babeuf, particularly since 1945. There is now a considerable historical industry based on the study of both Babeuf and Buonarroti. Yet for a long time they were neglected. Only a few of the writers on conspiracies and secret societies in the years following Babeuf's abortive plot found it necessary to mention him. Nor is this very surprising; his attempt is at first sight merely a matter of one of the many small groups of discontented ex-Jacobins seeking to reverse the direction taken by French politics after Thermidor and failing in their attempted putsch. Babeuf only came to enjoy prominence in the revolutionary story with the publication of Buonarroti's book about his conspiracy in 1828. It was then that the *Conspiracy of Equals* took its place in the hagiography and mythology of socialism and it is to that book that we must trace the origins of the huge bibliography the subject has recently acquired. Before Buonarroti wrote, Babeuf was almost forgotten. Nonetheless, even before that, he exercised an im-

[68] See the letter from a Tuscan correspondent to Buonarroti printed by Armando Saitta, *CS*, 1965, pp. 843–5.

portant though indirect post-mortem influence on the development of the first secret societies and, through that, on the shape of the mythology about them. This, too, was Buonarroti's work, thanks to the personal connexions formed between them. But Babeuf's plot had also another direct influence relevant to this discussion. Because the plot came when and where it did it did much to mould French government policy, particularly in Italy, and therefore to form, indirectly, the Italian secret societies and the men who joined them.

Babeuf was born in 1760 into a poor, large family whose father had come down in the world. In a post as a 'commissaire à terrier' he acquired a close and detailed education in the social and economic realities of the landed society on which the whole ancien régime was based. Not that this was the only source from which Babeuf began to acquire the egalitarian ideas for which he was later to conspire and die. Through the Académie royale des Belles Lettres of Arras he was also at least in touch with the ideas of 'enlightened' circles; perhaps he met Robespierre, who was a member of the Academy and for a time its Director. Soon, he began to seek to express in writing views with a highly radical social content. One other outlet which he sought (on two occasions) was membership of a masonic lodge, but he does not seem to have been admitted.[69] It is not surprising, therefore, that with the coming of the Revolution he threw himself into the local opportunities it presented. He helped to draw up the Cahier of Roye, in Picardy, and took part in the burning of seigneurial archives such as those which had once been in his charge. Almost inevitably for one so passionately concerned in what was going forward, he then went to Paris and began to earn a living as a journalist. He took up a radical position, attacking Mirabeau and denouncing the franchise arrangements of the new constitution for their restrictiveness (they were indirect and contained property qualifications). He then returned to Roye until 1792, when he moved to Amiens, to take up a job as archivist and administrator to the Departement of the Somme. This seems to have finished in a row with the local administrators and Babeuf was soon in Paris again, where he obtained a job in the Food Commission (bureau de subsistances). There were more rows.

Babeuf still had not found in the Revolution the satisfaction he sought. Even Robespierre, whom he was later to praise, seems to have left him dissatisfied; at all events, after Thermidor he launched attacks on the still Robespierrist Commune of Paris; he seems to have

[69] See M. Dommanget, 'Babeuf et la franc-maçonnerie' in *Sur Babeuf et la conjuration des égaux* (Paris, 1970), pp. 60–8.

been on good terms with Tallien and Fouché, two of Robespierre's destroyers. But the Comité de Sûreté Générale soon turned on him. He went into hiding, was discovered and imprisoned. It was at this time that he met Buonarroti.

In this life there is much which makes it easy to understand the bitterness and the social passion which came to possess Babeuf. As the son of a déclassé father he could understand the importance of privilege and station in France, and of the injustice which governed their distribution. He had to struggle all his life to earn a living and support a family in a society which, because of its privileges, seemed to make the task doubly difficult. In his daily work he had for years evidence at close quarters in the rawest form of the way privilege worked. When the Revolution swept away the privilege enshrined in law and based on birth, it left wealth intact. It is not surprising that Babeuf should turn against this so violently when so much of the Revolution seemed only to have strengthened its grasp. In this respect he only carried sans-culotte egalitarianism to a logical extreme; many agreed with him.

There was plenty of discontent to exploit. The failures of the last sans-culotte efforts in the days of Prairial and Germinal, the closing of the popular clubs, the harrying of the popular leaders and the economic hardships of the post-Thermidor era all turned people against the government. The resurgence of royalism suggested that even the bourgeois revolution might be in danger from reaction. The setting up of the Directory under the Constitution in 1795 revealed that France was now to be governed by the well-to-do. There was much outraged egalitarian sentiment lying about waiting to be used. Finally, there were plenty of discontented politicians, too, prominent among them the so-called 'queue de Robespierre'.

Babeuf and Buonarroti must soon have found common ground in their egalitarian sympathies. They were in jail together for about five months, from March to October 1795 (they were released after the attempted royalist coup of 13 Vendémiaire) and had therefore ample opportunity to develop their views to one another. These views were strikingly parallel in social content, although Babeuf derived his largely from experience, while Buonarroti his from reading and, possibly, from his temperamental bias. Whatever Babeuf had thought earlier they now agreed on the merits of Robespierre and his ideas. Buonarroti also brought something to their association which Babeuf might not have arrived at by himself. This was a conspiratorial technique. Buonarroti first put into practice a certain model of insurrectionary activity based on the notion not of a popular rising—the technique hallowed by the Revolution's own history and now beginning to be exposed as useless against a determined government—but on that of a revolutionary élite, acting, as required, against the wishes of the people until the people should be enlightened enough to understand its own best interests. This élite would, if necessary, conduct its true policy behind a façade of openly avowed intention; in it, not in the people, was to be found the seed of the new and just society.

This is the idea which runs from its sketchy adumbration in the doctrines of the Illuminati right down to the teaching and leadership of Lenin. On this idea Buonarroti was to build a dominance as a revolutionary leader which was to lead Bakunin to call him 'the greatest conspirator of the century'. Its first expression in action, imperfect and unclear though its form might be, was the Babeuf conspiracy. Its repercussions in Buonarroti's later career were enormous. He was to become the Grand Old Man of the secret societies and advise and coach them right down to the time when the young Mazzini entered political life. After that Buonarroti's direct influence was to live on through Blanqui for the next fifty years. This personal influence was coupled with the legend which Buonarroti built on Babeuf's plot; this was to give it its importance in socialist hagiography. It was also, because of its obvious relationship to the Illuminati ideal (and even to the masonic device of reserved secrets), to provide a powerful reinforcement to the legend of the timeless, tireless work of the secret societies.

The story of the actual conspiracy has now been almost unravelled. In October 1795, shortly after leaving prison, Babeuf founded with some friends and other disgruntled ex-Jacobins a body called the Society of the Panthéon. This group seems to have spent its time discussing egalitarian ideas and helping to publish and circulate a newspaper, the *Tribun du Peuple*, throughout France. In February 1796 the police of the Directory silenced the *Tribun*. The society ceased to meet, but almost at once Babeuf formed from its keenest members a small 'comité insurrecteur'. This drew up first a manifesto and then a plan for insurrection. The drafting of the *Manifeste des Egaux* was the work of Sylvain Maréchal. It set out as the primary aim of the group the realising of equality of social conditions by revolution and the restoration of the Constitution of 1793 which had never been put into effect. Meanwhile, conspiratorial work was pushed ahead on two fronts, the dissemination of propaganda and the penetration of the army, police and other branches of the governmental machine through the work of twelve revolutionary agents.

Most of this was known already in detail to the authorities who had

their own informer within the conspiracy.[70] Although some apprehension was felt lest the conspirators should be able to subvert some of
the troops from their loyalty, there was really very little danger of their
success. The Comité met on 8 May and agreed on a plan to seize certain
public buildings and officials, but the authorities moved first. On 10
May two hundred arrests were made. Buonarroti was taken just as
he was about to leave to join the Army of Italy at the head of a group
of Italian exiles who were to provide a political warfare wing for
Bonaparte's invasion. His trial and that of the other conspirators took
place in February 1797. The sentences were surprisingly mild. Only
Babeuf and one other were sentenced to death and executed. Buonarroti was sent off to prison at Cherbourg, where for the moment we
may leave him. He had completed his revolutionary education.

The Babeuf conspiracy was soon to be given a place in the chain of
intrigue central to the secret society mythology.[71] In fact, though, there
is a very faint masonic flavour about the episode. It seems at least
possible that Maréchal, formerly connected with the Cercle Social, had
been a mason and that the group to which he belonged was linked by
personal attachments to the Bavarian Illuminati. But it is unlikely that
we can ever be sure about direct masonic ties with the plot and not
much was said about the conspiracy until Buonarroti's account of
thirty years later. This was the starting-point of all subsequent investigation. It came after much more had been done and said to promote
acceptance of the mythology of the secret societies and then presented
a picture of an organisation and a technique of conspiracy which had
suggestive masonic analogies and at some moments used masonic
symbolism. It had by then been forgotten that Babeuf's own evidence
at his trial and after is flagrantly opposed to any masonic interpretation
of what he had done.[72]

As for the practical contribution of the Babeuf conspiracy to the
development of the secret societies, that lay in the future. Through
Buonarroti's Italian connexions, it quickly had European significance,
and began to influence events elsewhere. Buonarroti was known to the
Directory as the spokesman and contact-man for the Italian refugee
Jacobins with whom the French were about to co-operate in Italy.
The men brought together at Oneglia had worked together in a common

[70] It has been suggested that he may have been Maréchal (G. Pariset, 'Babou-
visme et Maçonnerie', in *Mélanges offerts à M. Charles Andler par ses amis et ses
élèves* (Strasbourg, 1924), p. 270).

[71] In *Le tombeau de Jacques Molay* and Barruel, for example.

[72] See G. Pariset, esp. pp. 273–5.

cause long enough to have generated a genuine sense of Italian nationality and to be interested in the unification of Italy. Their revolutionary activity had for a time seemed likely to help Bonaparte's army, when he began his invasion. One of the civilian commissaires politiques with that force was Saliceti, the Corsican who had already been associated with Buonarroti and the Italians at Oneglia. Now, suddenly, this idea was compromised. The Italians were henceforth suspect as potentially social revolutionaries, with Babouvist ideas. This was to lead to two results of the greatest importance in the development of the secret societies. One was that French statesmen and soldiers would almost without exception for the next three years distrust any attempt to advance the cause of Italian unity because, apart from the diplomatic and military disadvantages it might have for France, it was tainted with the idea of social egalitarianism. The second result was the disillusionment that this would produce in the Italian Jacobins themselves. Coupled with the actual experience of French occupation it would lead them to seek ways of opposing their former patrons and eventually to organise anti-French conspiracies. Thus, paradoxically, when, at last, real political secret societies came into existence, they were directed against France, the standard-bearer of the Revolution, not against the ancien régime which had been so terrified of them.

SECRET SOCIETIES AND CONSPIRACY IN ITALY 1796–9

Before 1796, the French Revolution only affected a minority of Italians. The launching of Bonaparte's first Italian campaign in May 1796 opened a new era, when the Revolution and the Italian population at large came into direct contact for the first time.

Certain institutions gave this contact a particular form and flavour and shaped in a special way the reactions of Italians to the Revolution. Much the most important was the French army (understood in the widest sense to include the civilian administrators and agents who sometimes accompanied and supplemented it) and its special administrative and political methods. At one time or other, every Italian state was invaded by French soldiers between 1796 and 1799 and some had long periods of occupation. The army's impact on the local population was made in part by the spontaneous behaviour of the soldiers themselves and in part as a result of deliberate policy. At the start Italy was an inviting prospect to the ragged and half-starved soldiers of the 'guerre des alpes'. Lombardy, the area in which they first established themselves for a prolonged stay, was one of the richest parts in Europe.

As it was the practice of the French to live off the country like locusts and not to be concerned about carrying discipline to the point of interfering seriously with looting, pillage, rape and the usual incidentals of eighteenth-century warfare, the French army quickly aroused dislike and even active hostility among the local populations. Its reputation for godlessness also played some part in this. On the whole, this pattern persisted through the revolutionary triennium, and wherever the French army went any welcome it might at first receive turned very quickly into dislike.

This was inseparably connected with the operation of French policy. One motive for invading Italy in the first place had been the need to find rations and pay for an army too expensive to maintain at home. Occupied territories were made to pay for the upkeep of the army by a series of forced loans, fines, obligatory contributions and demands for billets, arms, clothes and forage. The Army of Italy was soon making a net profit; it sent monthly contributions to the Directory which were at one time indispensable income. The official imposition of this policy of exaction made no practical distinction between 'enemy' and friendly territories; whatever local administration existed or was set up, even if it were one of the satellite states—the 'sister republics' of revolutionary cant—the burdens still had to be met. It was clear to all Italians that they were paying through the nose for the privilege of liberation from the past by the French army. The army and its exactions were therefore what the Revolution came to mean in the first place to Italians. The next innovation it presented was that of the satellite republics of the peninsula themselves, new states set up on revolutionary principles. Paradoxically, they had never been a part of French governmental policy in the original planning of an Italian campaign. They had been extemporised by French commanders on the spot, of whom the first was Bonaparte, who in 1797 created the most important of the satellites, the Cisalpine Republic.[73] After this, there came into being the Ligurian, the Roman and the Parthenopean Republics. Supported locally only by a revolutionary minority and installed by French arms, they were from the start fatally compromised. They were always, to most Italians, the creatures of France, run by those whom a later age would have termed Quislings.

To make matters worse, in so far as the republics pursued revolutionary policies they emphasised their exotic and dependent origins.

---

[73] The Cisalpine was preceded by the Transpadane and Cispadane Republics. There were, of course, also satellite republics outside Italy, of which the most important were the Batavian and the Helvetic.

The destruction of traditional boundaries to introduce the French departmental system was damaging in Italy where local patriotism counted for so much. Anti-clericalism, even if only expressed in rhetorical flourishes and ineffective in practice, nevertheless fell with a harsh note on Italian ears. The revolutionary calendar made nonsense of the familiar routine of saints' days which counted for even more in Italy than it had done in France. Above all, there was taxation, and here we return to the French exactions. The republics were quickly saddled with the job of raising the money the French demanded. They became the tax-gathering machines of the occupying power. Where they were effective, the Revolution meant heavier burdens than in the past and was therefore detested. Nowhere did the Republics compensate any large group of Italians for the new burdens they imposed.

As quarter-master and tax-gatherer it is not surprising that the Revolution made no appeal to the masses. Instead, there was during the revolutionary triennium a groundswell of popular discontent. Actual violence against French soldiers or the bureaucrats of the republics tended to be limited to sticky moments—the beginnings and endings of campaigns, for example, when the disturbance of normal conditions seemed to make it possible to escape retaliation. This was the sort of thing which occurred early in the first Italian campaign at Lugo and Pavia, and later at Brescia. The greatest outbreaks of popular anti-revolutionary violence came in 1798-9, during the ebbing of French power in Italy, outstandingly in the Sanfedist insurrection in the Kingdom of Naples, and the anti-French rising in Piedmont. But probably a lot of the rumbling disorder and crime which was going on during all these years can be traced to this source.

General prejudice against the French, their creatures and dependents, and the Revolution which they embodied was the seedbed of modern Italian political life. The great issue of the next sixty years was to be the national question; this was what Italian politics were said to be about until unification and this issue was first defined in the revolutionary triennium. The Italians who first formulated the national programme were the friends and advocates of France in 1796. Before three years were out many of them, too, had been alienated by French behaviour and French policy. Some others began to see in the national programme, or some reduced version of it, the only way in which the interests of the peninsula might be safeguarded from France as well as from the ancien régime. The tangled pattern of developments which brought about these changes, never a clear progression, always subject to twists and turns, was decisive in shaping the Italian secret societies.

The Italian Jacobins soon had cause for dismay about the behaviour of the 'Grande Nation'. Those who came back with the French were distrusted by them because of Babeuf. Buonarroti's friend Saliceti now had the job not of helping but of watching them as a possible danger. Their contacts with sympathisers in Paris, especially on the Left of the Chamber, were regarded with deep suspicion. Moreover, the development of French policy also began to irritate them. Far from acting in the cause of revolution, French arms and diplomacy seemed only too willing to deal with the ancien régime as an equal; the negotiations with the Sardinian 'tyrant' which led to the armistice of Cherasco were an ominous warning. This, of course, was only the natural development of French policy in launching the invasion of Italy. Its aim was to achieve a strategic success with a view to winning diplomatic concessions from France's main surviving continental enemy, Austria, not to carry out revolutionary change there in the interest of the Italians. Though Bonaparte forced a fatal twist in French policy by setting up the Cisalpine Republic—which tied French hands in so far as it made it impossible to treat all Italian territories simply as a bargaining counter —the actual treatment of the satellite states by the French dealt further blows to the hopes of the Italian Jacobins. Their position was bitter; while the French held them back from carrying out revolutionary policies in the satellites and entrusted office when possible to Italian moderates, the satellite republics were at the same time hated because they seemed *too* revolutionary to the deeply conservative Italian masses. Finally, there was the colossal disillusionment of the Peace of Campo Formio, when the French handed Venice to Austria.

Their frustrations and disappointments eventually led many of the Italian Jacobins to accept the views of the few early unitarists among them who believed that only an independent and united Italy could guarantee the preservation of a constitutional republic there against the pressure both of Austria and France, soon seen as an equally dangerous threat to Italian freedom. Unity became more and more the shibboleth of the most determined Italian Jacobins, those, that is to say, who also held the most advanced views on the political and social content of the Revolution. This, of course, made them still more suspect to the Directory. The plans of the unitarists increasingly seemed likely to traverse the diplomatic, military and economic interests of France. They strove more and more obviously to mobilise support at Paris among deputies there who were themselves suspect as left-wingers. Soon, the unitarists were referred to almost habitually in French and satellite official correspondence as 'anarchistes', 'furibondi', 'buveurs de sang'. Because of the distrust of them felt by the French government, Italian nationalism never became French policy, though, elsewhere, the propaganda of nationalism had been one of the major French weapons. The disappointment of the hopes of the Italian Jacobins thus paradoxically united with the general popular dislike of the French and the failure of the satellites to endear themselves either to their subjects or to the radicals. Together they provided the bases of the anti-French movement which gave birth to the Italian political secret societies.

The inheritance of the Italian societies from the pre-revolutionary past is still in dispute. On the whole, it had been the traditional and conservative view that in so far as the Italian secret societies of the revolutionary period had historical roots, they went back to the masonic lodges which existed before 1789. This is plausible: freemasons usually belonged to those 'enlightened', engaged circles in the Italian élite which were most committed to the reforms of the last decades of the ancien régime. Sometimes the association was only guessed at, but sometimes it became explicit. It was unfortunate, for example, that one of the leading Jansenist theologians should praise the freemasons for their sympathy for ecclesiastical reform.[74] This was exactly the sort of evidence which could fit easily into the general plot theories which began to gain ground as the revolutionary decade wore on. By 1798, for example, it could be asserted that the protection of the freemasons of Milan had secured to the university of Pavia greater freedom for Jansenist ecclesiastical reformers than was available elsewhere.[75]

Freemasonry soon suffered from this. Official attitudes in the Italian states had already hardened against them between 1790 and 1796. Some lodges—those at Milan, for example—have been alleged to have been still meeting regularly right down to the eve of the invasion, but in other places masonic activity seems virtually to have ended in these years. In any case, the lodges showed no special responsiveness to the arrival of the French, nor, in most parts of Italy, any special sympathy for the new régimes. The reason may be the predominantly aristocratic composition of most Italian lodges; only where, as in Naples, members of the nobility were already opponents of the régime was masonic involvement in the satellites to be very remarkable. It may

---

[74] Tamburini, *Lettere teologico-politiche*, I, pp. 77–8.
[75] G. Marchetti, anonymous author of *Che importa ai preti* (Cristianopoli [Rome], 1798), quoted in R. Sòriga, *Le Società segrete, l'emigrazione politica e i primi moti per l'indipendenza* (Modena, 1942), p. 38.

even be that freemasonry in most parts of Italy was only brought back to life by the arrival of the French. The lodge at Leghorn which has been studied because of the fortunate survival of documentation about it was, in fact, founded in 1796 only by French officers. It then recruited locally and eventually emerged as an independent lodge, no longer affiliated to one at Perpignan whose French members had founded it.[76]

It is not possible to trace any general organised continuity between the Jacobins of the triennium and the freemasons, then, though no doubt many of the Italian masons took employment with the new satellites. There is a certain masonic element observable in the symbolism and ceremonial of the new régimes, however. The floor of the room occupied by the Directory of the Cisalpine Republic is said to have been decorated with the signs of a masonic lodge.[77] The arms of the Cisalpine Republic show the same influence. Official stationery carried in its headings the conventional symbols of set-squares, plumb-lines, eyes of vigilance, long familiar to masons. Such facts impressed contemporaries, no doubt, but do not provide much to go on. But to expect more is to fall into the error of the mythology itself, of regarding freemasonry as a bloc, instead of as something containing different tendencies. Socially, as the Savoyard example showed, divisions between aristocratic membership of lodges and middle-class memberships became more emphatic with the withdrawal of many of the former during the Revolution.[78] Certainly, in that case, the surviving membership played a considerable part in the clubs and societies which appeared in the wake of the French occupation. Contemporaries found such connexions convincing evidence of masonic depravity and responsibility for the revolutionary régimes.[79]

A question also arises of different obediences within masonry; the Strict Observance had been strong in Italy and an interesting suggestion has been made by a modern historian, though it does not have appeared to have occurred to Italians seeking evidence of masonic culpability in the 1790s.[80] This is the suggestion that it is in Illuminati influence

---

[76] The *Amici della perfetta unione* lodge has been examined in a paper subsequently reprinted in Francovich, pp. 89–98.

[77] Sòriga, p. 36.

[78] Jews and foreigners seem prominent in the Leghorn example. Francovich, p. 93.

[79] 'Il sistema giacobino ha in ultima analisi comune con le società massoniche lo scopo ed i mezzi, emblemi, colori, l'uso dei ruoli, dei catechismi, l'istituto della fraternizzazione e della corrispondenza, la libertà, lo spirito di una riforma universale, d'indipendenza e d'eguaglianza.' *La vera nozione del giacobinismo* (Verona, 1799), quoted in Sòriga, p. 43. See also pp. 45–6.

[80] Francovich is the proponent of this view.

that a real revolutionary contribution through Italian freemasonry can be discerned in providing masons with a set of social egalitarian ideals and some models of conspiratorial technique. The most thorough and important recent study of this topic has established with reasonable certainty that Illuminati influences were at work in Italian masonic lodges after 1787. The author contends that these provided the first secret societies with a body of egalitarian ideas, a technique of cherishing secret revolutionary purposes not revealed to all members of the organisation and the existence, consequentially, of a hierarchy of initiates. The penetration of the masonic lodges, as in Germany, is presumed to have been the means adopted to further Illuminati ends; in particular, it has been suggested, Scots rite lodges seemed attractive, and specimens of their catechisms have been said to show Illuminati influence. So far as distribution goes, it is said that there was an Illuminati lodge at Naples, and that the Trentino, too, was a centre from which Illuminati influence was diffused. The Leghorn lodge, too, showed both Scots rite and Illuminati characteristics.[81]

There is little difficulty in agreeing that there is acceptable evidence of such contacts with Italian masonry. What is more difficult is to decide exactly what this may have meant in practice. We need not exclude the supposition that Italian freemasons were influenced by Illuminati ideas and modes of action, but it is not possible to find examples of this having results which can be decisively attributed to this and to no other source. Though there may be Illuminati influences in the background of the Italian societies, therefore, it is not easy to be sure about its effects. If it existed before 1796 it was, presumably, directed against the governments of the ancien régime; it would, therefore, lose its purpose after the French invasion.

All the evidence of the actual emergence of secret societies is that it was French invasion and the disappointments which followed which were the real sources of the Italian secret societies of the next thirty-odd years. In this sense, the Revolution brought the seeds of the Risorgimento to Italy—by providing for Italians for the first time a common enemy, France. It was not essential—though as a matter of historical accident it happened—that Austria assumed this role after 1814. France had already focused discontent before 1814. Into the anti-French conspiracies could flow the irritations of disappointed former exiles, frustrated employees of the satellite republics, outraged clergy with important influence on their flocks, and noblemen who simply wanted to get back to the ancien régime.

[81] Francovich, *passim*.

The first organisation of which there was talk was the Lega Nera. The historian and former Jacobin, Carlo Botta, said later that it sought the exclusion from Italy both of the French and of the Austrians and hoped that the confusions and upheaval of the war would facilitate this.[82] It was soon denounced to the French and began to figure among their obsessive concerns. In fairness, it must be said that for all but fifteen months of the French involvement in Italy, warfare was in progress, and it is not surprising that they should treat seriously the strategical threat of popular risings. Moreover, they quickly connected the Lega with political opposition inside France itself.[83] By September 1797 they were thoroughly alarmed and feared what one French agent called 'un vaste projet d'assassiner les Français depuis Seize jusqu'à Terracine'.[84] The Sicilian Vespers was a recurring memory.

Nevertheless, about the reality of the Lega Nera we remain very badly informed and it is not easy to see what lay behind the power of this phantom to frighten. That it could frighten Frenchmen so much is, of course, very significant for our purpose. They were ready to be alarmed and therefore to exaggerate the power of secret societies when they appeared. This readiness to exaggerate their strength was always an important factor in the growth of the mythology about secret societies. They did not, however, go to extremes; they did not associate the Lega with masonry or any other pre-revolutionary sect.

In 1798 there comes more plentiful evidence about a secret society attempting to act over a wide area of Italy, the Raggi. The circumstances in which it failed revealed quite a lot about the state of underground activity in Italy. The name was not current until 1798, but a pamphlet of 1796 may have suggested it, by a reference to Lombardy's possibilities as 'il fuoco donde doveranno emanare tutti i raggi che in breve illumineranno o poteranno l'incendio nelle tirannie finitime'. Lombardy was to be the centre of the Cisalpine Republic and was already at that time a gathering-place for exiles from other parts of Italy who would naturally feel solidarity with other exiles while there and thus arrive at a more conscious nationalist viewpoint. Furthermore, the Cisalpine government itself quickly displayed an interest in expansion which later led people to assert that the whole Raggi conspiracy was in fact an instrument of Cisalpine policy and an expression of Lombard imperialism towards its neighbours.

[82] C. Botta, *Storia d'Italia dal 1789 al 1814* (Italy, 1826), II, p. 9.
[83] See the comment of Bignon, quoted in G. Vaccarino, *I patrioti 'anarchistes' e l'idea dell'unità italiana* (Turin, 1955), p. 50.
[84] Quoted in Vaccarino, p. 38.

The part of Lombardy in the building up of the Raggi was, it has been suggested, encouraged from France, though not by the French government. French Jacobins were in 1797 urging Cisalpine patriots to spread 'patriotisme et lumières' throughout Italy and to make an enlarged Cisalpine the core of a future United Italy. The links between the French opposition and the Cisalpine radicals were very strong at this time. A famous pamphlet, *Le cri d'Italie*, shows this, and undoubtedly many of the French felt a need to form a common front with Italian Jacobins in view of the rising crisis in France where the Left grew more and more discontented with the Directory. Jullien (one of the acquitted in the Vendôme trial), Le Pelletier, Antonelle and Amar were among these. There is a clear set of parallels here with what was later said to be the Raggi programme and one historian has seen in this the origins of the first Raggi cell.

Further conspiracy certainly followed the coups d'état of 1798 carried out in the Cisalpine by the French authorities and the failure of the mission of a Cisalpine general, La Hoz, to Paris to plead against such interference with the internal affairs of the Cisalpine. What seems to have happened is that the Raggi organisation, as soon as it took shape, also linked up with other conspiracies already under way. One appears to have been in Tuscany, and possibly promoted by a Cisalpine diplomat, and another at Bologna, where a Società Platonica is said to have been founded.

After the coups in the Cisalpine, information about the society becomes more plentiful. Its association with the French Jacobins (it was not directed against the Grande Nation as such, but against the Directory and its policies) made it easy for disgruntled Italian radicals to turn to conspiracy against France with a clear conscience. They formed groups of five, communicating directly not with one another, but only with larger insurrectional committees in each provincial capital. Clearly, the eventual use of armed force was envisaged, and the basic aim was unitarist. They were in effect the first proponents of the maxim 'L'Italia farà da se'. Though suspected of socially radical aims by the French, this does not seem to have been of much concern to the Raggi. The main branches of the society were Bologna and Milan, but there were offshoots as far away as Rome and Turin. Membership was especially strong in the Cisalpine army and some of its members also had hopes of the sympathy of the French generals, Joubert and Championnet among them, because of these soldiers' rows with their own civilian liaison officers.

By December 1798, the French authorities had a great deal of information. Jullien, La Hoz and Joubert were all denounced to them by name. A number of arrests were made in February 1799. But by this time the society's position had been significantly changed by the re-opening of the war and Russian entry to it. By May Suvorov would be in Turin and the French locked up in Genoa. In these circumstances, Italian patriots had suddenly to make a harsh decision to support or oppose the French; the Russians and Austrians, after all, might well bring something worse. It is not surprising that the unity of the Raggi was split. Those of its members who rallied to France found it easier to do so since the change in the French Directory after Prairial and the news that Joubert had been appointed to command the army of Italy.

The difficulties this created for the Raggi are shown in the two most important episodes of anti-French activity by Italians in 1799, the Piedmontese risings of February and the defection of La Hoz. Piedmont had been annexed to France. This had not met with local resistance; the Piedmontese seem to have preferred this to the Raggi programme of unity because they feared a unity centred on Milan, which they distrusted. They turned back to the ideal of unity only much later, after annexation had failed, and had led to popular risings. But these risings, too, had little to offer the Raggi. They were led by conserva-tives—nobles and clergy, usually, and were prompted by such acts of the new administration as the introduction of the revolutionary calendar, the suppression of religious congregations and the intro-duction of new taxation, all of which were necessary consequences of the assimilation to the French departmental structure which, until 1798, the Piedmontese had not experienced. The result was an odd coincidence of opposition to the French. Royalist cockades and pictures of Marat paraded together and the places which had risen to greet the French in 1796—Asti, Alba, Acqui—now rose against them.

La Hoz had been discredited since his abortive mission to Paris. In the winter of 1798 his arrest was ordered, but he escaped. After the Austrian invasion he was recalled and readmitted to serve in the Cisalpine forces. With them he retreated across the Po into Romagna, taking command of Cisalpine troops there. From Forli he issued in May a proclamation against both the French and the Austrians. He then went to Ancona, the last stronghold on Roman territory still in French hands, and sat down to besiege it. His aims were obscure and he had already little to hope for. Former Raggi comrades in the army left him over the issue of fighting the French. The peasants' bands with which he co-operated were in any case not interested in national independence. He began to negotiate with the Russians, some of whose ships turned up at Ancona to help him. He may have been saved from complete disillusionment when he was killed, early in October.

The position of La Hoz had been impossible. But it illustrated a weakness of the Raggi as a whole: when it came to the crunch, the French alliance seemed a better bet to most patriots than a return to the ancien régime. One ironical circumstance at Ancona shows the difficulty of La Hoz and people like him; on the other side was fighting (and was wounded) his former adjutant, Cerise, deeply distrusted by the French only a few months before for his contacts with the Paris Jacobins. Under strain, most of the Raggi had to swing back to the French side. Radical tradition and republicanism explain this but, of course, they deprived the Raggi of the chance of using the one real popular force in Italy which might have been politically effective, the reactionary peasant masses.

The Raggi of the triennium were therefore important, rather as forerunners and inspirers of later secret societies than for what they did. In personnel, in the doctrine of nationalist unitarism and the linking of this to the preservation of the political and constitutional gains of the French Revolution (embodied in the independence and integrity of the Cisalpine) they set a pattern for their successors. They even had an importance for the distant future, too, for their linking of nationalism with liberalism and progress—instead of, as in Germany, with obscurantist romanticism and reaction—meant that from the start Italian nationalism was fundamentally healthy. The Raggi, feeble as they were, had their eyes on the future, unlike Ruffo's Sanfedisti. When the secret societies revived in Italy after 1800, they would remember this tradition. But so would the French authorities. They had been badly frightened. After 1800, they were always to be aware of the danger of subversion in Italy, though they were too realistic to be perturbed by anything except its potential as a conservative force.

Chapter VIII
The Napoleonic era

INTRODUCTION

BETWEEN 1800 and 1814 there was something of a pause in the development of the secret society mythology. These were the Barruel years; virtually nothing was said against secret societies that had not already been said by him or by writers like Starck who drew pictures much like his. A great deal of conspiracy went on but was not exploited by a new generation of writers on secret societies until the waning of the Napoleonic régime. When this happened, new elements were added once more to the picture most people held of the secret societies and their importance and thus the final refinements took their place in the myth. Some were to be very enduring indeed, especially in inflating the career of Buonarroti (which is the only part of the mythology still exercising power over the minds of sensible men today). But this lay in the future. During the Napoleonic era it was the positive activity of policemen or conspirators which helped to develop the myth, rather than the writings of publicists. The first had to cope with disaffection and opposition and sometimes found evidence of what looked like the activities of secret societies; the second drew on past experience of secret societies, often masonic, or on what had been said about them by the polemicists of the revolutionary decade in order to provide models for efficient organisations of their own.

Much of this chapter is therefore about positive conspiratorial history. The subject has a substantial unity between 1800 and 1814 because of what happened then to define these years as a distinct epoch. Its background is a Europe undergoing huge transformations, for it was under the Empire that the French Revolution exercised its greatest influence, stretching, at its widest, from Lithuania to Portugal and from Hamburg to Naples. Millions of Europeans had some experience of living under French institutions or under others shaped by French ideas. In some countries, the Codes or the departmental and prefectoral structure were the channels of such influence; in others, conscription, the police and the censorship might be more obvious. And all the time there operated the informal influence of French ideas and attitudes, permeating all levels of society as never before and achieving unprecedented circulation. Sometimes they provoked envy and resentment, sometimes admiration and emulation. Wherever they went, they drove great furrows through society and ideas. Nothing could ever be quite the same again.

This is, in essence and in general terms, the analytical case for treating the Napoleonic Empire as a great progressive and liberating force; it does not matter that it was often thus unintentional. The historical case for the same judgment is the history of the next fifty years, a long demonstration of the impact France had made, both by awaking aspiration and by stimulating her opponents to make changes if they wished to resist her. The upheavals which accompanied the process and the wars which carried it forward into new geographical regions are the presuppositions of political activity in every country in these years. They imposed on European politics a unity which cuts across national boundaries. No government could think about its domestic problems except in the light of the French Revolution. It is this which gives a special unity to the history of Europe in these years.

This is in part why Frenchmen were sometimes tempted to discern a unity which rarely existed in the plots and combinations against them. On the whole, they resisted this temptation; the French police were not so credulous as, for example, the Austrians after 1814. They were, it is true, ready to attribute to secret conspiracy things that can be more plausibly attributed to other causes. Simple hatred of French soldiers on the spot was more likely to provoke popular hostility than any amount of purposeful subversion by hidden agents, as Spain and Italy both showed. In Germany, too, the idée fixe of some policemen that conspirators were at work led them to underrate the effects of the Continental System as a provocation.[1] Nonetheless, whatever might be true or believed to be true locally, the directors of Napoleon's police did not worry about the sort of bogies to which the previous decade attributed the Revolution and from which Metternich was to spend so much energy and thought protecting Europe after 1815. There were in any case few countries which actually produced enough subversion and secret organisation to justify special care. The most important were France and Italy.[2]

[1] C. Schmidt, *Grand duché de Berg* (1905), pp. 440–52. See also Le Forestier, *Les Illuminés*, pp. 706–15.

[2] It is true that French officials were much preoccupied by fears of German secret societies. But actual evidence of conspiratorial activity (except by governments) against the Napoleonic hegemony is far slighter in Germany than in France and Italy.

OPPOSITION AND CONSPIRACY IN FRANCE

In the eighteen years from the exposure of the Babeuf conspiracy to the fall of the Napoleonic Empire France underwent two major formal changes of régime (from the Directory to the Consulate, and from the Consulate to the Empire) and several less dramatic modifications of its institutions. In the circumstances, and given the long period of time involved, it is not surprising that the activity of political opposition changed too. It may even be thought unreasonable to speak of this period as if it formed a whole. Yet in the history of both the secret societies and of their mythology these years have a unity. They bridge a gap between the Revolution and the ideas it encouraged of conspiracy influenced directly by freemasonry in one form or another, and the Restoration era when other new general influences were believed to have joined in the work.

During the whole of these years there were two major opposition interests in France, both linked to the world of secret organisation and conspiracy. On the one hand were the unreconciled legitimists, for whom Directory, Consulate and Empire were all revolutionary usurpations. Attempts (in some degree successful) were from time to time made to conciliate them and to draw off their potential support. Emigrés were already more leniently treated under the Directory; Bonaparte offered them a generous amnesty in 1802. He had by then made peace with the Church, the most important ally of legitimist intransigency, by the Concordat of 1801. Later, the monarchical principle came to be embodied in the Empire and the rallying to it of some of the old nobility was lubricated by places and favours. Then, as time wore on and the restoration of the Bourbon line seemed less and less likely, the authoritarian Empire came to be attractive to conservative Frenchmen. They might formerly have been loyal to the Bourbons but the Emperor guaranteed order after years of anarchy. Nevertheless, though the legitimist cause might be weakened by such influences, there remained alive in exile a Bourbon court and an intransigent legitimist movement which retained its sympathisers in France. They were one enduring source of the threat of subversion for French governments of these years.

On the opposite wing was an equally durable revolutionary and republican tradition. In its extreme form it was harried by the Directory after the Babeuf plot, but that régime was at least still republican and parliamentary; under it, opposition from the Left could voice itself in the Chambers. With the Consulate this ceased to be true and under the

Empire the principle of republicanism itself was abandoned. Yet many Frenchmen remained sure that republicanism was what the Revolution had been about and could not be reconciled to the new course. These republicans were divided; some were won over (like some legitimists) by Napoleon who had, after all, established firmly many of the Revolution's achievements. Yet there remained an uncompromising core of republican opponents of the régime. They were particularly entrenched in the army itself, many of whose officers liked neither the rapid rise of a former colleague nor the re-erection of monarchy on the foundation of the victories they had helped to win.

These two tendencies had to operate in the teeth of growing governmental strength and the growing skill and efficiency of the French repressive apparatus. Much had been done in 1794–5 to curb the discontented. The steam had already been taken out of the popular societies before the Directory closed them down. The political police of the Directory and its Napoleonic successors continued to scrutinise their former personnel closely. In the countryside, large areas were still disturbed and disorderly under the Directory, but the army began the work of reducing them which was accomplished under the Consulate. 'Chouannerie', which had flared up again in 1799, was finished off as a real threat by 1801 and the Army of the West which dealt with it was dissolved in May 1802. Brigandage was gradually reduced to tolerable levels under the Consulate. Meanwhile the press was closely scrutinised and muzzled, opponents of the régime were locked up in lunatic asylums and Fouché eventually came to preside over a European police network of unprecedented scope and efficiency.[3]

Freemasonry, it may be remarked, was consciously incorporated with this machinery of control. It had flickered into life again at the beginning of the Directory, but officialdom hardly seems to have taken it very seriously; one police report of 1795 is very offhand in tone.[4] By the end of 1796, it is true, the police had their eye on two Parisian

[3] But N.B. the comment of Desmarest: 'je préviens que ces mots, *la police*, dont je me servirai souvent, ne doivent point s'entendre d'une unité ou capacité individuelle quelconque, mais du système entier des fonctionnaires et agens publics, le ministre au centre, ayant en outre ses rapports sur les états étrangers.' (P. M. Desmarest, *Témoignages historiques ou Quinze ans de haute police sous Napoléon* (Paris, 1833), p. xxviii.) Desmarest served under Fouché and his successor, Savary, and showed exemplary ability and discretion.

[4] 'Le royalisme est une secte folle et dépravée qui, si le peuple jouissait du strict nécessaire, ne mériterait pas plus l'attention du gouvernement que la secte des Jansénistes ou des francs-maçons.' A. Aulard, *Paris pendant la réaction thermidorienne et sous le Directoire* (Paris, 1898–1902), II, p. 408, report of 21 November. See also the comments later reported in IV, p. 18, V, pp. 425, 524.

lodges which were working and were suspect as possible centres of royalism, but there still seems to have been no great official concern.[5] A newspaper then attempted to excite the public in language which deliberately evoked the old stories of the masons' complicity in the Revolution.[6] This provoked a long reply from the secretary of one of the two lodges, writing openly as a freemason under his own name.[7] Presumably because he addressed a right-wing newspaper, he not only denied that many lodges were in existence (he said that there were only two in Paris), but went on to point out that, as before the Revolution, 'la majorité absolue de la noblesse et de ce qu'on appelait la bonne bourgeoisie composait les sociétés maçonniques'. As this had been accompanied by the most conspicuous and loyal devotion to the laws and religion the reappearance of lodges should therefore be seen as a sign of returning social health. The freemasons urged the editor to seek admission to a lodge. The old canard about the Duke of Orléans was shrugged off as a matter of 'quelques intrigants' unrepresentative of the Craft as a whole. Perhaps such arguments appealed to the authorities,[8] who, though they kept a watch on the lodges, intimated in 1798 that no legal impediment existed to their meeting. From that moment the Craft steadily revived, though its position was for some time delicate. In 1799 an important historic weakness was corrected by the solemn alliance of the Grand Orient and Grande Loge. It was a revivified, but chastened and no longer aristocratic, masonry which was working at the beginning of the Consulate.

Under the Consulate there was a little evidence that masonic forms might be used as pretexts for the assembly of discontented ex-Jacobins.[9] It cannot have amounted to much, because although Bonaparte's first instinct had been to suppress masonry, he soon decided to use it in-

[5] *RH*, xxxvii, 1899, pp. 278–80.

[6] 'Les sociétés de francs-maçons se reproduisent et se multiplient même de manière à inquiéter de bons citoyens qui, las de révolutions, en redoutent tous les instruments.' *Messager du Soir*, 6 December 1796 (quoted in Aulard, III, p. 611). The editor later said (p. 624) that he 'a craint de voir dans les sociétés des francs-maçons une nouvelle affiliation jacobite' (i.e., 'jacobine').

[7] Aulard, III, pp. 623–4.

[8] The Left remained suspicious. See the satire printed by Aulard, IV, pp. 217–19, and the press comment of July 1799 (V, p. 613): 'Pitt vient de supprimer les sociétés politiques et maintenir les sociétés de francs-maçons. Raison de plus pour nous de supprimer les francs-maçons et de rétablir les sociétés politiques.'

[9] See, e.g., the report of the Prefect of the Pas-de-Calais, quoted by G. Bourgin in 'Contribution de l'histoire de la franc-maçonnerie sous le premier Empire', *RF*, xlix, 1905, p. 47, and the letter of the Prefect of the Department of Mont-Blanc printed by A. Mathiez, *RF*, xl, 1901, pp. 32–4.

stead. This delighted masons anxious for his patronage in order to re-establish the public respectability of the Craft.[10] His brothers, Joseph and Lucien, were successively Grand Masters, while the effective direction of the official structure was carried out by the Grand Master 'adjoint', Cambacérès. Almost all the great dignitaries of the Empire belonged to it, too. This led to a flourishing growth in the number of lodges and adherents; many of them were members of the lower ranks of the administrative hierarchy, thus confirming the official function of the Craft as a part of the machinery for the maintenance and dissemination of the Napoleonic cult. The Grand Orient was the beneficiary of this prosperity, more than 1200 lodges being affiliated to it by the end of the Empire. By then its attitude was in the eyes of the régime impeccable.[11]

Nor were the systems outside the Grand Orient's jurisdiction less assiduous in asserting their loyalty and in integrating themselves with the structure of official patronage. They enjoyed a similar benevolence. Meanwhile, the illuminist tendency which had done so much to animate unorthodox, breakaway masonry was ebbing and many of its leaders had gone: its adherents had sometimes come round to a conservative, anti-revolutionary distrust of any secret political activity as early as the mid-1790s.[12] By 1814, therefore, it is not surprising to find that, in the words of one scholar, 'les Maçons étaient devenus des courtisans toujours prêts à se tourner vers le soleil levant'.[13] No doubt the gelded, official, nature of freemasonry under the Empire explains why its effectives fell away so dramatically in the last few months of the régime: it was identified with a crumbling political interest and little else.

[10] Sòriga (p. 47) quotes the apostrophe of one master of a lodge anxious for Bonaparte's protection for the Craft:

> 'O toi! sur qui le ciel versa son influence
> Toi, de tous les Français la gloire et l'espérance
> Sur mes faibles écrits daigne jeter les yeux
> Aime les Francs Maçons, et tu combles mes vœux.'

[11] An official survey of 1811 gives a good overall view of masonry at that moment. Only one Prefect (who we shall meet again in another connexion) expressed suspicion. See Bourgin, pp. 51–77.

[12] Kirchberger died in 1799, Lavater in 1801, Saint-Martin in 1803. See Viatte, I, pp. 319–26 on the change of mood.

[13] Le Forestier, La franc-maçonnerie Templière, p. 869. It may be noted, too, that Willermoz, far from a mere courtier, nonetheless became a conseiller général of his Department, an office he retained during the whole Napoleonic era, and played a considerable local role, particularly in religious affairs (p. 930). Nor, in due course, did the Restoration much affect his standing.

Nonetheless, even the temporary success of official masonry means that there was nothing to be heard of a masonic danger during the Napoleonic period. This was true also of the débris which still lay outside it, left by the masonic efflorescence of the previous century; the Scottish and mysticising rites presented no threat. 'La police de Bonaparte connaissait trop bien la nullité de ce corps immense, main impuissant et frivole, pour se défier de la vaine importance qu'il attache à ses mystères,' remarked a contemporary observer.[14] Moreover, if O'Meara is to be believed, Napoleon even thought the masons in some ways positively valuable.[15] The masonic background to the history of conspiracy in these years was, therefore, of small importance and the idea of participation by regular freemasons in a great plot should have become even more implausible. What was really important was going on elsewhere and would contribute other, non-masonic, elements to the myth.

The régime was much more worried by evidence of direct conspiracy in the legitimist or republican interest, some of which led to the creation of special secret organisations. Of the two, the threat from the Right was the more dangerous in the early years of the régime. Legitimism could always exploit among the masses its two great advantages: the persistence of religious loyalties and the existence in rural areas of grievances arising from the demands of war, above all, from conscription. After 1796 these were never to produce trouble for French governments quite so severe as in 1793, when three-quarters of France were formally declared in a state of insurrection. Yet there were grounds for hope for legitimists seeking to exploit these possibilities.

One early attempt to do so had come under the Directory, when the first royalist organisation took shape. The curiously named 'Institut

---

[14] *Histoire des sociétés secrètes de l'armée et des conspirations militaires qui ont eu pour object la destruction du gouvernement de Bonaparte* (Paris, 1815), p. 249. On most matters Charles Nodier, the anonymous author of this book, cannot be relied upon (see below, p. 269), but he may well have formed this view after talking to Fouché himself. Elsewhere he says that apart from the Templars 'le reste ne presente guère qu'une farce sérieuse, jouée par d'honnêtes oisifs entre des châssis de bateleurs, et dont la réprésentation, bonne pour amuser les loisirs d'une vieille femme, n'a jamais ému le sommeil d'un tyrant' ('De la maçonnerie et du carbonarisme', *Oeuvres complètes de Charles Nodier*, viii, *Souvenirs et portraits* (Paris, 1833), p. 129). The whole essay shows that it was possible to arrive at a sensible and balanced judgment on freemasonry in the revolutionary era. Nodier's suggestion that Napoleon also used the Templar masons as a safety-valve ('en jeux de théâtre') for the more ardently political of his followers seems more speculative.

[15] B. E. O'Meara, *Napoleon in Exile* (London, 1822), I, p. 185.

philanthropique' was founded in 1796 with British financial support to exploit the parliamentary and electoral opportunities available under the new constitution.[16] Its aim was to bring about the legal subversion of the revolutionary settlement and it had one great success in the elections of 1797. It was also intended to provide some protection against the recrudescence of extreme Jacobin influences after what was seen as their defeat at Thermidor. Its debt to conspiratorial tradition was shown by an organisation centred on a secret directory in Paris whose members were known only to the presidents of each departmental section of the Institut, and by a conscious reminiscence of masonic techniques in other ways. The inner group of Fils légitimes were to be distinct from the general body of members known as Amis de l'Ordre and were not to communicate the true royalist and insurrectionary aims of the society to them. This was vital if the aim of recruiting conservatives who feared Jacobinism was to succeed, and it was to these men rather than committed legitimists that the Institut looked in order to secure the election of its adherents. Another masonic reminiscence, though possibly less important, was suggested in a letter from Louis XVIII's representative to Grenville in 1796 when he observed that it might be possible to use changed versions of masonic signs as means of recognition within the royalist conspiracy.[17]

Nonetheless, the Institut can hardly be regarded as a true secret society since its aims were so closely linked to overt electoral action. In this activity it prospered. It seems to have spread widely (police reported branches in thirty-one Departements) but the coup d'état of Fructidor ended any hopes its members cherished of legally subverting the régime. They therefore turned to the preparation of insurrection. In the year VII they again enjoyed the support and encouragement of the British agent Wickham, who thought highly of the organisation, but the failure of an insurrectionary attempt in that year was really the end of the Institut as a serious force. After 1800 it fell into decadence and its role as a threat to the régime was taken over by other royalist bodies. It perhaps belongs to the history of moderate royalism and of the type of conspiracy likely to be encouraged by a foreign enemy, rather than to that of secret societies, but it fed the continuing awareness of the danger of subversive activity which was felt in official

---

[16] No good modern study exists of the Institut. See G. Caudrillier, *L'Association royaliste de l'Institut Philanthropique à Bordeaux et la conspiration anglaise en France pendant la deuxième coalition* (Paris, 1908) for some information and a selection of documents. For further information see the early nineteenth-century publications mentioned below.

[17] Caudrillier, pp. xi and 2–3, where the letter to Grenville is printed in part.

circles.[18] It was the official press which in fact put information about the Institut into public circulation by publishing a document containing its name in 1800.[19] This can hardly have done much more than bring the knowledge of the existence of such a body to the notice of those who had not yet heard of it; nothing more, it seems, was heard publicly of the Institut until the first Restoration.[20]

The only other legitimist organisations of the Directorial period which demand notice are two whose aims were not primarily political subversion, but which nevertheless familiarised their members with the techniques of conspiracy and secret organisation and to this extent fed the secret craze. One was the Société du Cœur de Jésus, founded as early as 1790.[21] It purposed to provide a confraternity operating in lay society to sustain members of the religious communities suppressed in that year. Later it recruited laymen, offering them the benefits of a spiritual life while they continued to live in the lay world. By 1799, this society, too, had spread extensively.

After Brumaire and the creation of the Consulate, the conditions of political action were much changed. Increasingly, opposition could expect an effective outlet only in conspiratorial and even terrorist activity. None of the legitimist organisations so far mentioned responded in this way, but there were a number of important legitimist conspiracies, or conspiracies in which legitimists were importantly involved, sometimes, confusingly, together with republicans and Jacobins. The most celebrated resulted in the attempt by the 'machine infernale' on Bonaparte's life on Christmas Eve, 1800 (this was used with great success by the régime as an excuse to harry the ex-Jacobins[22]). The resumption of war with England in 1803 revived their hopes and

[18] Its exploitation by the British is discussed by H. Mitchell, *The Underground War Against Revolutionary France* (Oxford, 1965), *passim*, where there are helpful references. See also G. de Bertier de Sauvigny, *Le comte Ferdinand de Bertier* (Paris, 1948). See Caudrillier for various references to the Institut which continue to turn up in official papers where royalism at Bordeaux is discussed as late as 1804 (e.g., pp. 46, 61). Even for the police, though, it does not seem to have been very alarming or to have possessed much more than historical interest under the Consulate.

[19] In a collection called *La Conspiration Anglaise. Tome premier* (Paris, An IX). Only this volume seems to have appeared and the reference appears on p. 283.

[20] See below, p. 259.

[21] Bertier de Sauvigny, p. 42.

[22] Among whom, it may be noted, Bonaparte was not always concerned to make fine distinctions. Desmarest (*Témoignages*, p. 49) later recalled the First Consul specifically referring to the followers of Babeuf during discussions about security measures immediately after the 'machine infernale'. V. Daline notes other examples of Bonaparte's sensitivity to this threat in his article 'Napoléon et les Babouvistes', *AHRF*, 1970, *passim*.

a joint conspiracy with certain republicans was mounted that year which looked forward to invasion and popular risings against Bonaparte. Unfortunately, much of this negotiation was the work of the Napoleonic police themselves, who saw advantages in revealing to Frenchmen the peril in which they stood from legitimists. This exploded in the arrest of Cadoudal the following year, and led eventually to the execution of the Duc d'Enghien and the proclamation of the Empire. Cadoudal was executed.

In these events no part was played by some legitimists who did not envisage popular insurrection, but who, nevertheless, sought to maintain some sort of political organisation: not to promote the violent overthrow of Napoleon, but to enable themselves to act decisively at a moment of crisis by having adherents in positions of power and responsibility. Two different bodies successively sought to do this. The Congrégation was founded in 1801 by an ex-Jesuit to undertake pious and charitable works and to offer special devotions to the Virgin and it is not easy to see when its members, or some of them, began to see it in a more political light. What seems to be clear is that the arrest of the Pope and his removal to France in 1809 (which followed the occupation of the Papal States by the French in the previous year) did much to undermine Napoleon's success in winning former legitimists to his support. This seemed a good opportunity to some members of the Congrégation, who now sought to use it. Among these, one was pre-eminent, the young nobleman Ferdinand de Bertier.[23]

Bertier was the son of the Intendant of Paris who had been murdered by the mob soon after the fall of the Bastille. He came of age in 1799 and almost at once seems to have been involved in royalist conspiracy. Later, rejecting Bonaparte's overtures, he came under the suspicion of the Napoleonic police and was closely watched. He was a member of the Institut Philanthropique. In 1808 his brother was arrested. In the following year Bertier joined the Congrégation and seems to have taken part in the clandestine printing and circulation of the Papal Bull of excommunication against those who had taken part in the abduction from Rome and of other propaganda matter. In September he was arrested as part of a general clamping-down on the Congrégation which, though it was to remain formally in existence, now becomes of less interest to us than its successor, founded by Bertier after his release. He had already been toying with the idea of a secret organisation of his own and appears to have been much influenced by the ideas and enthusiasms of Barruel. He decided to join a masonic lodge in

[23] On what follows, see Bertier de Sauvigny, *passim*.

order to find out how it worked. After this he devised the most important of the royalist organisations of the period, the Chevaliers de la Foi.

This body had several remarkable features which place it in the masonic tradition, even though its aims were totally at variance with those of traditional masonry and with those attributed to the legendary conspirators in the Barruel tradition. The most striking similarity was the combination of different grades in the organisation with different levels of revelation about its purposes. The first grade of members were known as Associés de Charité, whose only concern was with works of charity and piety, the ostensible purpose of the whole organisation. Above these Associés came the second grade, of Ecuyers, to whom was revealed, together with much antiquarian and pseudo-historical nonsense, the purpose of re-establishing the chivalric orders of medieval society. Above these came the third and highest grade, that of Chevaliers, further divided into three sub-grades, Chevaliers, Hospitaliers and the Chevaliers de la Foi, who were cognisant of the political aims of the whole fraternity. (The reminiscences of Scottish and Templar masonry are obvious.)

The first political action of Bertier's society seems to have been to get into touch with both the so-called 'black' cardinals and with the royalist émigrés, who did not prove easy to impress. This may have been in part because of difficulties of internal communication; in order to preserve secrecy the society relied on word of mouth, a stipulation that cannot have made for ease or speed. The exiles, moreover, may have found it difficult to be sure of the priorities of the society. Was it really concerned with the interests of the Bourbons or with those of the Pope? Nevertheless, the organisation prospered. It is not clear, though it is possible, that it was in touch with some of the conspirators in the Malet affair of 1812 which is, arguably, the most serious conspiratorial threat ever faced by the régime, and by the following year it is certain that it had established itself strongly in many Departments. Its provincial subdivisions, called 'bannières', were strongest in Picardy, the west, the Midi and Provence, and in Franche-Comté. Many of these were crucial frontier areas and became decisive in the second half of 1813 as the allied armies began the invasion of France.

In the crisis of the Napoleonic régime, the Chevaliers proved to be not an insurrectionary instrument but an important means of liaison and intelligence for the invaders, and a crucial political factor. Preparations for a rising in the Vendée failed of effect, but a scheme to subvert the Paris National Guard may have impressed Talleyrand, with whom the organisation was in touch. The strong position of the society at Toulouse and Bordeaux became important as Wellington advanced from the south; the members in the Franche-Comté welcomed the Austrians. It has been claimed that the Bordeaux Chevaliers played a decisive part and that the rejection of the régime and the proclamation of the Bourbons there on 12 March, which they stage-managed, may have decided the allies to march on Paris. This episode, nevertheless, also shows that the Chevaliers were essentially not initiators but only taking advantage of the crumbling of authority inside France. This was shown again at Toulouse where the adherents of the society were able to make use of a virtual breakdown of government accelerated by dislike of conscription and requisitioning, but could not provoke a popular rising. For the future mythology of the secret societies this relatively restricted role was unimportant. What the Chevaliers seemed to have done was to have provided by adopting the legendary techniques and methods of the secret societies an instrument for the restoration of the moral order as effective as those which were believed to have overthrown it. Their example reinforced the widespread readiness to believe in the importance of conspiracy and clandestine organisation as political techniques. Many of their members were no doubt again reflecting a few years later how dangerous such devices might be in the hands of their opponents.

In the opposing camp, there is also some evidence of clear and unambiguous modelling of subversive organisation on masonic lines, but even when it is clearest, it is obviously much less important than in the Chevaliers de la Foi. It is very hard to disentangle the story of left-wing and republican opposition to Napoleon, for there is little continuous thread to grasp, though its constituent elements are not hard to identify. The three most important were predictable. First came the unreconciled and unreconcilable old Jacobins, living with a sense of grievance that went back to the beginning of the Directory and even before, to the winding-up of the Terror and the end of Revolutionary Government itself. Then there were the 'salon' republicans, clustered about such figures as Madame de Staël; some of them were the intellectuals who were to be known as the Idéologues. Finally, there were the disgusted soldiers, some angry through principle and some through spite or envy of a too-successful colleague. Moreau was already showing his irritation in 1800, and in 1801 a number of unreliable regiments were sent off to San Domingo.[24]

[24] Jean Victor Moreau, general, later died of wounds received from the French while serving on the allied side at the Battle of Dresden.

Here were the possible materials of conspiracy, but three further points should be made. The first is that confusion always made it possible for the police to attribute to republicans and Jacobins the doings of royalists. This confusion was long to persist and still clouds the subject. The true strength of republican conspiracy is therefore difficult to assess. It is important, therefore, to recall also that the evidence which does exist shows the republicans to have been small minorities unable to draw on any certain popular support. The third point is that among the republicans the soldiers had at least their professional connexions, loyalties and techniques to lean upon. In the circumstances, it is hardly surprising that organised opposition to the Napoleonic régime from the Left should have expressed itself most frequently and obviously through a series of attempted coups by soldiers.

Three or four such attempts or abortive attempts between 1800 and 1812 caused real anxiety.[25] In 1802 there was a stir over the so-called 'libel' plot. A number of the discontented soldiers had been discussing their grievances and were in touch with the salon group; among them were Moreau and Bernadotte, whose names continually recur in the rumours and gossips about disaffection in the army.[26] Bernadotte's chief of staff, a brigadier named Simon, began in 1802 to circulate posters among the garrisons in the west, attacking Bonaparte's new popularity with the clergy and émigrés. From Rennes, where he was stationed, they were sent to other commands; some of the placards mentioned Moreau and there seem to have been hopes of a military coup. But nothing happened; the authorities quickly reacted, Simon and a number of others were arrested and the whole business fizzled out.

Moreau's name came up again in connexion with the still-obscure Cadoudal plot of 1804. It was not clear what part he had played and it is even likely that he had withdrawn from the conspiracy when he realised that it was a royalist affair. Nonetheless, he was arrested and, eventually, exiled.

Napoleon's mildness in dealing with his republican critics in the army was to be shown even more decisively in the case of General Malet. He had already toyed in 1800 with a plot to kidnap the First Consul. In 1808 he joined a republican group at Paris and was subsequently arrested and put in prison. While in La Force he took part in a plot to break out while Napoleon was absent from Paris and to

---

[25] The not very satisfactory book of E. Guillon, *Les complots militaires sous le consulat et l'empire* (Paris, 1894), is still the most convenient summary.

[26] *Mémoires de A. C. Thibaudeau* (Paris, 1913), pp. 62–3.

announce the Emperor's death as a prelude to seizing power. This was discovered, but no important punitive measures followed. He was left in prison, the mystery undissipated; it may be that he owed something to Fouché, the Minister of Police at the time. Whether or not this is so, Malet was next allowed to leave prison and to remove to a nursing-home because of his health, though remaining there, too, under detention. At this establishment were a number of royalist conspirators (among them the brother of François de Bertier). Malet seems at first to have avoided them, but one of them, the Abbé Lafon, succeeded in the end in winning his confidence and involving him in another plot. It, too, turned on Malet's escape and announcement of Napoleon's death, and the Emperor's absence in Russia provided the opportunity.[27] Malet and some others escaped and achieved a remarkable degree of success in bluffing members of the Paris garrison. They managed to arrest the Minister of Police and had not one officer shown more sense than the rest, Malet might have succeeded. As it was, he was within a few hours again under arrest. More than a thousand other arrests were also made and Malet and his closest associates were hastily shot, long before the news reached Napoleon. This was effectively the end of what we know of republican plot and conspiracy against Napoleon.[28]

Such an account does not take us very far. It helps neither in assessing the contribution of secret societies to these plots, nor in understanding what happened to the legend of the secret societies in the Napoleonic period. Yet much was woven about it. A thread of republican secret organisation and a secret society were soon alleged to be traceable through these events. Yet because the strongest assertions of the importance of a secret society rested for a long time largely on the account of one man, the 'littérateur' Charles Nodier, they were disregarded even by many of those who were, in another context, likely to be sympathetic to a conspiracy interpretation of events. It was not until some years had passed that a few fragments more of evidence came to light which made it possible to say that it was at least possible that secret societies had been operating with limited effectiveness during the Empire and, what is more, operating internationally. The appearance

[27] The new government was to have been presided over by Moreau and Carnot was to have been one of its members.
[28] Mention should perhaps be made for completeness' sake, however, of a royalist plot to use the army in 1813, by subverting the newly-formed Gardes d'honneur. It, too, failed.

of this evidence was to be followed in the 1830s by the publication of accounts by participants providing further details.[29]

All these scraps of information have to be treated with the greatest caution, if they are to be used to throw light on what was going on and this has, unfortunately, not always been the case. This is particularly true in the areas where the materials most closely concern Buonarroti who, for certain historiographical and political reasons, is still today sometimes treated in a mythological way even by serious historians who in other questions show far more caution. Almost all the evidence we have about Buonarroti's involvement in the world of Napoleonic conspiracy is at best plausible and inferential. It is for the most part hearsay of unsupported personal assertion, thickened only to the slightest degree by official record. Yet there runs through much of the recent writing about Buonarroti a wish to believe that he was closely implicated in important and continuing subversion in France which at times has led even reputable scholars to push assertion and inference far beyond what the evidence allows. If we ignore Buonarroti, too, the evidence even for the general proposition that secret societies intrigued against Napoleon is poor, and has all the usual defects of inbuilt dramatisation by participants and officials. Nonetheless, it does at least make it easy to see how non-historians and unobjective observers should have been able to come to believe soon after 1815 that a continuous chain of secret societies could be traced through the Napoleonic period, linking the 'Jacobin' conspiracies of the 1790s to the bogymen of the Restoration.

Buonarroti is quite a good place to begin in order to assess what the authorities believed the truth to be. Here is the first paradox: the outstanding figure in the history of the secret societies was very mildly treated, and all but ignored. There are references to him in the records, but they are neither so frequent nor, usually, of the character our knowledge of his later reputation would lead us to expect. The events and supposed activities of this period of his life can be reconstructed fairly clearly from these references and from what he later said. He had

---

[29] The main post-Restoration materials bearing on this question are discussed below, in another context (Ch. IX); they are the papers seized by the Austrian police in 1823, when they arrested the conspirator Andryane at Milan, his own books of memoirs, published at the end of the 1830s, and the autobiography of an Italian conspirator, Prati, published in an English radical newspaper. All these materials were first brought together and studied by Dr A. Lehning, in an article 'Buonarroti and his international secret societies' reprinted in his collection *From Buonarroti to Bakunin* (Leiden, 1970), pp. 30–64. All references to 'Lehning' which follow are to this.

remained confined in a fort at Cherbourg from 1797 to 1800 and while there appears to have been able to keep in touch fairly easily with his friends outside; he later claimed that he began to organise secret societies while there. In March 1800, an order was given by the Consuls for his transfer to Oléron and for him to be given a daily allowance. Then, in December 1802, he was moved to Sospello in the Alpes Maritimes, where, according to what he told Andryane in 1821, he was able to pick up again the threads of his organisational work of conspiracy.[30] In 1806 he was released and allowed to go and live at Geneva, where he remained for the next fifteen years, except for a brief interlude at Grenoble, to which he went in January 1813, returning to Geneva in May the following year, at the first Restoration. He seems to have had powerful friends to be treated with such indulgence by the authorities. Fouché and Réal (who had defended him at his trial in 1797) may have been one source of this, though Napoleon himself was another. The Emperor always seems to have thought of him with some benevolence and certainly showed no suspicion that Buonarroti was engaged in continuing conspiracy against him, though he showed great distrust of Babouvards in general. It is also true, of course, that by twentieth-century standards, the Napoleonic régime was by no means harsh in its treatment of opposition, and this may only be another instance of it. Undoubtedly the mildness of his treatment ought to have made it easier for Buonarroti to pursue at each stage his chosen conspiratorial career.[31]

Each of these movements brought him new associations and was later said to have played an important part in enriching his revolutionary contacts. At Sospello he seems to have re-established links with Piedmont and Italy and he said later that he there joined an organisation called the Philadelphes. When he arrived in Geneva, in May 1806, Buonarroti was still under 'surveillance spéciale', though the Prefect's first reaction was to discount the suspicions which his charge aroused among the friends of order. 'Sa conduite n'est pas répréhensible,' he wrote, 'et il existe plutôt des inquiétudes qu'il ne mérite pas de re-

---

[30] A decision to send him to Elba was countermanded (Francovich, p. 117). Most of Buonarroti's own reminiscences of this period were to Andryane, who then printed them nearly twenty years later in two books of reminiscences (see below, p. 327).

[31] He continued to receive his allowance of three francs a day for some years at Geneva (Saitta, *Filippo Buonarroti*, i, pp. 47–8). P. Robiquet (*RH*, liv, 1928, pp. 502–3) has drawn attention to his somewhat equivocal status. A note prepared for the Minister of Police on 19 November 1812 says that 'Sa majesté' ordered that he should be set at liberty and sent to a town of the interior under 'surveillance spéciale', (AN, AF⁷ 6331).

proches.'[32] Buonarroti seems to have made a living quietly by giving lessons in music, an art to which he was devoted all his life and in which, as a boy, he had been noted by a teacher to be 'little less than a master'.[33] Yet he was soon thought to be engaged in conspiracy and the organisation of secret societies. Seemingly, he organised a Philadelphe group within a masonic lodge to which he belonged, the Amis Sincères. The Prefect, Capelle, became suspicious, and it is he who has provided the only evidence in contemporary official records that Buonarroti was a serious figure in the secret societies at this time.

He had in 1802 reported to the Minister that a group calling themselves Philadelphes existed at Geneva, though this, like most of his subsequent warnings, was ignored at Paris.[34] He was in 1811 the only Prefect who responded unfavourably to the official enquiry on freemasonry. 'L'ésprit de la maçonnerie à Genève est généralement mauvais,' he reported, going on, 'mais est-il bien meilleur dans les autres parties de l'empire? C'est toujours l'égalité, toujours nos frères, toujours de la philosophie, toujours des idées républicaines, etc. Telle est encore la maçonnerie en France.' It had been dangerous to the old monarchy in France, he ended, and so it would prove to be to the new.[35] It is clear from other papers that these views were connected with the Prefect's suspicions about Buonarroti's activities.[36]

In March 1811 one of the commissaires de police seems to have been the first to draw Capelle's notice to Buonarroti by alleging that he usually spoke at meetings of the Amis Sincères at which anti-despotic and egalitarian sentiments were voiced. The lodge was thus out of step with the official and traditional masonic principle of political nullity: 'les principes développés aux amis sincères ont indigné et révolté les autres loges, qui ne les considèrent plus comme frères.' On the strength of this, Capelle reported to Paris, he had decided to close the lodge.[37] A period of close scrutiny of its members appears to have followed, for in January 1812, the Ministry of Police in Paris was told that an informant had asserted that clandestine meetings of the Amis Sincères were still going on.[38] Worse still, there had been talk of a plot,

[32] Quoted in E. Chapuisat, RF, liv, 1908, p. 163.
[33] Quoted in Morelli, CS, 1965, p. 536.
[34] L. Pingaud, La jeunesse de Charles Nodier (Besançon, 1914), p. 175.
[35] Quoted in Bourgin, RH, xlix, 1905, p. 68.
[36] They are to be found in AN, AF⁷ 6331 and the references which follow are to this dossier when no other location is specified.
[37] Letter of 12 April 1811.
[38] Letter of 16 January 1812, from Mélun, commissaire spéciale de police at Geneva.

aiming at a coming military coup which would reactivate in France the constitution of 1793, but with Moreau as president. 'Le mot d'ordre serait l'anagramme de philadelphie.' There were other exciting details, among them the assertion that Buonarroti had said he would be governor of Strasbourg when the coup took place, and another that Madame de Staël knew all about it, too. Unfortunately, this evidence was not very good. To begin with, the informant was (like many informants) not a very reassuring figure, and, furthermore, all his details about the plot were hearsay, said by him to have been communicated to him by a friend who had been admitted by the superiors of the lodge to a higher, Rosicrucian grade which made him eligible for their confidence.

What followed never really went further than this. By March, the Prefect was asking for the immediate arrest of Buonarroti and two of his friends who led the group, now reorganised as a new lodge, the Triangle.[39] He was convinced that Buonarroti was the key figure, largely, it seems, because of his well-known views and the assertions of his informant. Soon, he was distinguishing in the group the political association from the masonic; the political was called the Philadelphes, or Amis de Moreau, and it had its special signs of recognition.[40] Oaths were taken to obey an unknown director and unknown statutes and there were said to be branches of the society in every Departement. The authorities at Paris, nonetheless, refused to be alarmed. In May, the Minister wrote to the Prefect to explain that though it was clear that although a sect of Philadelphes had indeed existed under the Directory, they had certainly ceased to operate soon after Brumaire.[41] Those whom Capelle especially suspected at Geneva—a trio of whom Buonarroti was one—would cause far less harm by being left alone than by being taken seriously: 'ils sont hors d'état de pouvoir troubler la tranquillité publique.' This remained for months the view of France's best-informed police. The Prefect was not even allowed simply to send his 'conspirators' away until after the Malet affair. This led him to further urgent demands for action, though he could still produce no evidence that the Philadelphes of Geneva were linked to what happened in Paris. The result, nonetheless, was that the Minister began at last to relax his opposition. The Prefect was finally ordered to prevent

[39] This may, incidentally, have provided a cloak for another circle, De la grille, to which Buonarroti belonged, according to a report made many years later. See letter of Sub-Prefect of Gex to Minister of Interior, 9 August 1819 (AN, AF⁷ 6685).

[40] AN, AF⁷ 6331, Capelle to Minister of Police, 20 March 1812.

[41] Letter of 29 May 1812.

any further Philadelphe meetings and to send away from Geneva Buonarroti and one of his associates. This was done; in January Buonarroti selected Grenoble for his residence and went there for the last year of the Napoleonic régime.

As the minister reported to Napoleon, the Prefect's views were not supported by good evidence, there was no reason to believe in Philadelphe activity elsewhere, and there had been no earlier complaints of Buonarroti's behaviour.[42] The Prefect had only seemed to detect some agitation among his suspects after the news of Malet's attempt. Nonetheless, he was a zealous official and it was best not to resist him further. So lightly did Napoleonic ministers take the Philadelphe threat.

Paradoxically, Capelle may have been in some small measure justified by what only became known later. There is no sign, it is true, of any effective or important secret conspiratorial activity by Buonarroti in Napoleonic Geneva, but there does exist evidence that while there he had founded, perhaps in 1809, an organisation which may be regarded, formally at least, as the first international political secret society.[43]

This was the Sublimes Maîtres Parfaits, of which the Prefect heard nothing. Only freemasons were admitted to it, and its ritual and structure was heavily coloured by masonic experience. It represented an abandonment of the idea of the coup in favour of an attempt to build a new community within a corrupt society which would eventually destroy it by undermining it at every point. This was, of course, the Illuminati ideal, and there were other parallels, too. The three grades of Perfect Sublime Master, Sublime Elect and Areopagite were modelled on the Illuminati grades, and, as in the earlier organisation, the lower grades did not know the full secrets of the society. The Elect were aware that they were to work for a republican form of government; only the Areopagites knew that the final aim of the society was social egalitarianism, and the means to it the abolition of private property. Buonarroti thereafter always clung to the essentials of this model of the secret society: on the one hand, the concentration of authority in a small group of directors and on the other the concomitant structure of graded initiation. These ideas, it has been truly pointed out,[44] distinguish his doctrine of revolutionary action clearly from later notions based on party or class.

[42] Draft report of 29 December 1812.

[43] Buonarroti said 1808–9; the earliest document is of September 1811 (Lehning, p. 42).

[44] Lehning, p. 36. See also his later ideas on secret organisation, quoted by Saitta, *Filippo Buonarroti*, ii, pp. 136–9.

Whether this society had any importance in conspiracy against Napoleon is doubtful. It has been connected with the republican opposition because the first members of the Sublimes Maîtres Parfaits seem to have been Philadelphes of neo-Jacobin and anti-Bonapartist origins. Given how little we know of the Philadelphes, though, this does not take us far. If we infer a deliberate attempt to penetrate and take over masonic lodges we have an Illuminati parallel, and this seems a reasonable inference. But from the start Buonarroti had in mind a new conception, co-ordinating and directing secret societies all over Europe. This was to be carried out through the 'Grand Firmament', the directing body whose name may have been taken from the Philadelphes. Still with this aim, the Sublimes Maîtres Parfaits survived the Restoration, being re-organised in 1818 under the name of the Monde (whose notebook is the main source of our information about its organisation and ideas), and built up connexions with almost every secret society in Western Europe. Thus, for the first time, reality was given to the myth of the great conspiracy. In the 1820s, when the society was discovered, this became public knowledge. The alarm which it provoked was consciously exploited by Buonarroti who, for the rest of his life, preached the doctrine of the international solidarity of the revolutionary societies. His achievement was to have put something real, at last, behind the fantasies of the plot of thinkers.[45]

Yet this reality was tenuous. Paradoxically, whatever suspicions the police had of them, the Sublimes Maîtres Parfaits cannot be shown actually to have *done* anything at all that mattered beyond this, especially before 1815. In 1812 they played no part, it seems, in the one attempt that offered some chance of overthrowing Napoleon. Buonarroti's later claim to have been involved in the Malet plot rests only on his own statement made eight or nine years later.[46] No one has yet shown, it has been wisely remarked by an American scholar, that the Sublimes

---

[45] Not that there is not, still, much dispute about what he actually did. The question, for example, of the exact relationship of the Sublimes Maîtres Parfaits with other societies is still unresolved. See the detailed discussion of Saitta (*Filippo Buonarroti*, i, pp. 83–99).

[46] A. Andryane, *Souvenirs de Genève* (Paris, 1839), ii, p. 207. It is just possible also that a remark by the conspirator Prati could bear this interpretation. See Lehning, p. 39. But on the whole question, scepticism is advisable. Buonarroti was always prone to dramatic exaggeration and self-deception when talking about 'his' secret societies and had good reason for conscious myth-making in the interests of prestige (as has been pointed out by Pia Onnis in 'Propaganda e rapporti di società segrete intorno al 1817', *Rassegna storica del Risorgimento*, 1964, pp. 495–6). A letter of 1828 suggests he knew little about Malet and had no acquaintance with Oudet (p. 489).

Maîtres Parfaits did anything positive of significance except (later) to strengthen Metternich's hand by being discovered.[47] All that mattered was that they existed.

The society whose name cropped up most frequently in this account, the Philadelphes, did, in fact, come to the public eye even before the Napoleonic accounts were quite closed. This was because of the publication in 1815, during the first Restoration, of the *Histoire des sociétés secrètes de l'armée* already mentioned.[48] It purported to provide an account of an organisation with this name which was the heart of the opposition to Napoleon. It was anonymous and successful; almost at once it went into a second edition. Its tone was authoritative and it seemed to draw on a living tradition, so that although it was recognised that it raised important critical questions—how could so big and successfully organised a conspiracy as it described have been so unsuccessful?—it was greeted with respect.

Its author was Charles Nodier, who was to enjoy his greatest celebrity as the leader of a literary salon under the July Monarchy, having by then been displaced from his informal primacy as leader of the French romantic movement in literature by the publication of Hugo's *Préface de Cromwell*. Under Charles X he was librarian of the Arsénal and recognition of his standing—and compensation for his displacement—came when he was elected to the Academy in 1834. His several books and the talents he displayed in conversation gave him an exaggerated reputation which may have contributed to the even more exaggerated repudiation which followed his death in 1844.

Nodier was born in 1780 at Besançon, where his father was mayor and president of the district criminal court during the Revolution. Charles, somewhat precociously, began at the age of twelve to attend the local Jacobin club. His published recollections and earlier autobiographical notes are unreliable,[49] but it seems that after Brumaire—which he welcomed as a moderate—he had the idea of transforming into a political body a small Besançon student group founded in 1797 to which he belonged. His aim was to use the Philadelphes (as they were called) as a centre of propaganda for the new régime.[50] The new society had a masonic flavour, but its original intentions were far from sinister; its

[47] Eisenstein, *The first professional Revolutionist: Filippo Michele Buonarroti (1761–1837)*, p. 48.

[48] See above, p. 254.

[49] Pingaud, pp. 55–7.

[50] Pingaud, pp. 42–4, p. 61. This association took the name Philadelphes to emphasise the bonds of friendship which connected its members. It was a fairly common name for such bodies in the eighteenth century.

most substantial activities had been picnics and the reading of members' literary works.

When Nodier came later to look back on this period, he gave an account of what followed this transformation of the Philadelphes which attracted much attention when, in 1815, he published it in his book on the secret societies of the army. It became a prime source for public discussion of clandestine opposition under Napoleon but has been much run down by historians. Nodier's sympathetic biographer, Pingaud, called the Philadelphes 'une institution dont l'inventeur a créé la légende, à côté de la sienne propre, sous prétexte d'en retracer l'histoire'.[51] There can be no doubt that Nodier may not be accepted as a serious guide.[52] Nonetheless, in tracing his contribution to the secret society legend it is worth remarking again that the post-Restoration evidence about Buonarroti's activities tends to confirm the suspicion that the Philadelphes were a reality, though probably of no positive importance.

Nodier begins his story at Brumaire and almost at once it loses contact with what we know about the Besançon student group. At that moment, he alleges, there came into existence a conspiracy of those who deplored the coup as an assertion of personal power; its members were finally to be successful in overthrowing the Emperor fourteen years later. The conspiracy was eventually of enormous extent, involving at least six thousand plotters; sceptics should consider the careers of Moreau and Malet and ponder how they could conceivably have survived so long without widespread and powerful hidden support. This great force derived ultimately from the chance that there existed at the moment of Brumaire an organisation founded in eastern France for social purposes in the mid-1790s which was to provide the framework for their efforts. This was the society of the Philadelphes.

Malet, who had been stationed at Besançon in the 1790s, had been a member of this organisation, said Nodier, but its possibilities as a vehicle for political subversion were not (according to Nodier) seen by him but by another soldier, Oudet. He is central to Nodier's account, which depicts him as a romantic and attractive figure, brave, intelligent and self-sacrificing. He was also a great ladies' man.[53] (He is presented very much in the style of the typical young romantic hero of

---

[51] p. 11.

[52] To almost anything: he never soldiered, for example, but claims in his *Souvenirs* to have spent twelve years in the army. Pingaud also says (p. 159) that he was 'impressioniste constitutionellement et de naissance'.

[53] 'Il était né Werther, et le monde l'avait fait Lovelace.' Nodier, *Histoire des sociétés secrètes*, p. 23.

the epoch and is altogether a much more attractive figure as a conspirator than had been Weishaupt.) On deciding that the Philadelphes could provide the organisation he needed to resist Bonaparte's ambitious march towards dictatorship, Oudet joined it, but soon found that it was already contaminated by members with political ambitions which were frequently at variance with his own. Some of its members were, in fact, legitimists. Others sought a separatist future for the Franche-Comté.[54]

Oudet accepted this situation while preparing his own takeover of the society. He studied literature about other secret societies for inspiration about methods and organisation and, interestingly, found little to take from them except the basic masonic legacy of a system of graded membership and secrets. He adopted an 'échelle philandelphique' of three grades, each with appropriate secrets, those of the leader of the whole society being known only to him. On this basis he began to recruit.

From this time, says Nodier, the geographical centre of the Philadelphes was no longer Besançon, but wherever Oudet was at a particular time. Around him grew up a nation within the nation, whose members had abnegated the obligations of civil society, symbolising their adherence to the new order by re-baptism under new names. Local branches made their appearance under different names in different areas, often embodying themselves in the illegal and semipopular resistance and criminal world of the Miquelets in the Pyrenees, the Barbets of the Alps, the Bandoliers of the Jura, Switzerland and Savoy. In the army they were known as 'frères bleus', and six regiments contained groups of them.

Oudet's next step was to secure Moreau's agreement to be elected as leader. Working through another officer, Oudet persuaded him; Moreau entered the society under the name of 'Fabius'.[55] Moreau's views do not seem to have been rigidly republican; at any rate Nodier thought he favoured a monarchical restoration. Moreau's imprudences soon led to his arrest, a hindrance to the development of Oudet's plans.

In 1804, nonetheless, Oudet was getting things under way again. He had been in touch with the legitimists and with the British agent Drake. There was talk of a restoration under the Constitution of 1791, plans for an insurrection in the Jura, for another in the Tirol and for

[54] Nodier seems to have got this idea from a sixteenth-century book by Gollut, *Mémoires de la république séquanaise* (1592), and he describes his conspirators as animated by the national ideal of a republic so-named.

[55] Pingaud (pp. 169–70) says there is no evidence for this, though Moreau did once help to found a masonic lodge, called Philadelphie.

an attempt to kidnap Napoleon on his way to his coronation at Milan. Moreau's exile led Oudet to choose another leader for the society. He now approached Malet who agreed to act but was, unfortunately, not popular with the other Philadelphes. Perhaps this contributed to the failure of the first Malet plot. Soon after this Oudet was recalled to service and was killed with the connivance of the authorities. Doubts about the value of the conspiratorial technique now grew among the Philadelphes and, says Nodier, 'à cette époque se termine sensiblement . . . l'existence politique des Philadelphes'.[56] Nonetheless, Malet was its chief after Oudet and his attempt of 1812, though not organised by the society, was, like the contribution of Moreau to Napoleon's final defeat, an expression of its aims.[57]

Although it is easy to see that there is enough here to feed the secret society mythology and to demonstrate continuities which would be impressive to those disposed to look for them (some of the false names cited by Nodier, for example, were names already used in the Illuminati conspiracy), it is very hard to take any of this account seriously. It adds virtually nothing to our knowledge of political opposition to the Empire and is on many points wholly misleading. Oudet's career, for example, though it brought him at one point under the suspicions of the authorities as a possible transmitter of seditious literature, was marked conspicuously by the favour and patronage of the Emperor. Nor does Nodier's account of Malet fit easily into the known facts.[58]

Nodier's motives in writing remain unclear, but he was always less than candid in his account of his own political past and it may be that he was anxious to demonstrate to the returning Bourbons what they owed to people like himself who had opposed Bonaparte. He certainly later made much of his imprisonment for publishing an anti-Napoleonic

---

[56] *Histoire des sociétés secrètes*, p. 220.

[57] pp. 231–8.

[58] Besides promotions in the Legion of Honour and the army, where he finished as a full colonel, Oudet also received monetary awards. See Pingaud, pp. 165–74 on him and Malet. On the other hand, it should be said that Buonarroti seems later to have believed that Oudet played the part described by Nodier. See the evidence documented by Saitta, ii, pp. 44–5. The debate on Malet began even before Nodier wrote, with the publication in 1814 of the Abbé Lafon's *Histoire de la conjuration du général Malet* (Paris, 1814). This was intended simply to remove 'l'imputation de jacobinisme' levelled at Malet by the Bonapartists. This established one pole of a controversy which was to endure for many years. See, e.g., H. Douville, *Histoire de la conspiration du général Malet* (Paris, 1840), where the republican view is stressed and the whole Philadelphe-Oudet legend taken for granted. By this time, Nodier had produced an acknowledged statement of his anonymous work of 1815 in two essays, 'Le général Malet, le colonel Oudet' and 'le colonel Oudet, continuation', both to be found in *Oeuvres complètes*, viii.

poem. Yet his actual relations with the Napoleonic régime were far from as simple as this would imply. His early enthusiasm for the Consulate has been touched upon; it was confirmed when, soon after Brumaire, he was taking an anti-Jacobin line in a local row at Besançon over the behaviour of the Prefect.[59] After this he went off for his first visit to Paris. Among his new acquaintance there was Bonneville to whose friendship Nodier was later to pay tribute. His may have been one of the influences persuading the always impressionable young man to become critical of the new régime.[60] When he published (in 1804 in an émigré paper in London) an anti-Napoleonic poem, Nodier seems eagerly to have courted martyrdom. Indeed, he was disappointed when it did not come and he had, instead, to denounce himself to the police as the author in order to get them to take any notice of him. His object seems to have been simply to bring his talents to Bonaparte's notice, but after a brief imprisonment he was ordered back to live under surveillance in Besançon.[61]

Here he must have been something of a local lion among the dis-contented. He became involved with some of them in a madcap plan to kidnap Bonaparte as he passed through the Jura on his way to coronation at Milan.[62] When this came to light, he was treated with con-siderable indulgence, receiving nothing worse than a ticking-off from the Prefect. After this, he never seems again to have been compromised. We find him soon with a job in the prefecture at Besançon and then, in 1808, teaching at Paris in the Napoleonic university. He did not remain in official employment but kept up good relations with the régime, especially with the friendly prefect of the Jura, who even sug-gested he became a mason, a proposal which was virtually a certificate of official approval. After various employments he was nominated in 1812 as the director of the official journal of the Illyrian provinces published at Laibach and went there (almost at the same time as Fouché)

[59] Pingaud, pp. 65–8.

[60] To say nothing of the influence of illuminism and occultism which may also have reached Nodier through Bonneville's circle. See Viatte, ii, pp. 147–58. Bonneville may be the original of the conspiratorial leader Dr Fabricius in Nodier's novel, *Mademoiselle de Marsan*, which was published in 1832. In a later essay on Oudet Nodier spoke of 'cet excellent Bonneville, le cœur le plus simple et le plus exalté qui j'aie connu de ma vie, avec son imagination de thaumaturge et sa science de bénédiction, sa façon de tribun et sa crédulité de femme' (*Oeuvres complètes*, viii, p. 333). Elsewhere he called him 'L'Isaïe de la maçonnerie' ('De la maçonnerie et des bibliothèques spéciales', p. 8).

[61] Pingaud, p. 82.

[62] Desmarest believed Malet to have been involved in a scheme like this (Des-marest, *Témoignages*, p. 293).

the following year. Nodier then returned to France before the collapse of the Empire, opening his post-Restoration career and plunging into ultra-royalist journalism with the *Histoire des sociétés secrètes de l'armée*, which he never openly avowed.[63]

The circumstances of Nodier's life and the uncertainty of his motives therefore justify the well-established distrust which this work has inspired among historians. Nevertheless, its account does at a few points coincide with suggestive facts and with what is later known of Buonarroti in a way which makes it easy to understand how well it was to fit the state of mind of those who were believers in the secret society mythology. It is still difficult not to be impressed, for example, with the way in which Nodier's account gives continuing emphasis on the role of eastern France and the Jura, which we shall meet again in other connexions, notably in the origins of the Charbonnerie.[64] There is the known discontent of many soldiers with the personal government of Bonaparte.[65] There are the ambiguous relations between legitimists and republicans which seem to have run from the Cadoudal conspiracy to Malet's last attempt. There are the suspicions of the Prefect of Léman. Finally, there are the grades, secrets and false names, all of which were constantly recurring in the secret societies of the next twenty years. Yet it remains almost impossible to separate fact and fiction in Nodier. All that can be done is to note faint parallels in other sources and to use them to control him.

The later revelations of Andryane and the continuing interest of the Prefect of Léman in the career of Buonarroti provide some small reason for not closing the door entirely on Nodier's basic assertion that a society called the Philadelphes was a continuing element in opposition to Bonaparte.[66] But there is no positive evidence for it, far less for asserting that Philadelphes had anything to do with Malet's attempt of 1812. Reports of secret societies were made from time to time by the

[63] A relic of the doubts over the authorship of this work appears in the catalogue of the Bibliothèque Nationale (s.v. 'Nodier'), where it is attributed to Lombard de Langres.

[64] It was also, of course, the happy hunting-ground of the mysticising sects before 1789 which we have already touched upon, 'province mystique englobant les pays de l'Est et du Sud-Est, en rapports étroits avec l'Allemagne et la Suisse, de Grenoble à Strasbourg, sans omettre Turin et Chambéry' (P. Leuilliot, *Annales E.S.C.*, 1953, p. 242).

[65] Spreading outside metropolitan France, of course. In 1807, the police of the Kingdom of Sicily were perturbed by reports of a secret society whose aim was said to be to set up a government under Moreau. (Sòriga, *Le Società segrete*, p. iii.)

[66] Buonarroti told Andryane that he joined it while at Sospello and he also said that it went back to 1799.

Napoleonic police; some officials at least treated the danger of secret societies with respect.[67] Nonetheless, it is clear that, for the most part, the authorities from Napoleon downward were virtually unconscious of any threat from enduring secret societies in France, however much they might be aware of the danger they presented in Italy and Germany.[68] Concern over the possibility of a royalist or republican coup was a different matter; here real dangers existed and precautions were taken against them, but such attempts as were made seem to have owed nothing to secret societies (whatever the connexion of Moreau or Malet with the Philadelphes) and no one high in the service of the régime thought that they did.[69]

This did not mean that, in due course, the usual gap which existed in Napoleonic France as elsewhere between appearance and reality in these matters would not develop and that there would not be forthcoming fresh grounds for those who wanted to believe. One extraordinary example even brings Barruel briefly back into the picture once more. In 1806 he received a long letter from Italy which urged him to remedy what the writer thought to be the one defect of his

[67] Pingaud says Desmarest reported on secret societies in 1803, 1808 and 1811 (p. 175). But in his *Témoignages*, besides pouring cold water on the Oudet story and 'ce qu'on a imprimé d'une ligue secrète, soit de Philadelphes, soit d'Olympiens, ou tout autre nom qu'on voudra, dont le colonel Oudet aurait été longtemps l'âme invisible et le génie tout-puissant. Comme l'auteur a écrit cela avec gravité, je croirais que c'est un cadre fictif où il a voulu réunir les principales contrariétés qui ont traversé la carrière de Napoléon' (pp. 329–30). It is also interesting that when d'Aubignosc, a former Napoleonic police official, published his *Conjuration du général Malet contre Napoléon* (Paris, 1824) using hitherto unpublished documents, he said and alleged nothing about any secret society in connexion with the affair.

[68] The distinction is important; certainly there were fears of secret societies and Illuminati in Germany. See, e.g., Desmarest's comments (pp. xxiii, 238, 251). Stein's reforms, for example, are singled out for praise 'si on n'y eût pas mêlé des conjurations et des sociétés secrètes' (p. 238). But in spite of some wild talk, Napoleonic officials were usually clear-sighted. D'Aubignosc, then serving in Germany, once admitted that it would be nice to blame all his troubles on the Tugendbund—'on n'aurait qu'un ennemi faible à combattre'. But he went on to acknowledge that it was not a sect but a whole populace which was anti-French (C. Schmidt, *Grand duché de Berg*, p. 504).

[69] Policemen interested themselves in many reported secret societies, of course, but a very rough guide to what Napoleon and his advisers thought the situation to be can be found by glancing through the five volumes of daily bulletins to the Emperor for the years 1804–9 gathered by E. d'Hauterive, *La police secrète du premier Empire* (Paris, 1908–64). They contain much trivia about freemasons showing how tame the Craft has become and no references to other secret societies in France. Buonarroti's name appears once, when he is asking to be freed from surveillance in 1804 (vol. iv, no. 106). *Brigandage* and *chouannerie*, on the other hand, like foreign agents, are the subjects of a very large number of reports and show what the régime really worried about.

book, his neglect of the Jewish 'sect'. The importance of the incident lies in the fact that this seems to have been the moment at which one can see incorporated in the myth for the first time a new element, anti-semitism, one day to be of great importance. We depend for both the text of the letter and for an account of what happened on another priest, Grivel, who said that Barruel gave him the letter and an account of what followed in 1817.[70] After consideration, Barruel had taken the letter to Desmarest (who, although himself formerly a priest, Barruel seems always to have liked and admired). No action seems to have followed, though Desmarest seems to have treated the matter gravely. But whether this was to save Barruel's feelings is not clear. Certainly *he* seems to have taken it seriously enough and later spoke of the Jewish danger in the secret societies. Only when the letter finally got into print in the last quarter of the nineteenth century, though, did it begin to influence the shape of the mythology, which almost at once assimilated anti-semitism to the anti-masonic legend.[71]

Where such material as this was being taken seriously, it should not be difficult to understand the credulousness with which Nodier's book was received. Even today there are attempts to salvage its reputation and perhaps (as has been suggested) this is no bad thing if not pressed too far.[72] In any case those who wished to believe in secret societies would find fresh causes for alarm and excitement under the Restor-

[70] 'Les souvenirs du P. Grivel sur les PP. Barruel et Feller', *Le Contemporain*, July 1878. The episode is examined in detail in Father Dechêne's unpublished life of Barruel (see above, p. 188) and a correct copy of the text of the letter (it has never yet been printed without substantial errors) will appear in it.

[71] It is interesting to speculate on the importance of this, though it falls outside the chronological scope of this book. It *may* be that by the addition of anti-semitism —for other reasons much in vogue at the end of the last century and in the first half of this—the old mixture was given a new lease of life and that this explains something of an upsurge in the literature, especially in the Third Republic. Professor Norman Cohn, who discusses the letter and Barruel's views in his book *Warrant for Genocide* (London, 1967), pp. 25-31, confirms the view that the episode was not exploited until the end of the nineteenth century. The presence of Jews at masonic lodges, of course, had not escaped unfavourable comment long before this. For an example in 1779, see M. Chobant, 'Les Juifs d'Avignon et du Comtat et la Révolution française', *Revue des Etudes Juives*, 1937, p. 33.

[72] The judgment of A. Saitta that the Philadelphes and Adelphes constituted the skeleton of all anti-Napoleonic plots, 'o almeno di tutte quelle che non son riconducibili a puri e semplici complotti militari' (*Filippo Buonarroti*, i, p. 81) not only overlooks royalism and rests on evidence too flimsy for so categorical an assertion, but is made meaningless by its qualification: there is no evidence of anything important after Cadoudal which was *not* primarily a soldiers' plot. Unfortunately, there are still people who *want* to discover secret societies at work under Napoleon, though the implicit aim is now the burning of further incense in the Babeuf–Buonarroti 'chapelle', rather than keeping alive the Barruel tradition.

ation when much greater official credulousness, too, would be forth-coming everywhere in Europe. The attitudes of Napoleonic police and administrators would then seem very sensible and balanced.

Traditionally, the history of Italy during the Consulate and the Empire has been sharply distinguished from the revolutionary triennium of 1796–9. This is meaningful, in that the two periods have different characters, and affected Italian development in different ways. On the other hand, it should not be allowed to mask important changes during the years of Napoleonic domination which divide them, too, into separate phases and in different ways affected the growth of secret societies and the legends about them.

After Bonaparte destroyed at Marengo the Austrian hopes of holding Lombardy, people in the north of Italy were disposed to welcome back the French. Great though the disillusionments of the revolution-ary years had been, the experience of Russian and Austrian occupation had been even more discouraging. Most moderate men had abandoned the idea that Italy (or some part of it) could go it alone; if there had to be masters, the French were the safest to choose. Moreover, the re-placement of the Directory by the Consulate seemed to promise a better deal for Italians. In the interests of France, the Directors had sacrificed Italian interests and had taken up rigidly anti-Italian positions; but, it was remembered, Bonaparte, the new ruler of France, had quarrelled with the Directory and had once before imposed his own policies on them against their will. Furthermore, one result of that insubordination had been the appearance of the new Italian republics. The other new factor in Italian history was the return to the peninsula of most of the refugees, many of them very radical, who had fled in 1798–9.

The first discernible stage in the unrolling of Italian history after Marengo lasts until 1804. The peace of Lunéville (February 1801) in large measure restored the Italian settlement embodied five years before in the Treaty of Campo Formio. A new 'kingdom of Etruria' was based on a union of Tuscany and Parma, and Piedmont was again incorporated in France. The Ligurian and Cisalpine Republics were restored, and from 1802 the name of the latter was changed to the more evocative 'Italian Republic' while it retained its hold on the former Papal Legations. In March 1801 these arrangements were rounded off by the Treaty of Florence with Naples, by which the

Bourbons agreed to admit a few French garrisons and to close their ports to British shipping.

These arrangements, first and foremost, gave the French effective strategical and diplomatic control of the peninsula. The old Piedmontese army had gone; though the Austrians remained in Venetia, France held the keys of the peninsula in the north and could depend upon the self-interest of her satellites to keep them loyal. A big territorial consolidation had taken place, too; Tuscany and Venice had now disappeared, perhaps for ever, for all people knew. Though Italian unitarists were unhappy over Venice and Piedmont, they had gained something. While the international scene remained quiet, Bonaparte would not have to court their favour.

In May 1804 the proclamation of the Empire opens the second phase of French control of the peninsula, lasting until 1807. The transformation of the Italian Republic into the Kingdom of Italy affronted both Austrians and Italian republicans, who still felt common cause with the French republicans. The treaty of Lunéville was swept aside by the incorporation of Liguria and Parma into the Empire. These changes helped to provoke the formation of the Third Coalition whose short life came to an end at Austerlitz; Venetia now passed into the Kingdom of Italy. The rashness of the Bourbons' Neapolitan intervention against the French was rebuked by their expulsion to Sicily. Napoleon's brother Joseph was enthroned as King of Naples in February 1806 and at once invited the return of all Neapolitan refugees in exile.

These years placed the French in physical control of an even larger area of Italy, while Austria was now completely excluded from it and the only native rulers who remained were the Pope and the Duke of Parma, now ruling over Tuscany. Further territorial consolidation had now left two important satellites, the Kingdoms of Italy and Naples; the rest was ruled directly as Departements of the French Empire.

The last phase runs from 1807 to 1814 and gave the French direct control of the whole peninsula. The machinery of the Continental System was imposed on it and in 1809 the Papal territories were annexed and the Pope himself was carried off to exile. The French hold was now even more complete and much stronger than had been the case in 1798.

The extension of French control had been within the peninsula a remarkably peaceful process. Little formal warfare had been involved, though in the consolidation of French authority considerable force had to be deployed to deal with banditry, and a few local risings occurred. The result, too, was a rationalisation of Italy's political structure which gave it a degree of practical and legal unity far greater than anything achieved since the days of the Roman Empire. This had great potential for the future. Common interests were insensibly nourished, common frustrations shared and common opportunities exploited by some Italians who for the first time began to think of themselves as members of a nation. The most important division left intact to cut across these germinating connexions was that between north and south, between Milan and Naples, between the two kingdoms which were to experience importantly different fates at the collapse of the Napoleonic régime. All these things, perhaps, help to explain the overall impression of popular acquiescence in the Napoleonic régime. Anti-grist tax movements in the Kingdom of Italy, bandits in the Abruzzi and the south are important qualifications of this, but they are qualifications only. No doubt it helped that the French no longer patronised the cranks and extremists who had, in some places, achieved prominence under the Directory and who had then helped to alienate Italian support. Many of them, in any case, had rallied to the administrations of Milan and Naples because they offered a chance of realising at least some of their aims. The background against which the Italian secret societies developed and matured was a very different one from that of the revolutionary triennium, when the behaviour of French soldiers and commissaries was constantly at work to fan the smouldering popular resentments with which the armies of occupation were surrounded.

As in France, freemasonry was put to use by the new order. The revolutionary triennium may have helped to revive masonry in that some new lodges were founded then under French auspices; some masons as individuals were certainly deeply implicated in the new régimes. It is also probable that, as in France, the Craft suffered from an exodus by the socially prominent[73] and that some lodges provided the cadres of the new patriotic societies which appeared after the French conquests. Yet the political role of masonry before 1800 was inconsiderable and in a corporate sense non-existent. Political activists who sought to put principles into action had turned to other organisations and possibilities for fulfilling their aims. The restored governments of 1799–1800 had nevertheless proceeded against freemasonry where they could unearth it. In September 1800 the members of the Leghorn lodge received sentences of imprisonment and banishment for their

---

[73] See the composition of the Leghorn lodge studied by Francovich, almost entirely a body of merchants and minor officials, and the list of the Bologna lodge printed by Sòriga, p. 60, for a Napoleonic example.

part in setting up the lodge, and although the terms of imprisonment were not severe, the government of the Grand-Duchy was acting in very much the same spirit as the other returned régimes. In fact the sentences were not served; almost at once, the French were back. Henceforth, the masonic structure in Italy was to be dominated by adjustment to French purposes.[74]

What this meant is implied by the fate of the Leghorn lodge. Of its former members we hear nothing more; they almost disappear from the records of Italian masonry.[75] This had been a lodge presided over by an Avignonese merchant who, there is reason to believe, was a keen revolutionary and such men were not to find the temper of Napoleonic masonry any more sympathetic in Italy than in France.[76] Napoleon came to hold the view that in both countries the Craft could be used; it was, accordingly, integrated into the official structures. Yet in Italy there were indications, if only sporadic, that this process was less unchallenged than in France. In 1802, Melzi, the Vice-President of the Italian Republic, closed the Milan lodge. It seems to have had members who flirted with ideas of political independence for Italy and Melzi was anxious to avoid provoking Napoleon to any further distrust of his Italian subjects. Elsewhere, on the other hand, there was even some encouragement for a fairly independent attitude on the part of Italian freemasonry from some French commanders and officials in the peninsula.[77] Nevertheless, official integration prevailed. The outstanding event was the organisation in 1805 of a Grand Orient for Italy in Milan. This pretended to authority over all rites, though it is not easy to see how far such authority could be made a reality.[78] The political nature of the new arrangements was much more

[74] Where, that is to say, the Napoleonic writ ran. In 1808 we find a police report to the Emperor that there is opposition in Rome to the opening of a bookshop which, it is feared, may be exploited as a cover for the Craft. 'Un franc-maçon est en horreur à S.S. et à ses sujets. Il courrait des risques d'être assassiné s'il était connu et surtout qu'il était étranger.' D'Hauterive, La police secrète, iv, no. 662. Certainly such evidence as there is of masonic activity at Rome after its incorporation in the empire as a 'free city' (1809) does not suggest that it had any success among the local population. See G. Bourgin, 'Une loge à Rome en 1810', RF, xlviii, 1905, pp. 412–36.

[75] But not entirely. The Avignonese master, François Morénas, went to Elba in 1801 and was one of the founders of a lodge there. Francovich, pp. 110–11.

[76] See also the contemptuous comments of a Piedmontese priest who was a mason, reported in Sòriga, p. 68.

[77] Miollis, at Leghorn, is perhaps an example. See H. Auréas, Un général de Napoléon Miollis (Paris, 1961).

[78] The claim is illustrated by the title of an Italian publication of 1805 listed by Kloss (pp. 269–70), Estratto de' primi travagli della gran Loggia Generale dell'ordine

K

evident. The distribution of lodges matched the new departmental structure. Sycophancy led to the creation of a lodge Napoleone at Leghorn and a Reale Gioseffina at Milan. There were special workings at Milan in 1811 to celebrate the birth of the King of Rome and the years of the Empire saw the appearance of a whole masonic literature glorifying the Emperor.[79] Freemasonry's best certificate of official respectability, of course, was its unpopularity with those who sought the return of the ancien régime. In 1814 the Leghorn lodge was sacked by an angry loyalist mob.[80]

Under these circumstances it seems strange that the Viceroy of the Kingdom of Italy should in 1813 dissolve all the lodges of the Kingdom in what seems almost a fit of panic. The explanation is probably that official confidence in Italian masonry was always less firm than it purported to be.[81] There was growing evidence that secret forms and oaths made possible the retention of a secret 'inner' structure of masonry, impervious to official influence. There were also important breakaways which reduced the area of its control. One was the so-called Misraism rite, said to have been founded in Milan in 1805 and to have spread to Naples, Dalmatia and the Ionian Islands in the next few years. One police informer in 1815 distinguished no fewer than five important masonic rites in Italy, some of them secret. Still another view is that the vice-regal government acted because of a sudden recrudescence of English masonic influences in the lodges.[82]

Such suggestions should not be over-stressed. The best evidence, perhaps, that Italian freemasonry was a political nullity is the appearance of other secret societies. Presumably they appeared because freemasonry did not provide an adequate structure for conspiracy. It was a point made by Nodier, who said that Italians turned to 'compagnonnage', for example, because freemasonry was an obvious non-starter for real plotting. It was new organisations, though, which soon attracted most attention from those alarmed by conspiracy. Dozens are claimed to have existed. Yet when we try to list the truly political secret societies in Italy we have to sift a mass of assertion containing very little hard fact. This, of course, *was* evidence of the im-

---

Rle∴ della Franca-Massoneria Scozz∴ al Rito antico ed accettato sotto la denominazione di G∴ O∴ in Italia. Steps taken at Naples are summarised in Sòriga, pp. 79–80.

[79] Some telling examples of what he disdainfully calls 'la sonora vacuità di questi officiosi prodotti del Parnaso massonico italiano' are given by Sòriga, pp. 49–58.

[80] Francovich, p. 114.

[81] Francovich has argued that this may be true in the case of the lodge founded by (among others) Briot, on Elba.

[82] Sòriga, p. 58.

portance Italy—'vrai pays de Cocagne' for the societies, as one observer later put it—was to have in the amplification of the mythology
and legend which surrounded them. Some names crop up again and
again: the Spilla Nera, the Knights of the Sun, the Society of Universal Regeneration, the Decisi, the Centri, the Adelfi, the Guelfi
and, of course, most famous of all, the Carbonari were much discussed.
Of the information about these bodies which now seems reliable,
most comes from a later period, when defendants in the political
trials of the Restoration were drawing upon their memories and invention. Not much of it arises directly in the Napoleonic era itself.
Moreover, we can never be sure about the distinctiveness of many of
the societies even to their members. As was said to be the view of the
Papal police in 1818, 'the adherence of any individual to one of the
secret societies suffices to ensure his reception with a corresponding
rank into all those that may be formed afterwards, so that one sect is
always merging in another, while procuring new proselytes'.[83]

Given these difficulties, it is fortunate that here we are concerned
only with the secret societies as sources of alarm and, later, as examples
to others who wished to run similar bodies. In spite of the generally
favourable conditions in which French government operated in Italy
in these years there were always French officials ready to be alarmed at
the thought of conspiracies which might rekindle the anti-French
feelings of 1799 among the masses.[84] But not all of what was known—
or suspected—provoked alarm. Some members of the Raggi, for example, undoubtedly rallied to the Napoleonic order, which offered
Italian patriots at least a more promising future than would the restoration of the ancien régime. Others, it has been suggested, remained
in contact with some of their French correspondents and other sympathisers—among them, Buonarroti—but did little else. Some authorities have insisted that, notwithstanding these probabilities, the society
still had from thirty to fifty thousand members in 1804.[85] It seems, in
any case, to have changed its name and to be known generally after
1802 as the Astronomia Platonica or, more frequently, the Centri.

[83] *Memoirs of the Secret Societies of the South of Italy, particularly the Carbonari*
(London, 1821), p. 20.

[84] e.g., the Prefect of the Department of the Mediterranean who warned the
Director-General of Police of 'dans presque toute l'Italie un vaste projet organisé
contre les Français et tendant à donner le second exemple des horreurs qui n'a
guère ont ensanglanté l'Espagne' (AN, AF⁷ 6523, letter of 12 May 1809).

[85] R. J. Rath, *The Provisional Austrian Régime in Lombardy-Venetia 1814–1815*
(Austin, 1969), p. 217. Sòriga quotes a statement that there were about forty
thousand members in 1802 (p. 193) and this is certainly the sort of scale on which
it was believed to operate.

But little more than this is known, though much was said. The directing body was alleged to be a 'Solar Circle', presiding over but having only oral communication with two 'hemispheres', one at Bologna and one at Milan. The presidents of 'segments', the next stage in the hierarchy, made up these hemispheres, and the segments were further divided into 'raggi' of which each member was a 'line'. By 1814 a society on this model seems to have been spread throughout the whole Kingdom of Italy.

Over the Adelfi or Filadelfi, confusion is still greater. Nodier asserted that there were no fewer than three organisations in Italy using these names, and, of course, there is the possibility of confusion with the Philadelphes as well. Some authorities maintain that the Italian society derived directly from the French and had a French Templar lodge as their origin.[86] They were alleged to be in touch with Paris and Geneva; Milan was supposed to be their Italian centre. They seem to have penetrated masonry to some extent and to have established cells within orthodox lodges and this fact and the use of the terminology of the 'Grand Firmament' to denote their directing body certainly suggests the possibility even before 1814 of contact with Buonarroti's Sublimes Maîtres Parfaits. Whatever else, they were certainly anti-Napoleonic.[87] Finally, we may remark that the aims of the Guelfi, a northern secret society, appear to have been influenced by British rather than French sources. This, at any rate was the story told to the Austrian police after the Restoration by those formerly involved in it.[88]

What does all this add up to? This is very hard to say. Certainly, the authorities sometimes believed that troubles they had to deal with arose from the work of secret societies.[89] Nor did they see these all as creations of what would be later called the 'Left'. In 1809 Napoleon

---

[86] Sòriga, p. 110.

[87] One conspirator, Joachim Prati, later said that he had joined in 1810 a Milanese secret society which was a 'masonry in masonry, unknown to the very grand-masters and deputy-grand-masters' which was the 'Great Firmament' of the Philadelphes. There he claimed to have met deputies from the 'committees of Paris and Geneva' who were engaged in preparing the Malet conspiracy (Lehning, p. 39). Dr Lehning states bluntly (p. 42) that the Adelfi were a derivation of the Philadelphes of France. For six or seven different theories of the origin of the Filadelfi see Rath, pp. 204–8. The chapter of which they form part, 'The Secret World', is probably the most level-headed and succinct summary of the mass of scholarship and speculation which has accumulated around the subject of the organisation of the Italian secret societies.

[88] Archivio di Stato, Milan: *Ricordanze Processuale* of the trials of 1819–20, entry 'Bentink William. Lord. Generale inglese'.

[89] See, e.g., the note of Melzi (undated and without attribution) quoted by Sòriga, pp. 195–6, on the 1802 troubles in Bologna.

was warned of a 'Ligue Italique', numerous in Piedmont, and reactionary and clerical in its composition.[90] But there is an a priori element
in all such assessments: conspiracy was normal, willing conspirators
existed among both the discontented survivors of the ancien régime
and the discontented Jacobins of the triennium. What more natural than
that both should turn to secret societies to accomplish their ends or
that, at least, they should talk about them so as to exaggerate their own
effectiveness and importance? Beyond this we can hardly go on to
precise statements about the real danger they presented. There is no
evidence that the governments of Napoleonic Italy had any reason to
fear any of the much-trumpeted secret societies until the crisis of the
régime. At that moment the only significant action by secret societies
in the whole Napoleonic period was taken, and it was that of the Carbonari, the most famous of them all.

The Carbonari must be placed with the freemasons, Jesuits and
Illuminati as the greatest contributors to the mythology of the secret
societies. It was not until the Restoration that they became well
known and not until the early 1820s that this society exercised its full
weight on the European imagination. Much that was nonsense was
said and written of it and no doubt uncertainty as to its true extent
and powers made the Carbonari, like its predecessors, all the more
alarming and portentous. The origin of the Carbonari still remains
very mysterious, but has to be sought in the Napoleonic era.

One obvious assumption, since the Carbonari emerged as a political
society, is that they spring lineally from the Raggi or Lega Nera of the
late 1790s, but this, while plausible—it is certainly very likely that
many members went from one to the other—raises certain difficulties.
The Carbonari's own version of their origins was mythological, going
back to St Theobald and to Francis I, and, as the name shows, to the
mythical origins of the confraternity of charcoal-burners. These
assertions are no more helpful than masonic evocations of Hiram and
Athelstan, but if we confine ourselves to recent history the charcoal-
burners provide the best clue. It suggests a connexion between the
'compagnonnage' of French charcoal-burners before the Revolution
with the Italian society, and this seems to be reasonably enough
established to be accepted.[91]

The story begins, interestingly, again in the Franche-Comté and the
Jura, before the Revolution. In this area there existed already in 1789

[90] D'Hauterive, v, no. 178.
[91] For one of the earliest published accounts, see Nodier, 'De la maçonnerie et
du carbonarisme'.

a semi-formal association of charcoal-burners called the 'Charbonnerie'. Its members, who referred to one another as 'bons cousins', met for social and philanthropic purposes and were preoccupied largely with professional concerns. They represented a survival of the medieval institution of 'compagnonnage' and their rituals were emphatically Christian. They met in lodges called 'ventes', which were sometimes held in the forests where the members worked at their trade. As in the case of operative masonry more than a century before, Charbonnerie had already attracted the attention of amateurs of folklore and antiquities. Nodier said that although its membership had been to some extent contaminated by the entry to its ventes of professional men and bourgeois, the organisation as a whole was uncorrupted and remained fundamentally an association of working men. It seems likely that a number of soldiers stationed in the area were initiated to the order during the Revolution, but the whole revolutionary epoch remains obscure.[92] During the Napoleonic era its existence was well known to the authorities and it is clear that its membership could by then have all but lost contact with the practical business of charcoal-burning. In becoming respectable, they also remained loyal to the régime and celebrated as one of their feasts the anniversary of Napoleon's coronation.[93] The authorities had no reason to fear them.

It has been asserted that it was suspicion directed towards the Charbonnerie as a possibly counter-revolutionary organisation during the Terror that in fact turned the interests of some of its members for the first time towards politics. Nodier suggested that it was awareness that masonic lodges would not do as vehicles for conspiracy which led plotters to seek to use the Charbonnerie for this purpose. However politicisation may have occurred, the influence of the Charbonnerie seems to have reached Italy by two routes. One is that provided by the movement of regiments. Some lodges of Carbonari appeared at Capua in 1808, and these have been connected with the stationing there of a Swiss French regiment from the area bordering on the Jura. The other link is personal, the arrival of Pierre Joseph Briot in the Kingdom of Naples in 1806.

Pierre Joseph Briot was a man of the Franche-Comté, born in Doubs

[92] The Piedmontese general Rossetti told Murat in 1814 that he had been affiliated in 1802 when his regiment was stationed at Gray, Haute-Saône. At this time, he said, it had no political object: 'le seul but louable de la secte était de reconnaître à certains signes le voyageur égaré et de lui prêter secours et assistance.' (Sòriga, p. 71.)

[93] See, for example, the list of members of a Besançon vente printed by Bourgin, RH, xlix, 1905, p. 62.

and educated at Besançon.[94] He threw himself keenly into the Revolution, having a brief, unenthusiastic and somewhat obscure career as a soldier before emerging under the Directory as a left-wing member of the Council of Five Hundred, the lower house of parliament. There, his friends included Lucien Bonaparte and the Corsican Saliceti, both idealistic republicans, the second the friend of Buonarroti. Briot was also the patron and supporter of the Italian patriots in exile and helped to present their case for a united and independent Italy in the Council of Five Hundred. By this time he had already become involved with the Charbonnerie though very little is known about this. Brumaire seems to have displeased him; he did not approve of Bonaparte's march towards personal power nor, eventually, of the Empire. After an appointment as secretary to the prefect at Besançon in 1800,[95] a commission to Elba in 1802 was the last employment by the French government which he was given and he seems henceforth under an official cloud, though he was soon popular in the island. In 1806, nonetheless, he was invited to Naples by Bonaparte's brother, Joseph. On arrival there he found Lucien Bonaparte and Saliceti and there he seems to have sown the seeds of the first Carbonari lodges. In 1808 he is known to have asked his wife to send him his masonic notebooks and it may have been in connexion with the setting-up of the Carbonari that he did this.[96]

The ritual similarities of Charbonnerie and Carbonari alone make it impossible to doubt the filiation of the two bodies. But by itself, this uncovering of Carbonarist origins does not take us very far. It does not explain why the Carbonari turned to politics, nor why its organisation and rites were so successful in the competition for the allegiance of Italians with other secret societies.

The connexion with the French opponents of Bonaparte may have been important. Here we may recall the Franche-Comté background. Nodier was known to Briot and the Philadelphes were founded there. The rites of the Charbonnerie may have been more attractive than those of other secret societies because less influenced by masonry, which had become discredited in some eyes by its official takeover. They embodied a historic tradition of simple mutual support and neighbourliness which was the legacy of the operative Charbonnerie. The organisation was democratic; there were only two grades, apprentice and

---

[94] See M. Dayet, 'Pierre Joseph Briot, Lucien Bonaparte et les Carbonari', *AHRF*, 1953.
[95] Pingaud, pp. 64–5.
[96] Dayet, p. 13.

master. The terminology of 'bons cousins' expressed it well. The practices of the ventes seem to have been far less elaborate than those of the masonic lodges.

Certain conditions in Naples and central Italy towards the end of the Napoleonic era made the implantation of a new secret society easier there than elsewhere and also may explain something of the later incoherence which it showed. The relative mildness of Napoleonic rule in Italy had some exceptions and in Calabria in 1806, for example, peasant resistance reminiscent of the Sanfedist movement of the late 1790s flared up and was cruelly and ruthlessly crushed. This was an area in which Carbonarism later showed itself to be well-rooted. Then there was the fact that Naples was a long way from Paris; as the presence of Briot showed, revolutionaries who disapproved of the general tendency of Napoleonic policy could there find lodgement where they could continue to try to advance the causes associated with the Revolution without abandoning their resistance to personal rule. This was much more attractive than moving over into a simple opposition which might favour the return of the ancien régime. Many of the French officials and soldiers at Naples, too, notably Joseph and Murat themselves,[97] encouraged the crystallisation of a sense of local patriotism and the building of a real political unit in southern Italy. This was likely to express itself, as it did, in dislike of many French exactions and of the Continental System of which the Kingdom was officially a part. It was therefore possible for the Carbonari to recruit from a wide spectrum of essentially anti-Napoleonic feeling. It drew at one margin on reactionary popular movements reminiscent of the Sanfedisti, whose leaders looked to a Bourbon Restoration; at the other it tapped a new, progressive, sometimes republican, patriotism among the middle and upper classes.

Two other factors in the south also may have contributed to a special atmosphere for the cultivation of new secret societies. One was the masonic tradition which seems in Naples to have been more resistant to the introduction of the official, gelded masonry of the Empire than that of the north. Murat had his own interests in view and wished in any case to bring freemasonry in the Kingdom of Italy under his own control. A number of clandestine lodges seem to have broken away from official masonry and coalesced with elements of dissident Scots rites. Some of these masons are said to have organised the Carbonari as a political instrument of Scottish masonry in 1810.[98]

<hr/>

[97] Joseph went to Spain in 1808 and Murat replaced him on the throne of Naples.
[98] See Sòriga, pp. 80–1.

The other background factor which was of enduring importance was the presence of the British in Sicily during the whole of the period after 1806. There is no evidence of the direct exploitation of clandestine organisations on the mainland by the British though this was alleged even before the lodgement in Sicily.[99] Nevertheless, their presence, the existence of the Sicilian constitution which they endeavoured to uphold, and the eventual prospect of a campaign from the island kept alive the hopes that there was a constitutional and independent future available for Italy if the British would support it. This was not the only result of the Sicilian occupation, it must be said. It was at this time that there also took root in Italian demonology an anglophobe legend (which was to persist until Fascist days) that the British sought to annex Sicily and then unify the peninsula in the interests of their own commerce. In this scheme, the exploitation of Scottish masonry and the use of the authority of a lodge at Edinburgh was said to have a major part. The original version of this said that the Carbonari proposed that the Duke of Sussex should be installed as King of the Two Sicilies—a good touch, for he was, of course, one of the several princes of the blood who were Grand Masters of English freemasonry.[100]

Yet this background still leaves it difficult to say what Carbonarism actually stood for. In part, perhaps, to ask about this is inappropriate. The Carbonari could find room for many tendencies; it was always attractive to dissidents of strongly contrasting aims who saw in it possibilities of action. It should be understood as a functional, rather than a doctrinal, unity.

This explains much that is ambiguous in its history (so far as can be established). It enjoyed a semi-clandestine life at Naples under Murat which suggests some degree of official tolerance.[101] Yet the Carbonari—or some of them—were later to turn to the exiled Bourbons and this caused confusion: one version of their origins current after 1815 was that they had been founded by Queen Caroline as an anti-Muratist society before she was pushed out of Sicily by Lord William Ben-

[99] In 1802, for example, Melzi, Vice-President of the Italian Republic, assumed the British were working through secret societies to produce the troubles at Bologna (which seem to have found their source in popular feeling against Frenchmen and high prices). See Sòriga, p. 194. In 1808 the French police were warned by an official in the south that the English and the priests were trying to stir up a rising like that of 1799 (letter of Radet, 12 November 1808, AN, AF⁷ 6523).

[100] Sòriga, p. 82.

[101] Briot may have pressed the cause of constitutionalism and unification on Murat. See Dayet, p. 22.

tinck in 1813.[102] Others looked to British support or that of the House of Este. Another difficulty is, of course, the confusion of secret societies at this period: undoubtedly some Carbonari were members of many other bodies and confused the nature and aims of one with another. What seems to be precisely and firmly attributable to the Carbonari is, in the first place, a body of rites and ceremonies and some concomitant doctrine. The influence of the old, pre-revolutionary Charbonnerie, can be detected in these, and so can a strong Christian element. Rossetti, the Piedmontese general of Murat's army, thought that the sect began to spread rapidly in 1812, as the Continental System was reaching its height and just before the start of the Russian campaign.[103] By 1814 hundreds of 'vendite' were in existence. We can also be fairly sure that by 1814 the political attitudes of the Carbonari boiled down to a generalised anti-French sentiment (especially in the army of the Kingdom of Naples, where the fiasco of the Russian campaign was deeply deplored) and a broad disposition to favour constitutionalism. Some Carbonari also favoured the unification of Italy.

It would be unwise to be more definite about aims and doctrine. It has been suggested that there were in Carbonarism Illuminati elements which envisaged much more sweeping revolutionary aims.[104] If they were there, they were not remarked by contemporaries and did not, therefore, contribute to the rapid inflation of fears and expectations of the Carbonari which was the result of their activity in 1814–15. What is reasonably certain is that an organisation which became so widespread in middle-class and professional circles cannot have wished to renounce the whole mass of reform owed to the Napoleonic régime. Whatever its faults, Napoleonic Italy had offered unprecedented opportunities to many Italians and to the more progressive intellectuals; it had given symbols and administrative reality to a greater degree of national integration than any of its predecessors. These things were true throughout the peninsula. Yet its rapid and complete collapse in 1814 is very striking. In both Milan and Naples, the centres where the régime had been most beneficial, it fell almost without resistance. The attractiveness of the restored régime does not at first sight seem a

[102] This is reported in G. Orloff, *Mémoires sur le Royaume de Naples* (Paris, 1819), ii, p. 284. Bentinck was sent out to Sicily by the British government in 1811 to try to put some order into its confused politics. In a measure, and at a cost of the goodwill of the Neapolitan royal family, he succeeded, but his attempt to impose a new constitution, modelled on the British, collapsed completely soon after his departure. The episode is discussed in J. Rosselli, *Lord William Bentinck and the British Occupation of Sicily 1811–14* (Cambridge, 1956).

[103] Sòriga, p. 72.   [104] By Francovich.

plausible explanation of why this should happen. Almost at once people began to look for explanations which went further. Many believed British influence must have been at work and this is hardly an audacious inference; where and how this influence expressed itself is, on the other hand, much more difficult to agree about. But the obvious explanations looked to the successful plotting of the secret societies.

The Milan collapse came first. At the beginning of 1814 a tired population, smarting under the vicissitudes of the last few months of fighting provided a poor background against which Napoleon's viceroy, Eugène Beauharnais, struggled to save the Kingdom from the disaster of a restoration. Some Italians were loyal to Beauharnais, though not to France; they provided a nucleus for a small party hoping that a separate and independent existence might still be retained by a Kingdom of Italy separated from France. But there were also Italians who wanted independence, but not under the Beauharnais régime, seeing it as merely a French imposition. The young Confalonieri and his friends were members of this group and it was divided about what should follow Eugène's deposition, some looking to Murat, some to an Austrian prince, and some even suggesting an English duke. Undoubtedly some of these were encouraged by Bentinck's ill-judged activities. He had crossed to Italy, landing in March at Leghorn where he almost at once issued a proclamation to Italians; 'be Italians,' he said, and the 'Italian Levy' he brought with him had a banner inscribed with the slogan of national union and independence.[105] Other Italians, not attracted by him, were encouraged by Murat's advance northward.[106] Opposed to both these factions was a third, that of the old reactionary nobility and a substantial section of the clergy, which simply wanted an Austrian restoration. The great mass of the population probably cared very little about which of these alternatives should in the end be successful.

Undoubtedly some of the members of the second faction—and possibly some of the others—were members of secret societies. But beyond

[105] Italian informers after the Restoration and Italian historians much later have always made much of Bentinck's supposed connexion with the secret societies (see, e.g., A. Capograssi, *Gl'Inglesi in Italia durante le campagne napoleoniche* (Bari, 1949) for a recent example). The difficulties of believing in the positive reality of this are succinctly summed up in an admirable note by Dr Rosselli, pp. 198–9.

[106] The various acts and pronouncements which produced a flurry of hope and excitement among Italians who thought that the moment had come to create an independent Italy are conveniently summarised by D. Spadoni in *Sette cospirazioni e cospiratori nello stato pontificio all'indomani della restaurazione* (Rome and Turin, 1904), pp. xi–xiii.

this it is not possible to say very much. At least three organisations seem to have been involved—freemasons, Adelfi and Carbonari—and their membership no doubt overlapped. Nor is the evidence about their activity very plentiful. The cautious verdict of the American scholar who has studied this matter most closely seems justifiable: 'No doubt the sects played some kind of a role in fanning the embers of discontent against Habsburg rule in the summer of 1814; yet their importance should not be over-emphasised.'[107]

That revolution was preceded by the allied entry to Paris in April and by the end of fighting between the Austrians and Eugène when roughly half the territory of the Kingdom of Italy was occupied by the Austrian forces. The party which wished to maintain the viceroy as ruler of an independent north Italian state now went into action. Melzi summoned the Senate, which sent off a deputation to Paris to ask the allies for the maintenance of Eugène. Nonetheless, there was opposition in the Senate from the pro-Austrians which imposed delay and prevented any undisturbed continued assumption of power by Beauharnais. An opportunity therefore existed for the fomentation of popular opposition to this course, and it was seized by leaders who appear to have believed that this would be favoured by the British. The culmination of their efforts was a riot on 20 April which led to the Senate recalling its deputation to Paris. In the course of this, the mob attacked and killed the Finance Minister of the former Kingdom of Italy, Prina. In Verona there were violent scenes, the Prefect being attacked, while at Brescia the retiring French troops were fired upon. All these indications of popular feeling seem to show that whatever directing minds may or may not have been at work, the viceregal régime was unpopular because it was identified with French domination and the continuance of the war. On 26 April Eugène concluded that he could not hope to control the Kingdom and, throwing in his hand, left the country.

There is little specific evidence of the activity of secret societies in any of this. Some of those who led the movement in Milan were freemasons, but by itself that means nothing. Certainly, too, the disorders and the events which they provoked suited what was later claimed to be the programme of national independence favoured by the Carbonari, but inferences would be dangerous, though they were soon to be drawn. And in any case, what had been done was in the long run highly damaging to this cause. Whatever irresponsible Englishmen on the spot like Bentinck might say, the British government was resigned to giving

[107] Rath, p. 242.

the Austrians virtually a free hand in Italy and the riot in Milan provided a pretext for the restoration of Austrian rule without more ado.
When Confalonieri went to see Castlereagh in Paris he received not,
as he had hoped, British support for an independent north Italian
state, but a bland assurance that in the history of the House of Austria
'there can be found no traces of abuse of power or force'. The British
government was already alarmed by the reports of the events in Milan,
which seemed to have gone far beyond mere anti-Bonapartist demonstration.

If the Carbonari or other secret societies had, therefore, helped
to engineer the collapse of the Napoleonic Kingdom of Italy, it is
worth observing that they were very good at promoting the ends
they had in view. This may be thought in some degree excusable in
that they were undoubtedly encouraged by the activities of Bentinck to
believe that they had England behind them when this was not the case.[108]
But it is also true that the plotters much overplayed their hand in
attempting to exploit popular resentment with the war in support of a
particular programme. As in other parts of Italy and for many decades
to come, popular movements in a generally anti-government sense
were essentially negative. The secret societies, though much feared
by the Austrians, had already shown by their failure to do more in the
crisis of the Kingdom, that they were not a widespread and popular
but an élite group and ineffective. A subsequent plot in August in
Brescia should have confirmed this.

Secret societies went to work somewhat more clearly and unambiguously in the south. The shape of future events had begun to emerge
there earlier than in the Kingdom of Italy. In 1813, the coincidence
of Murat's personal inclinations and interests with popular feeling
against the French and the continuation of the war was already clear.
In January 1814 he withdrew from the war. Down to this point Murat's
relations with the Carbonari had been almost those of patronage on
his side, while on theirs we can discern the hope that he would prove
their instrument. Yet soon after it became clear that the movement
was turning more and more against him. The reasons for this may lie
in the equivocal behaviour of Murat as he now sought to preserve
his own throne, in the increasing realisation that Great Britain did not
intend to leave him in possession at Naples, or in the brutal repression
of a rising in Calabria by one of his French lieutenants. Whatever they
were, the consequence was soon apparent.

[108] There may have been some belief in encouragement from London; rumours in
December 1813 spoke of Carbonari emissaries there at that time (Dayet, p. 21, fn.).

Increasing conspiratorial activity began to be noticed at Naples while Murat was just south of the Po with his army waiting on events. At this moment he occupied about half the peninsula and hoped to secure not only his own throne but an addition to his territories at the peace. He was disturbed by a revolt in the Abruzzi which was attributed to Carbonari. It may have been directly because of this, or as a manoeuvre in the diplomatic game, that he issued from Bologna in April an edict against the Carbonari as a conspiracy against the state. He was well aware of their strength, but thought it could be contained. Maghella, a Genoese who had been his chief of police and was a leading Carbonaro, was arrested, too. He, it seems, had hoped to exploit against Napoleon Murat's growing disillusionment with the cost of Imperial policy and the dangers it presented for his own survival. Murat's treaty of January 1814 with the Austrians and subsequent march north against the Kingdom of Italy gave grounds for hoping that such a policy would succeed. Yet this defection may have alienated Italians who at least preferred Napoleonic rule to a restored ancien régime. Then came the edict against the Carbonari. With this it seems that the society's alienation was definitely achieved (though he remained secretly in touch with them) and, more and more, they listened to the British and to Ferdinand, the exiled Bourbon king.

Murat probably calculated that at this stage it was above all important to ingratiate himself with the Austrians, and issued the edict with this aim. It is also true that he may have felt he could rely on other secret societies than the Carbonari.[109] Nevertheless, his position was far less strong than he had assumed and this was soon shown when a group of his generals tried to exact from him a new constitution. Though he was able to handle the situation, Murat was from this moment aware that he could no longer take the army's support for granted.

Rossetti still thought in June that there was something to be obtained by Murat from conciliating the Carbonari. Zurlo, a former servant of the Bourbons and Finance Minister of the Muratist kingdom, perhaps tried to do something towards this. Here matters stood at the collapse of the Napoleonic structure in Italy. It could hardly be said that the Carbonari had achieved very much, but they had become a force to be taken seriously. Signs of insubordination in his army had frightened Murat at least into issuing a decree requiring Neapolitan birth as a qualification for holding office. The events of the next few

[109] Years later, in the 1819–20 trials, a witness said that in Murat's time the hopes of the Guelfi were sustained by him and the English fleet. Archivio di Stato, Milan: *Ricordanze Processuale*, s.v. 'Bentink'.

months were to show that whatever they might look to, the secret societies had at any rate given up Murat by the summer of 1814.[110]

They had begun to negotiate with Palermo, believing that the Sicilian constitution which had been imposed by the British would be the basis for a restored Bourbon régime. This offset Murat's efforts during the remainder of 1814 to maintain his position by throwing out promises of a new, constitutional régime. On his other flank he had to demonstrate to the Austrians that he was valuable to them because he was in a position to guarantee order and control southern Italy—a matter of some difficulty after a revolt in occupied Papal territory in the Abruzzi had showed how precarious his hold actually was.

It is not easy to believe that Murat could in any event have succeeded in holding his throne, but in 1815, after the news of Napoleon's return from Elba, he threw his hand away by a rash declaration in support of Napoleon and an announcement that he would reoccupy the territory south of the Po which he had handed back to the Papacy. This was the end of the road for the Austrians. From Rimini Murat now issued a proclamation appealing to Italian national feeling against the Austrians. After defeat in the field he attempted to rally support among the liberals by issuing a new constitution. Neither move was successful. The masses were not interested in patriotic appeals and the Neapolitan Carbonari were by now sure that they could expect a constitution from Ferdinand. After returning to Naples, Murat fled at last on 19 May.

This can be and was interpreted as an important success for the secret societies. They seemed to have powerfully contributed to the collapse of Murat by their defection and to have imposed conditions for the return of the Bourbon dynasty. Those who were ready to be impressed by talk of secret societies found this significant. But there was not so much to this achievement. The real cause of Murat's overthrow was that the British opposed him, the Austrians lost faith in him, and that he was defeated in the field. In the absence of these factors it is difficult to believe that what the Carbonari did would have mattered much. Once again, too, there is no evidence of any connexion between the secret societies and truly popular movements. Finally, there is the sad story of the actual restoration to be pondered. Ferdinand did not actually make a formal promise of a constitution.

[110] Mention may be made here of another, anti-Muratist and pro-Bourbon society working already before the collapse at Naples. This was the Calderari, of which much more was to be heard after 1819. Its oath was said to denounce masonry, Jansenists, materialists, economists and the Illuminati (*Memoirs of the Secret Societies of the South of Italy*, p. 71). If this is true it embodied almost the whole range of the classical secret society demonology.

When he returned to Naples in June he made protestations of his benevolence and good intentions, but co-operation with the Carbonari soon broke down. By October they were again conspiring with the exiled Murat. They had achieved little except to have made their mark already in the mythology of the secret societies. They were to haunt the dream of the statesmen of the Restoration and dominate the mythology of reaction just after 1815 as much because of what they were supposed to have been and done before that date as because of what they were actually to do after.

A VIEW FROM ST PETERSBURG

At the end of 1811 a uniquely authoritative observer set down a considered assessment of the political significance of the secret societies and the danger they presented. This was the Savoyard, Joseph de Maistre. His early and close interest in freemasonry and the mysticising sects of the eighteenth century has already been remarked.[111] None of his contemporaries was better qualified to pronounce on the question of how seriously the secret societies should be taken. His own masonic activities had taken him deep into the curious world both of masonry and its affiliates and of the mystical, near-masonic sects; this gave him access to a body of information and personal acquaintance which he steadily enlarged by study, travel and correspondence. It seems reasonable to suppose that he was better informed than any other man of his era on this subject and he was in addition a man of judgment and intellect, his mind matured and stocked by a rich general culture.

De Maistre was a born student who always continued to read about the subjects which interested him, and he was also a man chosen by his king to represent him at the Russian court. He went to St Petersburg in 1802 and stayed there for fifteen years. This posting to a remote city on the periphery of a Europe undergoing changes and upheavals which Russia escaped must have made it easier to ponder at leisure and assess calmly his mature conclusions about the secret societies. It was there that he put them down in their final form after he had striven to sift the débris of half-truth and error which encumbered them. His scrupulousness and his learning both suggest that his views may provide a test case: de Maistre's final judgments show what a reasonable and informed observer might properly believe about the secret societies. He ought to be a limiting case, registering the extent of the mythology's strength.

[111] See above, p. 105.

De Maistre's own association with freemasonry and therefore with the world of the secret societies had of course been affected by the Revolution. But this did not happen startlingly or suddenly. Without breaking with freemasonry violently because of its supposed revolutionary responsibilities, far less condemning it, he rather drifted away from it, impelled by other preoccupations (and helped, perhaps, by maturing views to a certain benevolent detachment).[112] He continued, nonetheless, to fill his notebooks with quantities of masonic material drawn from the books on religion and esoteric sects which he continued to read. Among these were some of the works of the myth-makers already described: besides Barruel, he certainly read Proyart, Starck, Cadet-Gassicour and Lefranc. He read the Philosophes too, as well as their detractors. This reading, together with his huge correspondence and conversation with the Jesuit exiles he met in St Petersburg, led him to his final position on secret societies, which seems to have taken shape during the first decade of the nineteenth century.

Its history, nonetheless, is best traced back at least as far as 1793, after the proclamation of the Republic, the September massacres and the execution of Louis XVI, but before the Terror. De Maistre then wrote in defence of the Craft a 'Mémoire sur la franc-maçonnerie', for the information of a friend who was not himself a freemason. Qualifying his views in only one respect, de Maistre firmly asserted in this document the political innocence of freemasonry in words leaving no doubt of their sincerity. He drew on his own experience of Savoyard lodges to demonstrate that the Craft 'n'a certainement dans son principe rien de commun avec la Révolution française'. Even the higher grades possessed by a few masons were not sinister, but were only concerned with the pursuit of 'connaissances dignes d'occuper un homme sage et vertueux' (de Maistre had himself entered these superior grades in association with Willermoz). His only qualification of the innocence of freemasonry was commonsense: if freemasonry served the Revolution, it did so per accidens. It was an association of clubs, many of whose members sympathised with the Revolution (though this was not a function of their masonry). They were, therefore, likely to use the organisation to which they belonged as a natural channel or framework for their activity in forming revolutionary clubs.[113] This commonsense

112 As late as 1810 he declined with regret an invitation to take part in a masonic lodge at St Petersburg, giving as his reason the (implicitly mistaken) interpretation placed on such bodies by some 'personnes de mérite' whose good opinion he wished to retain (Oeuvres complètes de J. de Maistre (Lyon, 1884), IX, letter of 20 August 1810).
113 Dermenghem, Joseph de Maistre mystique, pp. 88–90.

view corresponds, in fact, to what is now the accepted view of the masonic role in 1789 and the early Revolution.

When Barruel's book reached him six years later, de Maistre thought it important enough to embark upon a full-scale refutation which has been conserved among his papers.[114] Like Starck, de Maistre regretted Barruel's failure to assert the innocence of orthodox freemasonry, but he disliked the book for other reasons, too. He found it in the most exact sense incredible; it corresponded neither to his personal experience of the sects nor to what he had learnt from his studies, nor to simple logic. He even refused to believe Barruel's assertions about the Illuminati. As he asked elsewhere, if the Illuminati were so unscrupulous and ruthless with their secret poisons and assassination plots, why were their announced enemies—such as Barruel—still alive? His refutation was remorseless, exploiting Barruel's bad logic and exposing his errors of fact. All that de Maistre would concede was that some members of the secret societies were wicked and corrupted by revolutionary principles; as for freemasonry, its French version was as innocent as the English. In any case 'la patrie de l'illuminisme, c'est l'Allemagne; cependant l'explosion révolutionnaire s'est faite ailleurs. J'en reviens toujours à croire que celle pourriture de l'illuminisme est un effect et non pas cause, sans prétendre néanmoins qu'il ne put réagir à son tour et renforcer la cause.'[115]

Sane though such a reaction was, the last sentence points to the evolution in de Maistre's thought which followed. He was always, as in 1793, ready to concede that certain errors and corruptions in masons might be the effects and symptoms of a revolutionary spirit and that some masons were culpable. These distinctions were to be taken much further by him. At the end of 1811 they were given their final development in his *Quatre chapitres sur la Russie* (which were not printed until 1859) the last of which is entitled 'De l'Illuminisme'.[116] He was moved to write by the observation of certain developments or likely developments in Russian society and institutions (especially in education) which he thought subversive and pernicious.

He begins with an irritated outburst over the misuse of the word 'illuminé'. This word, he says, 'trompe nécessairement une foule d'hommes parce qu'il signifie, dans les conversations ordinaires, des choses absolument différentes. Un franc-maçon ordinaire, un martin-

[114] M. Dermenghem says it bears the title *Illuminés* and I have followed his account of it here (pp. 85–8).

[115] Dermenghem, p. 86.

[116] *Oeuvres complètes*, VIII, pp. 325–45, and the 'Appendice du chapitre quatrième et conclusion' which follow, pp. 347–60.

iste, un piétiste, etc, etc, et un disciple de Weishaupt se nomment com-
munément dans le monde, des 'illuminés'. Il serait cependant difficile
d'abuser davantage des termes et de confondre des choses plus dis-
parates.'[117] Once distinctions between them were admitted then he was
sure that masonry 'simple' had nothing in it to cause alarm in church or
state. This was a reassertion of his original view. Nonetheless, de
Maistre said, it was certainly sensible and prudent to recognise a source
of possible danger in any clandestine meeting in times of disturbance.
Accordingly, such bodies should not be allowed to meet without the
knowledge of the authorities.[118] As for pietists and Martinists, de
Maistre said that he had observed members of the highest grade of
Martinists taking part in the Revolution (though not in its excesses)
and both groups must provoke disapproval as opponents of the hierarchical principle in the life of the Church. Nonetheless, that is not
enough for them to be blamed for the Revolution itself. Moreover,
in non-Catholic countries they have even a positive value; their
spiritual quality helps to stem the flood of unbelief and materialism.[119]

To these apologetic distinctions de Maistre was to hold fast. He in
large measure repeated them eight years later in the eleventh conversation of his celebrated *Soirées*.[120] But they excluded another class of
'illuminés' which he went on to attack violently in terms which showed
how much he, too, accepted the prevailing mythology. It is in discussing
Weishaupt's followers that de Maistre accepts the conspiracy mythology and he links it wholeheartedly to an attack on what he holds to
be the vicious principle at the heart of Protestantism and to the Enlightenment. This truly dangerous variety of 'illuminisme', he says,
speaking of this connexion, 'est *le philosophisme moderne greffé sur le
protestantisme*, c'est-à-dire sur le calvinisme; car on peut dire que le
calvinisme a dévoré et assimilé à lui toutes les autres.

'Voilà pourquoi l'illuminisme est beaucoup plus féroce en Allemagne qu'ailleurs, parce que le vénin protestant a son principal foyer
dans ces contrées. C'est aussi dans ce pays que le nom de la grande
secte a pris naissance. Les conjurés sont nommé dans leur langue,
auf Klarung, l'action de la nouvelle lumière qui venait dissiper les
ténèbres des anciens préjugés; et les Français ont traduit ce mot par
celui d'*illuminisme*.'[121]

De Maistre went on to say that this sect had begun, like the others

---

[117] VIII, p. 325.   [118] VIII, p. 326.
[119] VIII, pp. 329–30.
[120] *Les Soirées de St Petersbourg* (Lyon, 1874), II, pp. 265 ff.
[121] *Oeuvres complètes*, VIII, pp. 330–2.

he had discussed, only as an association based on shared opinions: unlike them, it had gone on to give them form in a secret society, whose best example was the Bavarian one. (Barruel, he now said, had written an 'intéressante' book expounding this.) Now similar societies have appeared in Italy and at Paris. Unhappily, de Maistre at this stage fell back on a feeble inferential argument which he would hardly have respected in another; the great crimes which have been committed cannot be explained except by the operation of great means. Secret societies must therefore be at work. Their organisation and extent are not, though, what matters. The aims are clear: the Illuminati are the enemies of Papacy and the House of Bourbon, which they see 'comme les deux clefs de la voûte européenne'. Fortunately, they have not so far penetrated Russia.[122]

De Maistre went on to say much more about the devices employed by the plotters to gain the ear of the King, about their exploitation of issues such as the reform of mortmain and clerical celibacy, about their plea for relief for the Jews and concluded with a series of specific 'maximes conservatrices' which Russia required to observe and a long series of damning quotations in his appendix (several from Kant, whose teaching he thought especially dangerous because it was at that time fashionable). He had also used the correspondence of Voltaire and d'Alembert in his text, as Barruel had done. These details, however, are less important than the general tone and its revelation of the power the myth could by now exercise over even so well-informed a man. Though he had explicitly rejected the myth in its grossest and most indiscriminate form, his work incorporates all the illusions about the Illuminati. True, it is unlikely that de Maistre would have accepted such crudities as the legend of the Duke or Orléans' admission to the grade of Chevalier Kadosch, or been frightened into seeing a Jacobin club in every masonic lodge before 1789. Nevertheless, all distinctions and allowances made, his words are wild and whirling. Hundreds of pages by lesser men can arouse a sense of despair of rationality and commonsense; it is much more shocking to find so much of the mythology taken seriously by so accomplished and clear-headed a man as de Maistre. There is not more telling evidence of the power of its images and the shock given to a whole outlook by the French Revolution and the historical epoch of which it was the centre and climax.

It even led him to make tactical recommendations. One was that Jesuits should be allowed to teach in Russia. His reason was expressed

---

[122] Though, thought de Maistre, they would if Protestants were allowed to teach freely. *Oeuvres complètes*, viii, p. 333.

in language which, ironically, shows how much the anti-Enlightenment mythology itself had absorbed of its opponents' version of history: 'l'ennemi capital, naturel, irréconciliable de l'*illuminé*, c'est le *Jésuite* .. il faudra que l'on dévore l'autre.'[123] This anticipated a dramatisation much favoured by writers of both Left and Right later in the century. So myth was piled on myth. De Maistre's testimony is a revealing indicator of the readiness even of educated men to see conspiracy at work on the eve of the Restoration. And it was to be then that real secret societies were to have more scope than ever before or after.

[123] Dermenghem, p. 81.

Chapter IX

The Restoration and after

THE RESTORATION ATMOSPHERE

In both the history and the mythology of the secret societies, the Restoration was an epoch. Within ten years of 1815 they reached and fell from the peak of their strength, influence and diffusion. For about ten years, too, governments showed their respect for them by fussing over them and harrying them harder than ever before or after. It was then that they received their greatest publicity—which was both a cause and an effect of what governments were doing—and one result of this was the extraordinary fact that in many people's eyes they became respectable. It was then that they were admitted to the liberal pantheon as the admired precursors of the nation-makers of the later nineteenth century, a role which exaggerated their effect and distorted their nature almost as much as the conservative slanders and misapprehensions.

There was also another way in which the Restoration marked an epoch in the mythology. Although the old grandiose view of the secret societies as the inheritors of a timeless, cosmic mission, great with theological and metaphysical implications, still persisted, many people after 1815 came to attribute to them a significance which, though still great, was much more narrowly political and slightly more realistic. The bloc view of conspiracy was beginning to break down; there was a growing willingness to accept that particular continuing conspiratorial organisations might exist without having to believe they were all aspects of the same great organisation. Oddly enough, this was taking place just when co-ordination of secret societies in many countries was to be attempted on a quite unprecedented scale for the first time.

The Restoration was, with these qualifications, the moment when the myth of the secret societies came to a climax. It was richly fed by new revelation and purported revelation from many sources, but there were also some forces at work which made new information and assertion specially effective just then. One of these may be called the new conservative state of mind.

Just before Christmas 1820 Metternich sent a remarkable 'confession of faith' to the Emperor Alexander, who was then at Troppau, where a congress of the powers was about to meet.[1] It was not a personal but a political document, written to prepare Alexander to join his fellow-sovereigns of Austria and Prussia in action against the revolutions of that year. Metternich presented it as a survey explaining the catastrophic state in which Europe found itself. Human presumption, 'that inseparable companion of the half-educated, that spring of an unmeasured ambition', was, he thought, the key;[2] the real aim of liberals everywhere was not even any longer, he averred, the cause of nationality which they once espoused; it was the emancipation of the individual from *all* authority. Their success could be explained in several ways. One was the feebleness of governments and sometimes their willingness themselves to touch pitch by trying to use the liberals' instruments.[3] One was the damage done by Napoleon in the Hundred Days and by the folly of French governments since. A third lay in the middle classes, 'wealthy men—real cosmopolitans'[4]—among whom presumption was especially rife. But even more alarming than all these were the secret societies, 'a real power, all the more dangerous as it works in the dark, undermining all parts of the social body, and depositing everywhere the seeds of a moral gangrene which is not slow to develop and increase'.[5] Metternich concluded that the only basis for safety lay in union between the monarchs of Europe against the levellers and the doctrinaires. This might hold Europe steady, though a big obstacle lay in the way because of the spread of liberty of expression; perhaps the existence of society would prove incompatible with a free press. Metternich closed with specific recommendations on how to be firm, among them one to suppress 'Secret Societies, that gangrene of society'.[6]

---

[1] *Memoirs of Prince Metternich* (London, 1881), III, p. 453. The title is misleading; this volume consists of selections from Metternich's correspondence.

[2] p. 465. Like most of Metternich's ideas, including those on secret societies, this was far from novel, let alone original. Cf., e.g., Burke to Sir Lawrence Parsons, 7 March 1793: 'The Evil of our time is in presumption and malice, the latter partly the Cause, partly the consequence of the former.' *The Correspondence of Edmund Burke* (Cambridge, 1968), VII, p. 359.

[3] 'Prussia committed a grave fault in calling to her aid such dangerous weapons as secret associations also will be' (Metternich, p. 463). Nodier later (1832) remarked in his novel *Mademoiselle de Marsan* (which has as titles for its first two sections, 'Les Carbonari' and 'Le Tungend-Bund') that secret societies had during the Napoleonic era 'pour la première fois dans le vieux système européen une autorité légitime' (*Oeuvres complètes de Charles Nodier*, VI, p. 22).

[4] Metternich, p. 467.

[5] p. 464.

[6] p. 475.

This document is characteristic of the Restoration state of mind, not least in its fears of the bogy of the secret societies. 'Restoration' here means more than the plain facts of the European settlement of 1814–15 and more, even, than the events of the ensuing four or five years. In these there was much variety: political changes which ran from, at one end, the monarchy of the French 'Charte' to, at the other, the attempted reversion of the Kingdom of Sardinia to the situation of 1798, do not easily fall into a neat institutional pattern. Nonetheless, certain general impressions remain; some enduring and pervading habits of mind stand out. Metternich himself contributed as much as anyone to giving posterity an impression of the Restoration as a bloc by his pressing concern with international precautions against the Revolution. It is the principle of conservatism in the Restoration which still makes it identifiable as a particular political standpoint. In its working out, conservatism, a new idea born of the French Revolution, combined with certain deep-rooted cultural and ideological tendencies in an atmosphere of fear and muted violence to produce the characteristic flavour of the Restoration era, the 'mingled odour of sacristy and police station' which Croce once remarked.[7] Not everyone succumbed to it to the same degree, of course, but it is striking how few were completely resistant to it. A seductive path led from this conservative standpoint back to the belief in malign human agency. Chateaubriand reprinted in 1815 a book he had first published in 1797, in which he had said that the Revolution 'ne vient point de tel, ou tel homme, de tel ou tel livre, elle vient des choses', but later in the same book he took up once more the tired old theme of 'la Secte Philosophique sous Louis Quinze'.[8]

A few years later the temptation and the readiness to believe in secret societies grew much stronger, and understandably so. Not only was there seemingly much new evidence of the secret societies' work, but there existed a stratum of conservative political thinking irrigated for years by the doctrines of men like Barruel and ready to interpret this evidence in a particular way. In the same year as Metternich's letter to Alexander, for example, there appeared a *Histoire des Jacobins, depuis 1789 jusqu'à ce jour* which showed just how much life there still was in the Barruel scenario nearly twenty-five years after its appearance.[9] Much material drawn from later events was added to

[7] B. Croce, *History of Europe in the Nineteenth Century* (London, 1934), p. 93.

[8] F. A. de Chateaubriand, *Essai historique, politique et moral, sur les révolutions, anciennes et modernes* (London, 1815), pp. 349, 379. He did not, it is true, attribute any of the events of the Revolution to secret societies.

[9] Paris, 1820. It is usually attributed to Vincent Lombard de Langres.

that basic plan, but to a remarkable degree the elements remained unchanged; the myth had hardened into what was virtually its final form. In a deliberate attempt to prolong the interpretation of the 1790s into a different period the author of the *Histoire des Jacobins* had no misgivings over fitting what seemed to him the corroborative evidence provided by events in the months immediately preceding his new book into the Barruel framework: 'dans le Tirol, le Voralberg, l'Espagne et l'Italie, on voit se renouveler les scènes horribles de la révolution française. Dans Milan, les têtes sont promenées au bout des piques.'[10] Behind all these dreadful events, as behind the French Revolution, could be seen the operation of one gigantic plot by an international sect spanning the centuries. '*Illuminé* est un nom primitif, générique, donné à la secte lorsqu'elle a paru sur la scène du monde. Ses affiliations ont pris noms divers, depuis deux siècles, selon les temps et les lieux. Puritains, niveleurs, frères rouges, deffendeurs, réformateurs, jacobins, idéologues, radicaux, carbonari, indépendans, liberaux, peu import; ces corporations aboutissent à un centre commun, qui est l'*illuminisme*.' The 'Jacobins' of the title are simply illuminés, under another name.[11]

This structure follows the Barruel model in principle, though it departs from it in important details. There is the universality and antiquity of the plot, there is the comprehensiveness which links so many sub-species of conspiracy, there is the huge climax of 1789 which is, in its turn, made all the more terrible by the revelation that it is not an end but a beginning. In its account of events leading up to 1789, too, the book by and large follows Barruel, arguing that all the nonsense of the freemasons, theosophists and so on simply served as a disguise and cover to the illuminés, who used these oddities to throw dust in the eyes of those they wished to mislead. But there is an important touch not to be found in Barruel, and for good reason: the

[10] p. 15. I do not know to what episode in Milan he refers; a sensational incident there in 1814 was, of course, the lynching of a former minister of the Napoleonic Kingdom of Italy who was poked and beaten to death by umbrellas, but, horrible as this was, no one cut his head off, far less paraded it about. But a connexion between Prina's murder and secret societies had, it is true, been asserted long before Lombard wrote (see below, p. 311) and he may have picked it up in a confused form.

[11] p. 24. 'Deffendeurs' (and 'Fendeurs') were a sub-species of Charbonnerie, 'crée en 1747 à Paris par le chevalier de Beauclaire', says J. Kuypers, *Buonarroti et ses sociétés secrètes* (Brussels, 1960), p. 115. For a defence of them against the charge of political subversion see the pamphlet of G. F. Cauchard d'Hermilly, *Des Carbonari et des Fendeurs Charbonniers* (Paris, 1822). 'Loin de conspirer contre les lois, la plupart des Fend[eurs] Charb[onniers] d'Artois ont applaudi à la restauration qui devait affranchir la France du despotisme' (p. 27). Barruel discussed them too (*Mémoires*, II, p. 361).

author thought that under Louis XV a struggle to rule the state was going forward in France, the illuminés on one side, on the other—the Jesuits. When it came, nevertheless, 'la révolution sortit des loges maçonniques';[12] among those taken in by the talk of constitutionalism and the English constitution was Lafayette (again, of course, a prominent and controversial public figure when the book appeared). The usual confusion over terminology shows itself again in a reference to Germany in 1792, where it is found significant that in Prussia an illuminé, Bischoffswerder, was in power. After this there is not much that is interesting or novel in the treatment of the revolutionary decade until we come to the 18th Brumaire, over which the author waxes lyrical. 'C'est cette journée qui retient pendant quinze ans la civilisation sur le bord de l'abîme, et qui jette une planche de salut à l'ordre social. Les jacobins n'ont jamais pardonné à Bonaparte de les avoir muselés.' This is a Bonapartist version of the myth. Until 1813 few traces were to be found of the Jacobins; they had gone underground again. Since that date they had emerged and were once more at work undermining royalty everywhere.

In surveying the recent scene the author is very gloomy. Russia is probably the country where there are most illuminés, he thinks, but 'l'Italie a toujours été pour la secte un vrai pays de Cocagne'.[13] In Germany, too, they are widespread, having been kept alive by Arndt's struggle against Bonaparte.[14] In England he finds all sorts of evidence of illuminé success; the radicals, Cochrane's enterprises in South America and the royal divorce proceedings all fit into the picture, and so, even, do proposals for the free distribution of bibles to the poor.[15]

Such an account was given additional plausibility in many people's eyes, of course, by the moment at which it came and which, no doubt, Lombard consciously exploited. In 1820 a new revolutionary wave was beginning to be felt. Its upheavals were to continue, recognisably linked to one another, for the next two or three years and, in the process, to throw up more information about the secret societies. This wave was to produce the greatest burst of revelations and publicity since the days of the Illuminati exposures and to give the secret societies their moments of greatest fame and notoriety. It appeared for a little while to justify all that those who thought like Metternich had feared. But

[12] *Histoire des Jacobins*, p. 39.

[13] *Histoire des Jacobins*, pp. 325, 332.

[14] p. 319. This is, interestingly, his only mention of anti-Napoleonic secret societies.

[15] pp. 324–5. Lombard de Langres was still taken seriously as an authority as late as 1901 (see Rinieri, p. 465, fn.).

the strength of the myth did not rest on it alone, nor on the diffusion of ideas such as Barruel's in the preceding quarter-century. There were also telling in its favour certain general forces wholly separable in principle from what secret societies might or might not do.

Mythological thinking was at bottom a response to what was, in spite of the name 'Restoration' a new and unfamiliar political world, an uncomfortable experience. For twenty-five years the statesmen of Restoration Europe and the ruling classes they represented had been exposed to a terrible series of shocks. In 1815 they sought, above all, stability, and were more sensitive to threats to it than ever before. Yet stability was just what could not be assured; however it might be controlled, the process of change was bound to continue. For twenty-five years Europe had been at war with the Revolution and in that time she had willy-nilly absorbed much of the Revolution into her public life. With the return of peace it was very difficult to recognise this. Yet it was there. The statesmen of the Restoration faced, for example, a new vitality of national feeling in many parts of Europe and even, sometimes, disappointment at the disappearance of the institutions of Napoleonic rule. In retrospect, the great man's work seemed more attractive than it had done at the time: Europe was full of Julien Sorels, even if they did not all keep the Emperor's picture under their mattresses.

The Restoration did not have adequate institutional or ideological equipment to deal with such problems. All it could do was reject them and repress their results in public disorder. Few countries except England, after all, had any notion of legitimate political opposition.[16] Furthermore, they usually imposed a virtually complete restriction of freedom of association and assembly, only slightly less sweeping restrictions of freedom of speech and in many countries there were still almost no representative institutions. The Restoration emphasis on police power is a logical consequence; so also is the rise of irreconcilable opposition in clandestine forms. As Nodier remarked in 1815, 'chez les peuples heureux par la longue influence des institutions . . . il y a ce que l'on appelle des *clubs*, des cercles, des coteries, des réunions . . . Chez les peuples malades . . . il y a des conspirations.'[17]

Exaggeration of the influence of secret societies was also likely to

[16] Even in England, of course, the phrase 'His Majesty's Opposition' provoked amusement when it was first used in 1826 as a 'bit of parliamentary persiflage', says A. S. Foord (*His Majesty's Opposition*, Oxford, 1964, p. 3); the same author points out (p. 5) that Alexander I was impressed enough after his visit to England in 1814 to declare that he, too, 'would have an opposition'.

[17] *Histoire des sociétés secrètes*, pp. 341–2.

follow another consequence of the Revolution, the new internationalising of politics. International affairs had been injected with an ideological issue or, rather, a series of issues: natural rights against prescription, nationality against dynasticism, liberty versus order, contract versus status, the past versus the future. These burst into the domestic politics of different countries in different ways, but, whenever they did so, helped to create a sense of common interests transcending national boundaries both on the Left and the Right. For various reasons the end of the fighting brought economic and social dislocation in many countries. In England it broke out in Luddism; in central Europe in emigration. Disturbances made governments more nervous still. In some instances—England is again a good example—a disposition to look for explanations in conspiracy and agitation cannot have made these problems easier to solve.

In such circumstances the exaggerated fear of secret societies shown by the men of the Restoration begins to become comprehensible. It should be understood not only in terms of the revolutionary decade of the 1790s and its violent shocks, but in terms of the different circumstances of 1815 and the different experience of the men who then grappled with politics. Almost everywhere these fears were shown in legal enactments. From 1801, for example, all officials, schoolmasters and clergy in the Habsburg lands had to take an oath that they belonged to no secret society.[18] The Papal government issued a formal prohibition of the Carbonari in its dominions in August 1814 and reiterated in it the anti-masonic provisions of the previous century's Bulls. (One reason for this, though, as the edict admitted, was a story put about by some Carbonari that the Pope had issued from Fontainebleau a special Bull in their favour.)[19] In Lombardy and Venetia, the provisions of the Austrian legal codes which concerned secret societies were imposed and the death penalty for membership followed in 1820.[20] The Spanish Inquisition began again to harry freemasons.

Even where such legal changes did not take place, the membership of secret societies was discouraged by all sorts of pressures. Yet the results were paradoxical. Evidence about the growth and expansion of these societies poured in to the governments of Europe: nowhere were they eradicated. This caused much alarm, led to more publicity, and then to more alarm. No one seemed to notice that the secret

[18] Rath, *The Provisional Austrian Régime*, p. 190. After 1806 this oath was required also of candidates for doctoral degrees.

[19] Spadoni, *Sette Cospirazoni*, p. cvii. A translation of the edict can be found in *Memoirs of the Secret Societies of the South of Italy*, pp. 206–12.

[20] Rath, pp. 190–4, has an admirable summary of the steps taken by the Austrians.

societies never succeeded in doing anything which would justify the attention given to them. They justified neither the hopes nor the fears they aroused. Yet governments went on worrying about them. Even Alexander was, in fact, won round in 1820 by Metternich's pleading.

In some instances, exaggeration and alarm went well beyond the reasonable and became ludicrous. Perhaps a Habsburg emperor was bound to find it hard to take a realistic view, but it still seems startling that as early as 1814 Francis should have been enquiring about certain tiepins worn at Florence which were, he supposed, of masonic design.[21] It may simply have been a manifestation of the special and peculiar anxiety the Austrians always showed about Italy. In 1816 Metternich visited Milan and noted that 'the troubled temper of Italy in general necessitates a ceaseless watch on the efforts of agitators in all parts of the peninsula'.[22] It was in the same year that the Austrian envoy at Rome used up much of his audience with the Pope to tell him at length about the danger of the secret societies and the likelihood that they would at once convulse Italy if Austria's attention was ever relaxed by war with another power.[23]

Behind this alarm was a solid truth; Austrian rule in north Italy was the implicit foundation of the whole Restoration there. Both the fragmentation of the peninsula and the maintenance of its institutions depended finally on the ready support of Austrian arms. In this sense, there was always an implicit national, anti-Austrian cause in Italy which might at any moment (it was feared) explode in a general disturbance. Yet this was only theoretically conceivable. Co-ordination and unity— as events were to show—were never to be achieved by the Italian revolutionaries.

Nor were there so many of them as the Austrians thought, though it is impossible to say how many discontented Italians there really were. Good evidence about the membership of secret societies is almost impossible to come by.[24] Opponents and members were equally anxious to exaggerate. Another basic problem is confusion: it is very difficult to know what is being talked about or even to make a complete list of names of societies. Byron (who was watched with great concern) was said by the Venetian police in 1819 to belong to a society called

[21] D. E. Emerson, *Metternich and the Political Police* (The Hague, 1968), p. 32.
[22] *Ibid*. p. 60.
[23] Lebzeltern to Metternich, 30 April 1816, in *Correspondance du Cardinal Hercule Consalvi avec le Prince Clément de Metternich 1815–1823*, ed. C. Van Duerm (Louvain, 1899), p. 128.
[24] One report of 1817 estimated that there were seven hundred thousand Italian *republicans*, alone! Emerson, p. 67.

Roma Antica and in the following year was reported to have joined something called the Cacciatori Americani at Ravenna.[25] Perhaps they existed, but the existence of other societies whose names were bandied about is at least non-proven. Many Italians must have belonged to more than one society, too, but it is hard and perhaps impossible to distinguish clearly among some of them. 'That they are all, however, no other than so many ramifications of Masonry, some of the best informed sectaries themselves allow' said the Papal investigations of 1818 into the Macerata disturbances, 'and none of them differ essentially as to the object they have in view: viz—Independence, or, at least, a constitutional government.'[26] This may be exaggerated, too, for masonry seems only to have been important as a soil which often made it easy for secret associations to take root, but it makes clear the difficulty of distinguishing bodies which so often shared similar forms and rituals. It is certain, too, that masonry was consciously exploited as a cover by other societies and this further deepened the mystery.[27]

Among the Restoration sects, besides the Centri and Decisi the most celebrated—or notorious—name was that of the Guelfi, often cited in the police records of the immediately past-Napoleonic years. It was always ill-defined. The head of the Austrian police believed that it admitted as members only Carbonari of the highest degree.[28] Possibly centred on Bologna, it was thought to have been the society most clearly involved with Bentinck in 1813–14, but certainty about its status dissolves when one reads that it was used as a front by another body, whose strength lay mainly in Piedmont, the Adelfi.[29] This mysterious sect, of uncertain origins (one suggestion derived it from the French Philadelphes) worked also under the name of the Società Delfica. The Austrians did not hear of it until 1816, but people concerned in conspiracy later said it had existed at least since 1812.

If this confusion were not enough, there hangs over the whole peninsula the vaguely defined shadow of the Carbonari. Undoubtedly, the Restoration brought it prosperity in that there were then more

---

[25] I. Rinieri, *Della vita e della opere di Silvio Pellico da lettere e documenti inediti* (Turin, 1898–1901), i, pp. 207–8.

[26] Quoted in *Memoirs of the Secret Societies of the South of Italy*, p. 20.

[27] For example by Buonarroti. See the document by him printed by M. Vuilleumier, *AHRF*, 1970, pp. 494–7.

[28] Spadoni, (pp. 95–116,) prints documents concerning it which fell into the hands of the Papal authorities.

[29] Emerson, p. 75, Sòriga, pp. 107–12. The possibility of English official support for Italian revolution continued to bother the Austrians as it had the French. See the letter of Apponyi to Metternich, 18 March 1817, in Van Duerm, pp. 276–7. The story turned up in the Papal States, too; see Spadoni, p. cxvii.

Carbonari than ever before. The organisation stretched as far afield as Spain and even Russia. In Italy they had spread north in the last years of the Napoleonic decade, and it seems likely that Murat's 1814 campaign helped to establish them in the Legations and the Po Valley. The first reference to them in the Tuscan police archives, too, we are told, is in 1814.[30] It was the greatest single spectre of the Restoration. One of Murat's advisers told his master in 1814 to conciliate and co-operate with it and did so in terms which would fully justify the alarm it inspired in the restored régimes. (He may, of course, have been exaggerating consciously, in order to win over his master.) Although he saw the Carbonari as above all an anti-Bonapartist body, he recognised in them universal aims and a core of republicanism, sustained by a ferocious discipline over members. He discerned in the society exactly the sort of bogy others had seen in earlier bodies and even hit on an alarming parallel: 'cette organisation a perfectionné avec une heureuse simplicité tous les moyens de correspondence employés en Allemagne par les *Illuminés et les Amis de la Vertu*.'[31]

Italian historians have devoted much time and scholarship to this period, and while it can hardly be said that they have either clarified our picture or come to agreement about its meaning, they have produced a body of literature which contains more information about secret societies than that available for any other period or country.[32] Fortunately, though the preceding paragraphs will appear wholly inadequate as a summary of the known and hypothetical facts, it is not necessary, in order to understand the history of the myth, to say much about what the true state of affairs was. What matters is what men believed it to be. Vague and confusing as the evidence was, the authorities had to try to make something of it unless they were to proceed on entirely a priori grounds. There was more than enough to confirm their fears.

Inevitably, the Austrians took the lead; they tried to amass intelligence material from all over Europe, not merely from their own dominions, and in Italy to organise liaison and co-operation between all the states. This was none too easy. Even within the Austrian dominions,

[30] Spadoni (p. xxiii) bluntly attributes the spread of Carbonarism to the Marches to the movements of the Napoleonic army and explores the question in detail. Francovich (p. 114) reports the Tuscan reference.

[31] General Rossetti, quoted in Sòriga, pp. 71–2.

[32] Fortunately, the reader need not at once plunge into it in order to learn more. There is an excellent introductory digest of much of the story which is the best place to begin in Professor Rath's chapter, 'The Secret World' (*The Provisional Austrian Régime*, pp. 190–242) already cited, p. 281, an admirably balanced survey.

co-operation and co-ordination was not always easy.[33] When different states were involved it is hardly surprising that things did not always turn out well. Co-operation with the Neapolitans, for example, was not made easier by the Austrian belief that its lack of success could only be explained by assuming that the Neapolitan chief of police was himself a member of the sects.[34] Of course, he may well have been: certainly many Roman officials were.

Nor were agents and informers always reliable. Many of them had formerly been members of secret societies, some had worked for Bentinck or the Napoleonic régimes, and there was a natural tendency on the part of such men to exaggerate the importance of the bodies they sought to penetrate. Some would believe anything; some had an interest in distortion and even invention, in seeking to ingratiate themselves with the restored régimes. At least one was a straight swindler; this was Codoni, who 'exposed' a masonic plot to rise in the Napoleonic and Muratist interest in the summer of 1814.[35] He was quickly exposed, but other lying—or merely gullible—agents were not, and the quality of intelligence available demanded the most critical evaluation at a time when, perhaps, it was never harder to assure it. On the whole, the Austrians on the spot in Milan and Venice seem to have kept their heads and shown critical judgment. Yet even when they rejected a report as false, it could leave its mark on the mythology. An outstanding example exists in a forged document which, though exposed almost at once by the Austrian police, nonetheless continued to be treated as genuine by historians until 1963, when its true nature was made clear by an American scholar.[36] This purported to be a constitution of the Guelfi, dated 1813; in 1816 this came into the hands of the Austrians who almost immediately perceived it to be false. Indeed, the officials at Milan consequently became much more sceptical about the existence of the Guelfi than they had been hitherto. This was going too far; there existed much independent evidence. For our purposes, though, it is interesting to note that a

[33] As late as 1822, irritation was felt in Venice over the lack of co-operation, in a series of important political trials which they felt at Milan. (A. Sandonà, 'Contributo alla storia de'processi del ventuno e dello Spielberg', *RI*, 1910, pp. 794–5.)

[34] Emerson, p. 71. The colleagues of Consalvi were even more credulous; the Austrian minister reported that in 1816 they were saying the cardinal was a freemason (Van Duerm, p. 129) though he in fact showed great willingness to co-operate against the sects.

[35] For details, see Rath, *The Provisional Austrian Régime*, pp. 194–5.

[36] R. J. Rath ('La costituzione guelfa e i servizi segreti austriaci', *Rassegna storica del Risorgimento*, 1963, pp. 343–76) brought this to light and discusses the case in detail.

forged document contributed (if only marginally) to the inflation of the secret society legend as late as the twentieth century. Moreover, in one respect, by a specific reference, it established a new detail of the myth. This was the allegation that the apparently spontaneous lynching of Prina, Eugène's Finance Minister, was in fact the execution of a deliberate sentence of the secret society. This was to be repeated in the ensuing decade by persons themselves engaged in conspiracy.

Given such difficulties it is perhaps creditable that Italian governments were not even more alarmed than they were. Yet such dangers crop up in all police work: experts should expect them. Even allowing for them, the exaggerations and misinterpretations of Restoration Italy still seem exceptional, though often echoed in patriotic liberal Italian historians. Often the result was unwise action; one example was the Austrian pursuit of freemasons in Lombardy in 1814 at a moment when many of them were actively sympathetic to the restored régime.[37] Confusion also led to suspicion falling on people who might have been expected to be co-operative. The Milanese authorities, for example, suddenly became excited in 1817 by the discovery of a secret society with the name Congregazione Cattolica e Apostolica Romana: it was said to be plotting to exploit the spiritual hegemony of the Pope in the interests of Italian independence, but virtually no further trace of it was then found until 1822, when its statutes were discovered.[38] Another, the Consistoriali, was talked of by a prisoner of the Roman police (who told the Austrians about it). It was supposed to be a reactionary society with the Duke of Modena at its head.[39] The Romans were inclined to be sceptical: the Austrians thought that it was a part of the scheme to use support for Papal supremacy against them! The crux of the matter was that very little certainly reliable information was available. When, in 1817, Cardinal Pacca proposed to arrest all the leaders of the secret societies in all Italian states on the same day, the Austrians turned down the scheme because their police could not identify the leaders to be taken up in such a swoop. Much was said, but little was known that could be depended on, and Metternich's policy of watching and waiting, rather than striking, was imposed largely by necessity.

Oddly, given all the efforts of the police and the informers, nobody

[37] Rath, *The Provisional Austrian Régime*, p. 193.

[38] See letter of the Commissione Speciale of Milan to Strassoldo, 3 October 1822, printed by F. Lemmi in *Il processo del Principe della Cisterna* (Turin, 1923), pp. 92–4. Also Emerson, p. 62.

[39] Spadoni, p. cxliii, and the letter of Apponyi to Metternich printed in Van Duerm, p. 296.

L

in authority seems to have wondered whether this might not be because not very much that was important was going on. Italian patriots who were actually engaged in the attempt to advance the cause of Italian constitutionalism could be far more sceptical about the secret societies. Silvio Pellico, the hero of the Spielberg, remarked to his older brother from Milan in April 1819 that the stupidities of policemen being infinite, it was believed at Milan as at Turin that the Carbonari must be behind all liberals though there was no connexion at all between them.[40]

Although the little that happened before 1820 caused much alarm, it is also true that even of such conspiracy as there was only a tiny amount actually resulted in action. A small and easily contained plot at Brescia was the first to alarm the Austrians and was nipped in the bud in 1814. In Naples the Carbonari seemed for some time almost stunned into disillusionment by the shock of what happened after Ferdinand's return; all the hopes they had cherished of co-operation with a constitutional Bourbon régime were then dashed. Their leaders ceased to meet in Naples itself and moved to Salerno. Plans made at Pompeii for a revolutionary attempt in the autumn of 1817 came to nothing, for the authorities anticipated it by making hundreds of arrests. Further north, a pitifully bungled plan for a rising in the Legations on the news of the Pope's death (which was expected) resulted only in a half-cock and bloodless fiasco at Macerata in June 1817. The investigations and the trials of the following year provided yet more evidence of the widespread nature of Carbonarism, yet this episode, like others, really showed how little danger threatened Italy from the societies during these years, whatever the fears of the authorities. Even Metternich came round to this view briefly, remarking, on a visit to Naples in 1819, that no political danger seemed to exist there.[41]

Though to a smaller degree than in Italy, the influence of Austria was also preponderant in Germany after 1814 and there, too, Metter-

[40] Rinieri, *Silvio Pellico*, i, pp. 330–1. 'Le sciochezze delle Polizie essendo infinite, s'e detto qua come se dice a Torino che tutto cio che e liberale in Italia e carbonaro; ma sta tranquillo che non v'e ne anche la piu lontana relazione tra una setta oscura che si nasconde e una societa schietta che professa pubblicamente e stampa (quando puo) le sue opinioni.' For another disparaging comment on the Carbonari by Pellico, see p. 401. (It is also interesting that in the letter he quoted he goes on to say that there is nothing more discredited in Italy as he writes than any kind of masonry. 'I buffoni che vi hanno brillato son una ragione per cui i galantuomini sdegnino d'aggregarsi a sifatte ciarlatanerie.') Two interesting statements by prisoners of the Papal authorities which give a good impression of the sort of information offered to the police have been printed by Spadoni, pp. 157–90.

[41] Emerson, p. 86.

nich was exaggeratedly fearful of the secret society danger. Much was said of the Tugendbund, a patriotic survival from the days of the anti-Napoleonic movement; even then too much had been made of its contribution to the defeat of the French and this exaggeration persisted. In fact, it seems to have had no practical importance during the Restoration. Yet Metternich saw its hand in the excitements among students which culminated in the Wartburg festival of October 1817 and was convinced, without any positive evidence for the view, that the murderer of the journalist Kotzebue in 1819 must have been a member of a secret society. One outcome of his convictions was the Carlsbad decrees and the setting up of a commission by the Federal Diet with the task of rooting out subversive forces throughout Germany. Something of a panic occurred. Not surprisingly, therefore, interpretations of what was going on in Germany soon became available which fitted the Tugendbund into the comprehensive mythology. The opportunity presented by the sensational murder of Kotzebue, for example, produced an anonymous pamphlet entitled *Des sociétés secrètes en Allemagne et en d'autres contrées* by Lombard de Langres.[42]

He had played a fairly active part in the Revolution and on several occasions published his observations on it. He was one of those former revolutionaries who had rallied to Napoleon after Brumaire and has some interest as one of those who made serious attempts to incorporate into the myth the work of anti-Bonapartist plotters.[43] In his account of the German movements he did not limit himself but touched on the whole range of the traditional mythology, borrowing heavily from Barruel, Robison, Luchet and others in order to provide a framework with which the recent occurrences in Germany could be integrated. He saw the Tugendbund as simply another manifestation of the age-old occult powers which had brought about all the miseries of recent years, though its great opportunity arose, he thought, by the folly of the princes themselves who had sought to use it against the French; now, the genie would not go back into the bottle. As a result, 'tout ce que l'Illuminisme a de plus exalté' was in the Tugendbund now turning Germany upside down.[44]

It was quickly pointed out in a reply by 'un ancien illuminé' that this was muddled and unoriginal stuff, whose only novelty was its

[42] Published Paris, 1819.

[43] He enthusiastically eulogised Bonaparte's seizure of power as a restoration of order and later asserts that his fall was in large measure due to illuminé influence (pp. 185-8, 203). The Bonapartist twist of the *Histoire des Jacobins* has already been noted.

[44] *Ibid.*, p. 102.

Bonapartist bias.[45] Over its pages are scattered all the old stage-props: a sinister poison for which a recipe had been found in the papers seized at the time of the Illuminati discoveries, 'aqua tofana' (and the attribution of the deaths of both Joseph II and Leopold II to it), Cromwell's ambitions, reserved secrets, Cagliostro and the Jesuits. But even these have a certain impressiveness. They testify to the strength of the myth in even its most banal forms. This was because, as the author of the reply to Lombard himself pointed out, secret societies were news, and so were the affairs of Germany.[46] Even an informal rebuttal of myth-mongering such as he provided was therefore liable to provide fresh fuel. The attempts made by the 'ancien illuminé' to disentangle what lay behind Mirabeau's mysterious statements about the Illuminati on the eve of the Revolution were just as likely to re-awaken suspicion that there *had* been something to hide as to allay it.[47] Stein might have failed to use the Tugendbund effectively, as he asserted, but to admit that he had tried to link it to freemasonry was bound to suggest that there was some real connexion after all.[48]

Frenchmen were much interested in secret societies under the Restoration, as such publications as these show. Yet the first French societies which were given publicity were royalist or anti-Bonapartist.[49] In the circumstances, it is hardly surprising that, by comparison with Italy and Germany, public opinion was much less provoked by governmental hysteria. The early governments of the Restoration were after 1816 mild and conciliatory. Freemasonry they knew all about and did not fear; demoralisation under the Empire made weather-cocks of the brothers of the Craft when it ended. Numbers had fallen as the end began to come more and more obviously in sight in 1813. At the allied occupation of Paris, the Grand Orient rushed to grovel

---

[45] *La vérité sur les sociétés secrètes en Allemagne, . . . par un ancien illuminé* (Paris, 1819), p. 5.

[46] p. v.   [47] pp. 9, 34–6.   [48] p. 61.

[49] Not only in Nodier's work, already discussed. It was during the first Restoration that the American-born Bordelais merchant, Dupont-Constant, rushed to print his *Mémoire historique des évènemens rélatifs à l'Institut philanthropique, établi dans toutes les Provinces du Midi, par ordre et en vertu des pouvoirs du Roi, en 1796* (Paris, 1814). By way of authenticating the claim he made for the importance of this body's enduring role in events culminating in the proclamation of Louis XVIII in the city in 1814, he reprinted some of the official collection, *La Conspiration anglaise*, of 1800. The Institut was not to be forgotten and received further publicity in 1816 in an *Exposé fidèle des faits authentiquement prouvés qui ont precédé et amené la journées de Bordeaux, au 12 mars 1814*, by I. S. Rollac (Paris, 1816). Dupont-Constant himself again went into print on the subject in 1817 so there can be little doubt that the case for the efficacy of at least one secret society was forcefully and continuously argued by supporters of the restored régime itself.

before the restored Bourbons, put back the fleur de lys on its seal, and urged its lodges to subscribe to the re-establishment of the statue of Henry IV which had been removed in the Revolution from the Pont-Neuf. This proved a little precipitate; the return from Elba and Waterloo soon imposed two more rapid changes of the seal. Once the Restoration was assured, however, freemasonry again looked forward in France to a career which, if not official, as it had been under the Empire, was nevertheless tolerated by the government. Décazes, Minister of Police, himself a high official of the Suprême Conseil du Rite Ecossais, gave semi-official notice of this in 1818, and it has been suggested that the new government hoped to find in the lodges some counterweight in opinion to the influence of the Ultras.[50]

Meanwhile, in spite of the White Terror which briefly ravaged some areas, Frenchmen seemed in the immediate post-Restoration era almost indifferent to politics after the exhausting excitements and turbulence of the Revolution and the Napoleonic years. The politics of the constitutional state set up by the Charter were those of a small social élite and of different tendencies within it, but attempted risings (such as one made at Grenoble in 1816) revealed that widespread support for the subversion of the existing order would not be found. Nonetheless, conservatives were easily frightened; it was always tempting to assume a large measure of pre-arrangement and organisation in movements which (like that at Grenoble) were largely spontaneous. At Lyon in 1817, gatherings of peasants in the neighbourhood in bands under the tricolour were put down to pre-arrangement (there may have been something in this).

In the circumstances, the coolness of the government is remarkable and even praiseworthy, for, after all, it had better and more rational grounds for fearfulness than that of any other country. This was largely because of important legacies of political diversion going back to 1789 which were deeper and potentially more dangerous than similar divisions elsewhere. France was where all the trouble had started. Many people had been alienated from other Frenchmen by the time it ended and not only along the simple dividing line of the Revolution itself. There were other important fissures, too. In the army, for example, there was still strong Bonapartist feeling. By 1817, when a plot was exposed in a Guards regiment against the lives of

[50] Le Forestier, *La franc-maçonnerie Templière*, pp. 869–70. Nomenclature is often an interesting guide to masonic attitudes. In 1805 the Marseille lodge 'Le choix des Vrais Amis' became the 'Loge française de Saint Napoléon'. In 1816 the saint's name became 'Louis'.

princes of the blood, the government had grounds for feeling that it could not be sure of the steadiness of its forces.[51] There was also believed to exist outside the army a specifically Bonapartist secret society, called the Chevaliers de la Liberté. On another flank were republicans who had been disaffected under Napoleon and now transferred their disaffection to the restored Bourbon régime. Some of these were believed to work inside specific masonic lodges, others through their own societies, such as L'Union founded by Joseph Rey in 1816, of which Lafayette and Voyer d'Argenson were members.[52] One of its derivatives seems to have been the Parisian Loge des amis de la verité, which exploited the masonic cover afforded by the régime's toleration of freemasonry. It is said to have had over a thousand members and to have linked the radicalism of the student world to the dissatisfied liberalism of the commercial classes. Carbonari were reported at Lyon in 1819 and Paris in 1820, and soon there was plenty of circumstantial evidence that many secret bodies existed in France. Later, at a famous trial in 1822, the prosecution referred to societies called L'épingle noire, Patriotes de 1816, Vautours de Bonaparte, Chevaliers du soleil, Patriotes européens réformés and La régéneration universelle, and there is no reason to suppose that bodies with these names were all that existed. Yet they achieved nothing. The government kept its head and did not become really frightened until the Charbonnerie became a serious proposition in 1821. By that time the climax had come. From 1820 onwards there burst on Europe a series of revolutions which seemed to many people to justify all that had ever been said of the secret societies.

REVOLUTIONS AND EXPOSURES

It was not only among conservatives that there existed attitudes predisposing acceptance of the secret society mythology. On the other side, also, of the great ideological division of these years were people who wanted to believe that secret societies were important. It is easy to understand this of participants in the societies, of course; no one

---

[51] E. Guillon, *Les complots militaires sous la Restauration* (Paris, 1895), p. 99.

[52] Joseph Philippe Étienne Rey, magistrate (until struck off the bench for his part in a conspiracy in 1820) was one of the first to introduce Owenite ideas to France. It has been suggested that it was first-hand acquaintance with the Tugendbund during the Empire which gave him the idea of his secret society (E. Pia Onnis, 'Propaganda e rapporti di società segrete intorno al 1817', *Rassegna storica del Risorgimento*, 1964, p. 482). Marc René Voyer d'Argenson was grandson of the famous eighteenth-century minister and a prominent liberal politician.

likes to believe that what they are doing is pointless. But there were also others willing to believe. Liberals in France, for example, were often in touch with secret societies and perhaps exaggerated their importance all the more the less they knew precisely about them. Or there were the little groups of disgruntled veterans of the republican régimes of the 1790s surviving all over Europe into the new world of the Restoration: such a one was the circle about Buonarroti at Geneva. They needed a myth to live by; they had to believe the battles of the 1790s were not lost forever, that the struggle continued, and that the secret societies they patronised would one day carry it to victory. The revolutions encouraged them as much as they horrified the conservatives.

This helps to explain why the series of events between 1820 and 1825 gave the mythology its last expansion and enhancement. These years legitimised the secret societies in the eyes of liberals and confirmed the worst fears of conservatives. The contribution of secret society and conspiracy to the assault on what was summed up, somewhat misleadingly, as the 'Holy Alliance' led to the incorporation of the failures of these years in the classical liberal reading of nineteenth-century history. That reading assumed a fundamental progress in European development: nations emerged as independent units after rightly struggling to be free and then showed their maturity by giving themselves formally liberal constitutions, and by guaranteeing the rule of public opinion (which meant, that is to say, the opinions of the liberal élite who claimed to be able to interpret it). The secret societies were in consequence widely admired and respected by many observers who saw in them the advance-guards and skirmishers of the battle in which modern civilisation was the victor over obscurantism and reaction. Undoubtedly, this view fitted the known facts in some ways much better than the nightmare visions of the Barruel school. It at least broke with the mumbo-jumbo of ancient, long-nurtured designs and transmitted secrets. But it was mythology, nonetheless.

It was mythology because it, too, exaggerated the power of secret societies and gave them a positive and instrumental importance which they cannot be shown to have had. By 1871 a federal German Empire based on universal suffrage and a united, constitutional Italy both existed; France was a republic. Such achievements were for fifty years the goals of German, Italian and French radicals and the secret societies contributed virtually nothing to them. Indeed, their occasional flash-in-the-pan successes sometimes actually endangered the causes they sought to advance by driving alarmed rulers back into more reactionary attitudes. This, too, was a development with a mythological dimension. Many conservatives were by 1815 far too sensible to swallow the whole Barruel bag of bugaboos, but they readily fell into agreement with liberals who exaggerated the power of secret societies, seeing them as merely political organisms, but ones of great power and effectiveness.[53]

The main factual basis of respect for the secret societies was the upheavals of the early 1820s. In January 1820 a mutiny among Spanish troops at Cadiz who were waiting there to go to South America began a wave of revolutions and disturbances. This was the detonator first of a Spanish revolution which, in its turn, inspired other rebels of that year. It did not, on the other hand, have anything to do with two well-publicised incidents which followed in February, the detection and stifling of the Cato Street Conspiracy in London and the murder of the Duc de Berry in France. Neither of these had any connexion with anything like the international secret societies so much feared by Metternich; nonetheless, they seemed to show the unrolling of a pattern which was to be the justification for the high period of the Holy Alliance. Alexander of Russia, though unmoved a little earlier by the murder of the German journalist Kotzebue, was thrown into great excitement by the Duc de Berry's death and swung round to the advocacy of international police action against revolution. A cabinet crisis followed in France; while the politicians manoeuvred, 'aux deux extrémités apparaissaient deux fantômes, la Révolution et la Contre-Révolution, se menaçant l'un l'autre et à la fois impatients et inquiets d'en venir aux mains'.[54] The emissaries to the Congress of Troppau met in an atmosphere of excited pessimism about the revived revolutionary danger, no one being more convinced of its origins in conspiracy by the societies than the Tsar, one of whose Guards regiments had just mutinied in St Petersburg. 'I attribute it to secret societies,' he wrote from Troppau.[55]

[53] A twentieth-century parallel is obvious: immediately after 1918, in a period of great political excitement, the hopes of the Left and the fears of the Right in many countries were equally aroused by wholly unrealistic assessments of the power of 'Bolsheviks'. Some people could even then still find the old framework capable of bearing new burdens of interpretation. See Nesta H. Webster's books already cited, where the Comintern, Sinn Fein and the Muslim Brotherhood are all seen as the last chapter of the Illuminati conspiracy. Bulldog Drummond, too, shows the fascination with the Bolsheviks: the appropriate counter-measure for him was the organisation of another secret society, The Black Gang.

[54] F. Guizot, *Mémoires pour servir à l'histoire de mon temps* (Paris, 1858), i, p. 226.

[55] Quoted in Hugh Seton-Watson, *The Russian Empire 1801–1917* (Oxford, 1967), p. 163. It must be said in defence of Alexander that masonry and its mystical derivatives had nowhere been more widespread and fashionable in high circles than in Russia, as readers of *War and Peace* will remember. Metternich's pleasure at the

Soon afterwards, revolution seemed to be roaring away like a gorse fire. In July one at Naples imposed the acceptance of the Spanish constitution on Ferdinand. Its success was celebrated by official processions in which appeared the banners and insignia of the Carbonari, and was accompanied by open avowals of the role of the sect by the new government. In August a revolution took place in Portugal which was to lead to a constitutional régime in 1822. In February 1821 a rebellion against Turkish rule broke out in Wallachia, to be followed a month later by Ypsilanti's in Moldavia and a Greek rising in the Morea. Also in March came another Italian coup d'état, this time in Piedmont, whose king abdicated. At the end of 1821 the French government claimed to have unearthed and scotched a conspiracy at Saumur for a Bonapartist restoration, and throughout the following year faced a major attempt to revolutionise the army and a series of minor, but still disturbing, plots and coups de main. No less than nine major conspiracies were detected in seven months. Also in 1822, in April, came the discovery by the Russians of a Polish nationalist movement, the Patriotic Society. Yet everywhere by the following December the worst was over. The Austrians had invaded Naples and overthrown the revolution there. The Piedmontese movement had also been checked. In 1823 the French invaded Spain with the approval of the conservative powers and the battle of the Trocadero in August brought the Spanish revolution to an end. In 1824 a counter-revolution took place in Portugal. Only the Greek revolution—a very special case—was now still alive. The last kick of the revolutionary wave came, belatedly, in Russia, with the unsuccessful Decembrist conspiracy at the end of 1825.

These alarums and upheavals had important positive effects on the secret societies, as well as on their reputation, yet it is still very difficult to be sure of the parts they played. Some fitted the traditional mythology better than others. The secret societies of Poland appear to have derived directly from that country's masonic structure, though freemasons there, as elsewhere, were divided between the loyalists who placed busts of Alexander I in their lodges and those who aimed at national independence and sought links with secret societies in other countries to this end. Some of these Poles were in touch, too, with one of the Russian societies which gave birth to the Decembrist attempt, though no co-operation resulted. The Decembrists themselves were

Tsar's change of tack appears in a letter to Consalvi printed in Van Duerm, pp. 311–12.

certainly a secret society (or, rather, two) but resembled military conspirators in other countries rather than ritualists such as the Carbonari. The Greek cause was assisted by a secret society, Hetaira Philiké, although the national movement did not spring from this. In Spain, there was a connexion between the mutinies in the army and the presence of masonic lodges.

Yet almost any one of the facts of these years would alone have been enough to confirm the views of those who, like Metternich, saw everywhere the work of secret societies as the explanation of disorder. And the revolutionary wave certainly goes some way to justifying the view that in these years, secret societies were at the peak of their strength and influence—though the little they achieved in the end shows how exaggerated were the fears they aroused. In Germany, indeed, they appear to have been able to achieve nothing at all (though Metternich in 1824 thought that he had identified a Prussian branch of the Sublimes Maîtres Parfaits). Even their activities in France and Italy, where they attracted most attention and publicity, make it clear that they were wholly inadequate as effective revolutionary agencies.

In France existed the best-organised threat to a régime and it was posed by a revival of the Charbonnerie which was soon given much publicity. Although the French police were receiving reports about it as early as 1819, it only seems to have been in 1820 that it took serious shape, after the return from Naples of two young Frenchmen who had gone there to join in the revolution.[56] They brought back, it is said, a copy of the statutes of the Carboneria, and the Loge des amis de la vérité then turned itself into the 'Haute Vente' of a new Charbonnerie. After this, the organisers of the new society spread throughout France in 1821 a structure of 'ventes'. These met frequently and were to organise a national rebellion against the Bourbons. Frequently they made use of the opportunites provided by masonic lodges and this, of course, led to renewed suspicion of freemasonry. The founders themselves formed the Haute Vente, though its membership (originally largely made up of students or journalists) was soon afforced by much

---

[56] Nicolas Joubert, son of a member of the Convention; Pierre Dugied, a member of Les amis de la vérité since 1818. See by an early account which is still one of the best available based on personal knowledge, 'La Charbonnerie', by U. Trélat, in *Paris Révolutionnaire* (Paris, 1838) (by various authors), ii, pp. 275–341. For a helpful historical introduction, see A. Calmette, 'Les Carbonari en France sous la Restauration (1821–30)', in *La Révolution de 1848*, ix, x, 1913, but this is now surpassed by Alan B. Spitzer's *Old Hatreds and Young Hopes. The French Carbonari against the Restoration* (Cambridge, Mass., 1971) which, unhappily, was not available to me until this book was in proof.

more prominent and experienced politicians, among them, it is said, liberal deputies, and, above all, Lafayette.

Whether these were leaders or led, however, is hard to say. Lafayette, said Guizot, was not the chief but the instrument and ornament of the secret plotters.[57] This introduces a major difficulty in establishing the precise aims of the organisation: many of those concerned were not even republican, let alone social revolutionaries, though they might be determined opponents of the régime.[58] Some wanted to bring in Napoleon II, others to crown the Duc d'Orléans (the son of the notorious former Grand Master of French freemasonry). Effectively, the former 'comité directeur' of the liberal opposition, a far from revolutionary body whose main achievements had been electoral, led the new Charbonnerie. While aims might be doubtful, however, there was agreement that political work in parliament might be combined with insurrection, and it was to discontent in the army that the leaders of the Charbonnerie looked for success in this.

Ventes were spread through many garrison towns, many of them coming to the knowledge of the authorities. They had good reason for alarm. The army was known to contain discontented soldiers; there had already been signs of disaffection when an expeditionary force was being got ready to move against the Spanish revolution. But although the conspirators tried hard to exploit this and subsequent irritations it soon became obvious that their efforts were marred by carelessness and over-confidence. Two outbreaks at Belfort and Saumur planned for December 1821 misfired badly. Much had already reached the ears of the authorities by then; reports of Carbonarist activities were coming in from all over France. Yet, as appeared eventually, there was no real danger. The most important legacy of the whole scare was, once more, a mythological one; the story of the Four Sergeants of La Rochelle who refused to save their lives by identifying the leaders of the Charbonnerie and were therefore executed, now entered radical hagiography. For the next half-century they would be invoked by radical orators seeking to move a popular audience. Practically, though, the ventes had not much mattered. They had not recruited many soldiers—above all, few officers—and of those who did join, too, some afterwards seemed to have far from revolutionary aims. There were also important continuing factors which always made the army an unpromising subject for conspiratorial cultivation.[59]

[57] Guizot, i, p. 239.
[58] Though Trélat (p. 283) says 'l'association était républicaine', he also admits (p. 303) that it contained crypto-Orleanists.
[59] See P. Savigear, 'Carbonarism and the French army, 1815–1824', *History*, 1969.

The whole episode is marked by incoherence, uncertainty and unrealism. Nonetheless, a spate of trials which followed, notably that of the Four Sergeants of La Rochelle, kept public excitement and alarm at a high pitch.[60] In France as elsewhere, too, mystery strengthened the myth; we have the paradox of people fearing the work of the secret societies all the more because no successful or unsuccessful revolution ever took place to settle the question of their power. Buonarroti, who knew a lot about them, was very contemptuous of the Charbonnerie.[61] Moreover, however reactionary French governments might wish to be, they ruled over a constitutional state in which certain legal opportunities for opposition were never altogether extinguished; to that extent a major influence strengthening the secret societies in other countries was absent. Nor was the régime very cruel. There were nineteen death sentences in two years of which eleven were carried out. After 1823 at latest, the Charbonnerie was moribund and other secret societies never succeeded in rivalling it in its extent or its power to alarm the authorities. Instead, it was the Chevaliers de la Foi who were now talked about; they were believed to be inspiring the seemingly theocratic reaction now in full swing. In 1824-5 the police began to relax their interest in conspiracies and less was heard of the danger of secret societies from officials. The Frenchmen who had joined them turned increasingly to other methods of opposition.[62]

In Italy, the successful movements in Naples and Piedmont did much more to make secret societies seem dangerous. Yet at Naples, though Carbonari had been meeting and plotting for years, the actual outbreak of the bloodless revolution of July 1820 was unplanned and, to all intents and purposes, accidental. General Pepe jumped in to take over its leadership; he was not himself a member of the sect but now joined it. An army of Carbonari soldiers and countrymen poured into Naples and the newly-appointed Regent, the Duke of Calabria, appeared before them wearing the Carbonari colours. The revolutionary movement nonetheless remained fundamentally divided; only the paralysis of will shown by the King had made its success at all possible. Essentially, it stemmed from two impulses, a real popular discontent, based on disappointment with promised land reform, and an upper-class constitutionalist movement, perhaps regretting the era of Murat and always present and discontented since 1815. This now gave the

---

[60] It was usual to print as pamphlets the proceedings at trials or speeches made at them. See, e.g., *Les Carbonari dévoilés, ou discours que M. de Marchangy, avocat général, a prononcé pour soutenir l'accusation dans l'affaire dite de la Rochelle* (Montpellier, n.d. [1822?]).

[61] Lehning, p. 51.   [62] Trélat, p. 334.

Neapolitan revolution its shibboleth in the Spanish constitution to which Ferdinand was required to swear loyalty. What the revolution showed before its suppression in March 1821 was that on the one hand it owed no central direction to the Carbonari or any other secret body (for, in effect, it had not had central direction at all) but that, on the other, the sect had adherents of every rank and station. As Metternich wrote after the suppression of the revolution, 'it counts among its initiates prelates, priests, citizens of distinguished rank'—and this was more frightening than popular discontent.[63] This very comprehensiveness in the movement makes it easier to understand the divisions and quarrellings which at once followed the Neapolitan putsch and indeed cut right across the Carbonari themselves, who turned out to be divided both from one another and from the soldiers who were the other major component of the 'revolutionary' coalition.[64]

In Piedmont, the story was not quite so unhappy, but the secret societies were again far from unambiguously helpful to the revolution. Here, too, the problem of responsibility is linked to distinctions among the revolutionaries. Some, young noblemen and army officers, are known to have had masonic backgrounds or connexions and they had been long at work to insinuate constitutional reforms in Sardinia. Some of them had connexions with the Adelfi and Federati. After the outbreak of the Neapolitan revolution the influence of the Carbonari can be detected, too, and this helps to explain the developing nature of the conspiracy, which was increasingly shaped by the need to divert Austrian attention from the suppression of the Neapolitan revolution. What followed is well known. The Austrian invasion of Naples in March 1821 detonated a Piedmontese putsch, only to reveal hopeless discordancy between those who should have supported it. Again, there was little ground for the view that the real revolutionary danger lay in the expert manipulation of discontent by the concealed masterminds of the secret societies. If it did, then the secret societies made a sorry hash of their opportunities; their achievement in 1820–1 was to install Austrian garrisons in the two important independent states hitherto without them.

This was not the end of the positive history of the Carbonari (they were even to achieve another substantial rising in the Papal States, in 1831), nor did people cease to believe in the danger it presented, but

[63] Quoted in A. Reinerman, 'Metternich and the Papal condemnation of the Carbonari, 1821', *Catholic Historical Review*, 1969, p. 60.
[64] Sòriga, pp. 90–1. Freemasonry at Naples showed the same factionalism. At one time in 1821 *three* Grand Orients claimed to direct it.

we may leave it here. All the evidence of 1820–1 should have told against the mythology of the secret societies. That it did not is a sad reflexion of human gullibility. It might however be argued, in part justification of those who clung to the myth that, whatever the practical importance of the secret societies, there actually was at this time, more than any other, a real attempt to co-ordinate the activities of revolutionary societies internationally.

This attempt (it has been argued) can be seen as the first step in a series of developments towards the internationalising of revolutionary movements which led logically to the creation of the First International. Yet Dr Lehning, who has put forward and strongly maintained this view, himself believes that the activities of the secret societies came to a climax at this point and were, even so, without revolutionary result. 1823 is, for him, practically the 'end of the activities of the revolutionary secret societies, and of their efforts to change the political régime of the Holy Alliance'.[65] This judgment is based, essentially, on the disappointment felt by Buonarroti and his associates, who had been striving for years to establish some sort of international direction of the secret societies and local revolutionary movements through the Sublimes Maîtres Parfaits. Even before 1815, Buonarroti's hopes for this body had gone far beyond the recreation of a French republic; he had seen it as the instrument of international social revolution, adopting different forms in different countries, but moving towards a universal goal. He seems to have remodelled it always with this in view, or, at least, so his opponents believed. During the early years of the Restoration he had kept up his contacts with France and Italy and had multiplied them, extending them to Swiss and German revolutionaries in 1819–20.[66]

In these years, Buonarroti seems to have succeeded in gathering into his hands the threads of conspiracies as distinct as those of the Parisian 'comité directeur' and the German republicans. Buonarroti was not, of course, the only person trying to co-ordinate the secret societies of different countries. The persisting belief of the Austrians that the Italian societies had a directing centre in Paris, for example,

[65] Lehning, p. 51.

[66] See Valtancoli's interpretation of Buonarroti's introduction of a special third grade in his order with the aim of issuing masonic structures to establish control over the Carbonari by the Sublimes Maîtres Parfaits (Saitta, i, p. 97). It has been said, too, that the Adelfi were taken over by the Sublimes Maîtres Parfaits in 1817 (Sòriga, p. 114). The authorities knew about this in the early 1820s; it became generally known with the publication of the memoirs of the police-spy Wit at the end of the decade (see below, p. 326).

may well have had as its germ contacts between Rey, the French founder of L'Union, and the Guelfi.[67] Another exercise in this view had been Wit's trip to Paris on behalf of German societies in 1820. Yet Buonarroti achieved more than they, though his successes were largely formal and meant little in practice. During his Geneva years he was not lost to the sight of the French police, though they did not begin to take serious interest in him until a relatively late date. For the most part his conspiratorial activities, marked by orthodox masonic activity, escaped notice until after 1821.[68] When they were then exposed, Buonarroti's reputation as a conspirator was enormously enhanced in the eyes of Metternich and his police. Now there can be little doubt that the 'Great Firmament' did have a brief, though ineffective, reality in that Buonarroti succeeded in knotting together the formal structure of secret societies of many lands under the Sublimes Maîtres Parfaits. It was, to that extent, a true international revolutionary centre. But it is not clear that it ever consisted of more than Buonarroti himself and one or two others, or that it ever directed events. In any case the revolutionary failures blew to the winds the hopes built on it. Yet by then enormous importance was being given to it by the European authorities.

One special factor helping to explain this was a sudden improvement in the information reaching the police in the turmoil of 1820–1 and the exploitation of this to get more information and make new arrests. More interesting material was forthcoming and it at once suggested a much higher degree of co-ordinated effort among the conspirators than ever before. In Italy, above all, they were obviously in touch across the frontiers of the different states, as the timing of the Piedmontese outbreak itself suggested. Confalonieri, the Lombard nobleman, whose trial and imprisonment was to give him so important a place in the martyrology of the Risorgimento, fell into the hands of the Austrians because of information given away by a prisoner of the Piedmontese police. A member of the Sublimes Maîtres Parfaits who was an Austrian prisoner similarly gave away a circle at Parma. Thus there swiftly emerged a picture of an attempt by a central international body to control operations throughout Italy, France and Germany. This was in principle true. Though the search for the location of this body was

[67] Pia Onnis, Rassegna storica del Risorgimento, 1964, p. 487. Buonarroti favoured freemasonry it seems both as a cover and as a recruiting ground (p. 495). The reminiscence of the work of Weishaupt and Knigge would have struck some of his opponents.
[68] On this period, see M. Vuilleumier, 'Buonarroti et ses sociétés secrètes à Genève', AHRF, 1970.

wrongly diverted to Paris, this was indeed what Buonarroti sought to do.

The name and a lot of the workings of the Sublimes Maîtres Parfaits soon came to light.[69] The society had, it seemed, begun to exercise some direction over other societies in 1818 (the date when, in fact, it appears to have been reorganised as Le Monde) and it had for effective purposes merged with the Adelfi. Although it seemed that the Sublimes Maîtres Parfaits were very lax about carrying out their own ceremonies of admission and precautions, an alarming picture of their activities was quickly available. In one blow it received its greatest elaboration when, in 1821, one of the most notorious figures in the history of the secret societies suddenly decided to talk to the Austrian military governor in Milan, Bubna.

This was one of the most celebrated informers of the period, Johannes Wit von Dörring, a Dane.[70] After acting as emissary to London and Paris for German secret societies he went from Paris in April 1821 to Italy, where he was to act as correspondent of a German newspaper. This was just after the Piedmontese revolution. The Prussians asked for his arrest at Turin; he avoided this, but gave a certain amount of information about the secret societies to which he belonged to a Piedmontese agent. Arrested finally in September in Savoy, he was handed over to the Austrians. At Milan, he was approached with some skill by Bubna who won his confidence and, said Wit, brought him to his senses.[71] To him he gave a lot of information. He then escaped to Switzerland and made his way to Bayreuth, where he gave the authorities even more information about the secret societies of Germany and their links with those of Italy: this was communicated to the Piedmontese government. Eventually, to cap his indiscretion, he wrote his memoirs and thus cashed in on the interest the secret societies aroused.

Wit's information was rich in detail and had to be taken seriously. He confirmed the existence of an international threat facing governments in the Sublimes Maîtres Parfaits, displayed some of the links between Germany, Switzerland and Italy, and averred the existence of a secret, anonymous directorate of subversive activities. As he was to

[69] On this see Sandonà, *passim*, and the declaration of Giovanni Manzotti of Reggio, quoted in Lemmi, pp. 64–78. An edition of Lefranc's *Le voile levé* (Liège, 1826), 'avec continuation des meilleurs ouvrages', may have been the first work to draw attention to them (p. 394).

[70] I use the spelling of his name on the German edition of his autobiography, *Fragmente aus meinem Leben und meiner Zeit* (Leipzig, 1827–8). 'Jean Witt', *Les sociétés secrètes de France et d'Italie, ou Fragments de ma vie et de mon temps* (Paris, 1830) is a version of part only of these memoirs.

[71] *Fragmente*, i, p. 292.

put it later in his memoirs, even secret societies themselves with revolutionary aims might be manipulated unknown to themselves by this central body because the central tendency of the Grand Firmament was to take over other secret societies even when their ends were not its own.[72] He explained, it is true, that he had never been formally received in any secret society except by virtue of passing into its membership as a freemason.[73] He also left the authorities with a clear impression that the Sublimes Maîtres Parfaits was anti-religious, as well as republican.

Wit was thus of the greatest importance in strengthening the fears of the authorities. But he may well have been surpassed in usefulness to them by another young man who fell into the hands of the Milanese police in 1823. The contribution of the police to the myths reached a climax in this discovery, for which Buonarroti himself must bear much of the blame. In the aftermath of the Piedmontese and Neapolitan revolts the Austrian police in Italy were especially alert. The régime had already made several arrests and had launched an important series of political trials. It was in these circumstances that a young conspirator and associate of Buonarroti, Alexandre Andryane, entered Italy at the end of 1822, only to be arrested by the Milanese police three weeks later.[74] Besides doing a great deal of damage to the network of international conspiracy, this arrest, it can be argued, did more than any other single event to substantiate and inflate official fear of secret societies in this period. This was because of the revelations which followed, which appeared to confirm the information supplied by earlier informants, and did so with documents.

Andryane was a wealthy young Parisian, of Belgian family and romantic temperament, who had no very obvious purpose in life until 1820.[75] Then, under his sister's influence, he decided to pull himself together and in 1820 went to Geneva to study. There he met the determining influence of his life, Buonarroti. Andryane went to him for lessons in Italian and singing. One day, in the middle of a lesson, Buonarroti began to talk about the Neapolitan revolution. Having said it was the work of the Carbonari he then fell silent and

[72] *Fragmente*, i, pp. 23–4. It is an interesting detail that he seems to have thought the Sublimes Maîtres Parfaits only to have been founded in 1821.

[73] Lemmi, pp. 31–2.

[74] Alexandre Philippe Andryane eventually published two books of reminiscences, *Mémoires d'un prisonnier d'état* (Paris, 1838–9) and *Souvenirs de Genève* (Paris, 1839). He was arrested 18 January 1823.

[75] Andryane, *Mémoires d'un prisonnier d'état*, p. 17: 'il m'était difficile d'échapper aux dangers que devait rencontrer à Paris un jeune homme de dix-huit ans, dont le père jouissait d'une fortune considérable.'

said no more.[76] Andryane's excitement was awoken. Some time passed, the older man continuing from time to time to drop hints of what he knew. Finally, in October 1821 Andryane was admitted by Buonarroti himself to a secret society, probably the Sublimes Maîtres Parfaits.[77]

Buonarroti's conspiratorial activity was at this time reaching its climax and Andryane began to be closely involved in it. He was greatly impressed by the accounts of the spreading influence of his society which now reached him as a member and nearly twenty years later paid tribute in his *Souvenirs de Genève* to Buonarroti's astonishing personal achievement, whose full extent was now becoming apparent to him. 'C'est une chose étrange, et sans exemple peut-être à notre époque,' he justly recorded, 'la persévérance de cet homme qui travaille depuis trente ans sans jamais s'arrêter, comme une araignée dans son trou, à ourder les fils d'une conspiration que tous les governements ont brisés tout à tout, et qu'il ne se lasse jamais de renouer.'[78] Certainly this was Buonarroti's own image of himself. It was during this period of their association that he told Andryane that he had been involved in the Malet plot.[79] Meanwhile, the younger man accompanied him on trips to Nyon and to the Jura to meet other revolutionaries, and was sent by himself on missions to Lyon and Paris. Nonetheless, he was beginning to feel some scepticism that so much activity should achieve so little and decided at the end of 1822 to go to Italy. Buonarroti who had been bothering him for some time to undertake further tasks, again commissioned him, this time as a messenger. Andryane was given letters and other documents to Italian revolutionaries whom Buonarroti hoped to galvanise into action to hinder the intervention about to be launched against Spain. All these documents were seized by the Austrian police when Andryane was arrested. The cipher which protected some of them was soon broken and the world of Buonarroti's international secret societies was suddenly revealed in detail; the efforts of the Swiss and German conspirators to co-ordinate their activities with the Italians and French were exposed. He said that the Sublimes Maîtres Parfaits had been in existence since the French Revolution. Furthermore, the documents included explanations of the grades and organisation of the Sublimes Maîtres Parfaits, the credo of the Sublimes Elus, descriptions of initi-

[76] Andryane, *Souvenirs*, i, p. 154.

[77] Andryane, *Souvenirs*, ii, pp. 1–12. The description of the ceremony is interesting because (among other details) the participants wore masonic insignia which, Buonarroti explained to Andryane, was for prudential reasons; if they were surprised, the gathering could be represented as an ordinary lodge.

[78] ii, p. 141.   [79] ii, p. 207.

ation rites and the statutes of the society. It was not the whole story—Andryane had not been initiated into the highest grade and could not, therefore, reveal that it was referred to as the 'Areopagus' and involved adherence to communist principles, and some of his documents were out of date—but it was more than enough. So highly did the Austrian government think of these that copies and summaries of the seized papers were at once circulated to other governments. Meanwhile, Andryane's case was linked—without justification, it seems—to that of Confalonieri and he was tried and sentenced to death. This sentence was then commuted to life imprisonment. After eight years in the Spielberg (where, even among much more grievous sufferings, it must still have been especially irritating to have a spiritual adviser who recommended, among other things, a work by J. A. Starck) he was pardoned and returned to France where he published the memoirs from which a wider public learnt still more about the secret societies.

There is much that remains mysterious about this episode, not least the difficulty of explaining Buonarroti's conduct in entrusting such dangerous materials to a young and relatively inexperienced emissary. Andryane was himself struck by this, as well he might be, given the compromising character of his portfolio of conspiratorial odds and ends. He put it down to Buonarroti's experience that men needed mystification to move them.[80] Whatever else may be suggested by the episode, however, this is not the place to pursue this topic. For our purposes the arrest was important because of the fresh and circumstantial confirmation it gave to the long-cherished belief of many officials that there really did exist a great international secret society, co-ordinating the movements of revolutionaries in all countries and analogous in its forms and rituals to the masonic systems of the eighteenth century about which so much had been written. It gave life to the spectre of one great force behind all the separate manifestations of Europe's revolution. Metternich and his police were as anxious to

[80] 'Etrange manie que toutes ces formules, ces statues, ces chiffres, ces diplômes auxquels il attache autant d'importance qu'on en mettait jadis à des titres de noblesse ou de chevalerie, comme s'il était nécessaire de s'imposer toutes ces vaines formalités pour bien s'entendre et bien agir! . . . Mais il pense, lui, que les hommes ont besoin, pour former une association politique efficace et permanente, d'être liés entre eux par des signes, des mystères qui flattent leur amour-propre, et donnent à la société dont ils font partie un air d'importance et de consistance que toute la moralité et l'estime réciproque des individus ne sauraient obtenir; il en appelle à son expérience, et peut-être a-t-il raison, car les hochets sont de tous les temps et de tous les pays, pour les grands enfants que nous honorons du nom d'hommes.' *Souvenirs*, ii, pp. 328–9. See also *Mémoires d'un prisonnier d'état*, p. 27.

be gulled as the enthusiasts for whom Buonarroti prepared his inspiring mystifications.

Moreover, Andryane's information fitted easily into the picture already provided in many different local variations by informers and spies. Many of these men had themselves belonged to secret societies and their evidence was specious. Their reports helped to give a special colour and apparent consistency to all the diverse conspiratorial activities on which they reported in these years. The career of one of them, the Italian Valtancoli, has been illuminated by the examination of his reports to the Tuscan police, for whom he had begun to work at the Restoration.[81] He was something of a specialist in masonic ritual, enthusiastically distinguishing rites and organisations in the underworld of Napoleonic Italy with all the collector's passion. Besides having much to say about Carbonari and Guelfismo, he appears to have revealed in 1820 the existence of the Sublimes Maîtres Parfaits, though he thought they were called Adelfia.[82] He also reported on the masonic rites which had remained unincorporated in the official Napoleonic structure; one of them, the Old Scottish Templars, has, it has been pointed out, ritual and legendary affinities with the Illuminati, whose influence it may well reflect. From his reports there emerged analogies between the egalitarian doctrines of the two bodies and the conspiratorial techniques employed. Similarly, his distinction of the third grade of the Carbonarist maestro as that of the 'ultra'-revolutionaries also suggested Illuminati connexions.

This ritualistic and symbolic emphasis was important and (the police believed) valuable because other sources were turning up fragments of information which could be fitted together in a way reminiscent of the full-scale mythologies propounded by people like Barruel and Lombard. The Illuminati elements were central to this and often make their appearance in the records. A Piedmontese agent operating in Strasbourg reported in October 1821 that 'la ville de Coire dans les Grisons fut pour longtemps un point où les Carbonari d'Italie venaient recevoir des Illuminati d'Allemagne de nouvelles instructions sur la manière dont il fallait se déguiser depuis que les affaires de Naples avaient dévoilés aux Gouvernemens les moyens de reconnaissance que les anciens Carbonari avaient entr'eux'.[83] A few years later, Wit was telling the public in his memoirs, too, that in the seventh and last grade of the Carbonari, reserved to very few (of whom,

[81] See Francovich, pp. 17–21, 26–7.
[82] Saitta, ii, p. 85.
[83] Quoted in Lemmi, pp. 29–30.

he said, he had been one), it was revealed that the sect's purposes were the same as those of the Illuminati. The prince-bishops of the Carbonari (as he describes the grade) coincided exactly, he said, with the 'homo res' of Weishaupt's sect and its initiates swore the ruin of all religion and all government, however it might be organised. All means were permitted to them—murder, poison, perjury. (Let it not be forgotten, he adds, that when the Illuminati were exposed there was found among other noxious substances 'tinctura ad abortum faciendum'.) The masters of this grade laugh over the mass of Carbonarists who only seek the liberty and independence of Italy which, for the initiates, are only means, not ends.[84]

At such a point, the power of the mythology is seen at its height in the easy integration of political conspiracies which had some reality with the whole inheritance from the previous century. The new 'facts' joined other evidence to become sources themselves, not merely for positive history of the secret societies (though historians have done much with such materials) but also for its mythology. Wit, Valtancoli and others fed it for the future by providing those familiar with the sensational literature of the preceding twenty years with material confirming it. There were, after all, confessions by men who had been deeply involved in the events they described. This had a cumulative effect. The reinforcement which the informers and spies gave to the myth was sometimes effective at a very high level indeed. So was the unhappy Andryane's evidence, and so at one further remove, were the untiring and practically ineffective labours of Buonarroti.

Plentiful information is then much of the explanation of the extraordinary atmosphere of the early 1820s. Otherwise normal, sane and balanced statesmen showed themselves capable of astonishing fearfulness and credulity. Almost everywhere, the danger was exaggerated and essentially sporadic and disjunct conspiracy was misread as evidence of the existence of central, co-ordinated direction. Those who were so inclined made the most of it. Metternich in 1824 circulated the German courts with a memorandum (drawing heavily on Andryane's information) explaining in detail his picture of the international conspiracy agency to which Buonarroti belonged.[85] The prosecution speech at the trial of the La Rochelle sergeants in 1822, the reports reaching the French government of the existence of eight hundred thousand members of the Charbonnerie,[86] the near-panic over student

[84] Witt, pp. 21–2.
[85] A version can be found in Rinieri, *Silvio Pellico*, ii, pp. 26–66.
[86] Savigear, p. 200.

unrest in Germany are all manifestations of the same alarm. The
Russian government (except in its worries over Poland) lagged a little
in succumbing, but in 1822 it, too, prohibited all secret societies and
masonic lodges. After the Decembrist attempt three years later, which
led to the final rejection by the autocracy of any compromise with the
liberals, there was, of course, to be no relaxation in this government's
almost hysterically excessive suspiciousness.

The Papal reaction was inevitably a special one; some smugness was
shown by officials who reflected that if only Clement XII and Benedict XIV had been heeded, much trouble might have been avoided.[87]
There was no unwillingness, of course, after the work of the Papal
police had revealed the almost total penetration of the apparatus of
state (including the police itself) by the sects, to take the secret society
threat seriously. Yet there was delay in taking spiritual action against
secret societies outside the Papal States.[88] The Bull *Ecclesiam a Jesu
Christo* which excommunicated members of the Carbonari (and
probably, therefore, did much to diminish the society's popular appeal)
was not published until September 1821, six months after the Austrian
invasion of Naples and the suppression of the revolution there. Metternich had always found Consalvi, the Papal Secretary of State, cooper-
ative, and at the outbreak of the Neapolitan revolution had urged
almost at once that the spiritual weapons of the Holy See should be
deployed against the secret societies as against the freemasons in the
previous century. Consalvi was not unwilling to help, but two difficulties stood in the way. However noxious the political doctrines of
the Carbonari might be, they asserted that they were loyal Roman
Catholics and there was no evidence that this was not true; they would
hardly be excommunicated as enemies of the Church and proponents
of philosophical error until it was provided. The second, practical,
consideration was that so long as the Neapolitan revolution was
unsuppressed, action against the Carbonari might lead to a Neapolitan
attack on the Papacy.[89] Time removed both obstacles. Though at
Laibach in January 1824 Consalvi still declined to issue a condemnation, the Austrians entered Naples two months later; all that remained
was to persuade the Papal government that the moment was now
ripe and that plausible evidence of the anti-religious nature of the
Carbonari existed. This still took another six months, in spite of urgings

[87] See Consalvi to Metternich, 23 August 1820, in Van Duerm, p. 397.
[88] On what follows, see Reinerman, pp. 55 ff.
[89] Consalvi summarised his views in a letter to Metternich of 3 August 1820
(see Van Duerm, pp. 264–5 and also p. 281).

from other governments besides that of Vienna. Finally, the Austrians found for Consalvi the evidence he wanted that religious charges could justifiably be brought against the Carbonari. Some of the rituals of initiation were prima facie blasphemous and possibly served only as a device to win over Roman Catholics by simulating Christian aims and doctrines. The preparation of the brief was now rapid. Metternich's criticism was solicited (he could only 'pay a just tribute of admiration to so excellent a work')[90] and it was promulgated.

Ecclesiam repeated much of *In Eminenti* and threw out the assertion that if not an offshoot of freemasonry, the Carbonari were certainly an imitation of it. Nonetheless, the condemnation rested on the blasphemous rituals, the allegation of a special hatred for the Papacy and the aim of overthrowing it. Excommunication was again reserved to the Pope himself. It was an important utterance, the first authoritative pronouncement to the Faithful everywhere that the Church believed the political secret societies to be a danger organically linked to that discerned by the eighteenth-century Popes in freemasonry. The Church to that extent—and it was by implication an enormous extent— had thus thrown its authority behind the secret society mythology.

Of course, this was far from the end of the story. Four years later, *Quo Graviora* condemned the sects as a whole, stressing their essential unity. Two more Bulls followed even before 1848, *Traditi* (24 May 1829) and *Qui Pluribus* (9 November 1846) and the climax was to be the renewed condemnation of freemasonry by Pius IX and Leo XIII.[91]

There were more immediate consequences, too, in that the Papal diplomatic activity was now deployed beside Austrian in urging other Italian governments to act against the secret societies. No doubt many Roman Catholics, laity and clergy alike, now felt obliged to abandon the Carbonari and this must have contributed to the sect's decline and, therefore, if the conservative interpretation was correct, to a declining danger. But the endorsement in the Papal pronouncement of what so many people believed about the secret societies and its reinforcement of the myth of their essentially anti-Christian nature was in the long run the most important result. The most extreme fears now seemed to be authorised; the Pope had endorsed the general assumption among conservatives in the mid-1820s that nice distinctions need not

---

[90] quoted in Reinerman, p. 65.
[91] Though vigorous denunciations by Pius did not scotch rumours that he was himself a freemason, supposedly after admission to a lodge in Uruguay during his residence there. See *AQC*, 1913, p. 218.

be made within the revolutionary movement.[92] It made it still easier for people to hold that its heart was a conspiracy built round the example, if not the leadership, of the freemasons, ancient enemies of order, civil and religious.[93]

The paradoxes and curious reversals in the growth of the mythology are very striking. Successful police action against the societies increased the authorities' alarm because of what they discovered. Papal condemnation led to greater fear of them though it probably cut deeply into their popular support. Their practical failures, among them those of Buonarroti (surely the most inflated of bogies) helped the survival and strengthening of old fears of the ever present danger the societies were supposed to embody. As the continuing popularity of Barruel and the transmission of his tradition through such writers as Lombard de Langres shows, the mass of new details exposed by the receding of the revolutionary wave found an accepted structure of interpretation readily to hand. That much of the new data was baseless did not make it less acceptable and influential. Moreover, at least in France there was now a considerable newspaper press to assure its circulation. The police, their informers, spies, their seizures of papers and interrogations threw up a mass of material and often resulted in trials, some of which were given much publicity.

There was also another important new source of information. This was the mass of publication which aimed to satisfy commercially the demand for explanation of Europe's turmoils. Much of it took the form of 'revelation' literature comparable to that produced after the Illuminati discoveries and during the French Revolution. Most of its expressions testify to the enduring sources of the myth's strength: the ideas of secrecy, subversion, hidden superiors, ancient historical roots which offered keys to rapid, accelerating and inexplicable change. Those who wrote in the opposing sense, who attempted to reduce the

---

[92] Some people pointed out, nonetheless, that Austrian diplomatic activity was what lay behind the portentous language of the brief. This was suggested by De Pradt (*L'Europe et l'Amérique en 1821* (Paris, 1822), ii, p. 208). Grégoire later said that *Quo Graviora*, too, had been published (against the advice of several cardinals) thanks to Austrian pressure (H. Grégoire, *Histoire des sectes religieuses* (Paris, 1828), ii, p. 381).

[93] See, e.g., the edict of Francesco IV, Duke of Modena, 1 March 1824: 'tutti queste sette non sono che emanazioni della presente setta dei Franchi Massoni o Liberi Muratori, la quale giudicando che il Mondo fosse ormai abbastanza imbevuto del veleno anticristiano negli animi, credette giunto il momento di poter finalemente, conspire il suo gran progretto di rovesciare ognuna Autorità Ecclesiastica e secolare ed immaginò a tal fine di dare diversi nomi, segni, diversi emblemi. . . .' (quoted in d'Ayala, *ASPN*, 1898, p. 818).

temperature and take a more balanced view did not achieve very much.[94] Success went to those who rushed to exploit a public avid for an 'inside' story. In 1822, for example, General Pepe published at Paris his account of the Neapolitan revolution.[95] It contained much about the Carbonari, its first reference being to the exiled Bourbons' encouragement of them in 1813. The society, he said, 'fut introduite par le pouvoir absolu, qui la propagea dans notre royaume, lorsque le roi, qui se trouvait en Sicilie, en eut besoin. Alors, l'Eglise de Rome, loin d'excommunier les Carbonari, faisait pêcher par les moines et les prêtres qu'il suffisait des signes de Carbonaro pour que saint Pierre ouvrit la porte du paradis.'[96] Pepe praised the society for its contribution to the maintenance of order in the countryside at a moment of popular upheaval and drew attention to the presence in its ranks of 'les principaux propriétaires, les hommes les plus recommendables, les ministres du culte, les artisans et les cultivateurs'. Undoubtedly, such an authority was a powerful advocate, but the implication for the mythology of the secret societies was the same as if he had attacked the Carbonari: that they were, indeed, an important and deeply entrenched force, which (he asserted specifically) was a branch of freemasonry.[97]

Pepe's remarks were incidental to a personal justification; there were others who wrote more directly about the secret societies. Material was readily available. The Naples Carbonari openly sold books and pamphlets containing accounts of their activities and financed them by this means.[98] The later decline into factionalism of the Carbonari after the revolutionary failures was another source of publicity as people sought to present their own version of events. Blatant sensationalists contributed to this flow of material, too. One such, writing under a pseudonym, published in 1821 a volume consisting largely of documents already available at Naples.[99] It was a blow in the political struggle of France for, it said, 'les jacobins de la république, les soi-disant libéraux de tous les temps et de tous les pays, les illuminés et les Carbonari ont toujours visé au même but, travaillé aux mêmes résultats'.[100] Its most interesting point today is its emphasis on the

---

[94] Nodier's scepticism about the role of freemasonry has been noted (above, p. 234); Peacock made fun of the Illuminati; De Quincey explodes the 'bugbear' in an essay.

[95] *Relation des événements politiques et militaires qui ont eu lieu à Naples en 1820 et 1821, adressée à S.M. le roi des Deux-Siciles, par le Général Guillaume Pépé.*

[96] p. 43.   [97] pp. 41–2.

[98] *Memoirs of the Secret Societies of the South of Italy,* p. vii.

[99] 'Saint-Edme', *Constitution et organisation des Carbonari* (Paris, 1821).

[100] p. i.

Carbonarist aims of national unity for Italy, but in 1821 its apparently solid documentation—and the Carbonari rituals were packed with their own mythological history—must have given powerful support to the historical mythology. The author also gave special emphasis to links between Carbonari and freemasons and his documents revealed once more the classical scenario of a secret only gradually revealed to the initiate.[101]

A much more objective and important book appeared in England the same year, the *Memoirs of the Secret Societies of the South of Italy*. This was to be one of the most celebrated books familiarising a wide public with the organisation and practices of the Carbonari. It was by an intelligent and well-informed observer, Bartholdy, the Prussian Consul-General at Rome.[102]

To begin by saying that Bartholdy contributed to the myth is misleading but true, for though his book remains one of the best on the subject it specifically and explicitly took as its point of departure the rubbish so often talked about it. As he pointed out in his preface, 'it is the mystery which envelops these Societies—it is the notions of extraordinary importance attached to them, which prevent impartiality, and may mislead those who are called upon to be judges in the cause. The veil of secrecy being removed from these Societies, it will readily be perceived, that the prison and the scaffold are not the arms with which to oppose them: and that persecution can only tend to exasperate the multitude to a degree which may lead them to sacrifice their repose, their conscience and their duty to the state, in order to maintain institutions puerile in themselves, yet dangerous because they open a vast field of influence, to the enthusiast, to the imposter, and to the ambitious man.'[103] This was a clear enough statement of the author's standpoint and a creditable one. In the execution of the book, too, there is a reassuring and unusual sobriety; a list of the materials employed (for the most part Neapolitan), including pamphlets, Carbonari

[101] pp. 7–8.

[102] The history of this famous and successful book is complicated. It has been helpfully clarified by V. Sperber in 'Il cavalier Bartholdy ed i Carbonari', *Rassegna storica del Risorgimento*, 1970, pp. 3–47, an article which argues powerfully for the objective quality of Bartholdy's book which first appeared in its English translation, published at London, in 1821. In the following year a pirated German translation of this version, with other material added, appeared at Weimar. (It was often said to be by Wit von Dörring.) Then in 1822, Bartholdy published the authentic German edition at Stuttgart and Tübingen and this, too, contains material not in the English edition. An Italian translation from the English did not appear until 1904.

[103] Bartholdy, pp. v–vi.

statutes and official documents, is followed by a cool and critical text which makes good use of substantial quotations from original materials. These provide the basis for a circumstantial and still helpful historical account of the Carbonari's role at the collapse of the Napoleonic régime; this firmly demonstrates the connexion of the sect with the aim of Italian independence. Bartholdy also stresses its links with constitutionalism—that is, with the desire of the dominant élites of the Kingdom of Naples to resist any recovery of royal power whether under Murat or the Bourbons. With this aim the Carbonari was spread among the peasantry of Calabria and the Abruzzi, to whom the religious symbols of the Order made a special appeal.[104]

Nonetheless, Bartholdy inevitably provided in the course of his argument sensational details which did much to corroborate what was already believed of the Carbonari as inheritors of the wicked designs of other secret societies. His illustration of a vendita in solemn conclave—wearing top hats—may have been reassuring, but the facsimiles of documents decorated with skull and crossbones and Phrygian caps must have been the reverse. His lurid account of passages in the history of the Decisi and Philadelphes, with their horrible crimes of assassination, would remain in the mind, all the more convincing because expounded in so sober a manner. This would make it all the more creditable when he asserted of some branches of the Carbonari that they shamelessly preached 'the disgusting doctrines of horror and jacobinism'.[105] He asserted the existence of an 'ultra' Carbonarism not satisfied with the Neapolitan revolution, grouped in 'Jacobine' lodges under the exotic name of the 'solitary and scattered Greeks' (I Greci solitari e dispersi).

Though Bartholdy's assessment of the future was cool (he did not anticipate anything but decline for the Carbonari), he drew attention to the astonishing growth of the sect in the previous year and, in particular, the number of clergy it succeeded in attracting. Possibly still more alarming, though, was the effectiveness of its disciplinary arrangements. A true state within a state, it possessed effective sanctions and an inspiring morality: 'no society, intended by its founders to be so widely spread, ever sought to detach its members so completely from the state, by imposing on them a legislation distinct in its form, and at variance with its laws'.[106]

This sort of material was more memorable than Bartholdy's exposure of gossip about the Calderari or his scepticism about the future of the Carbonari. The documents he printed, too (they included substantial

[104] p. 17.   [105] p. 99.   [106] pp. 49–50.

extracts from the Papal government's investigation into the Macerata conspiracy), were often sensational. In these respects, Bartholdy was again strengthening the mythology.

It was this which largely explained why, by the mid-1820s, books about the secret societies had proved so profitable. None was as good as Bartholdy's, or as objective. There were nonetheless books which praised them as well as books which damned them; there had begun the legitimising of the secret societies in the eyes of liberals. One of the earliest and more impressive attempts to place them in what was to evolve into the myth of the Risorgimento was *L'Italie au dix-neuvième siècle*, a little book published anonymously by F. S. Salfi as early as 1821.[107] Salfi's main theme was that Italians needed institutions which would reflect the operation of public opinion and this led him to sketch the history of the peninsula in the first years of the century in a way which was to become conventional. In this account an important role was given to the secret societies. The detonator of subversion was the experience of French rule; when the Neapolitans had become aware of its true nature, they turned to the secret societies. 'La franc-maçonnerie avait déjà pénétré jusqu'au fond de la Calabre: les partisans du nouveau gouvernement réussirent à dénaturer cette institution, et à la rendre inutile. Mais, aux *loges* succédèrent les *ventes*, et les Carbonari prirent la place des ancien maçons. C'est à eux surtout que l'on doit la propagation des nouveaux principes.'[108] This was the beginning of the moral promotion of the Carbonari, who were gradually to assume the status of a beneficent and powerful agency of liberalism of which traces still linger in many accounts of the Risorgimento. They seemed to Salfi to hold out promise even for the immediate future. 'La tâche que les Carbonari se sont imposée, est de propager leur doctrine; et leur doctrine est de nature à faire impression sur le plus bas peuple. N'est-il pas même à craindre qu'elle n'ait déjà pénétré dans les rangs des soldats autrichiennes qui ont longtems demeuré dans le royaume de Naples? Et ce qui n'est pas encore arrivé, ne pourrait-il pas arriver aujourd'hui? L'expérience que l'on a de la propagation de la doctrine des Carbonari, justifie, ce me semble, mes craintes et mes conjectures. Enfin, tout tend à prouver qu'après les nouveaux désastres auxquels les Napolitains

---

[107] *L'Italie au dix-neuvième siècle ou de la nécessité d'accorder en Italie, le pouvoir avec la liberté* (Paris, 1821). There is a copy in the Bibliothèque Nationale, but the book is not easy to find and it is worth noting that it was reprinted recently in *Critica Storica*, 1969, pp. 282–342. On Salfi, see B. Zumbini, 'Breve cenno sulla vita e sulle opere di Francesco Salfi', *Atti della reale accademia di archeologia, lettere, e belle arti*, Naples, 1896.

[108] Salfi, p. 41.

pourraient être exposés, ils recommenceraient encore leurs tentatives, et redoubleraient d'efforts pour recouvrer ce qu'ils avaient perdu.'[109]

Although the Carbonari was the great new bogy and discovery of the Restoration Salfi also took up other themes which corroborated older myths. While freemasonry might be 'dénaturé' in the south, for example, he did not think that it had no influence as a subversive force elsewhere. 'Tout différens des autres, les maçons d'Italie profitaient de la faveur que leur accordait en apparence le gouvernement, pour mieux propager encore leurs doctrines, qui transpiraient alors même qu'elles semblaient ménager leur protecteur.'[110] If Austrian officials read the book, they must have found in such statements confirmation from the mouth of a liberal of all that they feared. He would also have confirmed their fears of the co-ordinating role of the secret societies of the old Napoleonic Kingdom of Italy: 'Les sociétés secrètes de Milan, qui plus ou moins dirigeaient celles de tout le royaume d'Italie, quoique favorisées en apparence par le gouvernement [of Beauharnais], avaient toujours conservé un esprit d'opposition.'[111] They had looked hopefully first to Murat, then to Bentinck; clearly, the Austrian interpretation of their role in the collapse of 1814 must have been confirmed by such assertions.

In the light of such claims and of the alarmist literature which was also appearing, it might have been expected that people would have been struck by the apparent failure of the secret societies to live up to the claims made for them. The discrepancy was virtually ignored and a belief in the power of the secret societies lasted well into the next decade (when fresh impetus was again to be provided by the revolutionary wave of 1830–1). Then, the revolution in France released a flood of publication similar to that at Naples in 1820. The secret opposition of the Restoration was unmuzzled and the public was eager to hear about them. In 1831 there appeared F. de Corcelle's *Documents pour servir à l'histoire des conspirations* and two years later Trélat's essay: both were by members of the Charbonnerie. Between them came a book by one of the Saumur conspirators, Ganchais. And so the tide rolled on, since, as in the case of Italy a decade earlier, liberals began to integrate the story of the secret societies with the story of the advance of liberty—the outstanding example was Louis Blanc—while conservatives shuddered at the power the sects still possessed and (they thought) had shown in the overthrow of the Bourbons for the second time. Though the peak of the secret societies' activity was past, the revolutions still to occur would keep alive the

[109] Salfi, p. 81.　　　　[110] p. 51.　　　　[111] p. 51.

fear of subversion so fundamental to the mythology. It did not matter that the failures of the early 1820s were so palpable that even Metternich concluded in 1826 that no further danger existed. Neither those frightened by them, nor those they had inspired wanted to give up the myth of international conspiracy. With the last years of one of the old believers, the ageing Buonarroti, this essay can now be concluded.

MYTH-MAKING: BUONARROTI'S LAST YEARS

Soon after Andryane's arrest, Buonarroti was ordered to leave Switzerland. This did not happen only to him.[112] There was a widespread reaction by police forces in several countries; many of Buonarroti's friends were arrested or had to go into exile. Conspirators everywhere were on the run. He himself succeeded in remaining for a time in Switzerland under a false name, but finally left for Belgium, a country where police were more tolerant of political refugees than elsewhere. He arrived in Brussels in 1824 and began there the penultimate stage of his conspiratorial career. He was warmly received—there was a subscription to buy him a piano—and he settled down to the re-organisation of his network of secret societies and to hold court as the Nestor of the movement in the café to which he went every day to meet old friends and fellow-exiles.[113] This lasted until 1830. Then, although a Belgian revolution broke out (which led eventually to the independence of the country from Holland), he went to Paris after the July revolution to remain there for the rest of his life, being arrested once more, briefly and for the last time, in 1833. He died in 1837.

Although Buonarroti was himself very busy in these last two phases of his life, the practical importance of the secret societies was over in civilised Europe. They had passed their peak in the early 1820s.

---

[112] Switzerland had come to attract a lot of attention because of the comings and goings of conspirators. See, e.g., the report quoted by Saitta (*Buonarroti*, i, p. 58) from the French legation at Berne, November 1823, on the activities of Prati. 'C'est un des principaux agents du Carbonarisme; et il a été spécialement chargé d'inoculer cette secte en Suisse et en Allemagne. Il est lancé aussi fort avant dans les associations secrettes de ce dernier pays et dans les plus hauts mystères de l'Illuminisme . . . Le centre de ses opérations mystérieuses était les villes de Genève et de Lausanne.' (Joachim Paul de Prati, the Swiss associate of Buonarroti, is an important figure in secret society history. He was the conspirator cited above (p. 282), who joined a society affiliated to Buonarroti's at Milan in 1810. He was denounced to the authorities by Wit at Bayreuth, was said to have introduced the Carbonari to Switzerland and, eventually disillusioned, finished as a Catholic, exchanging letters on spiritual matters with Rosmini.)

[113] Kuypers, *Buonarroti et ses sociétiés secrètes*, p. 3.

But Buonarroti did not give up; indeed, he showed unflagging energy in encouraging other conspirators. He evolved yet more forms for his protean creations and exploited the opportunities offered by the presence at Brussels of large numbers of political refugees. The very names of some of his fellow-exiles (though he was not on good terms with all of them) were enough to frighten anyone who could remember the revolutionary decade. Vadier, the former member of the Committee of General Security, whom Buonarroti visited every day, Prieur de la Marne, Levasseur and other ex-conventionnels (including Barère, whom Buonarroti detested), were all to be seen in Brussels.[114] There were also younger, newer revolutionaries, some of whom had taken part in the movements of the Restoration and some of whom the Netherlands police looked at askance because they were the first generation of Belgian liberals. Yet whatever they or anyone who remembered Buonarroti's record in the secret societies might fear, we do not know very much about what Buonarroti was precisely doing at this time.

Records have been found which show that a secret society designated by the initial 'M' was operating in 1824–5 and that Buonarroti was closely involved in this.[115] It is also clear that in 1828 the Sublimes Maîtres Parfaits underwent another remodelling to emerge, changed in detail but fundamentally the same, as Le Monde.[116] All the old rigmarole of 'professions of faith' was still used to distinguish grades, and the higher grades were to be completely unknown to those below them. The main innovation was a clean break with masonry and the creation of a quadripartite 'grado di osservazione' which was to provide a sort of fringe membership of persons who might belong to other bodies and who knew very little of Le Monde itself.

On the Belgian front, his connexion with Louis de Potter, a leading figure of the revolutionary movement and provisional government of 1830, is established. Even after the July Revolution and his transfer

---

[114] Marc Guillaume Alexis Vadier helped to overthrow Robespierre but also compromised himself in the Babeuf conspiracy; Prieur, former member of the Committee of Public Safety; René Levasseur, 'de la Sarthe', terrorist and noted 'représentant en mission'; Bertrand de Barère, denouncer of Robespierre in the Convention on the 9th Thermidor. On Buonarroti's associates see the fundamental book by A. G. Garrone, *Filippo Buonarroti e i rivoluzionari dell' Ottocento (1828–1937)* (Turin, 1951).

[115] Kuypers, (pp. 16–23) prints relevant documents.

[116] The basic source of our knowledge of this—and of the Piedmontese authorities' knowledge, it would seem—is a notebook first studied by Sòriga and since printed by Saitta in his *Filippo Buonarroti*, ii, pp. 91–116, and discussed in i, pp. 103 ff.

to Paris Buonarroti did not slacken his efforts to organise international revolution. After producing in 1832 a Charbonnerie réformée, of only two grades, but again with an unknown circle of directors,[117] he set up the Charbonnerie démocratique universelle, with the same structure of grades and reserved secrets, in 1833. In this society, very little of the quasi-religious symbolism of the old Charbonnerie survived but its ideological flavour was even more obvious than in his earlier creations. Some have for this reason distinguished in the Charbonnerie démocratique universelle the first link in the chain leading to the First International. But this seems a somewhat formal point, for the crucial steps could be seen in other events. The essence of what Buonarroti was doing was still to keep alive the model of the secret society whose origins lay ultimately and remotely in masonic structure and whose essence was the existence of reserved secrets and hidden directors. At least in form, the new society had great success, spreading quickly with the establishment of 'ventes' in Italy, France, Belgium and Switzerland (some have added, in Spain and Portugal, too). It was an organisation marked in detail as well as in shape and structure by its inheritance of the mythology of the past. To the noms de guerre drawn from classical antiquity the Belgian Charbonnerie added, for example, those of Oudet and Malet. In 1835, it seems, Buonarroti was thinking of transferring the headquarters of the society back from Paris to Brussels but this was never done.[118]

This was an enormous exercise in myth-making, even if not consciously so. As practical revolution, all this activity meant almost nothing. The circumstances which had briefly favoured secret societies were no longer there. New and competing forces were claiming the loyalty of the discontented. Yet the inspirational impact of Buonarroti was enormous and through it he made his last contributions to the mythology of a secret international movement threatening every government in Europe.

To be sure, it remains difficult to decide whether Buonarroti ever recognised his myth-making role to be his most effective one. In part, it was generated spontaneously by his personality and his absorption in his task. It was impossible even for those who were sceptical about his plans not to be impressed by his moral force; it made them susceptible to the belief that some sort of revolutionary continuity really was embodied in his career. Certainly one conscious contribution to the mythology of the secret societies was made by Buonarroti in his

---

[117] Its statutes have been printed by Saitta, ii, pp. 117–24.
[118] Kuypers, pp. 35, 95, 101; Saitta, i, p. 77.

most famous act, the publication of the *Conspiration pour l'Egalité* in 1828.[119] This was not directly about secret societies, but it was an appropriation by the most conspicuous and celebrated of the leaders of the secret societies of the egalitarian revolutionary tradition of the French Revolution. Buonarroti's book confirmed for many people the association of the ideas of communism with the secret societies. This was not perhaps its major importance, which has been well described by Dr Lehning as 'a landmark in the historiography of the French Revolution . . . By exposing the social implications of the Terror, and by a detailed account of the organisation, the methods and the aims of the conspiracy of 1796, the book became a textbook for the communist movement in the 1830s and forties in France, and the fundamental source of its ideology. In fact, his *Conspiration* started the Jacobin trend in European socialism.'[120] Important though this was to be, though, it is not what we are concerned with here. What was important for the secret societies was that this laudatory endorsement of what Babeuf had (according to Buonarroti) tried to do confirmed the fears many had entertained of the secret societies; evidently they were not simply associations of liberals seeking liberal reforms in a clandestine manner because other means were not open to them. They were truly and deeply subversive of all social order, as their most forceful detractors had always said.[121]

But besides this important publication Buonarroti was all the time feeding the myth by his own conspiratorial conservatism. The methods he adopted were heavily stamped with the masonic and Illuminati traditions and could not but suggest that direct continuity between these movements and his societies existed. Much of this came from time to time to the knowledge of the police (at his arrest in 1833, for example, yet another important body of papers came into their possession). He continually generated material which would thus feed existing obsessions. In 1819, he prescribed that one of the grades of the Sublimes Maîtres Parfaits, the Diacres mobiles, should be initiated into Rosicrucian doctrine. In 1828, the full masonic panoply was, it is true, abandoned in Le Monde, but the catechetical methods inherited from the Illuminati can still be discerned in the Charbonnerie démocratique

---

[119] Ph. Buonarroti, *Conspiration pour l'Egalité dite de Babeuf* (Brussels, 1828), 2 vols. There have been many editions and one which is readily available because recently reprinted, the English translation by Bronterre O'Brien.

[120] Lehning, pp. 30–2.

[121] Buonarroti had hoped also to write a life of Robespierre, who figured in his *Conspiration* as the forerunner of Babeuf, another confirmation of the fears of conservatives. (See Saitta, *Filippo Buonarroti*, i, p. 72.)

M

universelle. This organisation still preserved a complex system of grades and initiation and soon became known to the police in 1835.[122] Even his admirers found Buonarroti's obsession with forms and rituals excessive, but they were loyal, and through people like Blanqui and O'Brien there passed on to another revolutionary generation—which was to abandon them—the concepts and language which tied Buonarroti to the classical past of the myth. All this was bound to lend support to the mythology of the secret societies in the eyes of those who believed in it already and expected to hear of such discoveries being made.

Not everyone, of course, admired him even when they might sympathise with some of his aims. A far greater revolutionary, Mazzini, had as a young man belonged to a society deriving from Le Monde. (He had also been a Carbonaro and at one time a mason.) As late as 1831 he was still in close touch with Buonarroti, a member of one of his societies, and clearly influenced to a considerable degree by the Babouvist doctrines of the master.[123] But this changed. Becoming disillusioned with the Carbonari and similar societies after the failures of 1831, he founded in that year his Giovine Italia, which, though ultimately unsuccessful, was to frighten conservative governments in Italy with better reason than any of Buonarroti's creations. Young Italy was radical in politics, but first and foremost nationalist. As such, it cut across Buonarroti's hopes of international social revolution and his persistent belief in the revolutionary primacy of France. It also probably wounded his vanity by its success in attracting recruits and, through Mazzini's belief in popular insurrection, offended his strategical doctrine of the conspiratorial dictatorship. Characteristically, Buonarroti chose to oppose Mazzini by subversion. He set up yet another society, the Veri Italiani, to provide an alternative focus for the loyalty of young Italian revolutionaries. If Mazzini should successfully organise a revolution, then the Veri Italiani would step forward, taking it over and giving it a democratic and egalitarian twist under the direction of Buonarroti. Mazzini was rightly suspicious of the new society and refused to allow it to control his own organisation. He went his own way, thus provoking a breach with Buonarroti. It did not come suddenly, and it was accompanied by a slow evolution of Mazzini's thinking. He was still speaking respectfully of the old man in 1833.[124] But when it came it was final and it meant the

---

[122] In the same year, its Statutes were printed in connexion with certain judicial proceedings, so that knowledge of the society was not confined to the police. Saitta, i, p. 108.   [123] Garrone, pp. 339–40.

[124] Garrone, p. 368. The whole chapter on Mazzini's relation with Buonarroti is very informative.

abandonment by the younger man of the mythology of the secret societies.

This episode, too, was to contribute its elements to the alarm the secret societies could still cause. The Veri Italiani soon became known.[125] Discoveries in Tuscany in 1833 and trials in the following year gave it publicity and presented evidence of a social and not merely political revolutionary danger; this caused much alarm.[126] (It is an odd detail, nonetheless, that Buonarroti's own name was not mentioned in the trial; it may have been because the Tuscan authorities did not wish to embarrass his brother, Cosimo, at that time a member of the Tuscan bench.) These trials were to all intents and purposes the end of the Veri Italiani and Mazzini went his own way as before, denouncing Le Monde and the Charbonnerie démocratique universelle, and having abandoned both the secret dictatorial centre as an instrument and the mumbo-jumbo with which Buonarroti had loved to enwrap his societies. Yet this did not prevent him from acquiring a far greater status in the eyes of European governments as the centre of international conspiracy than Buonarroti had ever done.

This breach only anticipated by a few years the collapse of the whole world of the secret societies which became evident at Buonarroti's death. Its structure, fragile as it was, then fell completely to pieces for it had possessed reality only in so far as he had been its centre. New forms and new causes were to replace the hopes of the Babouvards and the men of the Restoration. 'Le temps de la Charbonnerie et celui des sociétés secrètes est passé,' wrote Trélat in 1838. 'Chacun, à l'heure qu'il est, agit à la face du ciel; le plus puissant moyen d'action est la publicité, et c'est se condamner à l'impuissance que de mettre en œuvre d'autres agents que ceux de son époque.'[127] Nationalism, constitutionalism, and the organisation of the working classes were to be the waves of the future. Yet the mythologies of the past kept their allure for some. Secret societies would still be formed and would still worry policemen, but increasingly they would have real substance only in the politics of backward Balkan states or the great Russian autocracy.[128]

---

[125] Francovich, p. 149.

[126] Francovich, pp. 159, 165.

[127] In *Paris Révolutionnaire* (Paris, 1838), ii, p. 276. Some had taken less time to make up their minds, of course; there is an amusing account, which may be true, of the young Guizot lecturing a Carbonarist in 1821 who tried to resist him (Guizot, *Mémoires*, I, p. 309).

[128] Here as elsewhere in this book, of course, I exclude from consideration the positive and mythological history of secret societies outside Europe.

Buonarroti had kept alive a tradition and even passed some of it on; to link the bourgeois leaders of the Convention to the socialists of the future and to use their history and inspiration against the liberals was no small achievement. And, simply by believing—for he cannot be thought insincere, even if we think him deluded—he imposed a continuity on the revolutionary movement in his own person. Simply by being there, he renewed the life of the conspiratorial view of history. An admirer, the Swiss conspirator Prati, said in his memoirs that the society to which he had belonged was directed by a secret committee which was composed of the disciples of Babeuf. Whether true or not, this was what Buonarroti had made men believe and must have believed himself. A little more speculatively it might be said that Metternich himself was the best testimony to Buonarroti's efforts: in 1830 he was still talking of a European centre of revolution in Paris.[129] Buonarroti was the ultimate source of enormous quantities of alarming information which came eventually into the hands of the authorities and helped to keep alive the fears of men like Metternich. Paradoxically, then, there was after all a continuity in the secret societies, just as their critics had always said, though it resulted in no effective action against the existing order and was imposed largely by one man. Nevertheless, that was enough for the myth to pass to the next generation, in which Louis Blanc could seriously state (and be believed) that Buonarroti was the heart of revolutionary Europe in these years. Such reality as there was in this claim was a mythical reality woven from illusion and self-deception. If this is thought to be a harsh judgment on Buonarroti himself, than whom no one was more deluded, there can be set off against it the devotion and respect he awoke in so many of those who knew him.[130]

[129] Emerson, pp. 134–5.
[130] See, e.g., the praise given him by Prati, quoted in Lehning, pp. 62–4.

Chapter X

Conclusion

BUONARROTI's last years blended the myth and the reality of the secret societies as never before. Each, too, was then at the peak of its strength. This book has been about the first; it has argued that though secret societies existed in large numbers in Western Europe between 1750 and 1830 and strove to influence events, their main importance was what people believed about them. This always mattered more than what they did and their numbers and practical effectiveness were in no way proportionate to the myth's power. This is their true instrumental importance as well as their interest for the historian; what was believed about them was an important part of the information shaping men's reactions to great events.

If this is granted, then can we hope—ought we to try?—to understand any more about this fact than its historical context? The mythology is, after all, a historical artifact. It is one characteristic achievement and expression of a particular age, a collective dream of one particular culture. We feel able to understand quite a lot of the social context in which, over eighty years or so, it was born and grew to its full stature; we ought therefore to have a fair chance of discerning what there was in it that locks the mythology into that particular culture at that particular time. Most of what has gone before in this book perhaps expresses that view implicitly. Yet this does not seem to exhaust the matter. Although the mythology has its peculiar features it is also based on elements which recur in other historical situations and it has itself shown astonishing powers of survival and adaptation. Long after the years which saw its birth, these powers have renewed its life at many times and in many places.

The most cursory glance at the history of the mythology since the 1820s reveals this durability. Secret societies themselves in these years tended to wither in Western Europe and to be replaced by political forms expressing new social needs and possibilities. They appeared instead at its fringes and in its primitive south-east, and then in Europe's dependencies overseas. (There may be clues here to the sociological or political environments which particularly favour them.) Nonetheless, the mythology was still sustained by Western Europeans though any real threat had long since vanished. Some manifestations of its later phases were touched on at the outset, but many more could be cited. The flow of literature has never stopped. It was a winner for authors and publishers all through the nineteenth century. Some of it was cynically contrived, such as the influential book of de la Hodde, who cashed in on the 1848 revolutionary scare which so impressed Disraeli.[1] Others, such as the Roman Catholic author Jannet or the infatuated English radical, David Urquhart (who detected in Chartism the hand of the Tsar and a structure modelled on the Hetaira Philiké), were deeply sincere.[2] Such examples may be thought special; a French priest under the Third Republic wrote from a political context of quarrels between the lay and ecclesiastical spirit, and Urquhart from an obsession with the Russian danger which makes their inclinations to conspiracy views understandable. But there are many more examples to be chosen which register the determination to thrust all historical data into the same logical Iron Maiden even when there is no special reason to do so.

There is a typical and striking twentieth-century example in the Frenchman, Léon de Poncins. As late as 1936 he blamed freemasonry for the transformation of the first World War into a 'guerre sociale' directed against Austria-Hungary rather than Germany. (Those who reflect on the implications of Allied propaganda for the two countries will recognise again here the specious and plausible nature of this argument, which is typical of many which have always given the myth great authority.) After that, he contends, it was the Allies' aim to shape a new world on the principles of '89; Wilson's doctrines had a masonic origin and so, therefore, had the League of Nations (S.D.N.). 'L'arrivée au pouvoir du régime Hitlérien et la lutte entreprise par lui contre la F.. M.. et le judaïsme sont en train de tout changer. Affirmons donc notre volonté de ne pas faire la guerre à l'Italie pour la S.D.N., ni à l'Allemagne pour les Soviets.'[3]

This testifies to the enduring nature of the mythology, but this century provides more striking evidence still of its efficacy in its incorporation in policy-making on a scale not paralleled, perhaps, since the Restoration era. We need not turn merely to its diluted presence in the alarm over Bolsheviks after 1918. There is the far

---

[1] L. de la Hodde, *Histoire des sociétés secrètes et du parti républicain de 1830 à 1848* (Paris, 1850).

[2] See C. Jannet, *Les sociétés secrètes* and the words of Urquhart of 1873 quoted by T. Frost, *The Secret Societies of the European Revolution* (London, 1876), pp. vii–viii.

[3] L. de Poncins, *S.D.N. Super-Etat Maçonnique* (Paris, 1936), p. 49.

more precise and alarming evidence provided by the actual persecution of freemasons. Between 1918 and 1939 the Craft was banned in
Hungary, Italy, Germany, Portugal, Turkey and Spain. It was denounced by the Comintern. Elsewhere it was by no means safe:
French anti-masonry was politically almost as strong as ever and in
1935 a Parisian deputy proposed to amend the laws against the 'ligues'
so that they should also apply to the Craft. When the war came, the
German SS formed a special anti-masonic section which pursued
masonic records and closed down lodges. Not all of this, of course,
sprang immediately from the mythology, but the mythology was the
soil of such policies.

This should remind us of the danger of taking the recurrent irrational element in history too lightly. It is not enough simply to be
amused by a Barruel or a Nodier; it is even beside the point merely
to be irritated by them. Either reaction puts belief in secret societies
on the same level as the fantasies of the Flat-Earthers, and there is
more to it than that, for it taps very deep and very powerful fears.
They are still there, long after Barruel has lost his spell-binding power,
and they emerge informally but violently in such outbreaks as the
McCarthy scare of the early 1950s, the Russian purges of the 1930s, or
the present Chinese suspicion of the outside world. All these fears
rest on simplifying, dramatising visions of politics. In the background
there is still a belief in hidden manipulation. Those who hold them have
abandoned some of the stage machinery, but the plot is the same.
With the secret society mythology as such most of us may have dispensed, but it provides an outstanding example of a continuing
phenomenon, the readiness with which men can go mad when determined to dramatise their history.

All human institutions can be described in terms of function,
mythologies as much as any other. They are all responses to a need to
master reality. They do this by providing an interpretation of it which
seems satisfactory, and therefore gives the person who accepts the
myth a chance to separate himself from the flow of events he has
to interpret and a standpoint, as it were, on the outside of them. From
intellectual satisfaction at the liberation he has achieved he may move on
to acceptance of a fate he now understands (and can therefore will) or,
even, to manipulation of it. In either case he gains a sense of control
over reality, which may even be demonstrated by deliberate action in
some cases not to be an illusion.

This does not take us far. There are mythologies and mythologies;
some are more plausible than others. It does not require an enormous

effort of historical imagination to conceive that the picture of this world and the next held by a medieval monk was, to him, completely credible, satisfying and convincing. But Barruel and his like were the contemporaries of Laplace, and the people who believed in Mesmer could read the Encyclopédie. To put it in another way, other mythologies were available and this has always been true of the age during which the fear of the secret societies has persisted; Nesta Webster might believe that Sinn Fein and the murderers of Sir Lee Stack could be traced back to the Illuminati, but Lloyd George did not have to, nor did he. In the example studied in this book we deal with a mythology which even at its height was denounced on rational and empirical grounds and is clearly nonsense. Why then, were such ideas effective? Why are books embodying them still finding audiences?[4]

Two possible levels of explanation exist. We could assume that there are permanent human characteristics which predispose society to political irrationality of perverse and noxious kinds. It may be pointed out, for example, that the secret society mythology is not the only one to have shown the power to influence men's behaviour widely and deeply. It is not even the only version of the conspiracy vision of politics. Other societies than the modern European have had other irrational forces at work in them. An earlier Europe (to go no further afield) had different dramas in mind and harried religious heretics as the carriers of a fatal disease which might destroy Christendom if left unchecked. Another Europe burned witches. In a later age, we have had the even more monstrously irrational politics of anti-semitism. That is a very sobering episode to think about. It was one which had occasional points of contact with the legends of the secret society, too, but that is not why it is to be recalled here. Its importance is the outstanding evidence it seems to give of the continuing wish of men to be deluded.

This approach, because of this, looks at first sight promising. There seems to be so much data available for investigation. But it has grave difficulties and, in the end, the central hypothesis of continuing perversity can hardly be demonstrated, though it continues to impress us. Though many men and societies show a recurring willingness to adopt ideas and attitudes which now seem irrational or unbalanced, we can still reasonably ask why some people and some societies were better able to resist such appeals than others, who rushed to embrace them. Granted that political irrationality is a social constant, we still need to

---

[4] *Secret Societies and Subversive Movements*, by Nesta H. Webster, was republished in 1964 in its *eighth* edition, it may again be remarked.

explain why some individuals do not show it in a society where many do and why some societies are more able to control it than others.

One tempting avenue of escape from this problem is to hope for explanation in the mental state of individual believers in the myth, for some may be properly called unbalanced, on any reading of their behaviour. This is in some ways even better shown by members of secret societies themselves than by their fierce conservative critics. Anyone who could believe, for example, the sort of things which were bandied about as part of the Templar legend, must have been at least highly fanciful and impermeable to much of daily reality. The great Buonarroti cannot but strike us as at least unbalanced: perhaps 'enthusiastic', in the old sense, is a fair word. There is in his obsession with organisation and ritual something suggestive of the enclosed mental world of Dostoevsky's *Possessed*—and although Buonarroti's elaborate conspiratorial network had ramifications wider than the isolated cell which was all that really existed in Dostoevsky's book, its effectiveness showed almost as huge a gap between appearance and reality.

Unfortunately, this line of enquiry leads to a dead end. The evidence is not available to follow it. Were we to establish a list of deranged persons who believed in secret societies as the motor of history, it would rest only on our own subjective impressions. So much has been hoped for from the assistance of psychology to the historian that, even at the risk of digression, this deserves a moment's further attention. Much has been said about the usefulness to the historian of the 'insights' of psychology. This word is quite a good one, because it does not tie the user down to saying that he has got anything more useful than a suggestive analogy out of psychology, and thus far, I suppose, a historian could think consideration of that branch of studies helpful. On these lines, though, it is perfectly proper to say that equally and more valuable 'insights' may be gained from many other studies and psychology has no claim to be of special explanatory value.

But some historians mean much more than this modest recognition of the possible helpfulness of psychology. There already exists a very large body of literature (most of it recent) on the philosophy and 'methodology' of this association of history and psychology. Much of it is pretentious twaddle, mere padding of bibliographies, though the best of it is written with seriousness and responsibility by historians who have actually tried to deploy their psychological studies as an instrument in specific pieces of historical research. Their efforts are justifiable but seem in fact to demonstrate the inadequacy of the approach because there seems to be no ground for believing that the 'evidence' of the psychologists which they use is either good or significant. If I understand them aright, those psychologists who are actually doing something which other scientists would recognise as scientific are themselves unable as yet to provide statements of sufficient generality and based on a large enough body of experimental data to be useful to the historian. In so far as their facts are hard, they are tiny. As for psycho-analytical approaches, both clinical and speculative, the historian must apply an academic Morton's Fork: if the psycho-analyst speaks, it is hearsay or evidence about himself that he presents, rather than about his patient, and if it is the record of the patient's behaviour (including verbal behaviour) that we study, then it is no different in kind from any other statement with which a historian has to deal. Its special nature has only significance as something to be considered critically by the historian (as he must consider the special form of, for example, a legal record).

It is not possible to draw comfort from the assertion that the truth or falsity of what the psycho-analysed say can be checked by their subsequent response (in improvement or lack of it) to analysis. For this to be impressive it would have to be demonstrated much more rigorously than is usual that the response was indeed the result of the treatment. And even if this were to be demonstrated, we should have a technique of very limited value, for it can only apply to the living. To repeat an account of what someone said provides just another account to be read critically. What is distinctive about the psychologists' work is the experimental element: even an analyst can modify his approach in response to changing symptoms. But it is just here that it is furthest from anything likely to confront a historian. Such opportunities rarely, or never, present themselves to historians. We cannot put Cromwell or Napoleon on the couch, or give them drugs. These are problems so great as to be at least for a long time insuperable if political irrationality is attacked on the psychological front. There is even a difficulty of definition involved: in many cases, the 'evidence' that people were unbalanced would be the fact that they believed in a mythology at all, although everything else known about them seemed normal. This would not be an explanation, simply a restatement.

The other possible approach to explanation is historical and specific. It starts with particular manifestations of political irrationality and attempts to explain them by an exhaustive discussion of the peculiar circumstances of their contexts. The disadvantage seems to be that of the method in whatever context it is used; it peels the onion of historical fact to reveal at its centre the absence of any general theory, and this is logically dissatisfying to some of us. Perhaps it can be used more sparingly than this and can be employed at least so far as the isolation of the obvious circumstantial factors is concerned, without our going so far as to pretend to exhaust the question.

On these lines, it is best to begin by recalling briefly and for the last time the essential structure of the secret society mythology in its classic age, however crude the summary may seem. A myth (or mythology) in the sense in which I have used the words in these pages is a collection of images. Connected, interrelated in their derivation and elaboration, they reinforce one another's power, and this power is in large measure irrational. An effective myth is defined not by its correspondence with positive reality, but by its power to move men to action by giving them an interpretation of that reality. Political mythologies are only special instances of this, primarily affecting conduct conventionally called 'political'. Much of the content of the myth of the secret societies was political, but by no means all (here, perhaps, has lain one source of its remarkable power). There is no perfectly typical embodiment of the secret society myth; there are always special variations. We must construct its skeleton by abstracting the essential constituents from its statements because even its most comprehensive statements—Barruel's for example—have distorting special features.

At the heart of the mythology lies the recognition of delusion. Its central image is of a community unaware of its true nature. Apparently self-conscious and self-regulating, it is, unknown to itself, in fact directed by concealed hands. These are the hands of the secret societies, which are, typically, affiliated in a great network covering the civilised world. These societies have origins going back deep into history, sometimes into the very remote past. In the network they form freemasonry has a specially sinister significance, of which its members (or at least its leaders) are aware. The aims of these secret societies are unchanging and subversive; among the most cherished are the overthrow of the fundamental institutions of society: religion, morals, the family, property. Their means are covert, but always include the manipulation of unconscious agents who do not realise whom they serve but blindly further the destructive plans of their masters. Directly, the most blatant advocacy of bad principles is employed to agitate discontent and to bring about a general corruption of good order; this can be discerned above all in the repetition of great historical patterns for whether the beginning is the Protestant Reformation, the persecution of the Jesuits or the French Revolution, a mounting pattern of disorder is the clearest evidence of the design that links all the symptoms of upheaval in Western European society in one great conspiratorial success. Indirectly, the societies work through kings and powerful men, by no means all of whom are cognisant of what they do.

Such an account would probably be an acceptable statement of the essential mythology to anyone who accepted one of its particular versions. But before it is considered as a historical creation, there is an important rider to be observed. With only a change of colour, this mythology is structurally the same as the one which sustains a wholly opposed politics. The secret societies have spawned other, friendly, images, too. Here is an alternative version, acceptable to many liberals and revolutionaries:

A few enlightened and disinterested persons have always cherished humanitarian goals and have planned and striven to improve institutions cluttered and corrupted by history. They have recognised one another and co-operated to realise their common aspirations: this co-operation was first truly effective among the enlightened writers and Philosophes of the eighteenth century who, as it were, secularised an assertion of the individual's rights first expressed theologically by the Protestant Reformers. Many people who shared these ideals sought to satisfy them by joining together in freemasonry, whose statutes and institutions expressed tolerance, equality and enlightenment. Later, when tyranny and historic injustice had been brought to bay in armed struggle with the French Revolution, some of these men realised that it was no longer enough to rely on propaganda and education; they could no longer hope that political, social and ecclesiastical injustice would be sapped by such means. Revolutionary action was required. So were born the first liberal and national movements, and later the early communist societies. Their means were conspiracy against the gendarme and confessor, the revolutionary education of people, and the international co-operation of the masses. The cause was essentially the same from the Enlightenment to the conspirators of 1821 and 1830, though the mode of action was transformed.

This version of history is just as mythological and has just as little and as much to recommend it to the historian as the conservative scheme previously outlined. Yet it is the conservative version of the myth which is sometimes thought to be the only one which matters. The liberal version, it is true, had in its particular embodiments perhaps fewer traces of real paranoia than the other; its slightly greater plausibility assured it a place in a Whig-liberal historiographical tradition which is by no means dead today. Nonetheless, these are both types, even if distinct types, of the same genus. They both embody the secret society mythology and nourished one another. It is to the fact that they arose almost contemporaneously that we should direct our attention. They are products of the same historical situation and each illuminates their age. Why should such views have been so acceptable at a particular time?

It is essential to recall again the most important but often forgotten fact that we approach historical questions with assumptions about what constitutes an adequate analysis which are quite different from those of the late eighteenth century and the first decades of the last. This is obvious, but crucial. The writing devoted to the secret societies may have been rubbish, but it was also often an attempt at historical analysis, directed to explaining a historical problem. It usually started from certain generally accepted canons of explanation. The assumptions of its writers about what constituted an adequate explanation have now been blown to the winds by the professionalising of history. Nonetheless, there lies embedded in the secret society mythology a philosophy of history, though one few can now accept; we have our own mythologies which seem more helpful.

The problem with which the conscious contributors to the mythology of secret societies were trying to deal was one of change on an unprecedented, accelerating and ever-grander scale. Historical change was not new; there had been a place for it in theories of those who sought to explain the ups and downs of states, the comings and goings of dynasties and princes. But it was not assumed that it would be either so fierce or so sweeping that it would compromise the very foundations of society and shake its most unquestioned ideas and institutions. Some societies were to prove more resistant to alarm and more ready to accept a new view of historical change than others, but all were in some measure shaken first by what the Enlightenment did to educated Europe and even more by the upheavals which followed the French Revolution. Since then, of course, change has never ceased and has even accelerated.

If providential or theological interpretations were to be set aside (and they were not, altogether) men had canons of explanation available to interpret these changes which were, broadly speaking, of only two kinds. One looked to some kind of determining factor, but determinist theories were few and not held by many people. Moreover, since their most frequent forms were climatic or psychological, they tended to be more and more inadequate when applied to phenomena which appeared to transcend national and regional boundaries. They sometimes simply took the fashionable modern form of saying that all that could be recognised was the 'force de choses', the sheer inertia of the whole historical process. This left readers with a sense of helplessness but still with no sense of a key to the mystery. They were likely to be driven back on the other available major interpretation, classical and central to European civilisation, that men were responsible for their own history: things happened because people wanted them to.

This bias gave room for many varied views, of course. One obvious difference of interpretation could arise over the attribution of direct or indirect influence to men. The troubles (or blessings) of the era could be attributed to a few wicked (or benevolent) men in positions of power, or to the missionary activity of those who spread new ideas among large numbers of men. Nevertheless, any voluntarist interpretation made it easy for those seeking an explanation of complex change to fall back on the conclusion that a conscious agency was at work. This coincided happily with the bias of minds brought up in the Christian cultural tradition which located moral responsibility in the individual. Moreover, it corresponded to practical political experience. If we disregard the United Kingdom and certain moments in the history of some other countries, it is not too much to say that the idea of public politics was hardly known in much of Europe before 1789. What existed instead was the politics of courts and élites, a strong awareness of the importance of influence, intrigue, persuasion and plot in shaping the acts of a comparatively small number of people in whose hands lay the power to make the decisions needed at the centre of a loosely organised ancien régime. To control these few was what the struggle for power was about. The institutional structure, therefore, itself favoured the concentration of attention on the acts of identifiable individuals, too.

Moralists might qualify the primacy of individual will by calling attention to the inexplicable frustrations arising from chance or the intractability of human nature; commonsense and practical knowledge, too, suggested that the difficulties of execution might paralyse intention in a society whose technical scope for coercion was so small (by comparison with a later age). Nonetheless, the current was strongly in the direction of an analysis of events in terms of human decision and influence. The mythology of simpler, earlier societies, theological and even magical, might not have done this; that of our own day, asserting above all else the toughness of the web of necessity, whether seen in terms of economics or of social structure, certainly does not. To look for the conscious authors of events was, however, natural to most men in the eighteenth century and the romantic era.

This fundamental assumption was used over a wide range of events. The Enlightenment has been mentioned: it disturbed men not only because of its specific criticisms of ideas and institutions but because it seemed to some to threaten the whole sacramental, mysterious dimension which they apprehended as the essence of life. Moreover, it seemed to do so through acts which suggested an overall unity of standpoint and strategy among its supporters; they were therefore in a plot together. The even more shocking effect of the French Revolution which followed has already been sufficiently described. It is simply convenient to remark here that it also provided a new conceptual device which helped acceptance of the mythology. It threw up together with its spectacular and frightening drama the new politics which was to simplify its own interpretation. It not only created a need for interpretation, it also created its instrument; politics could henceforth be conceived as a huge but simple struggle for the Revolution or against it, and one which need never end. This polarisation could be rapidly extended and intensified; the pre-revolutionary debates soon lost their distinctive outlines in the blinding clarity it provided. It was the Past against the Future. It became hallowed in the antithesis of Right and Left as the basis of politics ever since.

That this vision of the revolutionary age should be generalised was made easier by the French hegemony, at first cultural and then, under Napoleon, political. The polarisation of politics created a sense of common opponents among those hitherto divided: the positive working of the Revolution as it was carried beyond France actually contributed to the positive growth of secret societies, too. When people came to look at the chain of events it seemed impossible to resist the simplifying, generalising tendency of the new interpretation. Doctrines and schemes which in fact and origin were deeply incongruous were marshalled together into two great ideological arsenals. And there was something in this. Critics of the Economistes of the French eighteenth century had not been wrong to see that their ideology had a moral dimension, and was not just a matter of technical proposals. Demands were generalised so that nationalists and liberals in one country could after 1815 make common cause with anti-clericals and free traders in another. The ideal model of eternal warfare between the 'infâme' and progress, or between presumptuous pride and historic wisdom, blurred all distinctions. As events unrolled, they did so in a way which favoured more and more a view of history as a whole as a struggle or a debate between two sides, one white, one black. The model became more and more persuasive and even the struggles of Greek city states and the trumpetings of medieval barons were strained out of context and re-read as acts in the universal drama of Left and Right. A political Manicheism resulted which has embittered our political struggles ever since. Today people still seek new extensions of its wondrously simplifying power and impose the terminology it has engendered on things as incongruous as the politics of modern Africa —just as, a century ago, they were imposed on the primitive convulsions of the Balkans.

Another circumstance which was soon to feed the myth did not precede the Revolution, but emerged from it. This was the appearance of the full-time, professional revolutionary, a new character in the political cast. He had been prefigured in Weishaupt, was supremely embodied in Buonarroti, and was to recur in Blanqui, Bakunin and scores of others right down to our own day. He is now so familiar that it is hard to recall how recent is the full-time agitator's appearance. He rose into prominence first to enjoy the possibilities presented by the Revolutionary decade, when the professional agitator was new and therefore strange; it was not then hard to think that similar activities by many men in different countries were best explained by supposing a common source and direction.

These are facts which help to explain the credibility of the myth. There were also other less enduring attendant circumstances which inferentially lent it plausibility. Plot psychosis dogged the revolutionary decade of the 1790s—and there really were, after all, lots of plots. The Machiavellian exploitation of agents who themselves do not comprehend the full purposes of their masters is a commonplace of revolutionary politics and could hardly be doubted by those who remembered the veiling of Mirabeau's bust in the Panthéon when his relations with the court came to light. Mystery and suspicion about motive is generated almost in exact proportion to the pace of change in revolutionary times. Survival, personal or political, requires sidestepping, ambiguous utterance, sudden volte-face; historians can still debate the honesty of the Gironde and the true aims of Robespierre.

Perhaps this can be thought enough to explain a great delusion. Were we to confine ourselves to the scale of the upheavals which needed explanation, to the bias men brought to the attempt to understand them, and to known and suspected circumstances, we should

already know much of the appearance and success of the mythology
of the secret societies. Such conjunctions are indispensable in explaining
any major historical fact. The fact that the mythology was later to
wane in Western Europe, but to enjoy fresh success elsewhere, in
different historical circumstances, further confirms the importance of
special influences. Yet something remains. The local and temporary
ascendancy of circumstance will not by any means take us the whole
way. Our central problem remains and perhaps reveals some ultimate
inadequacy in the idea of a historical 'explanation', if by that we are to
mean more than a translation of our questions in different terms.
Plausible and logical accounts of events 'explained' by the myth were
always available and some people were sensible enough to prefer
them. Why should many others choose nonsense, instead? Why should
even the 'enlightened' see the hand of the Jesuits in everything opposed
to them? Is there a Gresham's Law of the mind which explains why
bad ideas may always drive out good, though the particular content
and degree of intellectual viciousness of mythologies change from time
to time? We are back at our starting-point.

It is worth recalling again that the myth is available in Left and Right
versions. No one who studies it, therefore, should feel happy to throw
off the problem simply by defining as mythology the particular nonsense talked by his political opponents. What seems to be worth
considering is the possibility that there exists always a readiness and
perhaps even a need among many men to take a distorted, even paranoiac view of society, and that this is intensified at moments of great
stress, though it may be impossible to delineate and measure it by
historical methods. It would be sad if this were so, but it should at
least make us a little less likely to laugh at our ancestors, because we
should see more clearly that their preposterous credulousness and
alarm might belong to the same family as our own political fears and
dreams. This should not be construed only in the dramatic terms we
have been considering; we could consider not only the witch-huntings
and notorious injustices of recent history but (for example) the milder
and far less damaging, but equally irrational, desire of many Englishmen to see so complex and elaborate a process as a general election
presented as a conflict between the armies of darkness and light. Many
other myths and traditional evocations of conspiratorial and personal
demonologies could be cited. A modern publication such as *The Black
Dwarf* still certifies its claim to be on the 'Left' by the traditional
device of personifying such a shapeless abstraction as the notion of
international capitalism.

This may take us too far away from the secret societies and perhaps rob them of their special significance. If we grant the view that political irrationality is ineradicable, of course, then there is no need for further explanations: the circumstances alone will by themselves then determine which particular myths the irrationality exploits. Yet such a view is not a very comfortable one for many of us, because it points to a pessimistic conclusion. Mythologies will flourish if useful and some evil mythologies among them so long as they meet some men's needs. It suggests that when a civilisation rejects one sinister mythology, it gains no inoculation against another. 'When the unclean spirit is gone out of a man, he walketh through dry places, seeking rest and findeth none. Then he saith, I will return into my house from whence I came out; and when he is come, he findeth it empty, swept, and garnished. Then goeth he, and taketh with himself seven other spirits more wicked than himself, and they enter in and dwell there: and the last state of that man is worse than the first.'

Index of personal names

Index of personal names

Aiguillon, Armand, duc d' (1761–1800), freemason, 159

Aldini, Count Antonio (1756–1826), Ital. politician, 226

Alembert, Jean Le Rond d' (1717–83), philosopher, 55, 298

Alexander I (1777–1825), Tsar of Russia, 301, 305; q. 318

Amar, Jean Baptiste André (1755–1816), Fr. revolutionary, 181, 199, 245

Anderson, Dr James (1680?–1739), masonic antiquary, 22, 62

Andryane, Alexandre Philippe (1797–1863), 262, 263, 273, 327–30, 340

Antin, Louis de Pardaillan de Gondrin, duc d' (1707–43), Fr. Grand Master, 33

Antonelle, Pierre Antoine, marquis d' (1747–1817), Fr. revolutionary, 181, 245

Antraigues, Emmanuel Henri Louis Alexandre, comte d' (1753–1812), 149, 170; q. 200

Argenson, Marc René de Voyer de Paulmy, marquis d' (1771–1842), 316

Arndt, Ernst Moritz (1796–1860), German writer, 304

Artois, Charles Philippe de Bourbon, comte d' (1757–1836), later Charles X of France, 151

Ashmole, Elias (1617–92), Engl. antiquary, 20

Auckland, William Eden, 1st Baron (1745–1814), Engl. diplomat, 207

Auribeau, Pierre Hesmivy d' (1756–1843), Fr. priest, 178

Aurora, Enrico Michele L' (1764–1803?), Ital. revolutionary, 226

Babeuf, François Noel 'Gracchus' (1760–97), Fr. revolutionary and conspirator, 160, 181, 182, 197, 205, 232–6, 240, 256, 346

Babo, Josephus Marius (1756–1822), Bavarian writer, 127

Bahrdt, Karl Friedrich (1741–92), German publisher, 132, 212, 218, 219

Baissie, Antoine Estève (d. 1815), Fr. priest, 168, 186; q. 168–70

Bakunin, Mikhail (1814–76), Russ. anarchist, q. 235

Barère de Vienzac, Bertrand (1755–1841), Fr. revolutionary, 341

Barruel, Augustin de (1741–1821), abbé, 140, 170, 188–93, 204, 217, 248, 257, 274–5, 295, 302, 303, 313, 334, 350; main references to works: *Les Helviennes*, 189–90; *Le Patriote véridique*, 191; *Journal ecclésiastique*, 190–1; *Mémoires pour servir à l'histoire du jacobinisme*, 192, 193–7, 295–8; other writings, 189, 191–2

Bartholdy, Jakob Levi (1779–1825), Pr. diplomat, 336–7

Benedict XIV, Pope (1675–1758), 44; his Bull *Providas*, 68, 72–6, 81, 83

Bentinck, Lord George (1802–48), Engl. politician, 5

Bentinck, Lord William (1774–1839), Engl. agent in Sicily, 282, 288–91, 308, 339

Bernadotte, Jean Baptiste Jules (1763–1844), Fr. marshal, later King of Sweden, 160

Berry, Charles Ferdinand, duc de (1778–1820), 318

Bertier de Sauvigny, Anne Ferdinand Louis de (1782–1864), Fr. politician, 257–9

Bischoffswerder, Hans Rudolf von (1741–1803), Pr. minister, 103, 178

Blanc, Jean Joseph Louis (1811–82), Fr. politician, 339, 346

Blanqui, Louis Auguste (1805–81), conspirator, 344

Bode, Johann Joachim Christoph (1730–93), freemason and illuminatus, 114, 124, 132, 136, 139, 162, 196, 215, 218, 219

Bolingbroke, Henry St John, Viscount (1678–1751), 29

Bonaparte, Joseph (1768–1844), King of (1) Naples, (2) Spain, 253, 285

Bonaparte, Lucien (1775–1840), 253, 285

Bonaparte, Napoléon (1768–1821), Emperor of France, 147, 192, 204, 230, 238, 240, 250, 254, 256, 263, 304

Bonneville, Nicolas de (1760–1828), Fr. author and revolutionary, 139–40, 159–62, 177, 196, 272; q. 161

Botta, Carlo Giuseppe (1766–1837), Ital. historian, 244

Briot, Pierre Joseph (1771–1827), Fr. official, 284–5

Brissot de Warville, Jean Pierre (1754–93), Fr. revolutionary politician, 93

Brunswick, Karl Wilhelm Ferdinand, Duke of (1735–1806), 109, 113, 115, 154

Bubna von Littiz, Ferdinand Anton, Count (1768–1825), Austr. general, 326

Buonarroti, Filippo Giuseppe Maria Ludovico (1761–1837), 222, 226–37, 240, 248, 262–7, 271, 273, 281, 285, 322, 324–9, 334, 340–6, 351; q. 227, 231

Burke, Edmund (1729–97), Engl. pol. thinker, 192; q. 201, 206, 301

Bute, John Patrick Crichton-Stuart, 3rd Marquess of (1847–1900), 4

Cadet-Gassicour, Charles Louis (1769–1821), 187, 295; *Le tombeau de Jacques Molay*, 180–2; *Les initiés anciens et modernes*, 182–3

Cadoudal, Georges (1771–1804), Fr. royalist conspirator, 257, 260

Cagliostro, 'Count' Alessandro, *alias* Giuseppe Balsamo (1743–95), 93, 105, 135, 136, 168, 181, 196, 226, 314; *Vie de Joseph Balsamo*, 174–7

Cambacérès, Jean Jacques Regis de (1753–1824), Fr. Grand Master adjoint, 253

Capelle, Guillaume Antoine, baron (1775–1843), Fr. prefect, 264–5

Casanova, Giovanni Giacomo (1725–98), adventurer, 56

Castlereagh, Robert Stewart, Viscount (1769–1822), 291

Cerise, Guillaume Michel, baron (1769–1820), Piedmontese jacobin, 247

Championnet, Jean Antoine Etienne (1762–1800), Fr. general, 245

Charles, King of the Two Sicilies (1716–88), later Charles III, King of Spain, 77–8; q. 99

Charles XIII, King of Sweden and Duke of Sudermania (1748–1818), 109, 113, 124

Charles, Duke of Hesse-Cassel (1744–1836), 113, 124, 127

Chateaubriand, François René, vicomte de (1768–1848), q. 302

Chatham, William Pitt, 1st Earl of (1708–78), Engl. statesman, 185

Clavière, Etienne (1735–93), Fr. politician, 186

Clement V, Pope (1264?–1314), 100

Clement XII, Pope (1652–1740); Bull In Eminenti, 68–72, 76

Clermont, Louis de Bourbon Condi, duc de (1709–71), Fr. Grand Master, 39, 67

Clifford, the Hon. Robert, Engl. writer, 209

Clootz, 'Anarcharsis', Jean Baptiste du Val de Grâce, baron von (1755–94), revolutionary politician, 160

Cluseret, Gustave Paul (1823–1900), Fr. soldier, 5

Cobenzl, Count Ludwig (1753–1809), reputed illuminatus, 124

Cochin, Augustin (1876–1916), Fr. historian; q. 163

Collot d'Herbois, Jean Marie (1750–96), Fr. politician, q. 152

Condorcet, Marie Jean Nicolas de Carital, marquis de (1743–94), Fr. philosopher, 196; q. 99

Confalonieri, Count Federico (1785–1846), Ital. statesman, 289, 291, 325, 329

Consalvi, Ercole (1757–1824), Papal minister and cardinal, 310, 332

Corsini, Cardinal Neri (1685–1770), 71; q. 71

Cossé Brissac, Louis Timoléon, duc de (1734–92), Templar Grand Master, 165

Coustos, John, Br. subject and victim of Inquisition, 84

Cromwell, Oliver (1599–1658), Engl. statesman, reputed founder of freemasonry, 87, 181, 314

Danton, Georges Jacques (1759–94), Fr. politician and jacobin, 147

Décazes, Elie, duc de (1780–1860), Fr. prime minister, 315

Derwentwater, Charles Radcliffe, 5th Earl of (1693–1746), freemason, 32, 181

Desaguliers, John Theophilus (1683–1744), Anglican divine and freemason, 23, 25, 33

Desmarest, Charles (1763–1832), Fr. police official, 192, 272, 275; q. 251, 274

Diderot, Denis (1713–84), Fr. philosopher, 56, 136

Dietrich, Philippe Frédéric de (1748–93), mayor of Strasbourg, 220

Disraeli, Benjamin, Earl of Beaconsfield (1804–81), Br. statesman and novelist, 4–8; q. 3, 6, 9

Dostoevsky, Feodor (1821–81), Russ. novelist, 351

Dugied, Pierre (1798–1879), Fr. conspirator, 320

Duport, Adrien (1759–98), Fr. politician, 93

Eckartshausen, Karl von (1752–1803), Bav. writer and illuminatus, 211

Esprémesnil, Jean Jacques Duval d' (1746–94), Fr. politician, 93, 136

Fauchet, Claude (1744–93), Fr. 'constitutional' bishop, 152–62; q. 160

Ferrand, Antoine François Claude, comte (1751–1825), Fr. controversialist, 149, 183

Fiard, Jean Baptiste (1736–1818), Jesuit demonologist, 199–200

Fleury, André Hercule de, cardinal (1653–1743), 66–7

Folard, Jean Charles, chevalier de (1669–1752), 139, 182

Fouché, Joseph (1759–1820), Fr. statesman, 192, 234, 254, 263

Fox, Charles James (1749–1806), Engl. statesman, 181

Francis I, Roman emperor, formerly Duke of Lorraine, later Grand Duke of Tuscany (1708–65), freemason, 45–6, 49, 64, 71, 83

Francis II, last Roman emperor (1768–1835), later Francis I of Austria, 307

Frederick William II (1744–97), King of Prussia, 103, 127, 210, 214

Genovesi, Antonio (1713–69), Neapolitan writer, 74, 85

George, Prince of Wales, later George IV, King of England (1762–1830), freemason, 208–9

Gloucester, William Henry, Duke of (1743–1805), freemason, 209

Göchhausen, Ernst Anton von (1740–1824), freemason and writer, 134, 139

Goethe, Johann Wolfgang von (1749–1832), reputed illuminatus, 124

Grégoire, Baptiste Henri (1750–1831), Fr. 'constitutional' bishop and writer, 193, 334

Guadet, Marguerite Élie (1758–94), Fr. politician, q. 152

Guillotin, Joseph Ignace (1738–1814), Fr. humanitarian and freemason, 199

Guizot, François (1787–1874), Fr. statesman, 321; q. 318

Gustavus III, King of Sweden (1746–92), 181, 198

Hardenberg, August Karl von, prince (1750–1822), reputed illuminatus, 124

Hangwitz, Kurt von, baron, (1752–1832), Pr. minister, 114, 127

Helvétius, Claude Adrien (1715–71), 55, 136

Herder, Johann Gottfried von (1744–1803), reputed illuminatus, 124

Hiram, legendary master-mason, 18, 98–9

Hoffmann, Leopold Aloys (1760–1806), Bohemian journalist, 214, 215, 218

Holbach, Paul Henry Thiry, baron d' (1723–89), Fr. philosopher, 179

Hund, Karl Gotthilf, baron von, founder of Strict Observance, 106–7, 109

Joseph II, Roman emperor (1741–90), 46, 49, 91, 124, 127, 133, 138, 212–13, 314

Joubert, Barthélemy Cathérine (1769–99), Fr. general, 245

Joubert, Nicholas (d. 1866), Fr. conspirator, 320

Jullien 'de Paris', Marc Antoine (1775–1848), revolutionary politician, 245–6

Kant, Immanuel (1724–1804), philosopher, 193, 197, 218, 298

Kirchberger, Niklaus Anton (1739–99), Swiss illuminé, 93, 105, 188, 253; q. 133

Knigge, Adolf, baron von (1752–96), illuminatus, 124, 125–7, 129, 133, 143, 214, 215, 218

Kolowrat, Leopold, count von K. Krakowsky (1726–1809), reputed illuminatus, 124

Lafayette, or La Fayette, Marie Jean Paul Motier, marquis de (1757–1834), 93, 153, 158, 164, 195, 304, 316

Lafon, Jean Baptiste Hyacinthe (1766–1836), abbé and conspirator, 261, 271

Laharpe or La Harpe, Jean François de (1739–1803), Fr. writer, q. 160

Lahoz or La Hoz, Giuseppe (d. 1799), Ital. patriot, 245–7

Lauberg, Carlo (1752–1834), Ital. jacobin, 225

Lavater, Jean Gaspard (1741–1801), Swiss pastor, 93, 113, 133, 253

Le Chapelier, Isaac René (1754–94), Fr. politician, 158

Lefranc, Jacques François (1739–92), abbé, 162, 191, 295; *Le voile levé*, 170–4, 207, 326; *Conjuration entre la religion* . . ., 177

Lenoir, Jean Charles Pierre (1732–1807), lieutenant de police, 85; q. 203

Leo XIII, Pope (1810–1903), 16, 333

Leopold II, Roman emperor (1747–92), former Grand Duke of Tuscany, 168, 214, 215, 227, 314

Lombard de Langres, Vincent (1765–1830), Fr. journalist, 302–4, 313

Louis XV (1710–74), King of France, 188, 302, 304

Louis XVI (1754–93), King of France, 146, 147, 173, 188

Luchet, Jean Pierre Louis, marquis de la Roche du Maine (1740–92), Fr. writer, 93, 135–8; q. 160, 176, 177, 183, 313

Maistre, Joseph Marie, comte de (1754–1821), Savoyard philosopher, 82, 104, 150, 163, 199, 294–9; q. 105, 114, 155, 295, 299

Malet, Claude François de (1754–1812), general, 260–1, 267, 269–71, 273, 328, 342

Malouet, Pierre Victor (1740–1814), Fr. politician, q. 149

Maréchal, Sylvain (1750–1803), conspirator, 235–6

Maria Carolina (1752–1814), Queen of Naples, 45, 77, 78, 85, 224–5

Maria Theresa, Queen of Hungary and empress (1717–80), 65, 83

Marie Antoinette (1755–93), Queen of France, 151; q. 85, 168

Martinez de Pasqually (1755?–99), seer, 104, 110

Martinovics, Ignaz Josef (1755–95), 216–17

'Masaniello' (1623–47), Neapolitan popular leader, 181

Maupeou, René Nicolas de (1714–92), chancellor of France, 184

Maurras, Charles (1868–1952), Fr. writer, 163

Maury, Jean Siffrein (1746–1817), Fr. priest, 178, 192

Mauvillon, Jacob (1743–94), illuminatus, 131, 218

Mazzini, Giuseppe (1805–72), Ital. patriot, 4, 235, 344–5

Melzi, Francesco, duca d' Eril (1753–1816), Ital. statesman, 279, 287, 290

Menou, Jacques François, baron de (1750–1810), Fr. politician, 173, 187

Mesmer, Friedrich Anton (1734–1815), charlatan, 93, 102, 105, 115

Metternich-Winneburg, Clemens Wengel Lothar, prince (1773–

1859), Austr. statesman, 124, 210, 301–2, 311, 312–13, 320, 331, 346; q. 301, 323, 333, 340

Mirabeau, Honoré Gabriel Riquetti, comte de (1749–91), Fr. statesman, 131, 135, 152, 164, 177, 179, 233, 314; q. 54, 121

Molay, Jacques de (d. 314), last Grand Master of Knights Templar, 100, 184, 187

Montagu, John, 2nd Duke of (1689–1749), Grand Master, 25

Montesquieu, Charles Louis de Secondat, baron de la Brède et de, (1689–1755), Fr. philosopher, 33, 136

Montjoie, Galart de (1756?–1816), journalist, 173, 179, 183, 217; *Histoire de la conjuration . . . d'Orléans*, 183–4; *L'école des factieux*, 185

Montmorency, Guy André Pierre de Laval, duc de (1723–98), q. 52

Montmorin, Armand, comte de M.-Saint-Hérem (1745–92), Fr. minister, q. 168

Moreau, Jean Victor (1768–1813), general, 259–61, 265, 269–71

Mounier, Jean Joseph (1758–1806), Fr. politician, 200, 219

Mozart, Wolfgang Amadeus (1756–91), musician and freemason, 124, 215

Murat, Joachim (1771–1815), sometime King of Naples, 286, 289, 291–4, 309, 322, 339

Necker, Jacques (1732–1804), Swiss minister of Fr. crown, 185

Newcastle, Thomas Pelham Holles, Duke of (1693–1768), 46

Nicolai, Christoph Friedrich (1733–1811), Berlin bookseller, 124, 136, 214

Nodier, Charles (1780–1844), Fr. man of letters, 261, 268–73, 282, 285; q. 254, 301, 305

O'Brien, James Bronterre (1805–64), Irish agitator, 344

Orlando, Ital. monk, 45, 75–6

Orléans, Louis Philippe, duc de Chartres and duc d' (1747–93), Fr. Grand Master, 40, 131, 149, 158, 164, 171, 181–6, 195, 209, 220, 252, 298

Orléans, Philippe, duc d' (1674–1723), Regent of Fr., 35

Oudet, Jacques Joseph (1733–1809), Fr. soldier, 269–71, 342

Palmerston, Henry John Temple, 3rd Viscount (1784–1865), Engl. statesman, 2

Pellico, Silvio (1759–1854), Ital. political prisoner, q. 312

Pepe, Francesco, Jesuit priest, 72–4

Pepe, Guglielmo (1779–1849), Neapolitan general, 322–3; q. 335

Pérau, Gabriel Calabre (1700–67), Fr. abbé and writer, 87; q. 95

Philip the Fair, Philip IV, King of France (1268–1314), 100, 177

Pitt, William (1759–1806), Engl. statesman, 151, 185, 252

Pius VI, Pope (1717–99), 68

Pius VII, Pope (1740–1823), 192

Pius IX, Pope (1792–1878), 333

Pivati, Gianfrancesco (1689–1764), Ital. encyclopaedist, 45, 75, 86

Plot, Robert (1640–96), antiquarian, 19, 59

Poncins, Léon, vicomte de, Fr. writer; q. 348

Prati, Joachim Paul de (b. 1790), conspirator, 262, 267, 282, 340, 346

Prichard, Samuel, anti-masonic writer, 61–3

Prina, Giuseppe (1768–1814), Ital. statesman, 290, 303, 311

Proyart, Liévain Bonaventure (1748–1808), Fr. abbé and writer, 184, 295

Rabaut du Puy, Pierre Antoine (1746–1808), Fr. protestant, 186

Rabaut St-Etienne, Jean Paul (1743–93), Fr. protestant and politician, 186

Radcliffe, Charles: see Derwentwater

Rainsborough (Rainborow), Thomas (d. 1648), 87

Ramsay, the chevalier Andrew Michael (1686–1743), freemason, 34–6, 94, 101, 208; his speech and its influence, 36–8, 53, 55, 63, 96, 99

Restif de la Bretonne, Nicholas Edmé (1734–1806), Fr. writer, 160

Rey, Joseph Philippe Etienne (1779–1819), Fr. conspirator, 316

Rivarol, Antoine (1753–1801), Fr. journalist, q. 198

Robespierre, Augustin (1763–94), associate of Buonarroti, 230

Robespierre, Maximilien (1758–94), Fr. revolutionary, 147, 153, 177, 181, 230, 233, 343; q. 152

Robison, John (1739–1805), scientist and writer, 208, 313

Roland de la Platière, Jean Marie (1734–93), Fr. minister, 93

Rossetti, Giuseppe, Ital. soldier, 288, 292; q. 284, 309

St Florentin, Louis Phelypeaux, duc de la Vrillière, comte de (1705–77), freemason, 33, 67

Saint-Martin, Louis Claude de (1743–1803), 'the unknown philosopher', 103, 110, 136, 150, 160, 253

Salfi, Francesco (1759–1832), Ital. writer, q. 338–9

Saliceti, Christophe (1757–1809), Corsican revolutionary and Fr. official, 230, 237, 240, 285

Sansevero, Raimondo di Sangro, principe di (1710–71), Neapolitan Grand Master, 73–4

Schiller, Friedrich von (1759–1805), poet and reputed illuminatus, 124

Shelley, Percy Bysshe (1792–1822), poet, q. 201

Sieyes, Emmanuel Joseph (1748–1836), Fr. politician, 158

Sonnenfels, Joseph, baron von (1737–1817), reputed illuminatus, 124

Sourdat (de Troyes), François Nicolas (1745–1810?), conservative writer, 173; Les véritables auteurs, 185–7

Starck, Johann August (1741–1816), German conservative writer, 108–9, 113–14, 131, 248, 295, 329; corresp. with Barruel, 196–8, 218; and Eudämonia, 218–20; q. 218, 219

Sussex, Augustin Frederick, Duke of (1773–1843), Engl. Grand Master, 208, 287

Swedenborg, Emanuel (1688–1772), philosopher, 103–4, 181, 199

Tanucci, Bernardo (1698–1783), Neapolitan statesman, 76–8

Toland, John (1670–1722), Engl. deist and writer, 18, 23

Trélat, Ulysse (1795–1879), Fr. doctor, q. 345

Urquhart, David (1805–77), Br. diplomat and politician, 348

Vadier, Marc Guillaume Alexis (1736–1828), Fr. revolutionary, 181, 341
Valtancoli, Giuseppe, Tuscan informer, 330
Vaudreuil, Joseph François de Rigaud, comte de (1740–1817), q. 151, 178
Ventre de la Touloubre: alias of Montjoie, Galart de, q.v.
Victor Amadeus III (1726–95), King of Sardinia, 45, 84
Voltaire, François Marie Arouet de (1694–1778), writer, 56, 136, 140, 159, 298

Walpole, Sir Robert (1676–1745), Engl. statesman, 62
Webster, Mrs Nesta H., English writer, 145, 198, 318, 350; q. 3
Weishaupt, Adam (1784–1830), founder of Illuminati, 118–30, 135, 139, 142, 143, 196, 197, 214, 227, 331, 358

Wharton, Philip, Duke of (1698–1731), 25, 33, 43
Wickham, William (1761–1840), Br. diplomat, 255
Wieland, Christoph Martin (1733–1813), reputed illuminatus, 124
Willermoz, Jean Baptiste (1730–1824), masonic enthusiast, 110–15, 127, 136, 150, 177, 208, 209, 253, 295
Wilson, Thomas Woodrow (1856–1924), President of the United States of America, 348
Windisch-Grätz, Joseph Nicolas, count (1744–1802), Austr. writer, 142–4, 201
Wit von Dörring, Ferdinand Johannes (1800–63), conspirator, 325–61, 330–1, 336
Wöllner, Johann Christoph (1732–1800), Pr. minister, 103

Zimmermann, Johann Georg, Ritter von (1728–95), Sw. doctor and author, 139, 196, 197, 214
Zwack, Franz Xavier von, illuminatus, 123, 128